My Windows® 8

Katherine Murray

QUE®
800 East 96th Street,
Indianapolis, Indiana 46240 USA

My Windows® 8

ISBN-13: 978-0-7897-4948-2
ISBN-10: 0-7897-4948-3

Library of Congress Cataloging-in-Publication Data is on file.

Printed in the United States of America

First Printing: September 2012

Trademarks

All terms mentioned in this book that are known to be trademarks or service marks have been appropriately capitalized. Que Publishing cannot attest to the accuracy of this information. Use of a term in this book should not be regarded as affecting the validity of any trademark or service mark.

Warning and Disclaimer

Every effort has been made to make this book as complete and as accurate as possible, but no warranty or fitness is implied. The information provided is on an "as is" basis. The author and the publisher shall have neither liability nor responsibility to any person or entity with respect to any loss or damages arising from the information contained in this book.

Bulk Sales

Que Publishing offers excellent discounts on this book when ordered in quantity for bulk purchases or special sales. For more information, please contact

U.S. Corporate and Government Sales

1-800-382-3419

corpsales@pearsontechgroup.com

For sales outside of the U.S., please contact

International Sales

international@pearsoned.com

Editor-in-Chief
Greg Wiegand

Executive Editor
Loretta Yates

Marketing Manager
Dan Powell

Development Editor
Todd Brakke

Managing Editor
Kristy Hart

Project Editor
Betsy Harris

Indexers
Cheryl Lenser
Erika Millen

Proofreader
Sarah Kearns

Technical Editor
Laura Acklen

Publishing Coordinator
Cindy Teeters

Book Designer
Anne Jones

Compositors
Mary Sudul
MPS Limited

Contents at a Glance

	Introduction	1
Chapter 1	Wow, Windows 8!	**9**
Chapter 2	Preparing Your Windows 8 PC and Devices	**35**
Chapter 3	Beginning with the Start Screen	**59**
Chapter 4	Working with the Windows 8 Desktop	**81**
Chapter 5	Personalizing Windows 8	**97**
Chapter 6	Securing Your Windows 8 Computer	**117**
Chapter 7	Exploring Windows 8 Apps	**147**
Chapter 8	Managing Files with File Explorer	**173**
Chapter 9	Always Online with Internet Explorer 10	**203**
Chapter 10	Connect and Communicate with Windows 8	**227**
Chapter 11	Get Entertained with Windows 8 Photos, Music, Movies, and Xbox	**253**
Chapter 12	Connect with Other Computers, Devices, and the Cloud	**279**
Chapter 13	Windows 8 Care, Feeding, and Troubleshooting	**293**
Appendix A	Windows 8 App Gallery	**309**
	Index	**339**

Table of Contents

About the Author ... ix
Dedication ... x
Acknowledgments ... x
We Want to Hear from You! ... xi
Reader Services ... xi

Introduction **1**

Versions of Windows 8 ... 2
Highlights of Windows 8 ... 3
What You'll Find in This Book ... 5
Let's Begin ... 7

1 Wow, Windows 8! **9**

Exploring Windows 8 ... 10
  Touring the Start Screen ... 10
Using Touch in Windows 8 ... 13
Getting Around with the Mouse and Keyboard ... 18
  Using the Mouse ... 18
  Using the (Real) Keyboard ... 22
Shutting Down or Putting Windows 8 to Sleep ... 27
Finding the Help You Need ... 29

2 Preparing Your Windows 8 PC and Devices **35**

Adding Devices in Windows 8 ... 36
Connecting to Wireless Networks ... 43
Managing Your PC Power ... 46
Transferring Files ... 49
Refreshing Your PC or Reinstalling Windows 8 ... 53

3 Beginning with the Start Screen 59

Exploring the Start Screen....60
Understanding Windows 8 Charms....64
Changing the Way Tiles Look and Behave....66
Moving, Grouping, and Removing Apps....71
Searching in Windows 8....75

4 Working with the Windows 8 Desktop 81

Moving Between the Desktop and the Start Screen....82
Getting Ready to Work with Programs....83
Tailoring the Taskbar....87
Working with Windows on the Windows Desktop....89
Window Basics....89

5 Personalizing Windows 8 97

Personalizing Your Lock Screen....97
Adding Badges....103
Adjusting the Look of Windows 8....103
Changing Your Windows 8 Desktop....107
Tweaking Your Touch Experience....110
Adjusting the Mouse....111
Choosing Your Language....114

6 Securing Your Windows 8 Computer 117

Customizing Your Login....118
Working with the Action Center....129
Using Windows Defender....134
Turning on Your Windows Firewall....136
Working with User Accounts....139
Maintaining Your Privacy....143

7 **Exploring Windows 8 Apps** **147**

Getting Started with Apps ... 148
Finding and Starting Apps ... 151
Working with Apps ... 154
Exploring a Program "Window" ... 155
Checking Out a Windows 8 App ... 156
Closing Apps ... 160
Getting New Apps from the Windows Store ... 162
Starting and Stopping a Program from the Desktop ... 165
Repairing and Uninstalling Programs ... 167

8 **Managing Files with File Explorer** **173**

Getting Started with File Explorer ... 174
Starting File Explorer ... 174
Exploring the Explorer Screen ... 175
Using the Ribbon ... 178
Working with Windows 8 Libraries ... 181
Managing Your Files and Folders ... 188
Copying, Moving, and Sharing Files and Folders ... 194

9 **Always Online with Internet Explorer 10** **203**

Introducing Internet Explorer 10 ... 203
Starting Internet Explorer ... 205
A Look Around the Internet Explorer Window(s) ... 206
Browsing and Searching the Web—the Windows 8 Way .. 209
Navigating the Web ... 211
Searching for Information ... 216
Working with Tabs ... 220
Securing Your Browsing Experience ... 223

10 **Connect and Communicate with Windows 8** **227**

Getting Social with the People App ... 228
Staying in Touch Through Email ... 238
Checking Out the Mail Window ... 240

Keeping Your Dates Straight with the Calendar App 243
Messaging: When You Need Instant Contact 247

11 Get Entertained with Windows 8 Photos, Music, Movies, and Xbox 253

Let There Be Photos! 253
Grooving to Your Tunes 260
Watching and Sharing Video in Windows 8 269
Games in Windows 8 273

12 Connect with Other Computers, Devices, and the Cloud 279

Setting Up a Home Network 279
Gathering Your Equipment 280
Getting Started with a HomeGroup 283
Using Your HomeGroup 286
Saving Your Files to SkyDrive 289

13 Windows 8 Care, Feeding, and Troubleshooting 293

Getting Windows 8 Updates 293
Backing Up and Restoring Your Files 298
Using System Tools 302
Compatibility with Windows 8 305

A Windows 8 App Gallery 309

Appreciating Your Apps 310
Checking Out the Bing Apps 312
Finance App 313
Weather App 313
Maps App 314
News App 315
Sports App 316
Travel App 317

The Windows Store Revisited 319
  Getting App Info 322
  Installing Apps 324
The Windows 8 App Gallery 330
  Allrecipes 330
  ChaCha 331
  Dictionary.com 332
  HowStuffWorks 333
  OneNote MX Preview 334
  Paint 4 Kids 335
  StumbleUpon 336
  Wikipedia 337

Index **339**

About the Author

After writing about technology for 25 years, **Katherine Murray** believes there's never been a better time to be a tech enthusiast. With the advent of Windows 8, technology is more connected and more integrated with our daily lives than ever before. She's worked with every version of Microsoft Windows released, marveling with the masses at Windows 3.1, swearing at Windows ME, enjoying Windows XP, and threatening to throw her computer off the roof, thanks to Windows Vista. Windows 7 was her favorite version of the operating system, followed in a close second place by Windows XP. But now with Windows 8, she feels Microsoft is in sync with the times, offering a fast, fluid, and secure option for connecting with others, enjoying media, saving to the cloud, and integrating our work across multiple devices. She started writing about technology 25 years ago and still enjoys it, specializing in Microsoft Office technologies and the fascinating ways in which we stay in touch with each other through cloud technology, blogging, social media, and more. You'll find Katherine's blog, BlogOffice, at www.murrayblogoffice.blogspot.com. In addition to writing books, she writes regularly for CNET's TechRepublic and Windows Secrets.

Dedication

This book is dedicated to all of us who love change, color, and speed but also want reliability, security, and comfort. Bring it, Windows 8. :)

Acknowledgments

What a great project! As a tech author, I spend a lot of time peering into multiple monitors, working into the wee hours of the night and writing about what I find. Working with a team like the one at Que makes the writing process fun, collaborative, and something I always enjoy doing.

My thanks to the whole crew at Que Publishing for their hard work and cranked schedules, all the way through *My Windows 8*. Special thanks to Loretta Yates, as always, for being so great to work with, to Todd Brakke, development editor, for his spot-on insights and good humor; to Laura Acklen, technical editor, for her good catches and helpful suggestions; and Betsy Harris, project editor, for shepherding this book through the production process.

We Want to Hear from You!

As the reader of this book, *you* are our most important critic and commentator. We value your opinion and want to know what we're doing right, what we could do better, what areas you'd like to see us publish in, and any other words of wisdom you're willing to pass our way.

As Editor-in-Chief for Que Publishing, I welcome your comments. You can email or write me directly to let me know what you did or didn't like about this book—as well as what we can do to make our books better.

Please note that I cannot help you with technical problems related to the topic of this book. We do have a User Service group, however, where I will forward specific technical questions related to the book.

When you write, please be sure to include this book's title and author as well as your name, email address, and phone number. I will carefully review your comments and share them with the author and editors who worked on the book.

Email: feedback@quepublishing.com

Mail: Greg Wiegand
Editor-in-Chief
Que Publishing
800 East 96th Street
Indianapolis, IN 46240 USA

Reader Services

Visit our website and register this book at quepublishing.com/register for convenient access to any updates, downloads, or errata that might be available for this book.

Introduction

We expect certain things from our operating system. We want it to work, first and foremost. We want it to be fast and efficient and keep things running. We want it to be secure, and we want it to enable us to find and launch our programs, organize our files, and print, share, and beam our documents to the cloud whenever we choose to.

These are all reasonable expectations.

And if an operating system can do all this with movement and color, if it can make our computer as fun to use as our mobile devices, if it can respond to touch, stream media, give us updates on the messages and calls we have waiting, and can give us a choice about how we choose to interact with it, so much the better.

Welcome to Windows 8.

This revolutionary new operating system from Microsoft has had the tech world buzzing for more than a year, as the various releases of Windows 8 made their way into the public realm. Whether you've worked with Windows 8 before or not, chances are good that you've heard all the buzz about the huge changes—the colorful new user interface, the vibrant Start screen, the Charms bar, and more. Some folks question why we need such a drastic overhaul, but others cheer the new lease on life our ho-hum operating system has been granted. I'm in the "celebrating" camp, as you'll discover throughout this book. And it's my hope that as you work through the examples here and get to know your new operating system, you'll feel good about the change as well.

The way I see it, working with computers just got a whole lot more fun, thanks to Windows 8.

Versions of Windows 8

Some software manufacturers offer a whole array of program versions so that you can choose just the version you need for the type of tasks you do and the hardware you have. Microsoft is typically a big culprit in this area, offering a number of versions of Windows 7 that did little more than confuse users who were trying to decide what they needed. For Windows 8, Microsoft seems to have listened to the masses. This time around, we have only three versions of Windows 8 from which to choose:

- Windows 8 (32-bit and 64-bit), which is the standard operating system that will work for most users.
- Windows 8 Pro (also in 32-bit and 64-bit versions), which adds high-end features like BitLocker, Client Hyper-V, and a fully encrypting file system for advanced users; and now, Windows Media Center.
- Windows RT, which is the version of Windows available for tablets that run on ARM processors. This version of Windows contains a slightly different feature set and is available only when you purchase a new ARM tablet, so it comes preinstalled on the equipment for you.

>>>Go Further

WHAT'S ARM?

ARM processors are the "brains" of many mobile devices today, offering a simple design that works well in low-power situations. The Android smartphone and tablet are two examples of hugely popular devices running on ARM.

The significance of Microsoft developing an ARM version of Windows 8 is that this significantly extends the reach of Windows 8. Because Windows 8 is designed to work beautifully with touch capability, Microsoft needs to ensure that Windows 8 can be used on as many different touch-enabled devices as possible. Because so many devices today run on ARM processors, Microsoft needed to address this ARM space to be a serious contender in the mobile market. Windows RT also includes touch-capable versions of Microsoft Office, which is one big perk not included with the standard Windows 8 or Windows 8 Pro.

This book uses Windows 8 to demonstrate examples and give you the play-by-play for the various tasks you'll want to try with the operating system. The illustrations reflect both desktop and tablet versions of Windows 8. I'll also throw in some Windows RT bits along the way, but the primary narrative of the books focuses on Windows 8 proper.

Highlights of Windows 8

Everything in Windows 8, from the moment you turn on your computer to the icon you tap to shut it down, has been reimagined. Although the blogosphere bristled at first with so much change, so fast (we humans are typically change resistant, after all), folks who have been using Windows 8 for months find it functional, easy to navigate, and intuitive.

Although it can be overwhelming at first, things aren't *harder* to find in Windows 8; they're easier. We didn't lose anything big when Microsoft decided to retire the Start menu—we gained a quicker way to get to what we need. As you'll see throughout this book, the steps Windows 8 leaves out were just unnecessary steps anyway. Soon you'll be tapping and clicking and flicking your way through programs and media like a pro—and it will take much less effort that you might imagine right now. We'll start with the following tasks:

- Use the customizable Lock screen to get live information about the number of messages, calls, and instant messages you've received since you locked your computer.
- Play with the new Start screen, customize Start screen colors and designs, and show your favorite apps the way you want them to appear.
- Let live tiles give you the latest information for your favorite apps.
- Use touch, keyboard, and mouse techniques to personalize your Windows 8 experience as you work with files, folders, and more.
- Improve the security of your system by changing your Lock screen, adding a picture password, and creating a PIN logon.

- Tap or click your way into your favorite apps, cycle through open apps, dock apps, and close or suspend apps you no longer need.
- Let the Refresh and Reset tools to give your computer a fresh start if you're having computer problems.
- Shop for apps in the Windows Store, install apps on your computer, and add ratings and reviews to let other shoppers know what you think.
- Browse with the sleek and streamlined Internet Explorer 10 in the new, modeless style or—if you still are attached to your plug-ins—you can use Internet Explorer 10 for the Desktop to get a more traditional browsing experience.

In addition to all the new energy in Windows 8, the instant notifications, the connection between apps, and the fluid and colorful interface, Windows 8 makes media, games, and more easier to access and enjoy than ever. Note that for some tasks—such as pinching and zooming the display in Internet Explorer 10—you need to have Windows 8 installed on a touch-capable computer or device.

>>>Go Further

THERE'S TOUCH—AND THEN THERE'S WINDOWS 8 TOUCH

Windows 8 runs on any computer that previously ran Windows 7, which means there are a number of touch-capable devices you can use to get the Windows 8 experience. When you install Windows 8, the operating system does a quick check of your hardware to see whether it can make use of the new touch sensitivities in Windows 8. If your computer is a non-Windows 8 computer or device (you might be upgrading to Windows 8 on a system that previously ran Windows 7, for example), you will see a message that your system isn't optimized for Windows 8 touch. Don't worry—touch will still work. Microsoft is simply telling you that your touchscreen might not be as wonderfully responsive as it would be if you had hardware designed specifically for Windows 8. (Cue the Microsoft Surface commercial.)

If you are using a Windows 7 or ARM tablet with Windows 8, you may not notice anything missing in your machine's touch capabilities. But if you put the non-Windows 8 tablet up against one designed to run optimally with Windows 8, you will notice a greater precision in the way the system picks up gestures, as well as a larger area of the screen where it is most receptive to touch. (Windows 8 surfaces were designed so that the device is touch-capable all the way out to the edge of the screen.)

Microsoft's new Windows 8 tablet, called Microsoft Surface, was made available at the general availability of Windows 8, and this little device is designed to bring out the best of Windows 8. You can find out more about Microsoft Surface by going to http://www.microsoft.com/surface/en/us/default.aspx.

What You'll Find in This Book

This book shows you, in an easy-to-follow visual format, how to do the things you want to do with Windows 8. We'll focus first on the features you're most likely to want to know up front, and then explore some of the more specialized tasks, like organizing files, finding and playing media, and creating a HomeGroup for your computers and devices at home. The chapters unfold like this:

- Chapter 1, "Wow, Windows 8!," gets you started with the basics of Windows 8 and gives you your first look at the new operating system. You'll learn how to use touch gestures, as well as the mouse and keyboard, to navigate with Windows 8, and find out how to put Windows 8 to sleep, wake it up, and power down your computer.

- Chapter 2, "Preparing Your Windows 8 PC and Devices," shows you how to set up devices so that you can use them with Windows 8. You'll also set app notifications, make sure you have Internet access, learn about managing your PC's power, and find out how to refresh or reset your system.

- Chapter 3, "Beginning with the Start Screen," shows you how to navigate the new interface in Windows 8. You'll learn how to organize app tiles the way you want them, discover how to navigate in the way that fits you best, and learn how to tweak settings so that the Start screen launches you right into the tasks you most want to accomplish with Windows 8.

- Chapter 4, "Working with the Windows 8 Desktop," introduces you to the other face of Windows 8, where you will use programs you may know and love from Windows 7, tailor the taskbar to include the Quick Launch items you want, and more.

- Chapter 5, "Personalizing Windows 8," introduces you to the Lock screen and shows you how to change your picture, add badges, change your Start screen color scheme, and work with Windows 8 accessibility features.

- Chapter 6, "Securing Your Windows 8 Computer," helps you make sure your computer is as safe as possible by setting a password, customizing your login, creating user accounts, adding a PIN logon, setting location privacy, and telling Windows 8 how—or whether—you want apps to share your info.

- Chapter 7, "Exploring Windows 8 Apps," introduces you to the wide world of apps in Windows 8. You'll learn about the apps included with Windows 8, find out how to work with multiple apps on the screen at once, search for and download new apps in the Windows Store, and install them on your computer and devices. You'll also find out how to rate the apps you download so that others can benefit from the information and experience you share.

- Chapter 8, "Managing Files with File Explorer," spotlights the tasks you need to know to organize your files, folders, and libraries in Windows 8. Along the way, you'll learn about the changes in File Explorer (now that it has its own Ribbon), and discover how easy it is to copy, move, and share your files with others.

- Chapter 9, "Always Online with Internet Explorer 10," introduces you to a new, sleek, modeless browsing experience with Internet Explorer 10. You'll learn how to navigate with touch and mouse, save and choose favorites, and touch up your security settings in IE10. You'll also discover what browsing is like on the Windows Desktop, where the version of IE10 you're using is more traditional and allows plug-ins.

- Chapter 10, "Connect and Communicate with Windows 8," helps you get into the fun stuff—social media—and make sure you can use your Windows 8 PC to get email, manage your calendar, and send instant messages to friends and family.

- Chapter 11, "Get Entertained with Windows 8 Photos, Music, Movies, and XBox," takes you into all things media as you set up, work with, and personalize the Photos, Music, Video, and Xbox Live Games apps in Windows 8. You'll learn how to view and organize photos from all your photo-sharing sites; find, download, and play the music and movies you want; and explore and play games on the Xbox Live Games app.

- Chapter 12, "Connect with Other Computers, Devices, and the Cloud," shows you how to set up a home network and create a HomeGroup so that you can easily share files among all the PCs and devices in your home.
- Chapter 13, "Windows 8 Care, Feeding, and Troubleshooting," gives you some basic pointers on how to regularly back up your files, update your copy of Windows 8, and use Windows 8 system tools to improve your computer's performance and clean up your hard drive.
- Finally, Appendix A, "Windows 8 App Gallery," Gallery gives you pointers on finding, downloading, and reviewing apps from the Windows Store. You get a look at some popular apps and find out how to explore and add to the Store on your own.

The chapters are organized so that you can jump in and read about whatever interests you most, or you can choose to go through the book sequentially if you like. Along the way, you'll find tips, notes, and two kinds of sidebars: Go Further, which gives you additional information about getting more from the topic at hand, and It's Not All Good, which lists common pitfalls and trouble spots you can watch out for.

Let's Begin

If instead of purchasing a new computer with Windows 8 pre-installed, you want to upgrade your Windows 7 computer to Windows 8, your first step is to install Windows 8 on your desktop or tablet PC. Be sure to back up any existing data before you install the new operating system.

When you're ready to download Windows, go to one of the download sites (www.preview.windows.com) and choose the version of Windows 8 you want to use. The site provides instructions on how to download and install Windows 8.

Depending on the speed of your Internet connection, it might take an hour or so to download and install Windows 8. When the operating system is finished installing, the process restarts your computer and walks you through a series of setup questions called Express Setup. After you make those initial choices, you'll get your first glimpse of the Windows 8 Lock screen. That's where we'll begin exploring Windows 8 together.

Launch apps, change settings, and get the latest info from the Windows 8 Start screen

You can easily display thumbnails of all the apps you have open

In this chapter, you learn how to get started with your Windows 8 PC and use touch, mouse, and keyboard to perform tasks such as

- → Exploring Windows 8
- → Using touch in Windows 8
- → Getting around with the mouse and keyboard
- → Shutting down or putting Windows 8 to sleep
- → Finding the help you need

Wow, Windows 8!

It's probably safe to assume that you've already learned something about Windows 8—maybe you've heard about the high energy, the colors, the touch interface, and the new styling. You may be feeling excited to try something completely different in terms of the way computer operating systems typically behave. Or you might be a bit anxious—what if it's so much of a change that Windows 8 makes your life more complicated than it already is? Nobody needs that!

Relax. That's what this book is here to help you do—learn the basics of Windows 8 in a way that helps you keep your stress level low and your productivity level high. I personally think Windows 8 is smart and fun. I love the color, the movement, the touch capability, and the flexibility. I hope as you go through the chapters in this book, you'll feel a bit of that "fun vibe" rubbing off as you expand your experience and increase your mastery of Windows 8.

Perhaps you are just now getting a chance to try Windows 8, either as the sleek operating system on your brand-new Windows 8 PC or Microsoft Surface, or as an upgrade you've added to your Windows 7 computer. This chapter opens the door on your Windows 8 experience and gives you a chance to navigate the operating system using touch, mouse, and keyboard. You'll also find out how to put your computer to sleep (no, don't worry—no singing required) and power down the system completely, when you're ready to do that.

Exploring Windows 8

If you've just upgraded to Windows 8, the utility will restart your computer after installation is complete. When your computer restarts, Windows 8 quickly appears on your screen, and, after asking you a series of Express Setup questions (which help Windows 8 get you connected to the Internet, set your sharing preferences, and turn on the Do Not Track setting in Internet Explorer), you are ready to start exploring.

If you're powering up your brand-spanking-new Windows 8 computer for the first time, Windows 8 launches (and very quickly, too!) and asks you those same Express Setup questions. Just respond as prompted and soon you'll be looking at the beautiful new Windows 8 Start screen. That's where we'll begin our exploration.

A First Look!

Your computer needs the operating system in order to do what it does, which means that powering up your computer and launching Windows 8 are really the same thing. Here are the simple steps required for starting your computer and getting to the Windows 8 Start screen:

1. Press your computer's Power button. Your computer starts and your Windows 8 Lock screen appears.
2. Swipe up on the screen (if you have a touch-capable computer) or press any key to display your login information.
3. Enter your password and press Enter or click the arrow.
4. Now you're ready to review the various elements on the Windows 8 Start screen.

Touring the Start Screen

You've probably seen pictures online that show how colorful the Windows 8 Start screen is, but it's likely when you see it with your own eyes for the first time, you're going to be wowed. Or confused. Or both. The beautiful color and easy, smooth movement of the screen are really something to see. But once you get over that first glimpse, you're going to wonder how you actually use this beautiful tool. Here are some of the big features in Windows 8, which you'll find described in more detail throughout this book:

- **Use the Windows 8 Start screen.** This is where all the fun begins. You can get an enormous amount of information from this one screen in Windows 8. You can see at a glance the number of email messages you have, what your day's appointments look like, what the news headlines are, and much more. Plus you can start your favorite apps, play media, change system settings, and even customize the look of Windows 8, all from this one screen. You'll learn more about the Start screen in Chapter 3 and find out how to personalize your Start screen in Chapter 5.

- **Go to your Windows 8 Desktop.** The Windows 8 Desktop will look familiar to you if you've used previous versions of Windows. Here you'll work with programs designed for Windows versions prior to Windows 8 (known as *legacy* programs). You find out how to use and personalize the Windows 8 desktop in Chapter 4.

- **Launch and work with apps.** The colorful tiles on the Windows 8 Start screen represent apps, or programs, you can launch with a simple click or tap. Some apps display "live" information and update on the Start screen, and others don't. You learn how to work with, organize, and get new apps in Chapter 7. Also be sure to check out the Apps Gallery in this book's appendix to find out more about the apps included with Windows 8 as well as popular apps in the Windows Store.

- **Browse the web with Internet Explorer 10.** The IE10 is the newest web browser from Microsoft, and in Windows 8 it comes in a newly designed version and a Desktop version. Both allow you to surf the web, find the information you want, and connect with others—they just look different depending on whether you launched the browser from the Windows 8 Start screen or the Windows 8 desktop. You find out more about using Internet Explorer 10 in Chapter 9.
- **View, organize, and share photos.** The Photos app in Windows 8 enables you to easily view, organize, and share *all* the photos you take, whether you've stored them on your computer, in photo-sharing sites, or in your favorite social media accounts. You'll be learning more about managing your photos in Chapter 11.
- **Stay up to date with friends and family.** The People app pulls together your favorite social media contacts and displays updates in live feeds that you can use to stay in sync with what your favorite folks are posting. You'll learn more about using the People app in Chapter 10.
- **Find new favorites in the Windows Store.** The Windows Store is a new addition in Windows 8, and it's where you can find apps of all sorts, free and otherwise. The Windows Store offers apps in the following categories: games, social media, entertainment, photos, music and video, sports, books, news, health, food, lifestyle, shopping, travel, finance, productivity, tools, security, business, education, and government. You're sure to find something you like! You'll find out more about browsing and shopping in the Windows Store in Chapter 7 as well. You'll also get additional information about the Windows Store in the appendix to this book.
- **Display the Charms bar.** A simple swipe in from the right side of the screen (or moving the mouse to the lower-right corner of the screen) displays the Charms bar, where you'll find the tools you need for searching for files, apps, and settings; sharing content and apps; returning to the Start screen; connecting devices; and changing system settings.

These items don't represent all there is to do in Windows 8, certainly, but they give you a quick bird's-eye-view of some of the major places we'll be stopping along the way.

Using Touch in Windows 8

If you've seen any of the videos about Windows 8 (you can watch one I created using Windows 8 Developer Preview by going to http://www.quepublishing.com/articles/article.aspx?p=1766168), you have probably noticed that you can tap, drag, flick, and pinch your new operating system to get it to do the things you most want it to do. That's a great change for Windows, when you consider that we've been pointing and clicking mouse buttons for decades.

Touch capability is no longer the wave of the future—it's the way many of us navigate today. In case you haven't noticed, human beings are touchy-feeling animals. We like to make good use of our fingers and opposable thumbs, and (or so my theory goes) we feel more in control of our world when we have a tactile sense that we are operating it correctly.

If you have a smartphone, you already know about touch. You tap the surface of your phone to dial a friend's number, you swipe through photos, you pinch a webpage to make the print larger (so you can read it on that small screen). The gestures you'll use on your tablet or multi-touch monitor are similar to the ones you're probably already using on your smartphone, but for good measure (and for those readers who don't go for the smartphones), let's go through the gestures you're likely to use most often in Windows 8.

Single Tap

You tap the screen to launch an app on the Windows 8 Start screen, select a setting, or choose an item to display.

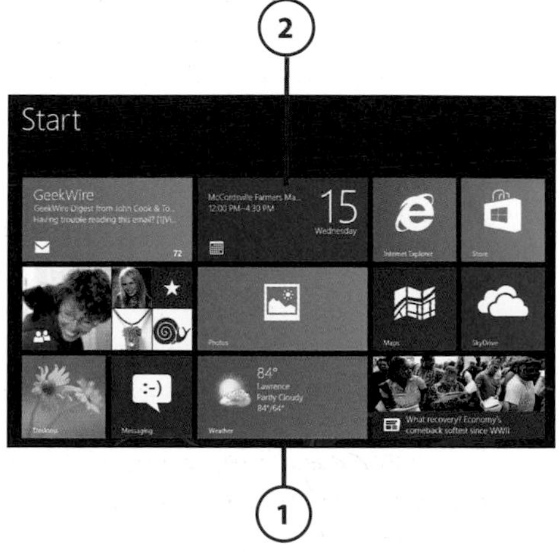

1. Display the Windows 8 Start screen or the app with the option you want to select.
2. Tap the display once quickly in the center of the tile or icon. If you've tapped an application on the Start screen, the program opens; if you tapped a setting or option, the item is selected or displays additional choices, if applicable.

Tap and Hold

If you want to select an item (and not activate it, as you did with the single tap) or perhaps display more information about an item, you can touch the item and hold your finger there until you see a small square surround the area. When you release your touch, a popup list of options appears. You can then tap the item you want to select.

Swipe Left

The swipe left gesture enables you to scroll screen quickly, from right to left and back again, and, if you're using Internet Explorer to browse the web, up and down as well.

1. Display the Windows 8 Start screen.
2. Touch a point toward the right side of the Start screen and drag to the left. The screen scrolls to the left, displaying additional apps.

Scroll Too Far?

One of the great things about touch is how natural it feels to make corrections. If you scroll the screen too far one way or another, simply reverse your swipe direction slightly to correct the display. It happens so easily you won't even have to think about it! Nice.

Swipe Right

You use the swipe right gesture to cycle through open apps in Windows 8.

1. Display the Windows 8 Start screen.
2. Launch at least two apps by tapping their tiles on the Start screen.
3. Drag in from left to right and the first open app moves onto the Windows screen.

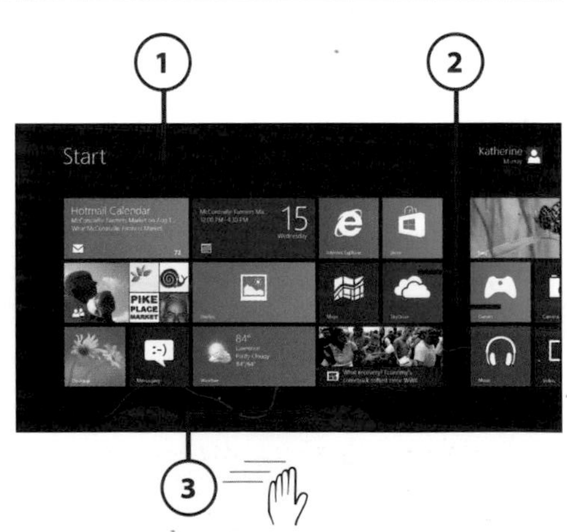

4. Drag in from the left to right a second time to replace the first open app with the second. You can repeat this gesture as needed and also dock apps in the Start screen so that you can see more than one at one time.

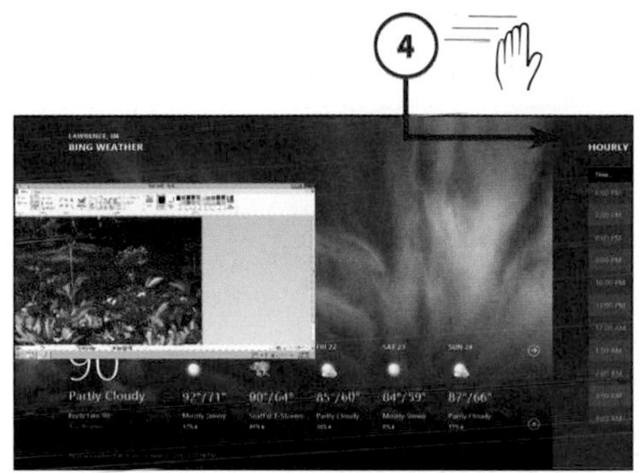

Docking Open Apps

You can continue scrolling through apps as long as you like; and you can also dock an app so that it stays visible in the Windows Start screen. You'll learn how to dock apps in Chapter 7, "Exploring Windows 8 Apps."

Swiping Charm

When you swipe in from the right edge of your screen, the Charms bar appears, giving you the tools you need for searching for apps and files, sharing apps, choosing program settings, and using other devices.

Swipe Up and Down

Swiping down from the top and up from the bottom of the Windows 8 screen enables you to unlock your Lock screen, select or close apps, and choose options.

1. To open the Windows 8 Lock screen, touch toward the bottom of the display.
2. Drag up and the Lock screen image scrolls up off the screen, displaying your login screen.

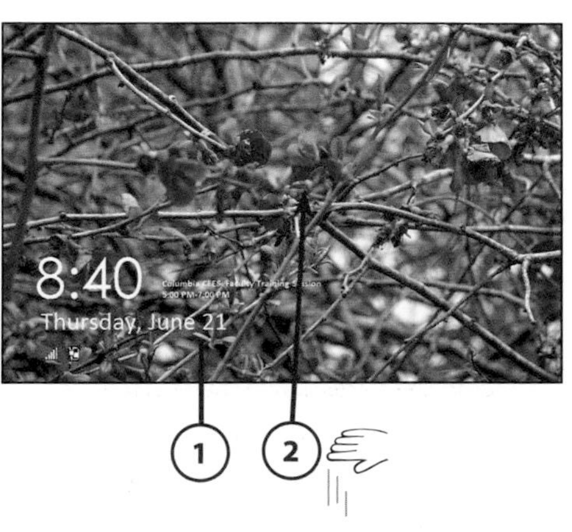

3. Swipe down when you are using an app to display options related to that app.

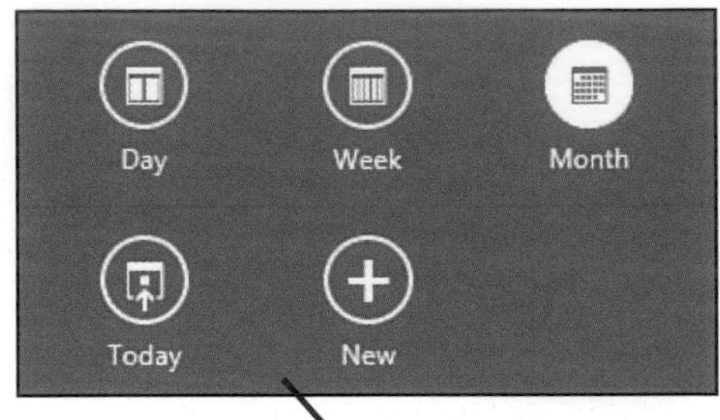

Options for Calendar app

Options for Maps app

Options, Schmoptions

Don't be dismayed if the options you see available for the particular app you have open differ from those shown here. Different apps offer different choices. For example, the Calendar app gives you different choices than the Maps app.

Swipe Down to Close

One of the big criticisms of Windows 8 Developer Preview was that initially Windows developers didn't provide a way to close apps because Windows 8 actually suspends apps not in use. Now in Windows 8, you swipe down, from the top to the bottom of the screen, to close an open app.

Pinch Zoom

The Pinch Zoom gesture enables you to enlarge and reduce the size of the content on the screen. On the Start screen, for example, when you pinch your fingers together, you reduce the size of the tiles so that you can easily move them around or group them the way you want them. When you want to enlarge an area of the screen, you use your fingers to expand the area, and the screen magnifies along with your gesture.

1. Display the Start screen or the app you want to use.
2. Reduce the size of the content displayed by placing your thumb and forefinger on the screen and "pinching" the area together.
3. Enlarge an area of the screen by placing your thumb and forefinger together on the screen and expanding the distance between them.

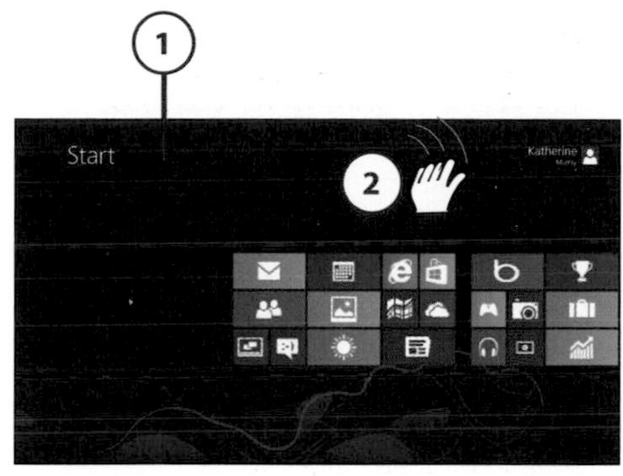

Semantic Zoom

You might see this feature referred to as *semantic zoom*, so named because it allows you to magnify a specific region of the display without disturbing other parts of the screen. If the app you're using was designed for Windows 8, chances are that it supports the pinch zoom gesture so that you can use two fingers to change the size of the content displayed on the screen.

>>>Go Further

INTRODUCING MICROSOFT SURFACE

On June 18, 2012, Microsoft unveiled the new Microsoft Surface, a state-of-the-art tablet with a built-in keyboard in the smartcover. Although you can use many tablets and touch devices with Windows 8, Microsoft Surface is beautifully optimized to work with the new operating system. Multiple touch points on the screen make navigating by touch as responsive and accurate as possible; and a live screen all the way out to the screen margins gives you the largest touch surface possible.

No matter what touch device you're using with Windows 8, if the device was capable of running Windows 7, you will be able to successfully navigate Windows 8. If you want the best Windows 8 experience on a tablet you can get, get in line for a Microsoft Surface tablet.

Getting Around with the Mouse and Keyboard

Windows 8 developers took a lot of heat initially when they talked about the touch interface of the new operating system. People talked and wrote about the "split personality" of the operating system, and mouse users worried that opening and closing programs, working with files, and changing system settings would be more difficult if they opted not to use touch techniques to carry out the tasks.

As the versions of Windows 8 have continued to evolve, however, Microsoft has made it clear that mouse users aren't being left in the dust. Windows 8 works equally well with touch, mouse, and keyboard.

Using the Mouse

The mouse can get you anywhere you want to go in Windows 8. Anything you can do with touch, you can do with your mouse—and then some. Whether you have a touch-capable device or not, you can still use your mouse for all of the common tasks you'll perform in Windows 8: start apps, find and open files, and choose program settings. By now, this operation may be old hat, but here's a refresher.

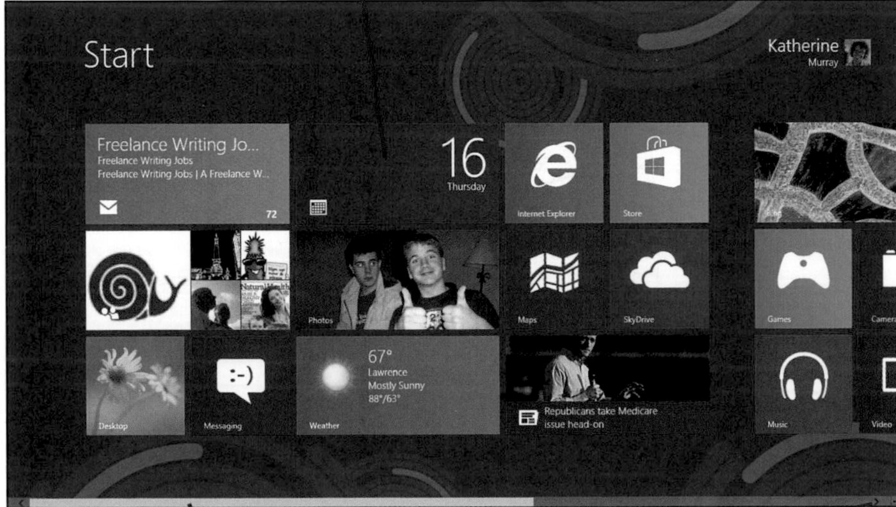

- Move the mouse to the bottom of the Windows 8 Start screen. The horizontal scroll bar appears. You can click the right arrow to move the display one screen to the right.

Right-click an app...

...to reveal options for that app

- To see the options for an app in the lower-right corner of the Start screen, right-click an app tile. From there, you can click the option you want to use.

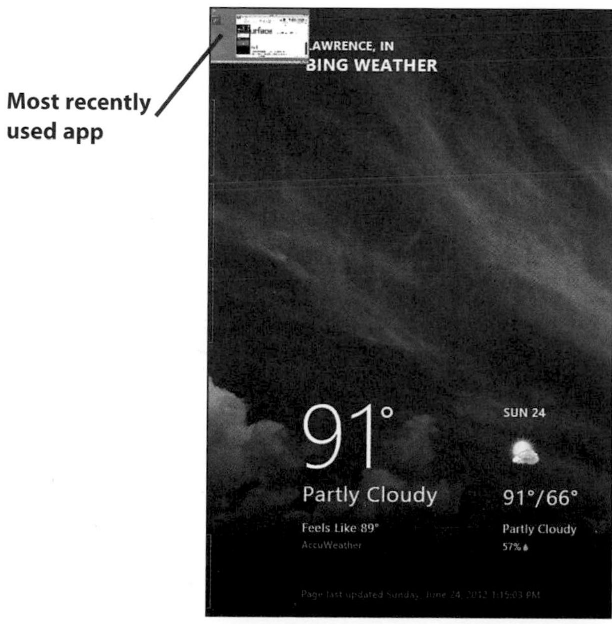

- Point to the upper-left corner of the screen to see a thumbnail of the most recently used app.

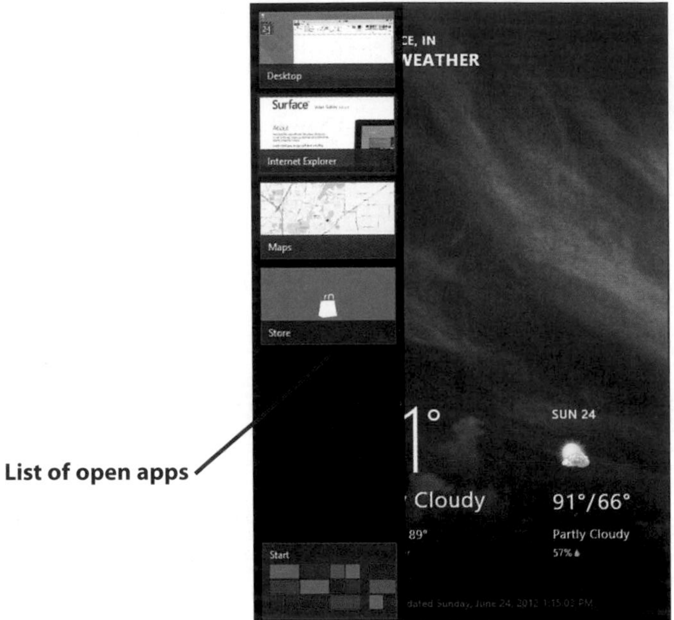

- Click and drag the mouse down the left side of the screen to display the thumbnail strip of open apps. Click the app you want to display.

Selecting Multiple Items

In File Explorer, you can use the mouse and keyboard together to select multiple items at once. If you want to choose several files in a folder, for example, you can click the first item and then press and hold the Shift key and click the last item you want to select. All items between the two clicked items are selected.

If you want to select multiple items that aren't next to each other, click the first item and press and hold the Ctrl key; then click all the other items you want to include.

Mouse Shortcuts for Navigating Windows 8

To do this:	Do this:
Unlock your Lock screen	Click any mouse button.
Display the Charms bar	Point to the lower-right corner of the Start screen.
Scroll the Start screen	Click and drag in the horizontal scroll bar at the bottom of the Start screen.
Show "power user commands"	Right-click in the lower-left corner of the Start screen.
Display app options on the Start screen	Right-click the app tile.
Display app options in an open app	Right-click anywhere in the app window.
Show a thumbnail of the next app that will appear if you drag in from the left	Move the mouse to the upper-left corner of the screen.
Display a thumbnail strip of open apps	Point to the upper-left corner of the screen, and when the first thumbnail appears, drag the mouse down the left side of the screen; the thumbnail strip appears.

>>>Go Further

GETTING TO IT

How do you feel about the disappearance of the Start menu? Lots of people are wringing their hands about that change, because the Start menu has stood for the place everything seemed to begin in since Windows 95. Now in Windows 8, we can just jump in and start anywhere, tapping and scrolling and flicking and zooming to our hearts' content. But as you already know if you've ever stood in front of a 31-flavors ice cream counter, sometimes having too much choice has a paralyzing effect.

>>>Go Further

If you know what you're looking for in Windows 8 and want to get right to it, you may enjoy using what some people are calling the "power user commands" in Windows 8. You'll find it by pressing Windows + X on your computer keyboard or your tablet's on-screen keyboard. The list of features includes many of those you are accustomed to working with in the Control Panel: Programs and Features, Mobility Center, Power Options, Device Manager, Command Prompt, Run, and more. Click the feature you want to use, or, to hide the feature list, simply tap or click anywhere outside the list.

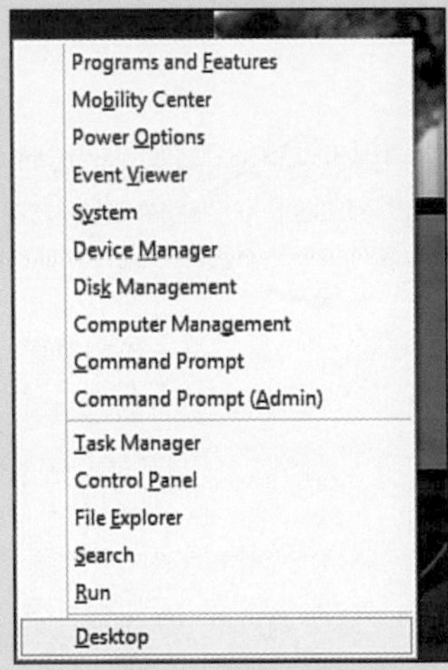

Using the (Real) Keyboard

Some things you'll need to do in Windows 8 you'll want a real, live keyboard to do. Sure you can type a quick memo or answer an email message on your tablet, using the on-screen keyboard. But when you need to write a 10-page report for a departmental meeting or you have lots of work to do storyboarding the next team presentation, chances are good that you'll want to use a real keyboard.

In addition to using touch and the mouse, you can also use your keyboard for navigating in Windows 8. When you use your keyboard to navigate the Start screen, move among apps, and manage windows, you use special keys, shortcut key combinations, and function keys.

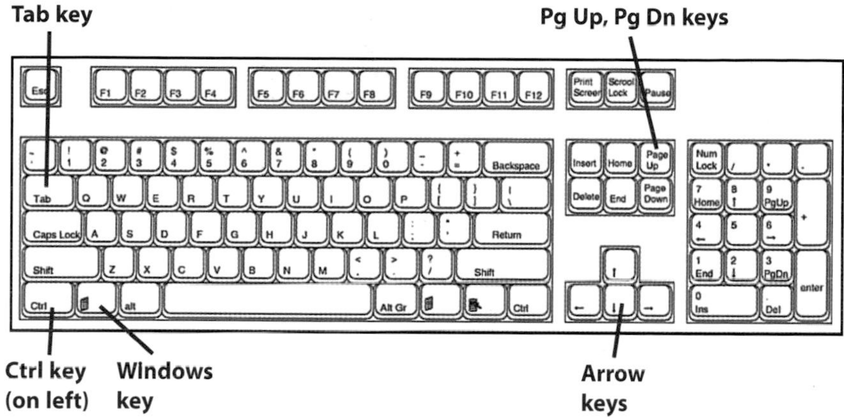

- The Windows key, located on the lowest row of your keyboard on the left side between the Ctrl and Alt keys, takes you back to the Start screen no matter where you are in Windows 8.
- You can use the Pg Up and Pg Dn keys as well as the arrow keys to move among apps on the Windows 8 Start screen.
- You use the Tab key to move from option to option in a dialog box.
- You can press key combinations (such as Ctrl and the letter assigned to a specific menu option) to perform operations.

Keyboard Shortcuts for Navigating Windows 8

To do this:	Do this:
Unlock your Lock screen	Press any key on the keyboard
Display the Charms bar	Press and hold the Windows key and press C
Display the Settings charm	Press Windows + I
Show the Search charm	Press Windows + Q
Return to the Start screen	Press the Windows key
Display the desktop	Press Windows + D
Lock Windows 8	Press Windows + L
Display "power user commands"	Press Windows + X
Cycle through open apps	Press Windows + Tab
Move to the next open app	Press Alt + Tab

A Keyboard Is a Keyboard Is a Keyboard...Right?

Depending on the type of computer you are using, you may notice some differences in the ways certain keys appear on your keyboard. The keyboard mentioned here is a "basic" keyboard layout. Your keyboard may or may not have a separate numeric keypad, function keys across the top, and a set of cursor-control keys that are separate from the alphanumeric keys. Additionally, you may notice that your Delete key or Backspace key is in a slightly different place than other keyboards you see. Take the time to learn where to find the common keys on your Windows 8 keyboard—once you know the lay of the land, finding the right key at the right time will be second nature.

Using a Touch Keyboard

In addition to the physical keyboard attached to your computer, there's also another kind of keyboard on touch devices like tablets you can use to add information and navigate in Windows 8. When you're using an app on a tablet that requires input—whether that input is a status update, a tweet, or a document—the touch keyboard appears in Windows 8. You can type on the touch keyboard as you would a normal physical keyboard, with one added benefit: You may also be able to display the keyboard as a "thumbs" keyboard, where the keys are arranged within the reach of your thumbs if you are holding a tablet device. Very smart!

Begin by launching an app that will require you to type something on your tablet. For example, you might open the Calendar app and start a new appointment. Then follow these steps to display and work with the Windows 8 touch keyboard:

1. Tap in the Add a Title area. The full keyboard appears along the bottom half of your screen.
2. Type the title of the new appointment.
3. If you want to change the type of keyboard displayed, tap the keyboard button in the lower-right corner of the keyboard.
4. A set of five choices appears. You can choose from the on-screen touch keyboard, a thumbs keyboard, a drawing tablet, the standard keyboard, or no keyboard. Tap the keyboard style you want to use.
5. The keyboard appears in the style you selected. Now you can type or draw your message.

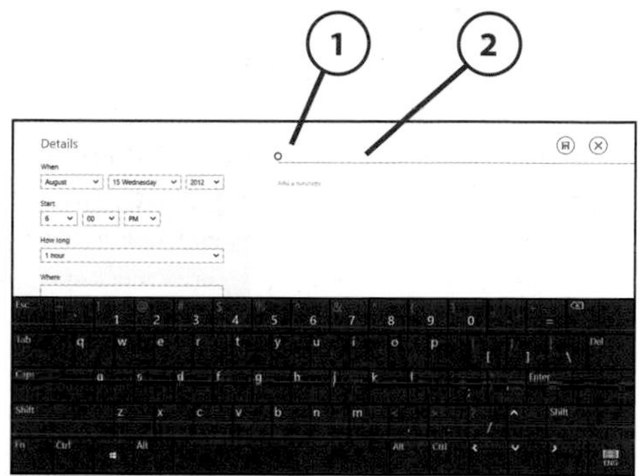

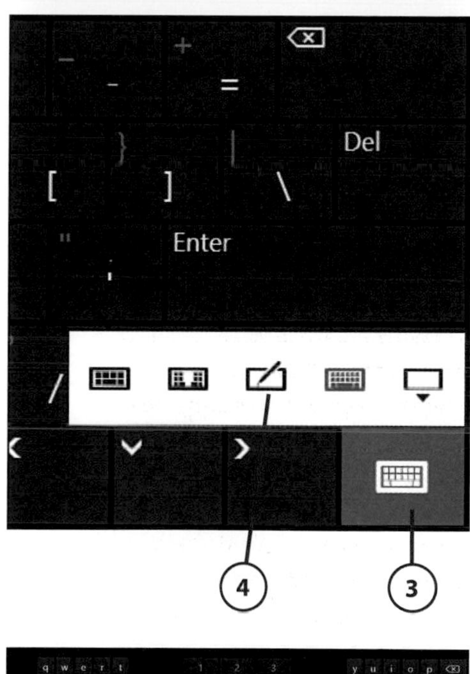

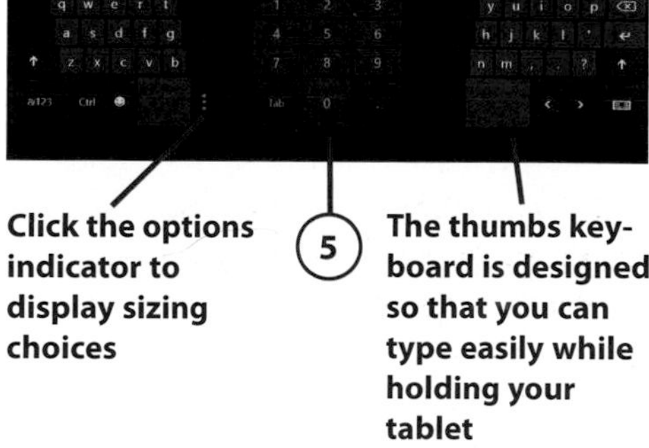

Click the options indicator to display sizing choices

The thumbs keyboard is designed so that you can type easily while holding your tablet

Displaying the Standard Keyboard

The first keyboard option available to you displays the on-screen tablet keyboard, which doesn't include function keys or special keys like the Windows key or Alt. The standard keyboard options is available to the left of the drawing pad icon, but if this keyboard isn't enabled in your PC settings, the item may be unavailable to you.

If the standard keyboard icon is grayed out, you can have Windows 8 display it as an option by swiping to display the Charms bar, tapping Settings, tapping Change PC Settings, and selecting General. Scroll down to the Touch Keyboard settings, and move the slider for the Make the Standard

Keyboard Layout Available to the On position. When you return to the on-screen keyboard display, you'll now be able to select and use the standard keyboard as one of the keyboard options.

Resizing the Thumbs Keyboard

Windows 8 lets you change the size of the thumbs keyboard so that typing is as easy as possible. To display your sizing choices, tap the three vertical dots just to the right of the keyboard segment on the left side of the screen. Medium is selected by default, but you can tap Small or Large to change the size of the keyboard.

>>>Go Further

SAY WHAT?!

Windows 8 has made some improvements to its Narrator accessibility feature, which reads the screen so that people with visual challenges can interact successfully with Windows 8. Narrator now offers a smoother performance and offers more natural-sounding voices (you can choose from three different PC voices—two female voices and one male voice). You can also control the speed at which Windows 8 narrates your experience, which can be helpful if you're just learning the lay of the land.

You can turn on Narrator as soon as you open the Lock screen, before you even log in to your computer. Simply tap the button in the lower-left corner of the login screen to begin the narration. You can also turn on Narrator by pressing and holding the Windows key and tapping the Volume Up button on your keyboard.

Internet Explorer 10 now includes Narrator support as well, so users can listen to web content, understand links, and make choices about commands on webpages.

Shutting Down or Putting Windows 8 to Sleep

One of the other basic tasks you'll need to do regularly with Windows 8 is turn your computer off. There's no obvious Shut Down command like the one placed so conspicuously on the Windows 7 Start menu.

The secret is that Windows 8 tucks away the Shut Down command in the Settings charm in the Windows 8 Charms bar. You can easily turn the computer off—or just send it off to sleep—by selecting the option of your choice from the Settings charm.

Putting Windows 8 to Sleep

When you're going to be away from your computer for a period of time but you aren't ready to turn everything off for the day, you can put your computer in Sleep mode to conserve energy and protect your files and programs while you're away.

1. Display the Charms bar by swiping left from the right edge of the screen or by pointing the mouse at the lower-right corner of the Start screen.
2. Tap or click Settings.
3. Tap or click Power. A list of options appears: Sleep, Shut Down, Restart.
4. Tap or click Sleep.

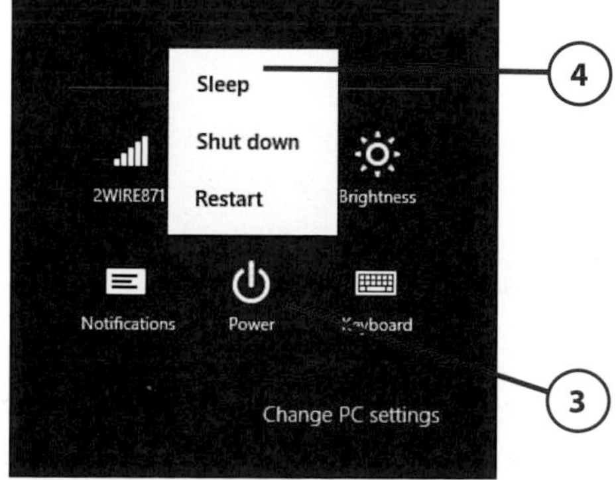

Wake Up, Little Fella

One of the great things about Sleep mode is that it is designed to help your computer spring back to life quickly as soon as you're ready. So even though it's a little distressing to see everything fade to black so fast after you tap Sleep, you'll be pleased to know a quick tap of the Power button on your PC brings everything back to full wakefulness almost instantly.

Shutting Down Windows 8

When you're ready to power down your computer, just tap or click Shut down instead.

1. In the Settings charm, tap Power.
2. Tap or click Shut down. If you have any open, unsaved files, Windows 8 prompts you to save them before shutting down.

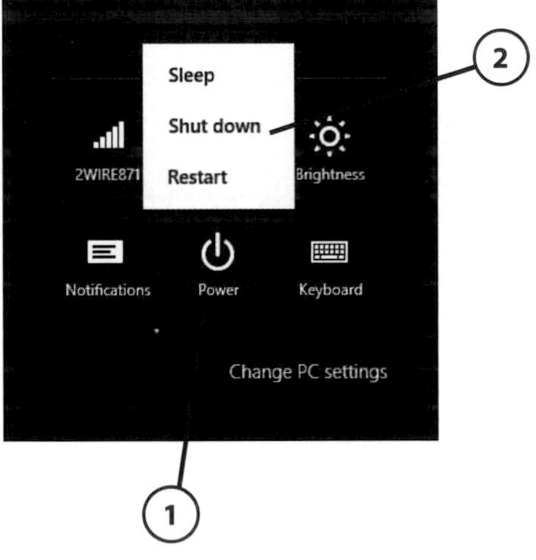

Starting Over

Of course you have one more option when you tap or click the Settings charm and select Power. If you want to restart your computer, you can tap Restart, and Windows 8 will power down and then reboot. You may be asked to restart your computer after you install an app or make a system setting change.

Finding the Help You Need

Windows 8 has revamped the look and feel of Help and Support to make finding articles, tips, and troubleshooting techniques easier than ever. If you've been looking for the little Help icon in Windows 8 you won't find it on the Start screen (it does still appear in File Explorer, though). But as you'll see getting Help in Windows 8 is as easy as typing four little characters.

Displaying Windows Help and Support

What's the first thing to do when you feel like yelling "Help!"? How about this:

1. On your computer keyboard, type *hel*. Before you even get to the letter P, Windows 8 instantly opens a search and displays the characters you typed in the search box.
2. Tap or click Help and Support. The Windows Help and Support window appears.

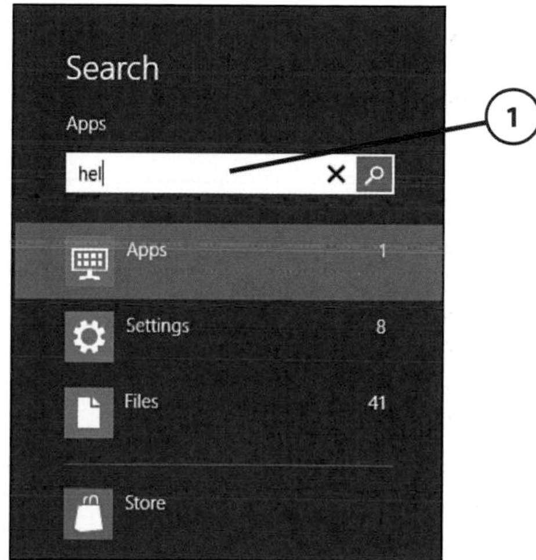

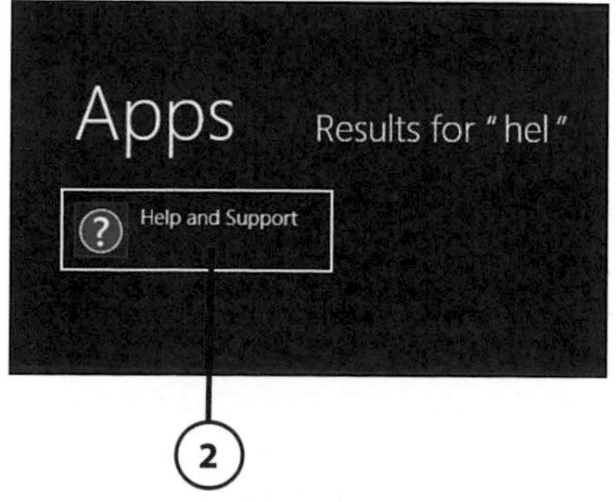

3. You can click one of the three displayed categories: Get Started, Internet & Networking, or Security, Privacy, & Accounts.
4. Or click in the Search box and type a word or phrase that reflects the type of information you want to find.
5. Click the Search tool.
6. Click a link to display a help article that looks as though it would offer the information you seek.

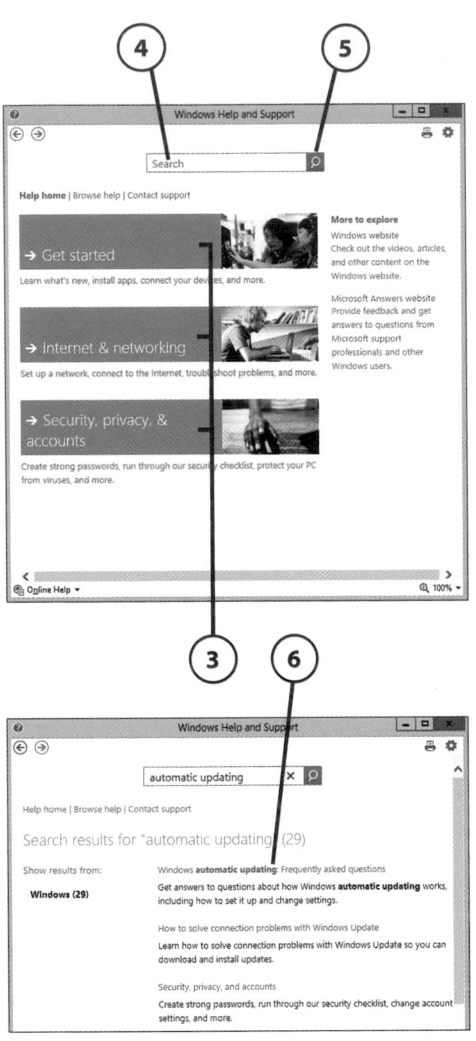

Changing Text Size

You can easily increase the text size in Help and Support by displaying the Windows Help and Support dialog box and then clicking Change Zoom Level in the lower-right corner of the Help window. Click Zoom In to magnify the text or Zoom Out to reduce the size of the text. You can also choose one of the other zoom percentages listed or click Custom to enter a zoom percentage of your own choosing.

Printing Help

If you find that you are looking up a certain task repeatedly, you might want to print the help information to keep close to your computer until you commit it to memory.

1. Search for the help information you need.
2. Click Print at the top of the help window.
3. Choose your printer.
4. Set your print options.
5. Click Print.

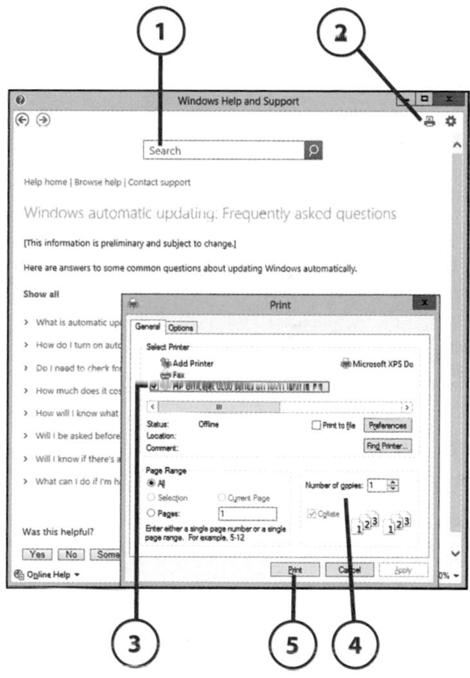

Including Online Resources

To the right of the Print tool in the Help window, you'll find a Tools icon. When you click or tap that tool, the Help Settings dialog box appears, displaying two help settings: Get Online Help, and Join the Help Experience Improvement Program, both of which are selected by default. The first option gives you access to the latest online help content when you search for help in Windows 8, and the second gives Microsoft permission to collect data about the way you're using the Help feature. If you don't want to send that type of information to Microsoft (even though you cannot be personally identified from the data collected), simply click to uncheck the box. Click OK to save any changes you made.

>>>Go Further

AND THAT'S JUST THE BEGINNING...

In addition to the help that's available to you in Windows 8 on your computer, you can visit Microsoft's Windows 8 site (www.windows.microsoft.com) to learn more about Windows 8 features, watch videos, and learn about basic tasks.

Check out the Windows Community forums to find out what other users are asking about Windows 8. You'll see responses from Microsoft MVPs (Most Valuable Professionals) that might just help solve a problem you're having. Check it out if you have one of those hard-to-answer Windows 8 questions that has been keeping you awake at night.

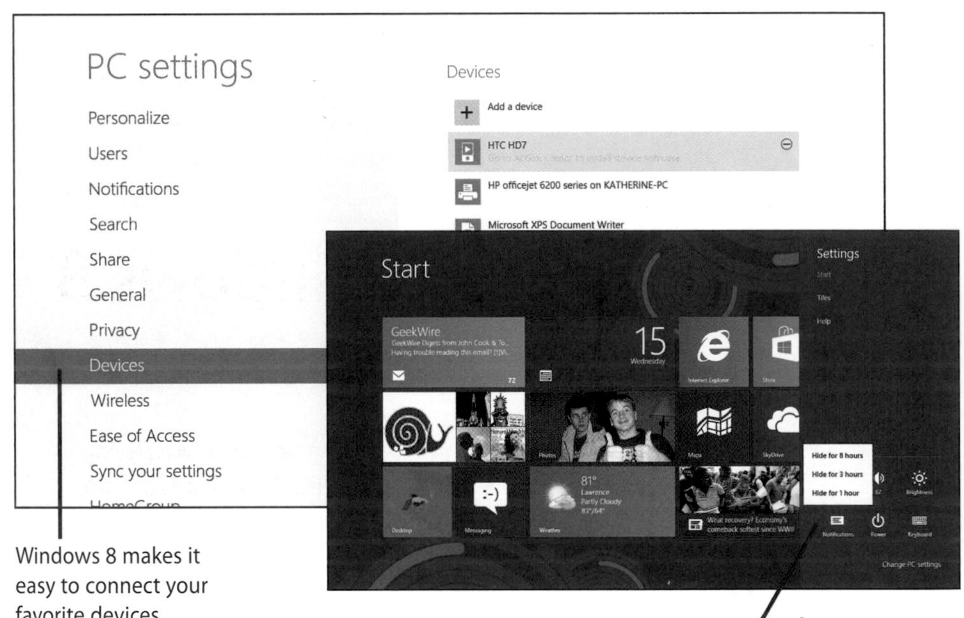

Windows 8 makes it easy to connect your favorite devices

You can change the way notifications appear in live tiles on the Start screen

This chapter shows you how to get your computer ready to use by demonstrating the following tasks:

- → Adding devices in Windows 8
- → Connecting to wireless networks
- → Managing your PC power
- → Transferring files
- → Refreshing your PC or reinstalling Windows 8

2

Preparing Your Windows 8 PC and Devices

Windows 8 makes it easy for you to get things up and running. When you plug a printer into your Windows 8 PC, for example, Windows 8 automatically detects the printer and installs the necessary drivers. You can also set up devices that Windows 8 doesn't recognize right off the bat.

In addition to setting up your devices to work with Windows 8, you can add new wireless connections and choose a power management setting that enables you to conserve as much power as possible while still giving you the computing performance power you want.

One other important aspect to preparing your PC involves knowing what to do if your computer begins behaving badly and you need to remove system changes or return to the way you'd previously configured it. Windows 8 makes this easy with the new Refresh and Reset tools. You can use Refresh or Reset to wipe away files and settings that are causing problems on your PC and restore your computer to its former functioning glory. Sound too good to be true?

It's not. Read on to finish preparing your Windows 8 PC so you can get on with all the fun stuff you want to do.

Adding Devices in Windows 8

Windows 8 includes an auto-discovery feature that scans for all devices connected to your PC or your network, detecting and connecting to printers, TVs, Xbox systems, and more. This means that Windows 8 may be able to find and install all your computer peripherals automatically, without you needing to do anything at all!

You'll begin by using the Settings charm in the Charms bar to see which devices Windows 8 has already discovered and added to your system. You can then add a device if you have one that isn't included on the generated list.

Flummoxed by the Start Screen?

If you find the Windows 8 Start screen a bit overwhelming and you'd like to know more about the lay of the land before you begin changing settings, take a look at Chapter 3, "Beginning with the Start Screen." That chapter introduces you to this important first screen and provides some basic navigational techniques (and some tweaks you can try) as you're acclimating to the new interface.

Viewing Installed Devices

You can take a look at the devices that Windows 8 has found and installed automatically as part of your setup. And then, if needed, you can add a device or remove devices that were added that you no longer need. To display the list, follow these steps:

1. On the Windows 8 Start screen, swipe in from the right or press Windows + C to display the Charms bar.
2. Tap or click Settings.

3. Tap or click Change PC Settings. The PC Settings window appears.
4. Tap or click Devices in the categories on the left. The devices installed with Windows 8 appear on the right side of the window.

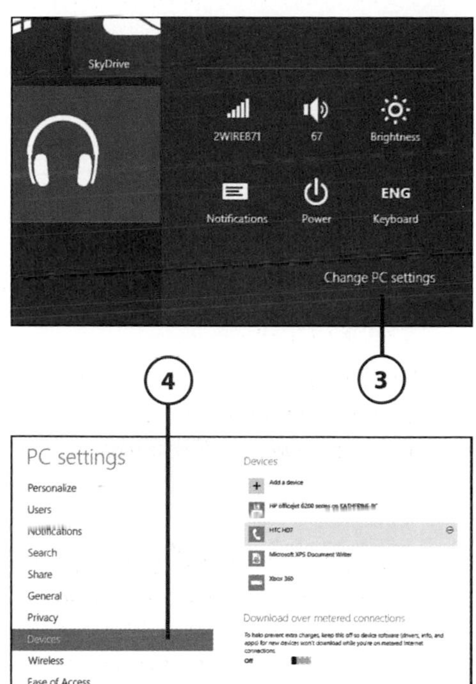

Checking Device Status

Notice that for some of the devices in the list, a status indicator shows whether the device is ready, offline, or needs your attention. This helps you know, for example, whether your printer is turned on and ready to receive files you send to be printed.

Adding a Device

If Windows 8 missed one of the devices that you feel should be on the device list, you can scan again to see whether the device is discoverable. Before you tap or click Add a Device, be sure that the device is connected to your computer or your home network and turned on. After you choose Add a Device, Windows 8 scans your computer and displays any found devices in a popup list. You can then select the item you want to add to the Devices list in Windows 8.

Connecting a Device

You can also add a device by simply connecting it to your Windows 8 computer and letting Windows 8 do the setup for you. For example, you might want to connect your Windows Phone so that you can easily sync your files, contacts, and media.

1. With the Devices category selected in the PC Settings screen, connect your phone.
2. After a moment, Windows 8 displays the device in the Devices list. Tap or click the device. In this case, Windows 8 displays a message that setup needs to be finished in the Action Center.
3. Click the link to go directly to the Action Center. The Action Center shows you that one of your devices needs installation software.
4. Tap or click Install. A Windows Phone popup appears (assuming you've connected a Windows Phone).
5. Tap or click Get Software.

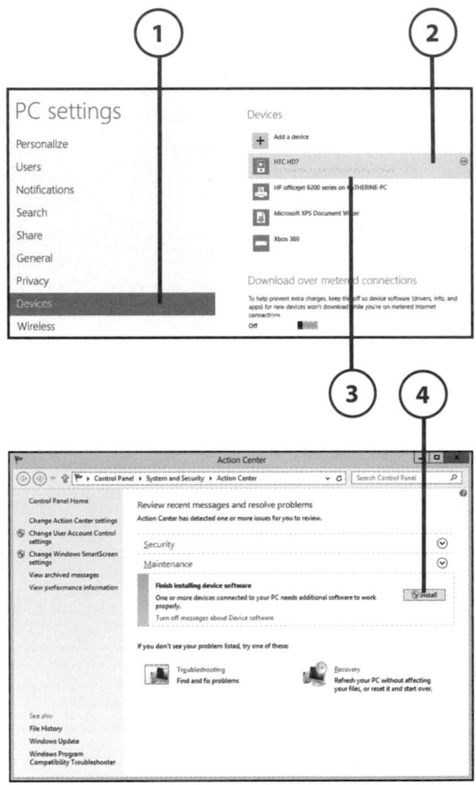

6. On the Zune web page that appears, tap or click the Download Now button.

7. A message box appears, asking whether you want to Run or Save the software. Click Run.

After you click Run, the Windows 8 download process takes over. The process prompts you to unplug your phone from your computer before the software is installed. When the download is finished, Zune displays the Microsoft License Terms; click Accept to continue and then click Install to install the Zune software.

After the install is complete, the Zune software launches and your phone synchs automatically with your Windows 8 computer.

It's Not All Good

HANGING ON THE DOWNLOAD

The first few times I tried to download the Zune software to Windows 8, the whole process hung up and sat lifeless on my computer screen. If this happens to you, you can try to get the download moving again by clicking the Pause button on the Downloads screen and then clicking Resume. If that doesn't start the download process, clear the Zune download by clicking Clear List in the Downloads dialog box, close your browser, and start the process again.

Removing a Device

You can also remove a device you no longer need from the Devices list. Having extra devices in the Devices list doesn't do any harm, but if you want to keep the list short so that you can easily find what you need, you may want to take any unnecessary items off the list.

1. Tap or click the small symbol to the right of the device you want to take off the list.
2. If you're sure you want to remove the device, tap or click the Remove button. Windows 8 removes the item from the list.

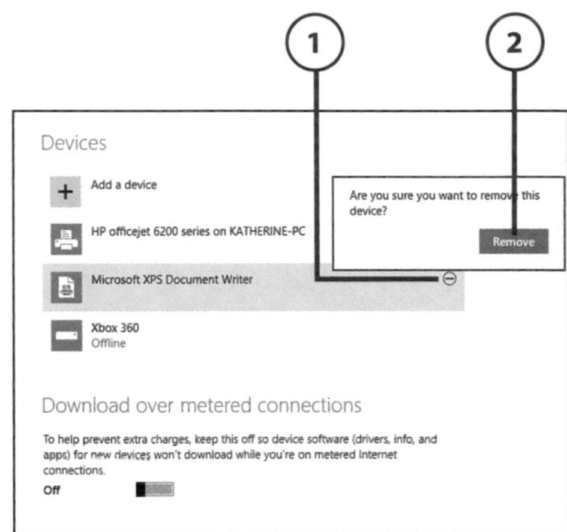

Troubleshooting Hardware Devices

Luckily, most of the time, your printer, router, scanner, camera, and drawing tablet function the way they're supposed to. You plug them in to your Windows 8 PC, Windows finds the right drivers, and they're ready for you to use. Piece of cake.

But once in a while, devices have trouble. Your printer doesn't print anything. Your router is blinking, but you have no Internet connectivity. Windows 8 doesn't seem to be recognizing your MP3 player.

If you have trouble installing a device, you can use a Windows 8 troubleshooter to sleuth out the problem. Here are the steps:

1. On the Windows 8 Start screen, type *troubleshooter*.
2. Tap or click Settings.
3. Tap or click Find and Fix Problems. The Control Panel opens, displaying the Troubleshoot Computer Problems dialog box.
4. Tap or click Configure a Device. In the Hardware and Devices screen that appears, click Next to begin the troubleshooter. Windows 8 detects and then displays a report of findings. The type of information you see depends on the device you're using and the problems Windows 8 finds. When Windows 8 locates a problem, it asks whether you want to apply the selected fix or skip it.

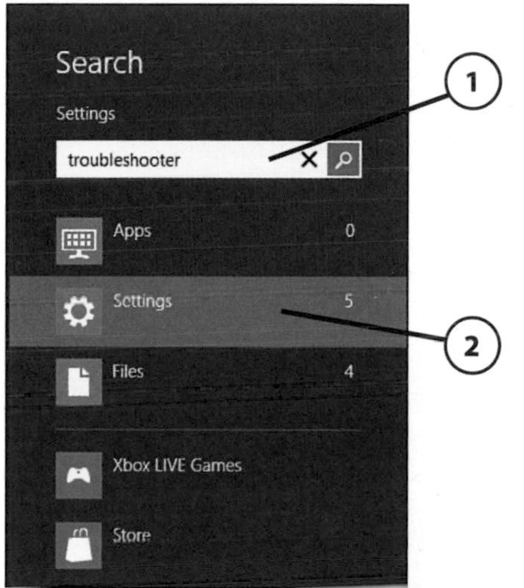

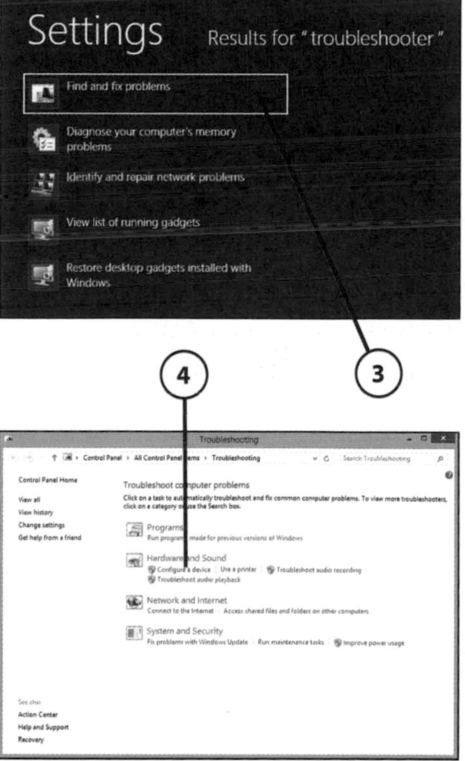

5. Click or tap Apply This Fix to have Windows 8 take the suggested action.
6. Click or tap Skip This Fix if you want to bypass the suggestion and see another alternative. When the troubleshooter completes, a list of problems and actions is displayed.
7. If the troubleshooter didn't correct the problem you're having, tap or click Explore Additional Options to display a list of other ways you can find help for the hardware problem.
8. If the hardware issue has been fixed, tap or click Close the Troubleshooter.

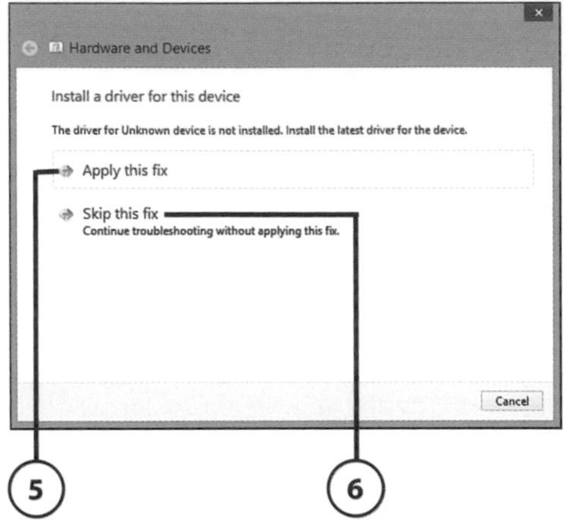

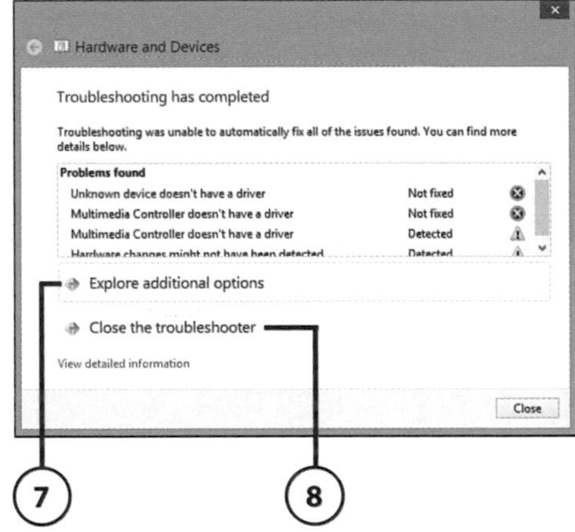

>>>Go Further

STILL YELLING HELP

If you've been through the troubleshooter and tried exploring additional options and nothing is fixing the problem you're having, you can search online for help in the Windows Community, available at www.windows.microsoft.com. In addition to other Windows users, you'll find Microsoft MVPs (Most Valuable Professionals) who may be able to offer insight into the problem you're having. You also may be able to find a fix to the problem by searching for information about it using your favorite search engines.

Additionally, you can visit the website of the hardware manufacturer to see whether there are any known fixes for your particular issue. You may find it's something as simple as a driver that needs updating, and the manufacturer site will be able to walk you through that process (or help you connect with tech support in some way).

Connecting to Wireless Networks

Today, it's unusual when we *aren't* online. We go from the corporate network at work to Bluetooth or mobile connectivity on the road to Wi-Fi at the neighborhood coffee shop. Windows 8 is good at discovering networks in your area and giving you the ability to connect (if you have the password or network key, of course) by simply tapping the connection you want to make. You can easily switch among networks by using the Networks tool in the Settings charm.

Connecting to an Available Network

Your first step to getting online involves taking a look at all the networks Windows 8 is aware of and choosing the one you want to use.

1. Swipe left or point the mouse to the lower-right corner of the Start screen to display the Windows 8 Charms bar.
2. Tap or click Settings.
3. Tap or click the network icon displaying your current Internet connection. Windows 8 lists all network connections in your area.

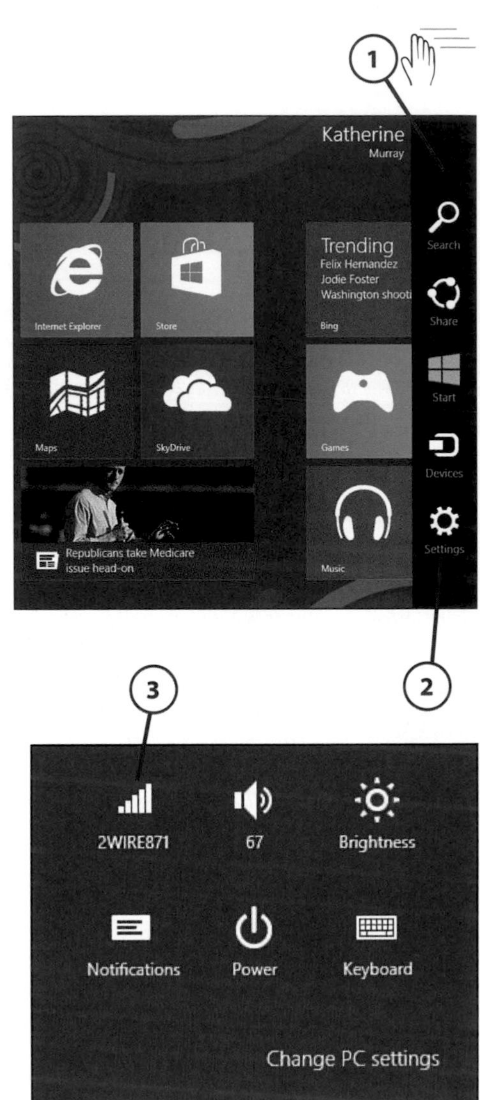

4. Tap or click the connection you want to change.
5. If you want Windows 8 to connect to the network automatically whenever it's present, click or tap the Connect Automatically checkbox.
6. Tap or click Connect to connect to the network immediately. Similarly, if you want to disconnect from a network to which you're connected, tap or click the Disconnect button.

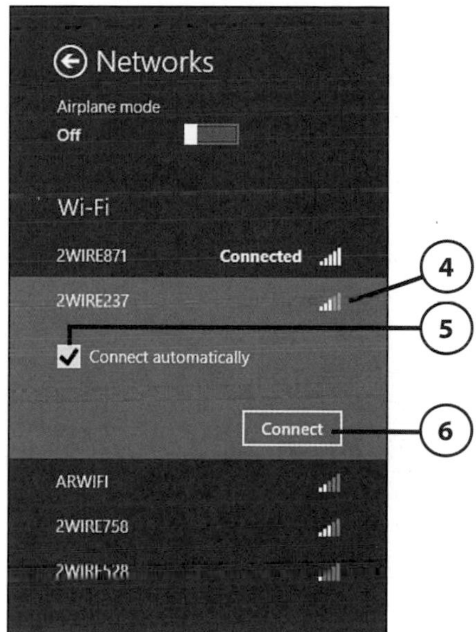

>>>Go Further

REPAIRING NETWORK CONNECTIONS

If for some reason you're having trouble connecting to the Internet, Windows 8 can help you identify the problem and correct it. On the Windows 8 Start screen, begin typing *repair network connection*.

The phrase appears in the Search Settings box. Tap or click Settings. In the results list on the left side of the screen, tap or click Identify and Repair Network Problems. This launches Windows Network Diagnostics and a troubleshooting utility investigates the connection problem. Complete any steps as suggested by the troubleshooter; if no problems are found, the troubleshooter closes without any further action from you.

Managing Your PC Power

Thank goodness, we're thinking more these days about the amount of power we use. This is good not only for our bank accounts but also for our planet. Computers today are created to be more energy efficient than ever. We want the batteries in our laptops, netbooks, and smartphones to last as long as possible. The more power we conserve, the longer our power lasts—and that's a good thing.

One thing we've learned in green tech is that small changes can really make a big difference. Changing the brightness of your screen, or turning off Wi-Fi or roaming when you can, may save a lot of processing going on behind-the-scenes. Even reducing energy consumption on your home desktop PC can have tangible benefits, like reducing your electric bill. Those simple techniques, added to steps like thinking through what happens when you close your laptop cover, can add up to smarter energy use for us all.

Windows 8 is the most energy efficient version of Windows yet, with careful attention paid to apps that are in the foreground. Apps that cycle to the background and go into suspended mode have no impact on power usage at all. And because Windows 8 boots so efficiently, you won't experience any lag time while you wait for an app you select to load up. That's a big change from the days you could push the power button and then go to the kitchen to get a cup of coffee while waiting for your computer to boot up.

Choosing a Power Management Plan

Windows 8 supports the same power management plans that were available in Windows 7. The Balanced power plan balances usage with performance, and Power Saver reduces computer performance a bit to lower your energy use. Selecting a plan is as simple as pointing and clicking.

1. On the Start screen, type *plan*.
2. In the Search Apps panel, click Settings.
3. Click Choose a Power Plan. The Power Options dialog box appears.
4. Click the power plan you want to use.

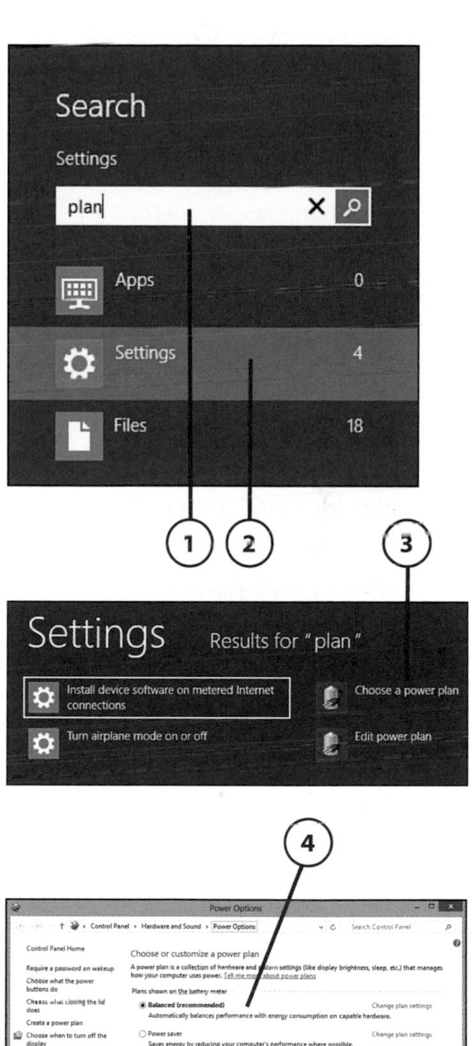

Wait, Reverse That

If you change the power settings and then have second thoughts and want to undo your changes, you can click the Restore Default Settings for This Plan link that appears in the same window where you modify the plan settings. Windows 8 returns the plan to its default settings.

Screen's So Bright I Gotta Wear Shades

One easy way to save some power right off the bat is to click the slider in the Screen Brightness control at the bottom of the Choose or Customize a Power Plan dialog box and drag it to the left. This dims the display relative to the slide setting on the bar. This setting is applied to all of Windows, so your apps will reflect the same level of screen brightness you set here. You can change the brightness level at any time by returning to this screen and adjusting the brightness level more to your liking.

Changing Power Settings

Each of the power management plans you can choose with Windows 8 enables you to set priorities about the way you use Windows 8 and the type of power you use and save. For example, you can choose a plan that saves as much power as possible or select a plan that balances the power use with your computer's performance.

You can view and change the settings to fit the plan you have in mind and tweak individual settings along the way.

1. On the Start screen, type *power options*.
2. Tap or click Settings in the Search Settings panel. A number of choices appear related to power management for your computer.
3. Click or tap the setting you want to change. Different dialog boxes will appear depending on the option you select. The System Settings dialog box appears when you choose either Change What the Power Buttons Do or Change What Closing the Lid Does.

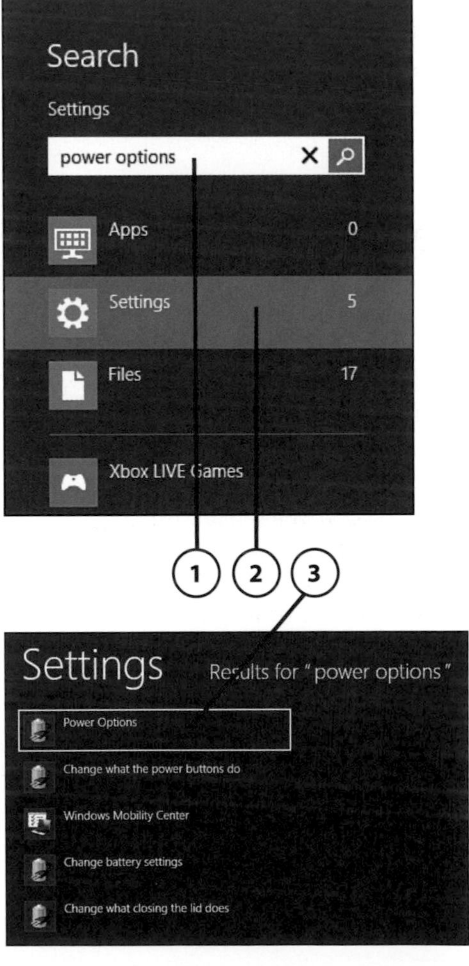

4. Choose whether you want your computer to sleep, hibernate, shut down, or do nothing when you press the power button. Choose the setting first for your computer when it is running on battery and then when it is plugged in.
5. Select what you want the computer to do when you press the sleep button in battery and plugged-in modes.
6. Choose what you want the computer to do when you close the computer lid (again, for both battery and plugged-in scenarios).
7. Click Save Changes.

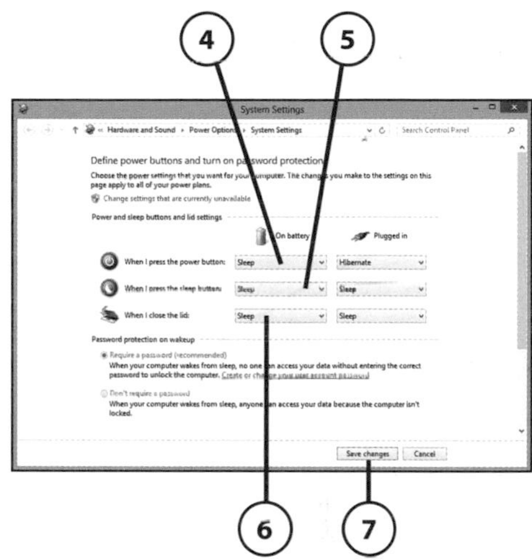

Transferring Files

If your new Windows 8 computer is the latest in a line of computers you've used at home or at work, it's likely that you have files you'd like to transfer from one computer to another. How do you move the things you most need to be able to carry on your work? You have a few options:

- Use Windows Easy Transfer.
- Save the files to Microsoft SkyDrive or another online storage space.
- Add both computers to your home network and transfer files from one to the other.

You'll learn about saving files to Microsoft SkyDrive and setting up a home network and establishing a Homegroup in Chapter 12, "Connect with Other Computers, Devices, and the Cloud," so this section focuses on using Windows Easy Transfer to move files and folders from your old computer to your new one.

Transferring Programs

The process for moving programs from one computer to another sometimes involves uninstalling the program on one computer and installing it on the new one, due to the licensing issues involved in legal copies of software you may have purchased. Some programs enable you to log in to your account online and download the software from the company's website. Be sure to gather the following information from programs on your old PC before you uninstall the programs:

- Your user ID and password
- Your software registration number
- Any toll-free numbers or websites related to the software
- Any identifying information that shows your legitimate ownership of the software

Using Windows Easy Transfer

Windows Easy Transfer transfers files, settings, Internet favorites, email, and more from your old computer to your new one. Before you begin using the utility, log in to both computers as an administrator and make sure both have Windows Easy Transfer installed. (If not, you can download the tool from the Microsoft Downloads site.)

Begin by using Windows Easy Transfer on your old computer to prepare a transfer file that you can then install on your new Windows 8 PC. Then, when you have saved the transfer file (you can use these steps for both computers), add the transferred files to your computer by following these steps:

1. On your existing computer, search for *Windows Easy Transfer.*
2. Tap or click it in the results list.
3. Skip past the Welcome to Windows Easy Transfer screen by clicking next and, on the next screen, choose the way in which you want to make the transfer. You can use an Easy Transfer Cable (this is a specific cable from Microsoft designed to work with Windows Easy Transfer), transfer files over your network, or use an external hard disk or a USB flash drive.
4. Choose This is My Old PC. The next screen gives you a chance to assign a password to the transfer file you create. Type the password and then retype it to confirm it. If you choose not to assign a password, leave the fields blank. Tap or click Save.

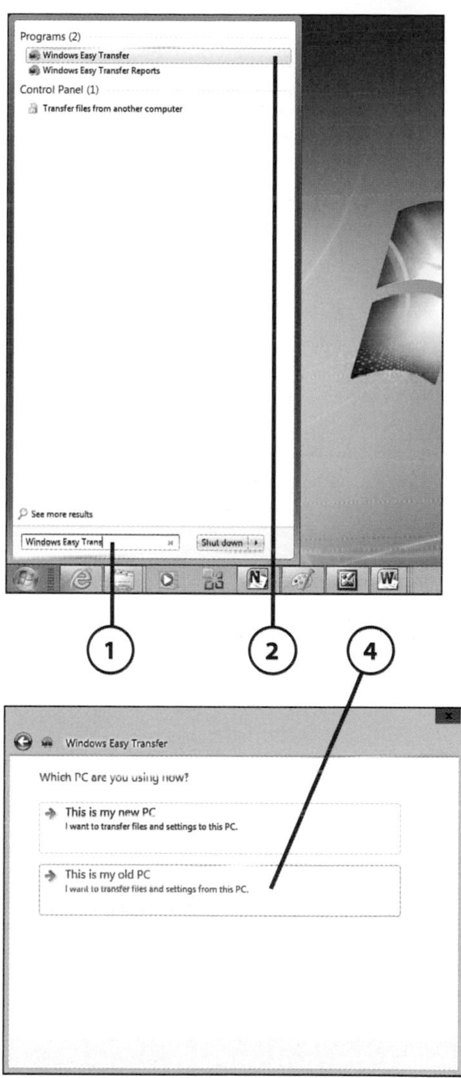

5. On the Windows 8 Start screen, type *Windows Easy Transfer*.
6. Tap or click it in the results area.
7. Click or tap Next and choose the method you selected for moving the files; then choose This Is My New PC. Windows Easy Transfer asks whether you've already saved the file to an external hard disk or USB flash drive. Choose Yes and in the Open dialog box, navigate to and choose the Easy Transfer file and click Open. The next screen enables you to enter the password for the file, if you assigned one.
8. If you specified a password when you created the transfer file, type it in the space provided.
9. Click Next. Windows makes the connection and begins copying the files from one system to another (if you elected to transfer files over your network). When the transfer process is complete, your files will be installed and ready to use on your Windows 8 PC.

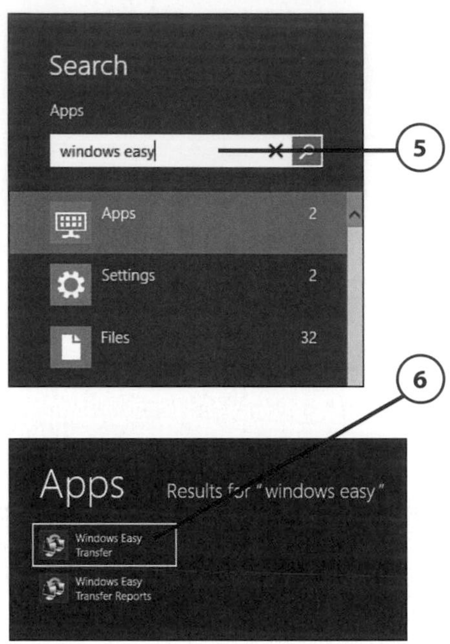

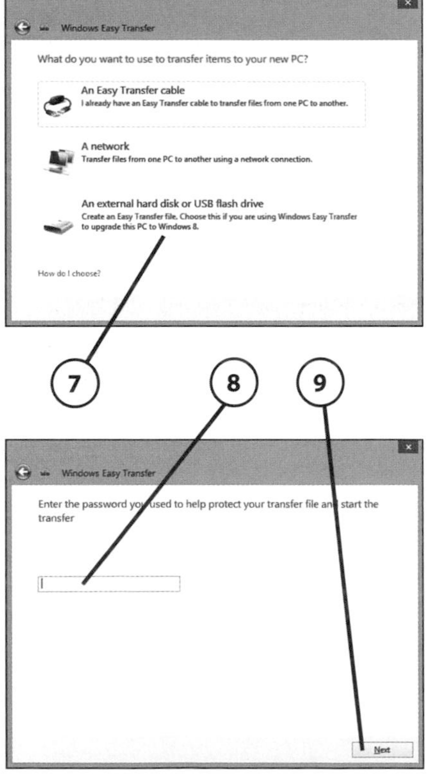

Checking Administrator Status

To make sure you're logged in as the administrator, type User Accounts on the Windows 8 Start screen; then tap or click User Accounts. In the Search screen, tap Settings and tap or click User Accounts in the results list. Your user account appears, listing the account type assigned to your account. If you need to change the setting, click or tap Change Your Account Type and select Administrator; click or tap Change Account Type to save your change.

>>>Go Further

CHOOSING THE RIGHT TRANSFER METHOD

Windows Easy Transfer gives you three different ways to transfer your files, depending on the type of setup you have and how you want to copy the files:

- If you bought an Easy Transfer cable when you purchased your computer, you can use it to connect the two systems you'll be using to transfer the files. (Note that this is not a standard Universal Serial Bus [USB] cable. You can purchase an Easy Transfer cable online or by visiting your local electronics store.)
- If you've set up a home network and both computers are part of the network, you can transfer files as easily as you would copy them from one folder to another. You learn more about home networks in Chapter 12.
- You can also use a USB flash drive or an external hard drive to store the file Windows Easy Transfer prepares for you. You can then move the flash drive or external hard drive to the new computer and transfer the files.

Refreshing Your PC or Reinstalling Windows 8

The way you deal with your computer when it is behaving badly has been dramatically improved in Windows 8. Now instead of crossing your fingers and rebooting—or perhaps arbitrarily choosing a Restore Point and hoping your journey back in time will fix the trouble you're having—now you can use Windows Refresh to simply refresh your Windows 8 installation without wiping away any files or settings. Or, if necessary, you can reinstall Windows 8 and return your computer to its pristine, out-of-the-box state.

Refreshing Your PC

If you find that a few of your apps aren't working the way they should or your computer has been behaving unreliably, you can refresh your computer to restore the files and settings to their original state without losing your files, media, and settings.

1. On the Windows 8 Start screen, display the Charms bar.
2. Tap or click Settings.
3. Tap or click Change PC Settings. The PC Settings screen appears.
4. Select General from the list on the right.
5. Scroll down and tap or click Get Started for the Refresh Your PC Without Affecting Your Files. Windows displays the Refresh Your PC message, letting you know what will happen to your files and program changes.

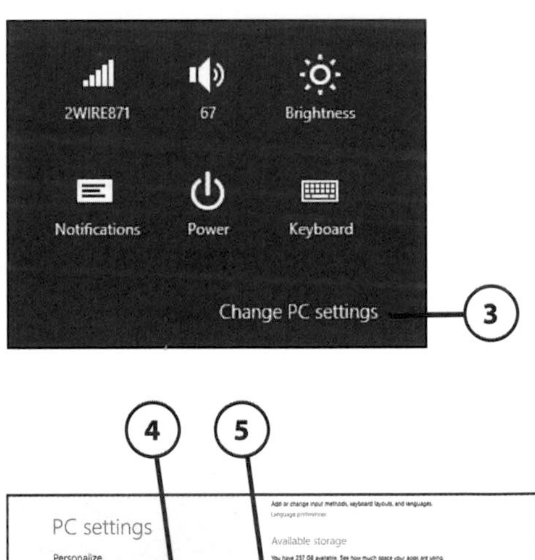

6. Tap or click Next. Windows 8 completes the refresh process, restarts your computer, and returns you to the Windows 8 Lock screen so that you can log in.

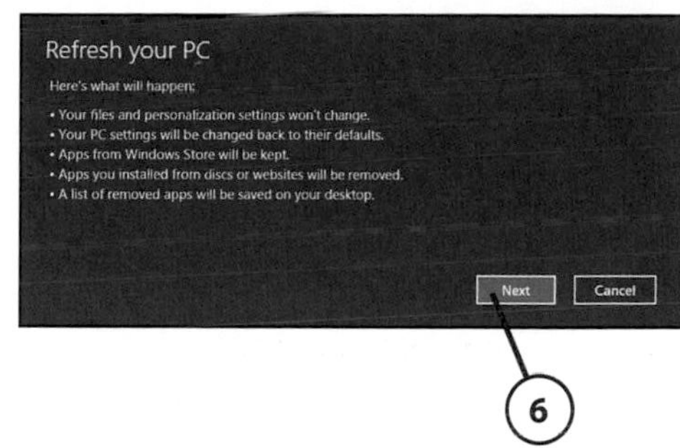

When You Need to Start Again: Reinstall

When all else fails and you need to wipe away everything on your computer and start again, you use Reset to do that. You can also use Reset when you want to donate your computer to someone else—Reset cleans all your data, settings, and personal information off your computer, which is an important thing to do before donating it.

1. Display the PC Settings screen and tap or click the General category.
2. Scroll to the bottom of the General list and tap or click the Get Started button in the Remove Everything and Reinstall Windows area.
3. The Reset Your PC and Start Over message appears, letting you know that your personal files and apps will be deleted and all PC settings will be returned to the factory default settings. Click Next to continue.

   Windows 8 launches the reset process, and all your files and settings are removed from the computer.

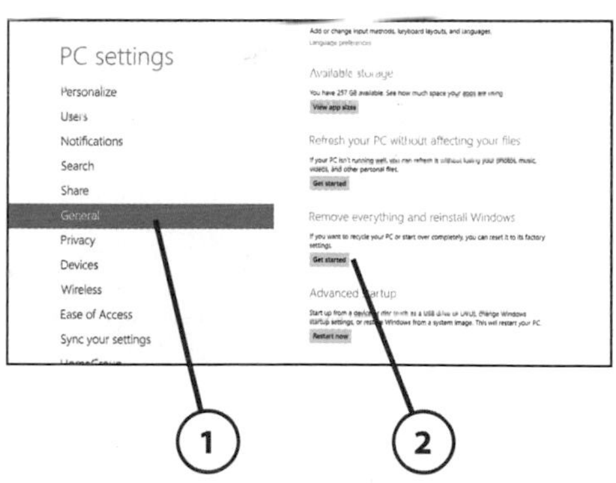

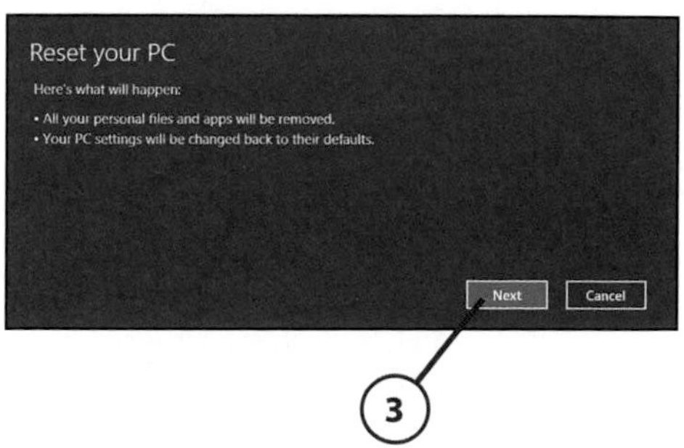

Starting Windows or Restoring from Other Media

If you have previously created a Windows system image or want to start Windows from a USB or a DVD, you can use the Advanced Startup setting at the bottom of the General category in the PC Settings screen.

>>>Go Further

USING THE WINDOWS MOBILITY CENTER

If you are looking for one central location where you can go to find the settings that control the way you use your computer on the road, you don't need to look any farther than the Windows Mobility Center. You can display the center by typing *Windows Mobility Center* on the Start screen and tapping or clicking Settings. Select the app to open the Windows Mobility Center window.

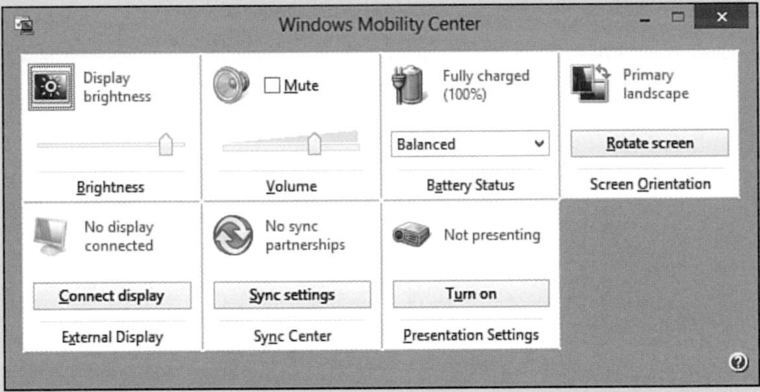

You can change options for Brightness, Volume, Battery Status, Screen Orientation, External Display, Sync Center, and Presentation Settings in the Windows Mobility Center. Simply tap or click the control of the item you want to change and select your choice.

If you use the Windows Mobility Center often, add it to the Start screen so you can reach it easily by swiping the app or right-clicking it. Then choose Pin to Start to add it as a tile on your Start screen.

You can easily search for apps, settings, and files from any point in Windows 8

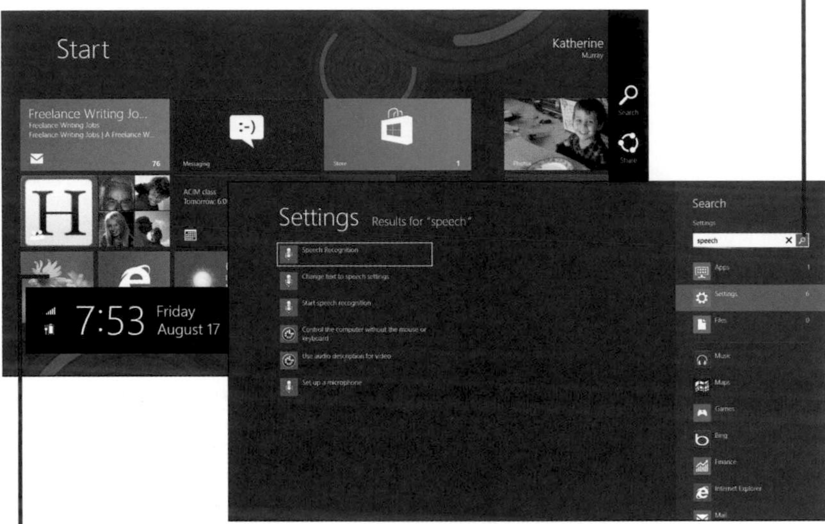

The Windows 8 Start screen brings everything you need to one colorful place

In this chapter, you find out everything you need to know to use and personalize your Windows 8 Start screen by performing these tasks:

- → Exploring the Start screen
- → Understanding Windows 8 charms
- → Changing the way tiles look and behave
- → Moving, grouping, and removing apps
- → Searching in Windows 8

Beginning with the Start Screen

As you have no doubt realized by now, the Windows 8 Start screen is a whole new animal in operating systems. Instead of the (boring) Windows 7 desktop, you've got a lot to feast your eyes on in Windows 8. The desktop moves and the display changes every few seconds as its app tiles update headlines, show social network statuses, and cycle through new photos. What's more, you can easily move the whole screen by swiping a finger to the left (if you have a touch-ready device) or by dragging the scroll bar along the bottom of the display, if you're using a mouse.

Also on the Windows 8 Start screen, you'll find the tools you need to change program settings, search for what you're looking for, and control the way apps behave. Where are these tools, you may wonder? This chapter shows you how to display the Charms bar and the Apps options and make all the tools you need magically appear.

Exploring the Start Screen

Okay, we've been sneaking around the edges of the Start screen in previous chapters, but let's really dig in. This beautiful, moving interface brings a great deal of information to you right off the bat. With live tiles, a scrolling screen, and access to all your favorite Windows tools (yes, even though you may not see them at the moment), you'll be using the Start screen as the beginning point for much of what you do in Windows 8.

What's the Difference Between an App and a Program?

Yes, the new lingo comes with the territory on Windows 8. Actually an app *is* a program, but now we're saying it in a more hip, cooler way. An app might also mean a smaller, more focused tool, like a photo app or a calendar app, that instead of doing everything under the sun focuses on doing one thing really well. That being said, however, you'll notice that even bigger desktop apps that run on your Windows 8 Desktop—like Microsoft Office—are still called applications, or, sometimes, apps.

The Start screen gives you access to apps on your Windows 8 computer and makes it easy for you to get to the programs you use most often. You'll discover when you first fire up your Windows 8 PC or tablet that a number of apps appear by default, but you can also add apps, create new groups or apps, and remove apps from the Start screen you don't think you'll need.

Also on the Start screen, you can display the Windows desktop, get to your photos or music, begin browsing with Internet Explorer 10, or start shopping in the Windows Store.

Notice that in Windows 8 your system icons—for example, your power indicator and the icon showing network connectivity—appear when you display the Charms bar. When you display the Charms bar, the system information icons appear to the left of the clock on the left side of the Start screen.

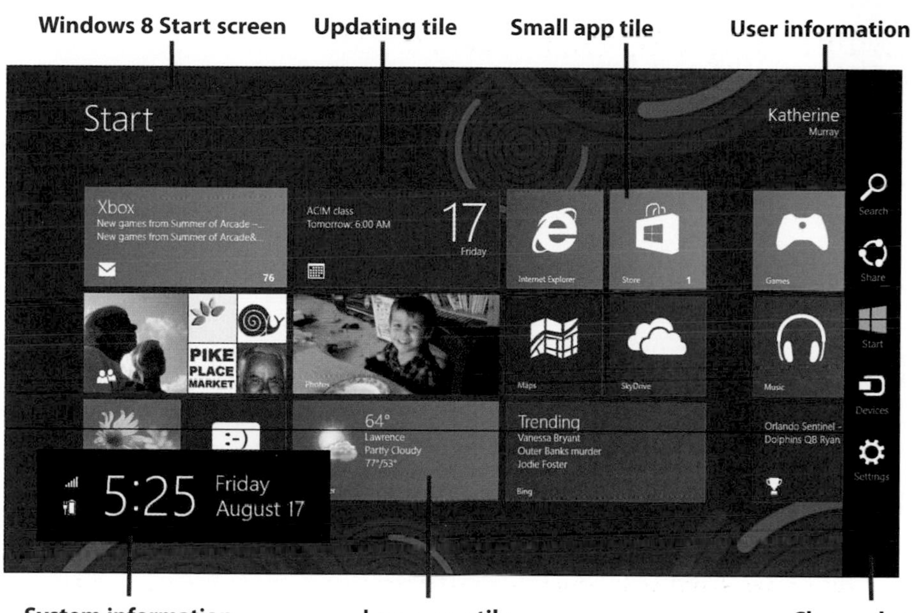

Diving Deeper on Windows 8

This chapter shows you how to use the Start screen as the starting point for the apps you'll use in Windows 8, but later chapters in the book go into more detail on the specific tools. For example, you'll learn more about working with the Windows 8 desktop in Chapter 4, "Working with the Windows 8 Desktop," browsing for new apps in Chapter 7, "Exploring Windows 8 Apps," working with the File Explorer to manage files and folders in Chapter 8, "Managing Files with File Explorer," and beginning to browse in Chapter 9, "Always Online with Internet Explorer 10."

Viewing All Your Apps

If you don't see a specific app that you would like to use—Windows Paint, for example—you can use the All Apps tool to find and launch it. You can also use the Search tool to locate the app you're looking for, which you'll learn about later in this chapter.

1. Swipe up from the bottom of the Windows 8 Start screen. If you're using a mouse, right-click at the bottom of the screen. The apps bar appears.
2. Tap or click All Apps.

3. Swipe the screen or use your mouse to browse through all available apps.
4. If you want to launch an app, tap or click it.

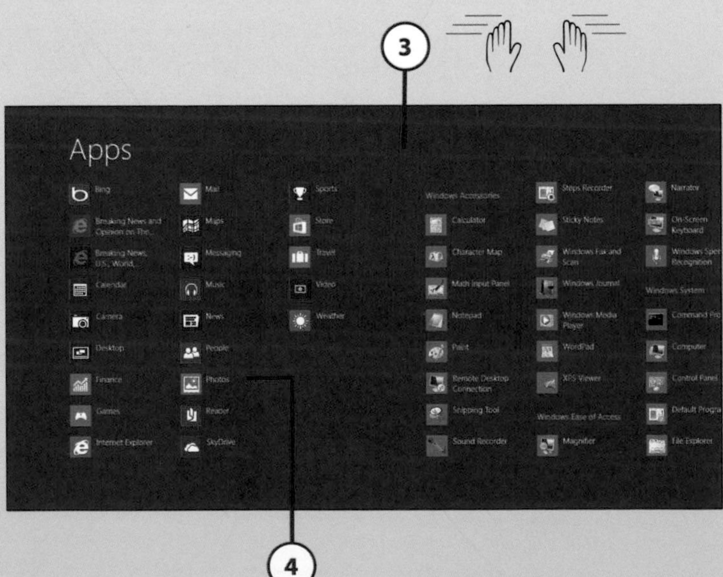

Displaying Administrative Tools

The app tiles that you see on the Windows 8 Start screen by default are actually only a portion of the tools available to you. Administrative tools are apps that you use to keep your computer healthy. To make them appear on the Start screen, follow these steps:

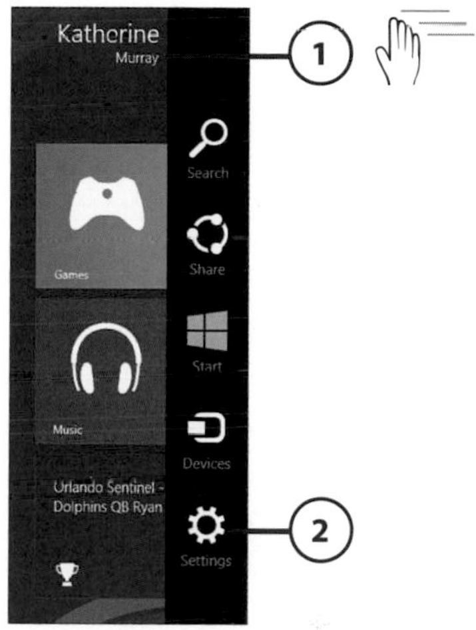

1. On the Windows 8 Start screen, swipe in from the right or move the mouse pointer to the lower-right corner. The Charms bar appears.
2. Tap or click Settings.
3. Tap or click Tiles.
4. Drag the Show Administrative Tools slider to the right, which changes the setting to Yes.

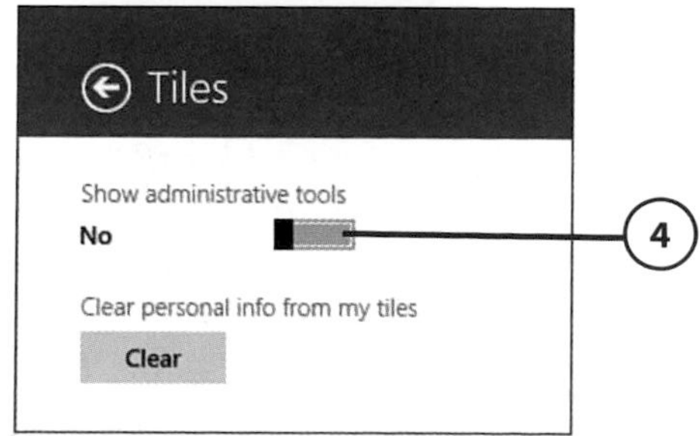

>>>Go Further

OH, THE GLORY OF THE ADMINISTRATOR

So what kind of special privileges are you in for, now that you've displayed the Administrative tools? If you swipe or click your way to the far-right side of the Windows 8 Start screen, you'll see that the operating system has added a number of tools for you: Event Viewer, Task Scheduler, Resource Monitor, Local Security Policy, Performance Monitor, Component Services, Computer Management, Disk Cleanup, Defragment and Optimize Drives, iSCSI Initiator, System Configuration, ODBC Data Sources, Windows Memory Diagnostic, System Information, Print Management, Services, Windows PowerShell ISE, and Windows Firewall with Advanced Security.

I know, I know! You'd better skip lunch today. You have way important stuff to do. Or, if you're rather not deal with all this serious business right now while you're learning (and a bit enchanted by) all the color and movement in Windows 8, you can hide the Admin tools and come back to them in Chapter 13, where we talk about "Windows 8 Care, Feeding, and Troubleshooting." For most day-to-day operations, you don't really need access to these tools, anyway, so you may want to hide them to keep them from cluttering up your Start screen.

Understanding Windows 8 Charms

The Windows 8 Charms bar is Microsoft's answer to the challenge of giving us easy and instant access to the tools we need without cluttering up the Windows 8 Start screen. If you're using a touch-capable monitor or device, you can slide out the Charms bar by swiping your finger from the right edge of the screen toward the center. If you're using a mouse, you can display the Charms bar by pointing to the lower-right corner of your Windows 8 Start screen. The charms give you access to several different worlds of tools you may want to use as you tweak and tap your happy way through Windows 8.

A Ghost of a Charms Bar

If you're using the mouse, when you position the pointer in the lower-right corner of the screen, you see the white shapes of the charms, but the whole Charms bar doesn't appear until you move the mouse up into the Charms bar area. Then the black background appears and you see the full effect of the Charms bar.

Windows 8 charms appear along the right side of the Start screen when you swipe in from the right using touch or right-click in the lower-right corner of the screen. You can also press Windows+C on the keyboard.

From here, you can tap or click the charms you want to change. The charms available to you are the following:

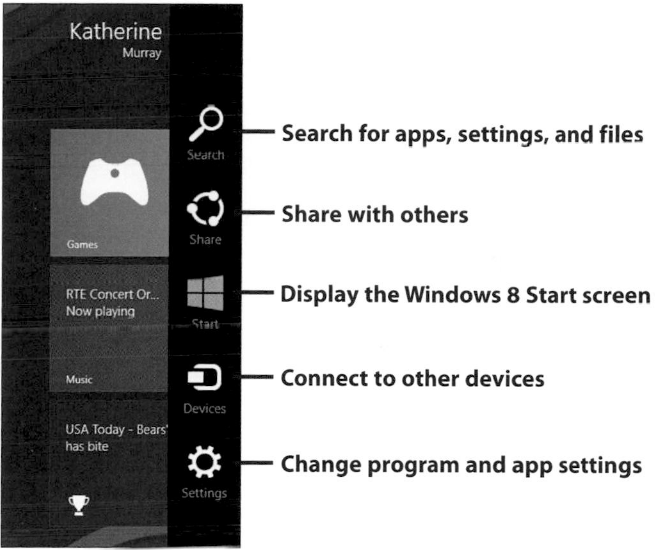

- **Search** enables you to search for apps (and also search *within* apps). You can also search for settings, files, and folders in Windows 8.
- **Share** enables you to share the selected app with other programs. This feature needs to be supported by the app you're using, though, or you'll get an annoying message that says "This app can't share" or "There's nothing to share right now."
- **Start** returns you to the Windows 8 Start screen, which, of course, is helpful only if you aren't *already* on the Windows 8 Start screen.
- **Devices** gives you the option of connecting the app to a device you've installed in Windows 8. For this to work, you need to have a device installed that Windows 8 can recognize, such as a second screen. I talked in detail about devices in Chapter 2, "Preparing Your Windows 8 PC and Devices."
- **Settings** enables you to change the way your system is functioning, changing your network connection, for example, or the brightness and volume of your computer. You can also display help information and change the information on your app tiles by using the Settings charm.

>>>Go Further

SILLY RABBIT, CHARMS AREN'T FOR KIDS!

One of the neat things about the Charms bar is that it is context-dependent, meaning that the Settings you see when you tap the Settings charm depend on what you're viewing in the rest of your Windows 8 screen. If you tap Settings when you're looking at your Photos app, you'll see the categories Settings, About, Help, Permissions, and Rate and Review. If you tap Settings when you're instant messaging a colleague, you'll see Account, Options, Permissions, and Rate and Review categories.

So even though the charms may appear to be consistent no matter where you display them or what you're doing at the time, know that Windows 8 is tailoring the options you're seeing—in Search, Share, Devices, and Settings—to fit the context of what you're working on.

Changing the Way Tiles Look and Behave

Even though the Windows 8 Start screen may be so mesmerizing when you first see it that you just want to sit there and stare at its cycling notifications (which is actually the *opposite* of productive, you know), pretty soon you're likely to begin thinking about how you can improve it. You might want to make some of the app tiles larger—or smaller—or maybe stop the updates on the ones you find distracting and irrelevant. (No, really, it can happen.)

Making Big Tiles Small (and Vice Versa)

The Windows 8 Start screen is colorful and varied. Some app tiles are large and some are small. You can reduce the size of the large app tiles on the Start screen if you want to condense the number of apps that appear in the various groups. This enables you to fit more apps on one screen area so that you can see them without scrolling. You may get a trade-off for this change, however; when you change a tile from large to small display, if the tile previously displayed app notifications (meaning the information on the tile updated automatically), the live notifications might disappear, depending on whether the app has been programmed to provide updates in both sizes.

1. To change the size of a large tile, swipe down on the tile or right-click it to select it. The apps bar appears along the bottom of the screen.
2. If the large app allows you to change the tile size, you'll see a Smaller option. If no Smaller setting appears, it means that settings isn't available for that app. To change the size of the tile, simply tap or click Smaller, and the tile is changed on the Start screen.

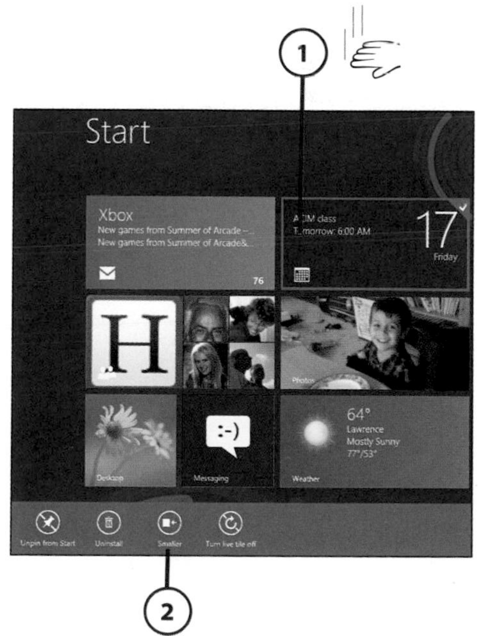

3. If you want to make a small tile larger, begin by swiping down on it or right-clicking to select it. The apps bar appears.
4. Tap or click Larger. Note that not all apps are capable of displaying large tiles, so if you select an app and don't see the Larger setting in the apps bar, you'll know that option isn't available for that app. Also note that not all apps that are capable of displaying in the larger view will display live updates.

Turning Off Live Updates

You can also turn off the live tile updates for a particular tile if you like by selecting the tile (by swiping down on it or right-clicking it) and then tapping or clicking Turn Live Tile Off in the apps bar at the bottom of the screen. To turn on the live updates later, simply reselect the app tile and tap Turn Live Tile On.

Getting a Rest from Notifications

Suppose that a deadline is hanging over your head, you've had too much coffee, and the rotating, flipping updates on the Windows 8 Start screen are making you crabby. Notifications push new information to the live tiles on your Windows 8 Start screen. You decide you'd like to turn them off for a while so they'll stop distracting you so you can work. Here's how to do that.

1. On the Windows 8 Start screen, swipe in from the right side of the screen or right-click the bottom-right corner to display the Charms bar.
2. Tap Settings.
3. Tap Notifications. A popup list appears, giving you the option of hiding the live tile notifications for 8 hours, 3 hours, or 1 hour.
4. Tap or click the setting you'd like to apply. Now you won't see new information for the period of time you've selected.

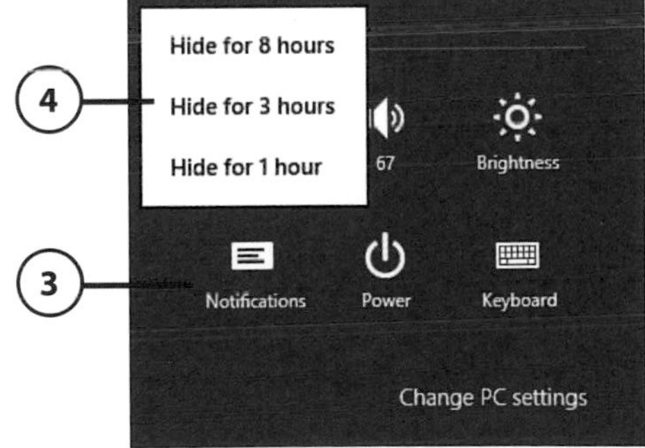

A Little Less Lively

After you reduce the size of a large app tile, you may notice something you're not too crazy about: Apps that previously functioned as live tiles, providing continually updating information, now simply display a logo. The "aliveness" is gone. Windows 8 does allow developers to create live tiles for the smaller, square tile, but fitting updating information into that small space is a bit of a challenge, so at this point most live tiles are of the larger variety. When you want to restore the tile to its larger, livelier state, simply swipe down on the tile or right-click it and click or tap Larger in the apps bar.

Hiding Personal Information on Your Tiles

If you regularly share your computer with someone else or have people forever looking over your shoulder (doesn't that bug you?), you can have Windows 8 hide the personal information on your tiles.

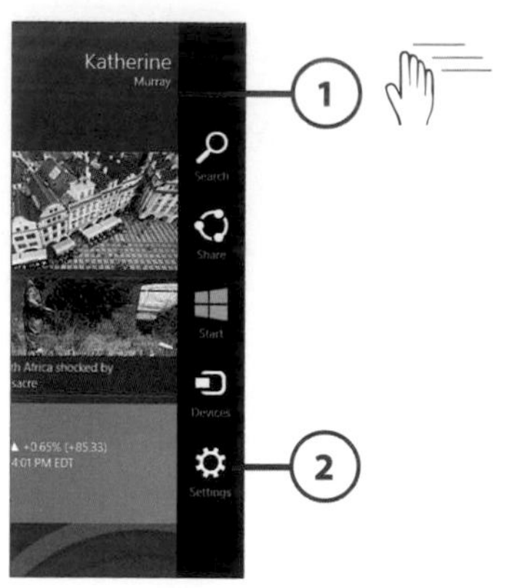

1. On the Windows 8 Start screen, swipe in from the right or right-click in the lower-right corner to display the Charms bar.
2. Tap or click Settings.
3. Tap or click Tiles.
4. Tap Clear. Tiles like Mail, Messaging, and Calendar, which had been showing your latest email messages, instant messages, and upcoming appointments, now should the plain-Jane app logos instead. So those folks looking over your shoulder won't be able to see much.

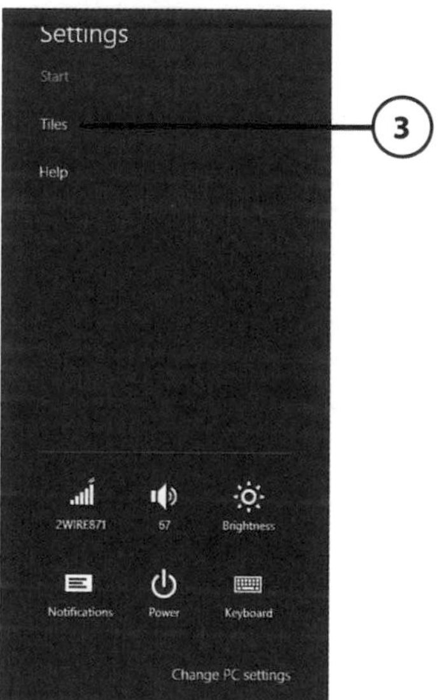

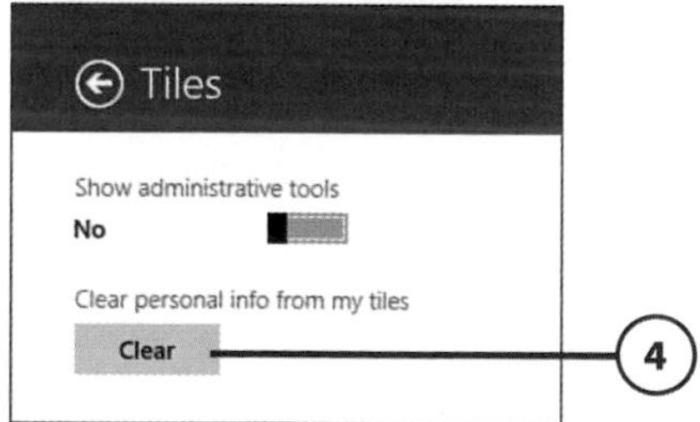

For One Brief Shining Moment

It's important to realize, however, that your live tiles—if you haven't turned the live tile off at this point—will continue to display your personal information as you receive new email messages, instant messages, and appointments. If you want to suppress the display of personal information for a longer period, such as the entire time you're at work, turn off notifications for eight hours or turn off the live tile display.

Moving, Grouping, and Removing Apps

Another way you can improve the Windows 8 Start screen and make it more to your liking involves moving apps around on the screen, grouping them in ways that make sense to you, or removing the ones you don't need. (Don't worry, if you remove an app from the Windows 8 Start screen, you aren't actually removing it from your computer altogether—you'll need to uninstall it using the Control Panel to do that.)

Installing and Uninstalling Apps

You will learn how to download, install, and uninstall apps when you take a closer look at them in Chapter 7.

Moving Apps on the Start Screen

You can rearrange the apps on your Start screen if you want to put them in a specific order that better suits the way you work. For example, one of my pet peeves is having wide and square tiles arranged on top of each other, resulting in blank space in the columns. So, I rearrange things to make the best use of space. The nice thing in Windows 8 is that you can put them in any order that suits you.

1. Select the app you want to move by pressing and holding Ctrl and tapping or clicking the app.
2. Drag the app tile to the new location.
3. Release the app tile and the other app tiles are rearranged to make room for the new app tile position.

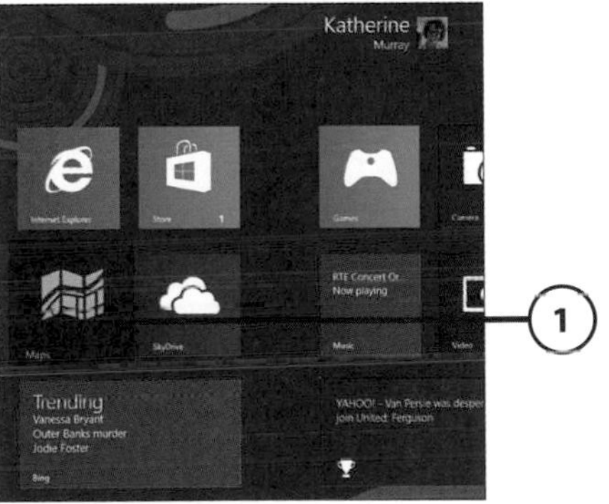

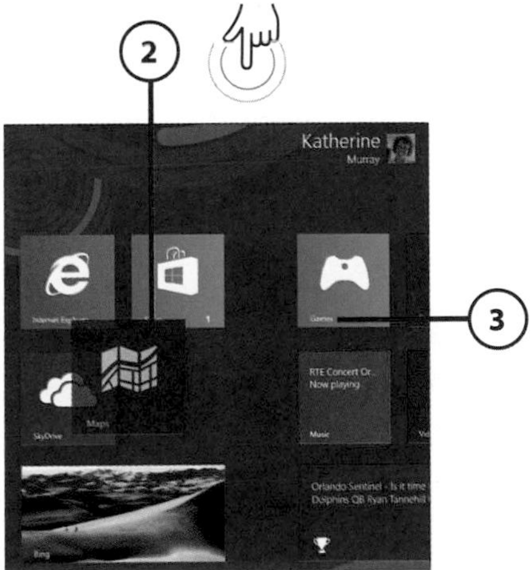

Creating an App Group

You'll notice that the Windows 8 Start screen includes a couple of "islands" of app tiles—some are grouped together with a little space between groups. You can change the way the groups are organized by moving app tiles from one group to another. You can also create your own groups, which is a great idea if you have a set of apps you use often together. Once you create a group, you can name it so that you can remember at a glance how you've grouped the apps on the Start screen.

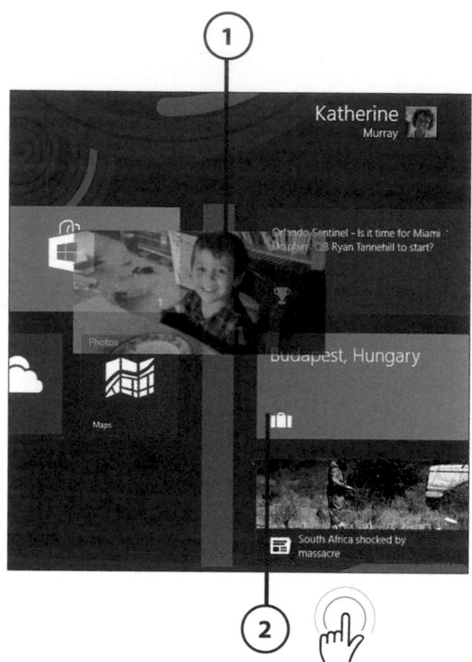

1. Press and hold Ctrl and click or tap the tile you want to move.
2. Drag it to the space between one of the app groups on the Start screen and release the tile. A horizontal bar appears to show you where the tile will be placed when you release it.
3. Grab other apps and drag them to the same space and release them. Windows 8 adds space around the group so that you can see it easily as a group.

Name Your App Groups

Once you've created your app groups, you can further organize them by assigning a group name to the Windows 8 Start screen. Naming groups is a three-step process: First you zoom out to see all the apps on your Start screen, and then you'll choose the group you want to name, and name it.

1. On the Start screen, pinch to reduce the size of the apps on the Start screen, or move the mouse to the bottom-right corner of the screen and click the Zoom tool (which looks like a small dash in the corner).
2. Swipe down or right-click the group you want to name and the apps bar appears.
3. Tap or click Name Group. A small popup window appears.
4. Type a name for the group.
5. Tap or click Name. The name appears above the group you selected. When you want to return the Start screen display to normal, press the Windows key or tap or click Start on the Charms bar.

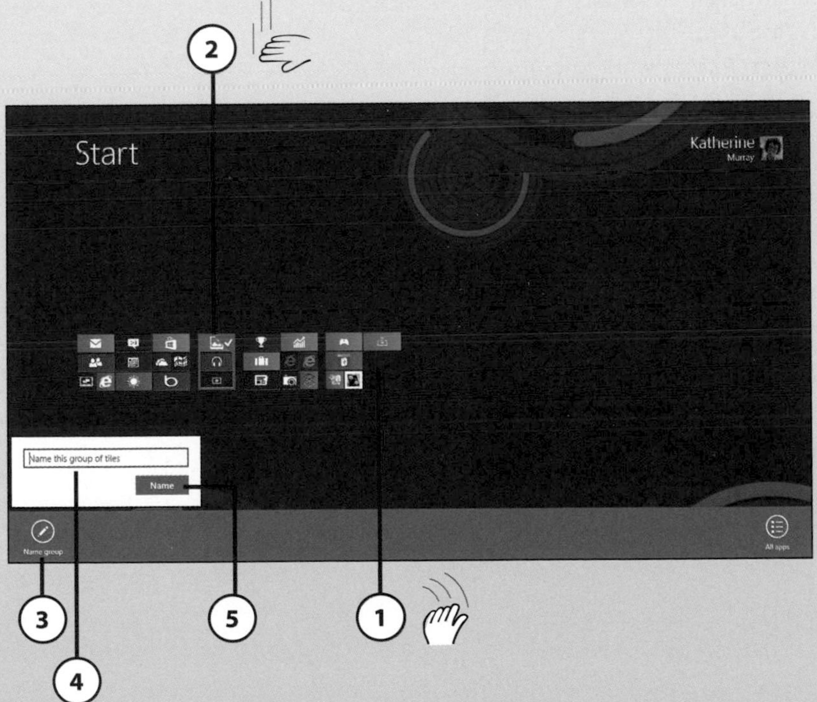

Removing an App from the Start Screen

Right off the bat, Windows 8 gives you a number of apps that you may—or may not—use in your daily computing tasks. If you want to remove some of the unnecessary apps, you can do that easily and pick up a little extra real estate on the Start screen.

1. Select the app you want to remove by swiping down on the app tile or right-clicking it.

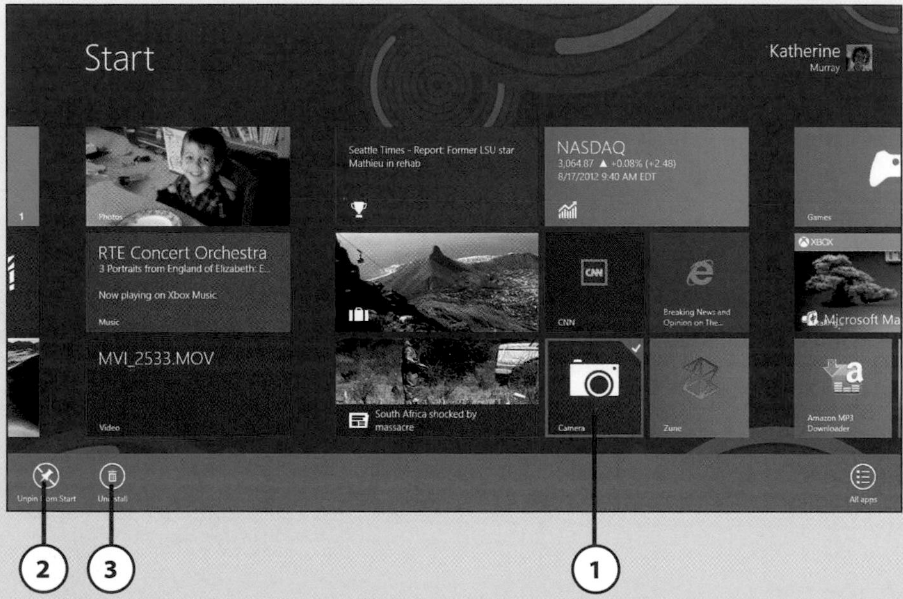

2. The apps bar appears along the bottom of the Start screen. To unpin the app, so that it is still installed on your computer but simply not visible as an app on the Start screen, tap or click Unpin from Start.

3. To uninstall an app you know you'll never use, tap or click Uninstall.

Searching in Windows 8

One of the disconcerting things Windows 7 users have noted in the new design of Windows 8 is that there is no Start menu, which means the All Programs folder is gone, gone, gone. I don't know about you, but I used All Programs a lot, maybe more than I needed to. In the good old days, it was so easy to just click Start, All Programs, and scan that long, delicious list of all the installed programs on your computer. Then one more little click did the trick of opening your looked-for program on the Windows 7 desktop.

And even though it feels a little odd to have that measure of security taken from us, Windows 8 actually makes it easier and faster to find the apps, settings, and files you need.

Just type it.

No, really. You don't have to launch a search tool or anything. If you're on the Windows 8 Start screen, you can simply type what you're looking for and Windows 8 picks it up and runs with it. Why? Because Windows 8 is awake and *listening*.

Finding What You Need, Like Magic

To search for something you want in Windows 8, you can simply type it. You don't need to go anywhere special. You don't have to click this or that. If you're on the Windows 8 Start screen, as soon as you start typing, Windows 8 begins searching for what it thinks you want (which you have an opportunity to correct, of course, if you change your mind mid-stream).

1. On the Windows 8 Start screen, if your computer or device has a keyboard, type *notepad*. Before you even get to the letter E, Windows 8 displays the Search screen with two search results: Sticky Notes and Notepad. (Not pictured.)

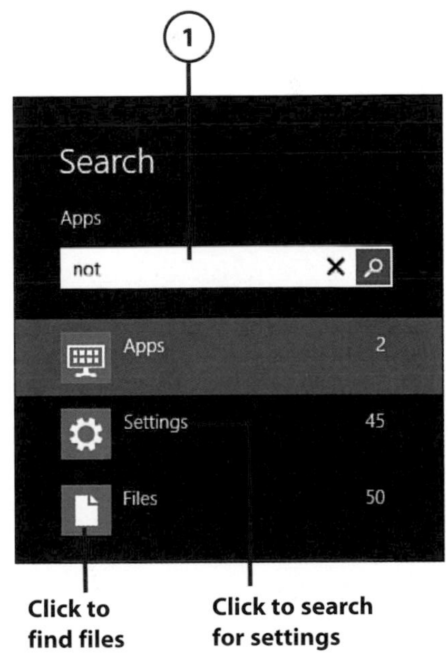

Using the Virtual Keyboard

If you're using a touch device with no keyboard, swipe in to the left from the right side of the screen to display the Charms bar, tap Search, and tap in the Search box. The onscreen keyboard appears.

2. Tap or click the app you want to launch.

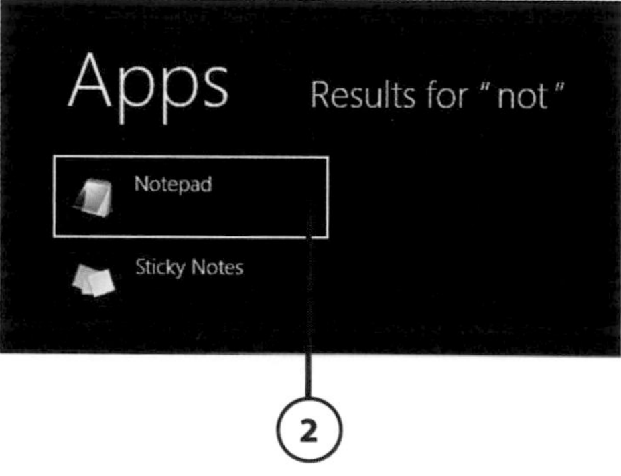

You Can Search for Settings or Files, Too

Below the Search box on the right side of the Search window, you see Apps, Settings, and Files. Each of these items serves as a filter to help you narrow the search results you receive for the word or phrase you entered. The number off to the right indicates the number of results in each of those categories related to your search. To change the type of result shown in the results list on the left, click one of the other categories.

>>>Go Further

SEARCHING FROM THE WINDOWS 8 DESKTOP

The Windows 8 Desktop is a little clunkier than the Start screen, which means that you can't do something as quick and simple as typing what you want and having it appear. When you want to search for something from the Windows 8 Desktop, you really wind up going to the Windows 8 Start screen to do it.

You can begin from the Windows 8 Desktop by pressing the Windows key or swipe in from the right side of the screen. You also can press Windows+Q to display the Search screen. That displays the search panel, where you can enter your search word or phrase in the Search box, and click the category (Apps, Settings, or Files) for the results you want to see.

Searching within an App

When you're working with a particular app, you can use the Charms bar to search for what you're looking for within the program. This works equally well whether you're looking for a tool that is part of the actual app itself or you're looking for something you want the program to find—like a certain destination in the Maps app.

1. Display the app you want to use.
2. Display the Charms bar.
3. Tap or click Search.

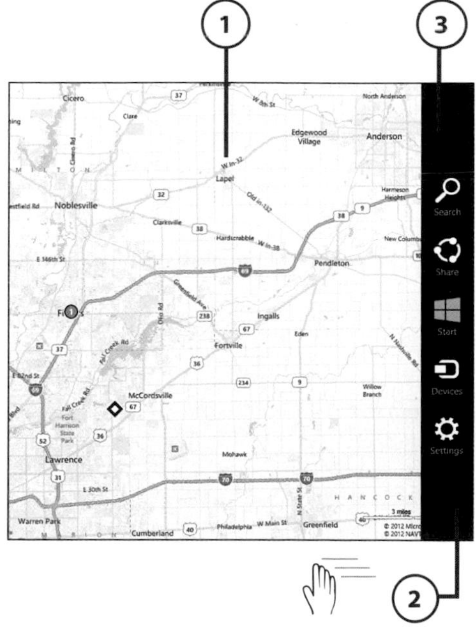

4. In the Search box, type a word or phrase you want to find. Notice that the app name appears above the Search box.
5. Tap or click Search.
6. The app displays the result you want in the left side of the screen.

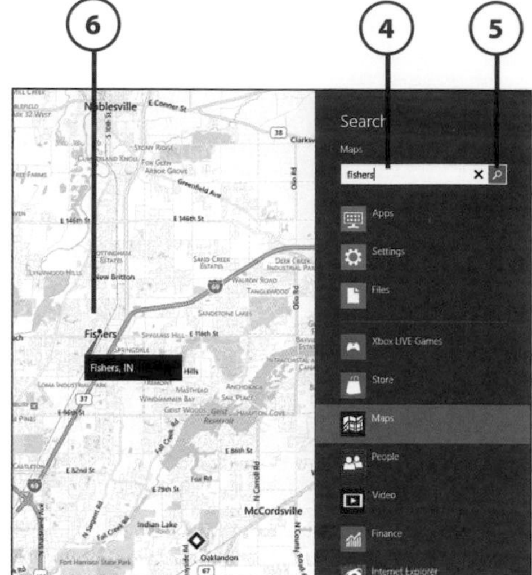

Or Skip the App Altogether

The Windows 8 Search tool is powerful enough that you can search within a specific app without even opening the app itself. Suppose, for example, that you are wondering what paint programs might be available in the Windows Store. You could press Windows+Q to display the Search charm, enter *paint* in the Search box, and tap the Store icon that appears in the lower portion of the Search panel.

Windows 8 instantly opens a results list on the left side of the screen that displays all the paint programs currently available in the Windows Store. Nice. You'll learn more about working with programs—and find out more about the Windows Store—in Chapter 7.

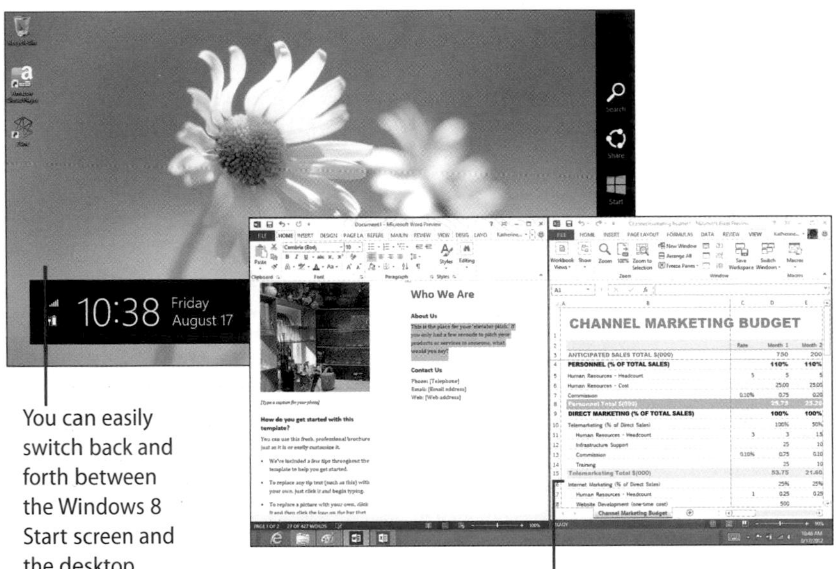

You can easily switch back and forth between the Windows 8 Start screen and the desktop

You can put your window-wrangling skills to work on the Windows 8 desktop

In this chapter, you learn how to find your way around the Windows 8 desktop PC by performing tasks such as

- → Moving between the desktop and the Start screen
- → Getting ready to work with programs
- → Tailoring the taskbar
- → Working with Windows on the Windows desktop

4

Working with the Windows 8 Desktop

If you were (or are!) particularly fond of Windows 7, you may be relieved to discover that the Windows 8 desktop, tucked away and accessed with a tap or a click to an app tile on the Windows 8 Start screen, has a bit of the same look and feel. Using the Windows 8 desktop, you'll use File Explorer to manage files and folders, work with the desktop version of Internet Explorer, and be able to launch programs—known as *legacy programs*—that run on the desktop but not in the Windows 8 Start screen interface.

One big difference about the Windows 8 desktop, as compared to Windows 7, is that the trusty Start menu is missing. Instead of the Microsoft orb you used to display the Start menu (with its handy All Programs list), you'll see only the icon that launches Internet Explorer.

Yes, times, they are a-changing.

Moving Between the Desktop and the Start Screen

The first thing you'll need to do when you access and work with the desktop is know how to move from the Start screen to the desktop and back. When you log in to your computer or device, the Windows 8 Start screen appears. You can then display the Windows desktop by tapping or clicking the Desktop tile or by typing *desktop* and tapping or clicking the Desktop app that appears in the search results.

Displaying the Windows 8 Desktop

When you first start Windows 8, the desktop doesn't get much fanfare. Instead you'll need to find it, a small app tile on the colorful Windows 8 Start screen. But even though the tile is small, the desktop still packs a lot of punch. That's where you'll be working with most of the familiar applications you use every day, like Microsoft Office and other favorite programs.

1. On the Windows 8 Start screen, tap or click Desktop.
2. The Windows 8 desktop appears. Here you can see any legacy programs you've installed with Windows 8, as well as the programs you've pinned to the taskbar.
3. Tap or click an icon to launch a program.

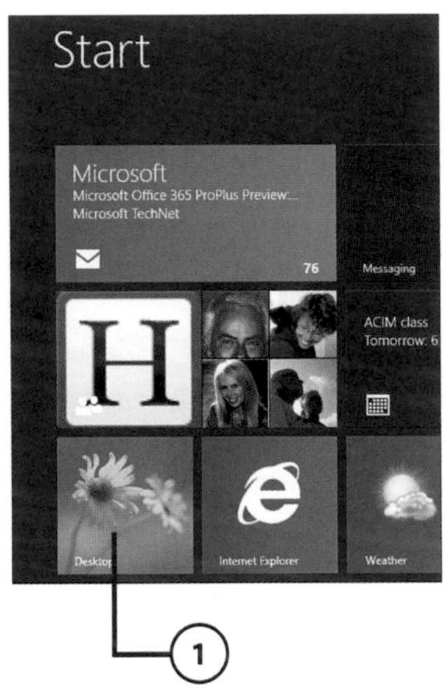

Returning to the Windows 8 Start Screen

At first it may seem a little jolting to be moving among screens like this, especially when the button you may be tempted to click or tap out of habit will launch Internet Explorer 10 instead of taking you to the Start screen. Don't worry—you'll retrain yourself soon enough to either press the Windows key or tap or click the Start charm.

1. Swipe in from the right side of the screen, or press the Windows key.
2. Tap or click the Start charm.

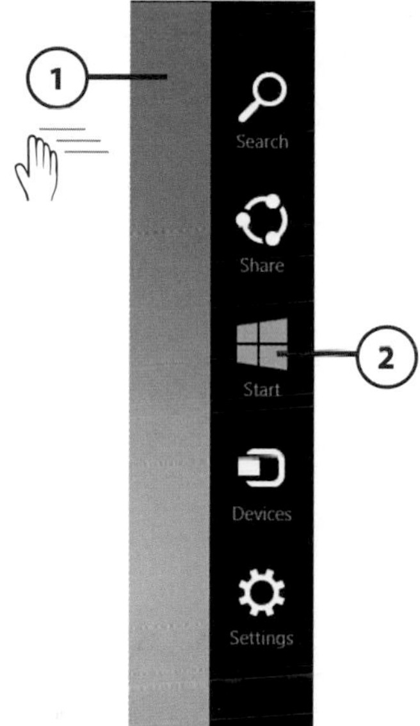

Getting Ready to Work with Programs

As you no doubt know, there is a whole world full of programs that currently run on Windows 7. Although developers are designing and introducing Windows 8 versions of their popular programs, this software typically takes a while to get to market. When you install and run one of your favorite Windows 7 programs on Windows 8, you can launch the program by tapping or clicking its tile on the Windows 8 Start screen, using the Search charm to locate it, or by double-tapping or double-clicking a shortcut on the Windows 8 desktop. In any case, the program opens in a window on the Windows 8 desktop.

More About Working with Programs

You'll learn more about downloading, installing, and working with programs in Chapter 7, "Exploring Windows 8 Apps."

Adding Shortcuts

A shortcut is a program icon Windows places on your desktop that gives you a quick way to launch a program, and you can add shortcuts for your favorite programs so you can start them right from the Windows 8 desktop. Here's how.

1. Tap or right-click the desktop.
2. Tap or click New.
3. Tap or click Shortcut. The Create Shortcut dialog box appears.
4. Click or tap the Browse button. The Browse for Files or Folders dialog box appears.
5. Navigate to the folder that contains the program you want to add as a shortcut. Click the program.
6. Click OK.
7. In the Create Shortcut dialog box, click Next.

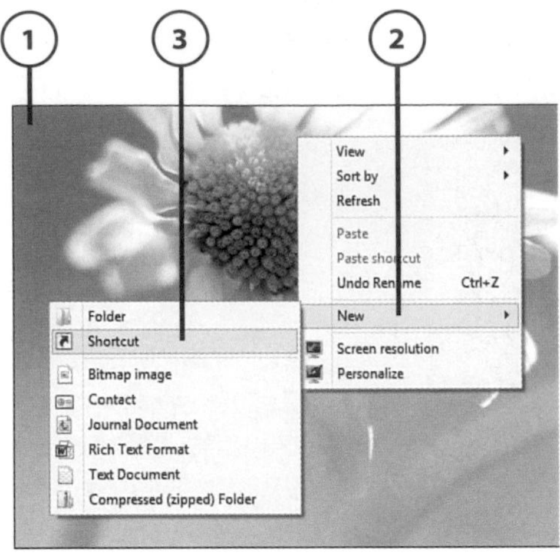

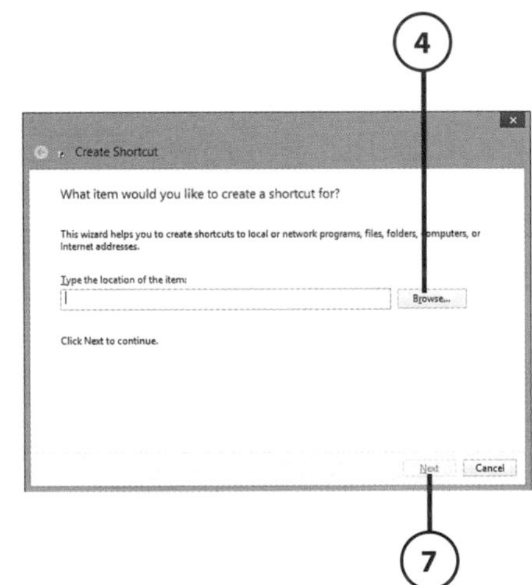

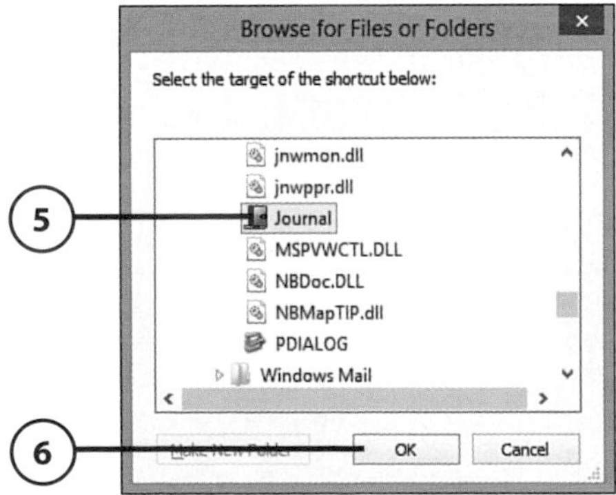

8. Enter a name for the shortcut.
9. Click Finish. The shortcut appears on the desktop, and you can launch the program by double-clicking (or double-tapping) the shortcut icon.

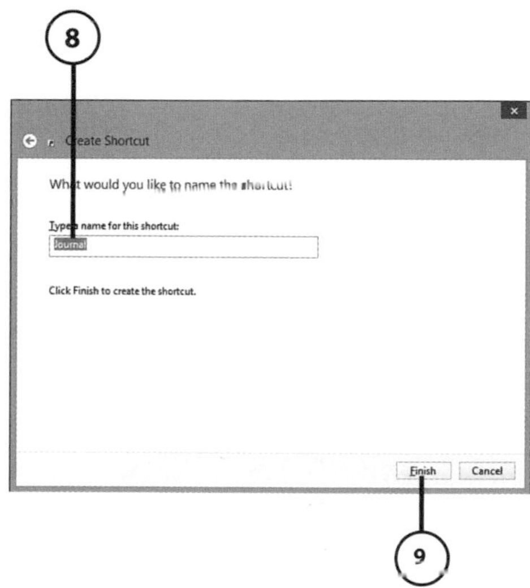

That Was a Dumb Shortcut

If you decide after you create a shortcut that you really aren't going to use it and it's just taking up desktop space, you can easily delete it. Click the shortcut icon one time to select it on the desktop, and then press Delete. (Tablet users can tap and hold on the shortcut to open an option list from which you can delete it.) Windows 8 deletes the shortcut with no further ado or prompt. (You can open the Recycle Bin and drag the shortcut back to your desktop if you change your mind and decide you want to keep it, however.)

Launching File Explorer

At first glance, you might be wondering where to find File Explorer in Windows 8. Because that program runs only on your desktop, you first need to display the Windows 8 desktop before you can start File Explorer.

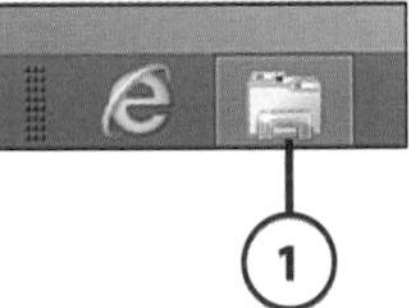

1. On the Windows 8 desktop, tap the File Explorer icon in the taskbar.
2. File Explorer appears, offering the familiar three-column layout (familiar, that is, if you used File Explorer in Windows 7), but you'll notice something new: Now File Explorer sports its own ribbon, with tools and settings you can use to manage your files and folders in Windows 8.
3. When you're ready, swipe right to display the Charms bar.
4. Tap Start to return to the Windows 8 Start screen.

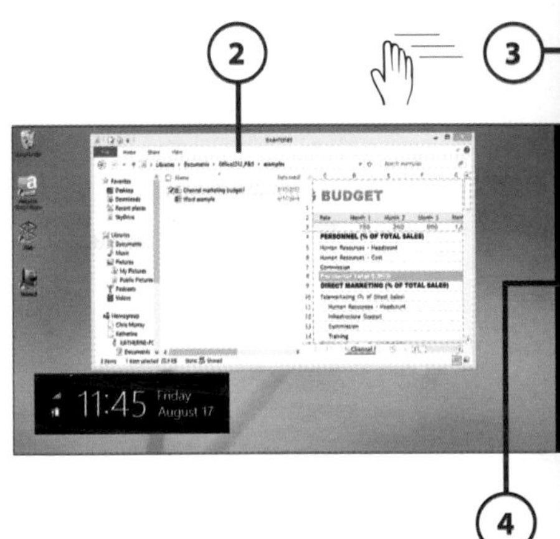

More About File Explorer

Chapter 8 tells you all about organizing and working with files and folders in File Explorer.

Tailoring the Taskbar

The desktop taskbar is a place for lots of activity on the Windows 8 desktop. By default, you'll find two icons in the QuickLaunch area, to the far-left end of the taskbar: Internet Explorer 10 and File Explorer. You can start either of those programs by clicking or tapping those icons. You can also add programs you use often to the desktop taskbar so that you can launch them. For example, if you record audio notes regularly, you might want to add Sound Recorder to the taskbar; or if you work with illustrations, you could add Windows Paint.

Adding Apps to the Taskbar

The first step in adding an app to the desktop taskbar is to launch the program you want to add. You might start the program from either the Windows 8 Start screen or the desktop.

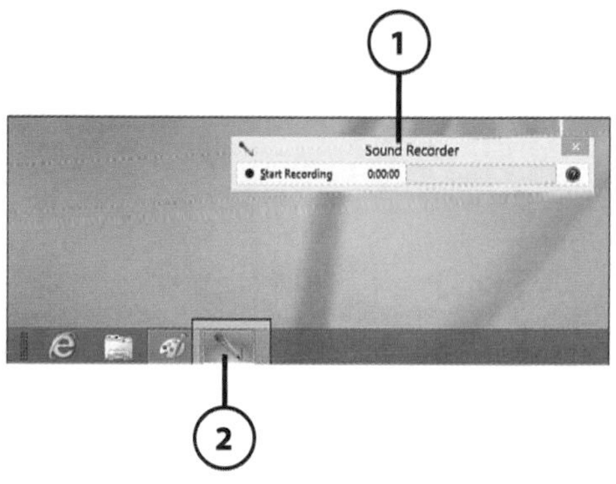

1. Open the desktop app you want to add to the Windows 8 desktop taskbar.
2. Right-click the app icon in the taskbar or tap and hold the icon until a square appears around it. A list of options appears.
3. Tap or click Pin This Program to Taskbar.

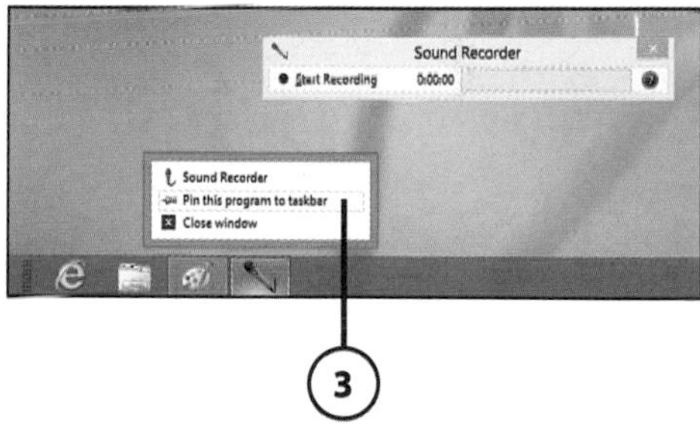

Unpinning, After the Fact

If you decide that your taskbar is getting cluttered or you want to remove items you've pinned there, right-click the pinned item (or tap and hold your finger on the item until a square appears around it and then release your touch to display the options list), and choose Unpin This Program from Taskbar. Instantly it's gone—like it was never even there.

Using Jump Lists

Jump lists are popular features in Windows 7 that enable you to get right to documents and files you've worked with recently without opening menus or launching new programs. A jump list keeps track of the most recent files you've worked with in a program you've pinned to the taskbar, and you can display the whole list by clicking the icon on the taskbar. You can then click the file you want and move right to it.

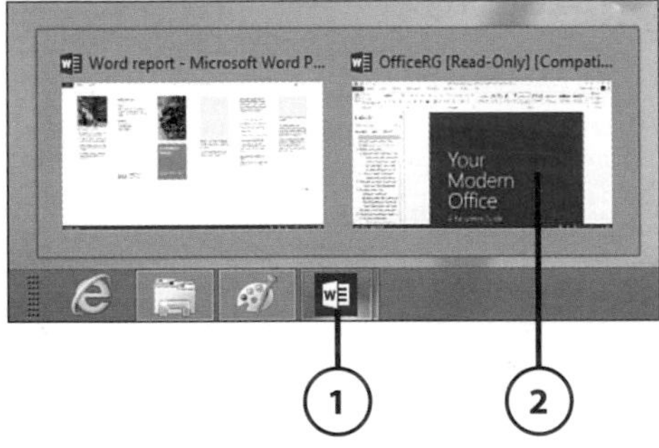

1. Hover the mouse over the program icon in the taskbar.
2. Alternatively, tap the program icon in the taskbar. The files currently open in that program appear above the taskbar.

Jump List Display

If you have only a few files in your jump list, the files will appear as thumbnails; when you have a whole slew of files (the default setting in Jump List properties is 10), you'll see a list of files instead of thumbnails.

>>>Go Further

KEEPING YOUR JUMP LISTS ON THE DOWN-LOW

In Windows 8, you have additional control over what gets displayed in your jump lists. If you'd rather others who use your computer not be able to see the files you've worked with recently, you can uncheck the Store and Display Recently Opened Items in Jump Lists checkbox. Here's how to do that.

Right-click the Windows 8 desktop taskbar. Click the Jump Lists tab in the Taskbar Properties dialog box. You'll find the option you want in the Privacy area. Click Store and Display Recently Opened Items in Jump Lists checkbox to clear the selection. Now click OK to close the dialog box, and you're all set.

Working with Windows on the Windows Desktop

When you work with programs on the Windows 8 desktop, they will appear in the type of windows you'll be familiar with if you've used previous versions of Windows. You can open, close, minimize, maximize, arrange, and resize the windows. You'll be able to click or tap the title bar of the window and move it from place to place. And you'll also be able to arrange more than one window on the screen at the same time.

Window Basics

The windows you'll open on the Windows 8 desktop have a number of elements in common:

- The title bar displays the name of the program and may display the name of the open file.
- The Minimize, Maximize, and Close buttons control the size of the window. Minimize reduces the window to the taskbar; Maximize opens the window so that it fills the screen; and Close closes the window.
- The Quick Access Toolbar gives you access to commands you may want to use with the program. You can customize the Quick Access Toolbar by clicking the arrow on the right and choosing additional commands from the list.

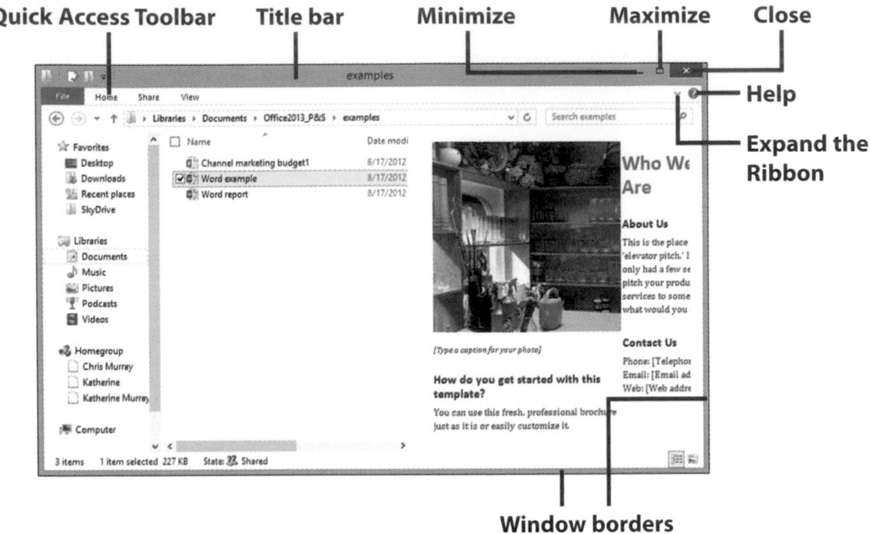

- Click the Help button to display help information related to the program you are using.
- By default, the Ribbon in File Explorer is hidden, given you the maximum amount of room to work with libraries, files, and folders. To display the Ribbon, tap the Expand the Ribbon tool.
- Click the Hide Ribbon to reduce the display of the Ribbon so that only the tab names show. When the Ribbon is hidden, the tool changes to Expand the Ribbon.
- The Ribbon tabs offer different sets of tools related to the tasks you're likely to want to perform in the program.
- You can click and drag the window border to resize the window.

Moving a Window

Moving a window is as simple as tapping or clicking and dragging a window in the direction you want it to go.

1. Tap and drag—or click and drag—the window's title bar.
2. Drag the window in the direction you want to move it, and release it in the new position.

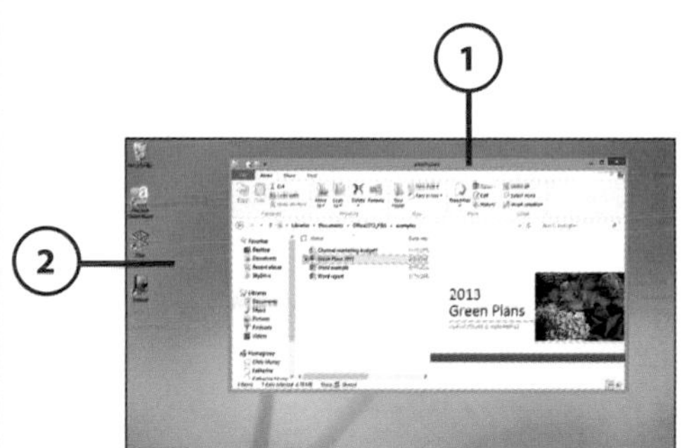

Resizing a Window

The easiest way to resize a window—from small to large—is to use the Maximize button in the window controls in the upper-right corner of the window. You can also resize a window by positioning the pointer on the window border or corner and dragging in the direction you want to resize the window.

1. Tap or point to a corner or side of the window.
2. Drag the border in the direction you want to resize the window, and release the border (or the mouse button) when the window is the size you want it.

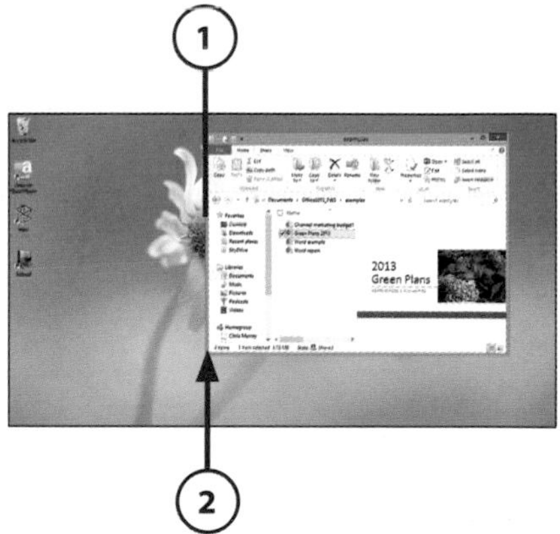

Switching to a Different Window

While you're working on the desktop, you can easily have many different windows open on the screen at once. These windows might be program windows or folders of files. If you work with a number of programs open at one time, of course, you need to be able to get to the program you want when you need it. If several windows are open on the screen at once, you can click any part of the window you want to bring to the top, or you can click the taskbar icon of the window you want to view. Alternatively, you can press and hold Alt+Tab to display a pop-up box and then press Tab repeatedly to cycle through open programs. When the window you want is selected, release Alt+Tab and that window opens on your desktop.

Arranging Windows

Another important task when you are working with multiple windows open on the screen at one time is having the ability to arrange the windows the way you want them to appear. If you want to compare two documents, for example, it would be nice to show them side by side. You can arrange windows the way you want on the Windows 8 desktop.

1. Right-click the taskbar and choose Cascade Windows.

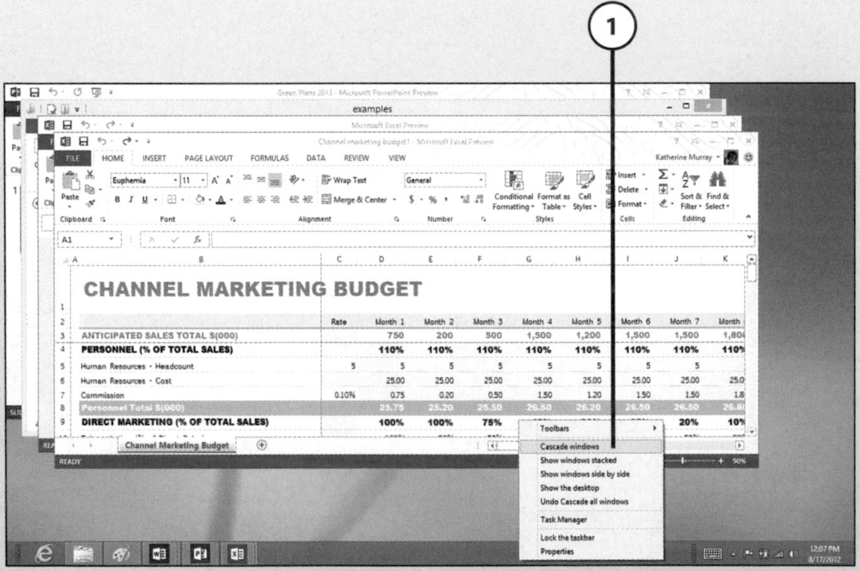

2. Right-click the taskbar and choose Show Windows Stacked.

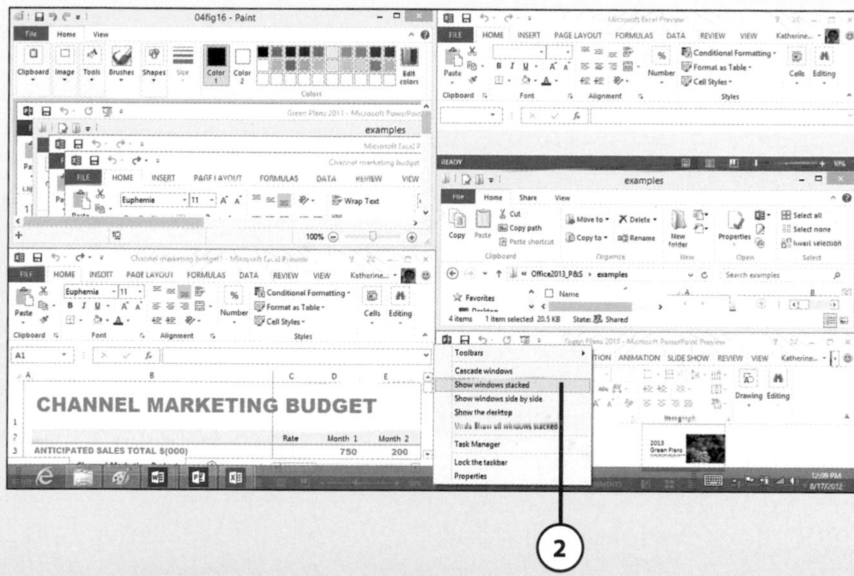

3. Right-click the taskbar and click Show Windows Side By Side.

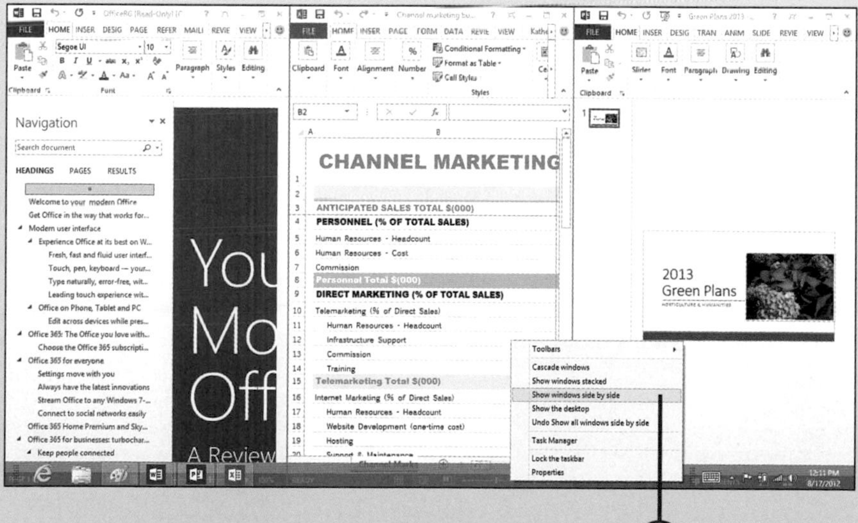

>>>Go Further

SHORTCUT KEYS AND SNAP FOR WINDOW WRANGLING

You can also work with the windows on your desktop without ever taking your hands off the keyboard. Here are the shortcut keys you can use:

- Alt+spacebar displays the shortcut menu for the current window.
- Windows + M minimizes all open windows.
- Windows + E opens your computer library.
- Windows + D displays the desktop.
- Windows + Home minimizes all but the active window.

Quick-Changing Windows

You can change the size of a window quickly by double-clicking (or double-tapping) the title bar. If the window was full-screen size (that is, maximized), it returns to its earlier smaller size. If the window is smaller than full screen, double-clicking the title bar maximizes it.

Old-Style Resizing

Sure, all these double-click tricks are fancy and fast. But if you prefer to choose commands from menus, you can display any window's control panel and choose the command you want—Restore, Move, Size, Minimize, and Close—from the list of options. You can find the control panel for the window in the upper-left corner; you can't miss it because it resembles a small program icon (in Word, you see a Word icon; in Excel, you see an Excel icon; and so forth).

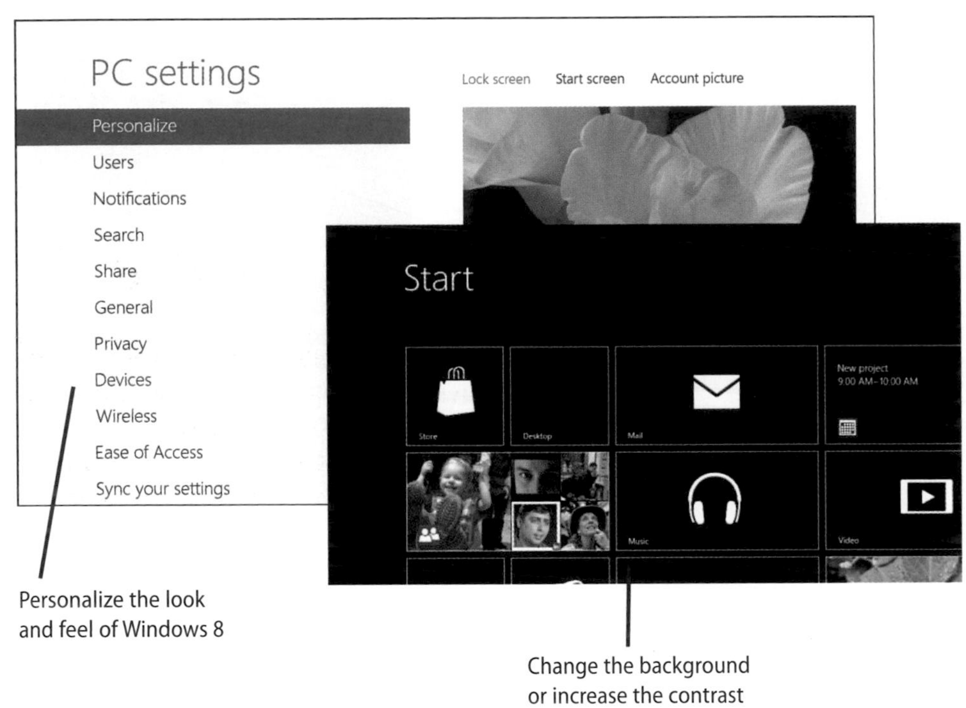

PC settings
Lock screen
Start screen
Account picture
Personalize
Users
Notifications
Search
Share
General
Privacy
Devices
Wireless
Ease of Access
Sync your settings
Start
Store
Desktop
Mail
New project
9:00 AM–10:00 AM
Music
Video
Personalize the look and feel of Windows 8
Change the background or increase the contrast of your screen

Do you want to put your own touches on Windows 8? In this chapter, you learn to personalize your Windows 8 experience by performing the following tasks:

- → Personalizing your Lock screen
- → Adding badges
- → Adjusting the look of Windows 8
- → Changing your Windows 8 desktop
- → Tweaking your touch experience
- → Adjusting the mouse
- → Choosing your language

Personalizing Windows 8

After your eyes adjust to the colorful palette of the Windows 8 Start screen, you may begin wondering how you can put your own stamp on the experience. Can you change the background color that your live tiles float in? Can you change the Lock screen to include a photo that has more personal relevance for you? Do you want to add badges that display updates at a glance, even before you log in to your computer?

All this is possible, and more.

Personalizing Your Lock Screen

The first screen you see when you log in to your computer is the Lock screen, which displays an image along with system information and perhaps a few notifications from your email, messaging, and calendar apps. You might push the Power button and see instantly that you have 27 new email messages, 12 instant messages, and a meeting invitation to respond to. That's a great feature—you can see what needs your attention before you even unlock your computer!

You can also customize the look of the Windows 8 Lock screen by changing the picture that is displayed or choosing your own favorite badges. Windows 8 gives you a number of photos to choose from, or you can use one of your own personal images if you like.

Choosing a New Lock Screen Picture

You use the Settings charm to get to the tools you need to personalize your Windows 8 startup experience.

1. On the Windows 8 Start screen, swipe in from the right or move the mouse to the lower-right corner of the screen to display the Charms bar.
2. Tap or click Settings and the bar expands to display a number of setting icons.
3. Tap or click Change PC Settings. The PC Settings window appears, with the Personalize category selected.

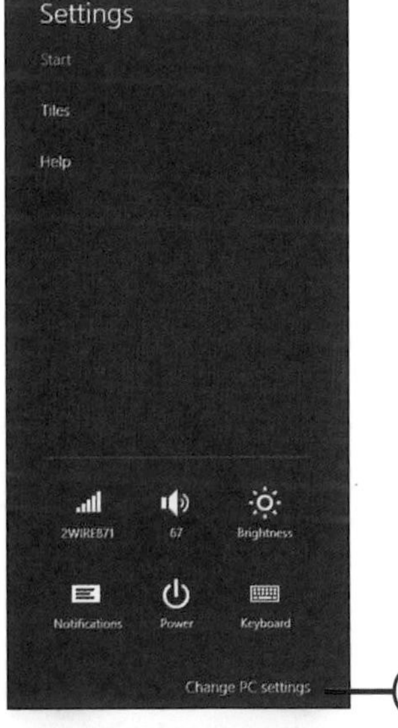

4. Tap or click one of the thumbnail pictures below the selected photo if you want to use an image displayed below the selected picture.
5. If you want to use one of your own images for your Lock screen, tap or click Browse. The Files window appears, displaying pictures and folders in your Pictures folder.
6. Tap or click the photo you want to use. If you want to choose a photo that is in one of the folders displayed, tap or click the folder and then select the photo. A small checkmark appears in the upper right corner of the image you selected.
7. Tap or click Choose Picture. The new image is added to the preview area in Personalize settings.

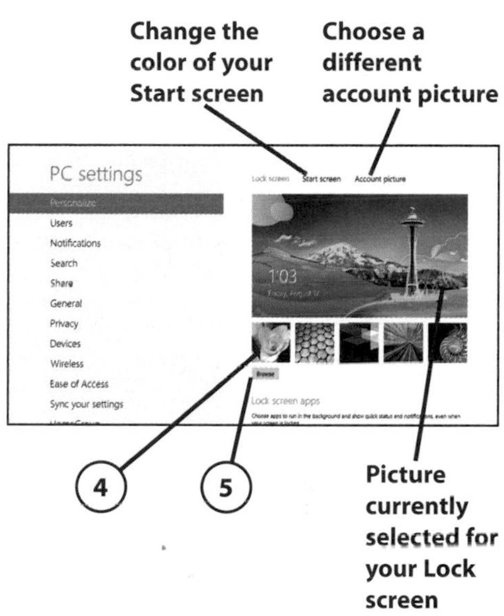

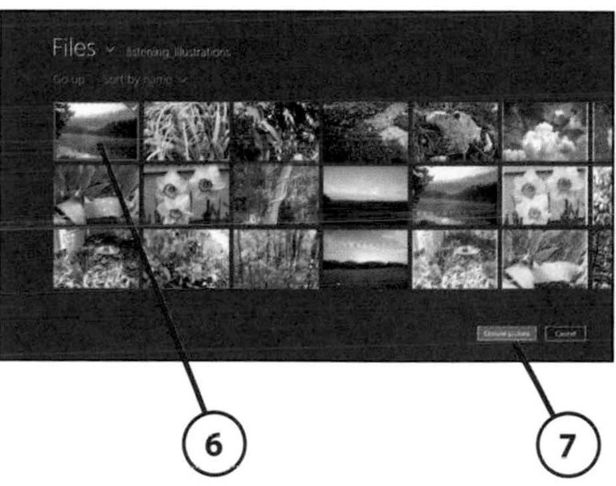

Saving Your Changes—Not

Yes, it's a little hard to get used to, but there's no Save Changes button in the Personalize settings. Windows 8 is designed to save incrementally as you work, so it's not that unusual that you wouldn't need to take a specific action to complete the operation. If you're one of those people (like me) who likes to wrap things up neatly, not having a Save button is a little disconcerting, but we'll get used to it (hopefully).

Starting Over

If you decide you don't like the Lock screen images you've added, you can go back to the pictures provided by default by right-clicking or tapping and holding a thumbnail and choosing Revert to Defaults.

Adding a New Lock Screen Picture on the Fly

If you're viewing photos on your computer and see an image you particularly like, you can make that photo your Lock screen image instantly, if you like. Here are the steps:

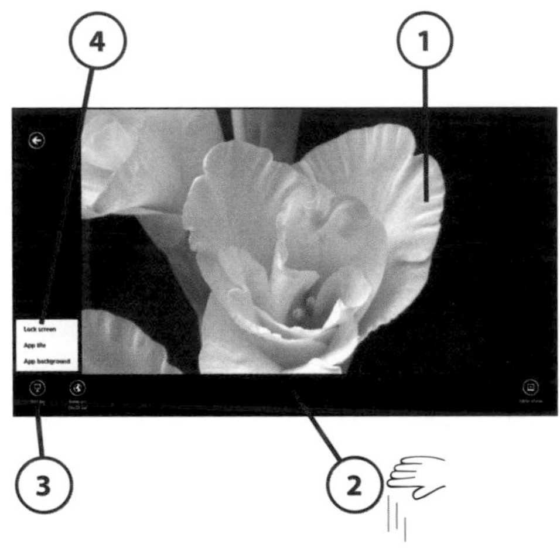

1. Display the photo you want to use as the Lock screen. To learn more about working with photos in Windows 8, see Chapter 11, "Get Entertained with Windows 8 Photos, Music, Movies, and Xbox."
2. Swipe up from the bottom of the screen to display the photo options.
3. Tap or click Set As.
4. Tap or click Lock Screen. The new photo is applied instantly as your Windows 8 Lock screen image.

Changing Your Account Picture

Your account picture appears—in a tiny size—in the upper-right corner of your Windows 8 Start screen. You'll also see it when you swipe up on your Lock screen. Similar to your profile picture in your favorite social media account or your avatar in Windows Live Messenger, your account picture is your own personal expression of who you want to be today. You can change your account picture in Windows 8 by switching it out in your Personalize settings.

Begin by displaying the Charms bar, tapping or clicking Settings, and choosing Change PC Settings.

1. In the Personalize screen, tap or click Account Picture.
2. To choose a new picture from the files on your computer, tap or click Browse.
3. In the Files screen, tap or click the photo you want to use.
4. Tap or click Choose Image, and Windows 8 adds it to your Account Picture preview.
5. If you want to add a picture using the camera on your laptop or tablet, tap or click Camera.
6. When the picture you want to capture is displayed, tap or click anywhere on the screen to take the photo.

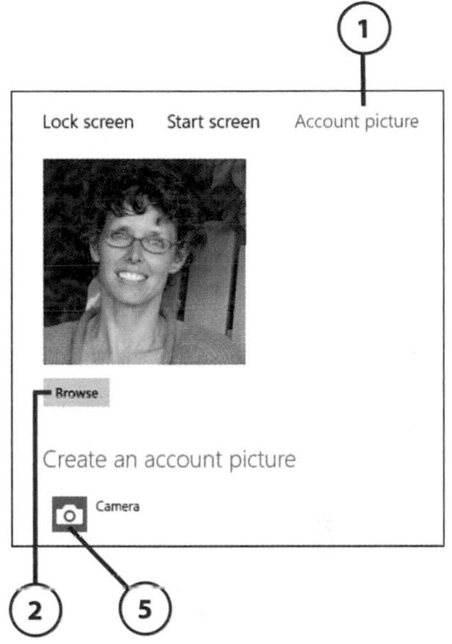

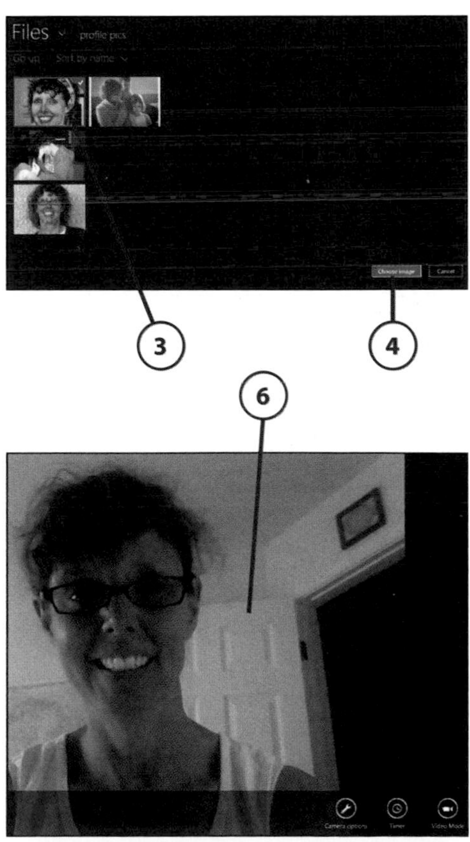

Fewer Choices, Please

If you go through a whole slew of possible account picture choices and aren't particularly happy with any of them, you can remove the ones that appear as thumbnails beneath your chosen picture in the Account Picture screen. Simply right-click the picture and choose Clear History and Windows 8 wipes away the images you've added like they were never there.

7. Windows 8 displays the picture in a preview screen. Click the cropping handles to adjust what remains visible in the picture.
8. When the picture is displayed the way you want it to appear, tap or click OK.

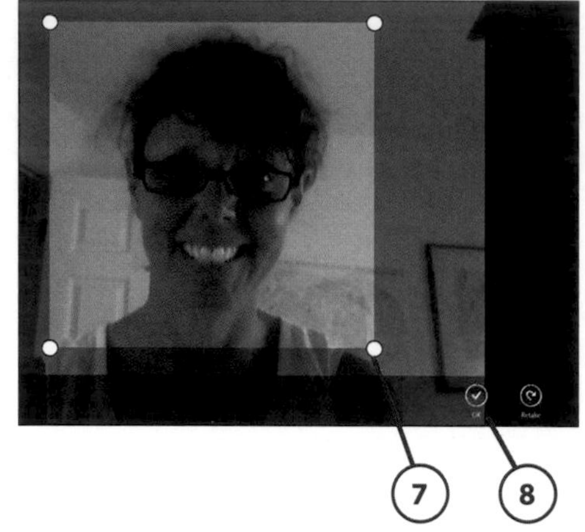

Retaking a Photo

If you want to replace the photo you just captured, tap or click Retake and repeat steps 6 through 8. Windows 8 then substitutes the new webcam photo for your Account Picture in the Personalize settings.

Where Are These Things Stored?

If you go to the trouble of creating and saving different account pictures, are they stored somewhere so that you can switch them as the fancy strikes you? Yes, thankfully, all the images you use as account pictures—whether you browse for them or capture them using your webcam—are stored in an Account Pictures folder. To see all the images that are available to you to use as account pictures, display the Personalize settings, tap or click Account Picture, and choose Browse. You can then change the account picture by selecting the image you want to use and tapping or clicking the Choose Image button.

Adding Badges

Badges are another name for the notifications that you see on the Lock screen, letting you know how many email messages and instant messages you need to respond to. Other badges are available as well. You can change the number and selection of the badges on your Lock screen.

1. Display the PC Settings window and tap or click Personalize.
2. Choose Lock Screen.
3. In the Lock Screen Apps area, tap or click a + in the apps area. The Choose an App popup window appears.
4. Tap or click the app you want to add as a badge on your Lock screen. Windows 8 will display the information related to that app on the Lock screen.

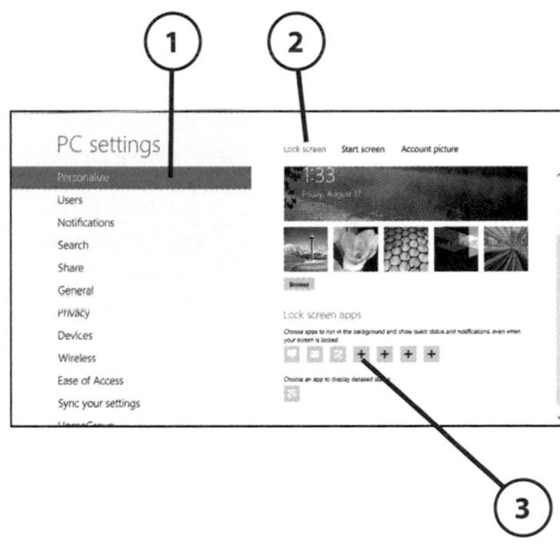

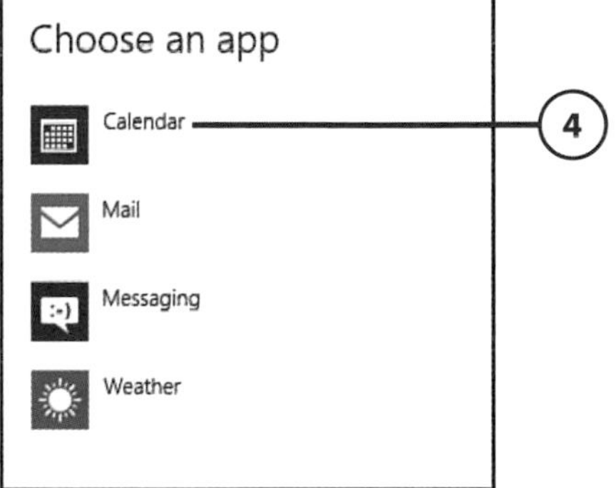

Badges Show Up Other Places Too

Badges also are the tiny items that show the notifications on the live tiles on your Windows 8 Start screen. For example, when you notice that your Messaging app tile suddenly shows 3 in the lower corner (when just a minute ago it didn't show any number at all), that's because the badge received and is displaying an update.

Adjusting the Look of Windows 8

In the preceding section, you learned how to personalize your Lock screen by changing the Lock screen picture, switching out your user image, and adding badges to your Lock screen. You can also change multiple aspects of the Start screen's color, contrast, design, and magnification, to give Windows 8 the kind of zest and flash (or zen quiet) you like.

Windows 8 takes an interesting approach in offering color schemes and patterns for the Start screen. You can choose from a large variety of color schemes, each of which has a color for the background and a color for items in the foreground. Then after you choose a color scheme you like, you can choose a background design, each of which offers a different design. Some of the designs are fairly sedate; others are bold and fun. (The last selection of design doesn't have any swirls at all, in case you're a no-swirls kind of person.)

As much as you may love the vibrant colors and enjoy the easy way Windows 8 moves, it can cause you trouble with making out the small words on the tiles or making things blurring as they pass (not saying you need to have your eyes checked or anything, *ahem*). There's good news—Windows 8 has other options that can make your computing experience a bit easier, and I show you how to work with them in this section.

Changing the Wow of the Start Screen

To change the Start screen's color, start off by displaying the Windows 8 Charms bar, tapping or clicking Settings, and choosing Change PC Settings.

1. In the Personalize screen, click or tap Start Screen.
2. Drag the color selector to a new color to see the effect of the change. The preview area shows you how the new color will look, along with the color highlights. The PC Settings title and the Personalize category also change to reflect the color choice.
3. When you've settled on a color, select the background design you want to apply to the background of the Start screen.

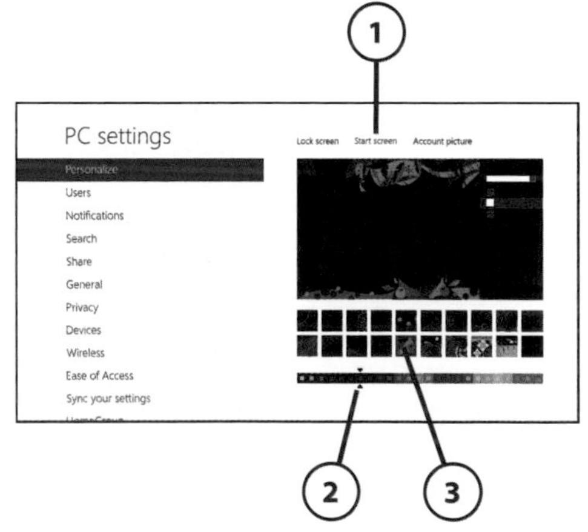

It's Not All Good

BEFORE YOU CHANGE THINGS...

If you like the color you've already got on the Windows 8 Start screen, make a mental note of which color scheme is selected before you change it to something else. The first time I changed the color configuration in Windows 8, I wasn't completely happy with the new selection, and after I changed the color back, I wasn't 100% sure I'd chosen the color scheme I had before. (This is one of those places where having a Cancel button would be nice.)

Up the Contrast, Baby

Windows 8 includes a High Contrast option so that you can display Windows 8 in a way that heightens the contrast on the screen, which hopefully makes things easier to read.

1. In the PC Settings (which is accessible from the Charms bar), scroll down to the Ease of Access category on the left side of the screen.
2. Drag the High Contrast slider from the left (Off) to the right (On).
3. Return to the Start screen to get a good look at how the background changes from white to black and the text appears in white and gray.

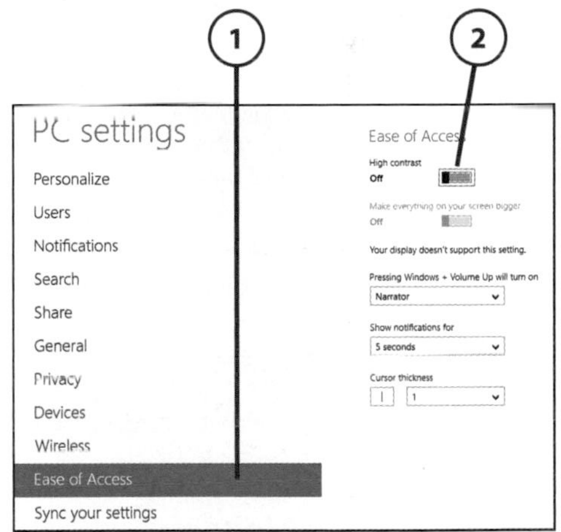

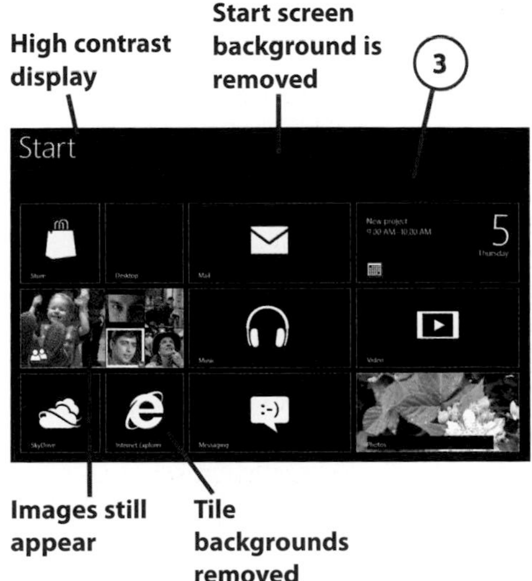

Magnifying Your Display

Another way you can enhance the readability of your Windows 8 screen involves magnifying the entire screen. You can do this by changing another of the Ease of Access settings.

1. Tap or click Ease of Access in the PC Settings window.
2. On the right side of the screen, drag the slider in the Make Everything on Your Screen Bigger setting from Off to On.
3. Your screen magnifies instantly, and you can navigate as normal (but you may need to do a lot more scrolling).

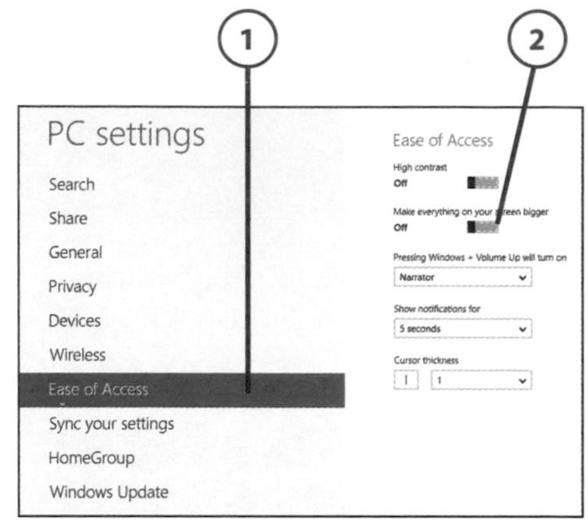

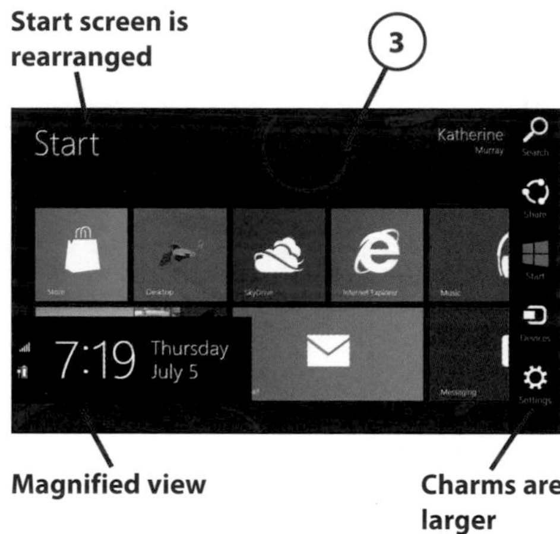

Changing the Time

It's likely that the first time you log in to your new Windows 8 computer (or the first time you fire up Windows 8 on your old computer), the program will ask you to verify or choose your time zone. But if necessary, you can let Windows 8 know what time it is where you are so that you're in sync no matter who you're chatting with online and where in the world they may be. (This becomes especially important if you're a big traveler and you take your Windows 8 computer or device on the road with you.) Having the time set to your local time is also helpful when you are scheduling calls and online meetings with others who may be in different time zones.

1. Display the PC Settings window and tap or click General.
2. In the Time Zone area, tap or click the time zone arrow to display a list of available time zones and choose the zone you want to use.
3. Leave the Adjust Clock for Daylight Saving Time Automatically turned on if you want the time to be adjusted for you when Daylight Saving Time changes.

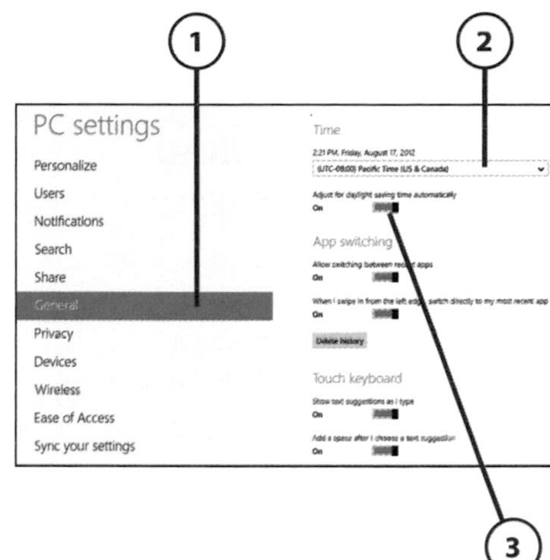

Changing Your Windows 8 Desktop

Now that you know how to change the look of the Start screen, you may also want to tweak the look of your Windows 8 desktop. Depending on the type of computer you purchased and the choices of the manufacturer, you could have a different customized desktop (for example, showing your computer manufacturer's logo in addition to the traditional Windows color scheme). You can modify the background—and choose some great new looks—with other themes and backgrounds available for your desktop in Windows 8.

Bring on the Screens

With Windows 8, you can set up multiple monitors and display different images on each screen. In fact, Windows 8 makes it easy for you to work with apps on one screen and desktop programs on another, all without giving up the ability to display the Charms bar and access the scroll bars and apps bars on each display. You use the Devices charm to set up a second screen for use with Windows 8.

Choosing a New Desktop Background

Windows 8 offers you a number of different choices for your background image. You can select a single image or multiple images, which display at increments you set, like a slide show.

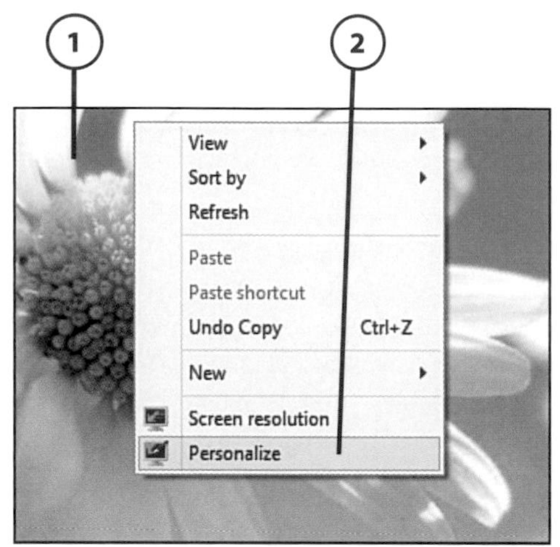

1. Tap the Desktop app on the Start screen, and right-click (or tap and hold; then release) the desktop area. A list of options appears.
2. Click or tap Personalize.
3. Click or tap Desktop Background. The Choose Your Desktop window Background appears.
4. Click the Picture Location arrow to choose the choices for backgrounds displayed in the Background window. If you choose Pictures Library, you can click Browse to choose the folder containing the images you want to use.
5. Drag the scrollbar to view all the choices in the display window.
6. Click at least three background images by clicking the check box in the upper-left corner of the image.
7. Click the Picture Position arrow and choose whether you want the image to fill the screen, fit the screen width, stretch, tile, or center.
8. Click the Change Picture Every arrow and choose how often you want pictures to change on the

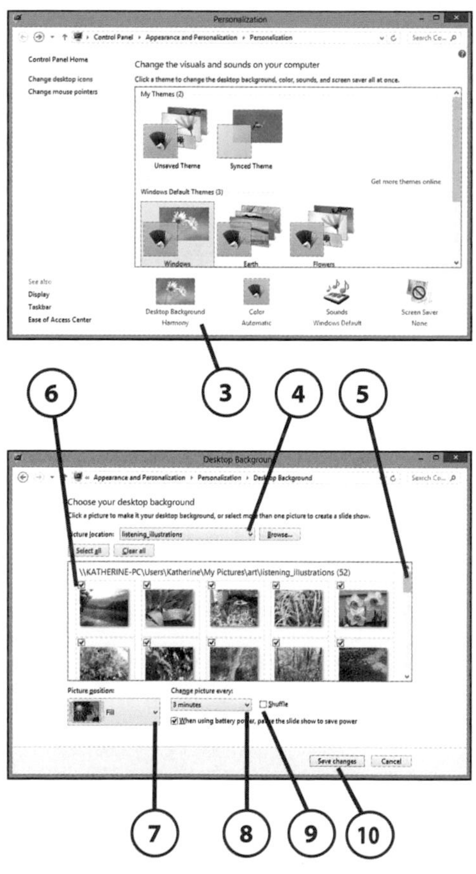

desktop. Your choices range from changing every 10 seconds (which is fast!) to changing once a day.

9. Click the Shuffle check box if you want the order of the images to be shuffled so they appear in different orders.
10. Click Save Changes.

Going Green with Your Slide Show

By default, Windows 8 is set to pause the slide show if your laptop or device is running on battery power. If you want the slide show to continue whether your computer is plugged in or not, you can uncheck the When Using Battery Power, Pause the Slide Show to Save Power checkbox.

>>>Go Further

CHOOSING A DESKTOP THEME

A theme for your Windows 8 desktop coordinates the desktop background, color scheme, sounds, and screen saver. You can choose the theme by displaying the desktop, right-clicking or tapping and holding and choosing Personalize, and then clicking the theme you want in the My Themes area of the Personalization dialog box.

If you don't see a theme that suits you, click the Get More Themes Online link. You'll find a variety of theme categories—new themes, animals, art, automotive, branded themes, games, holidays and seasons, movies, nature, and places and landscapes—to view a collection of different themes related to the various topics. To find out more about a specific theme, click the Details link. To download a theme you like, click the Download link just beneath it and click Open in the notification bar that appears at the bottom of the screen. The theme is stored in your My Themes area of the Personalization window in the Control Panel.

Tweaking Your Touch Experience

If you're using Windows 8 on a touch device, you can tweak the way Windows 8 interacts with your hardware so that you get just the kind of responsiveness you want. Windows 8 already takes care of a number of key (and common) tasks for you because it:

- Suggests words as you type
- Adds a space after you accept a text suggestion
- Automatically adds a period when you double-tap the spacebar
- Capitalizes the first letter of each sentence by default
- Puts your text in ALL UPPERCASE when you double-tap the Shift key
- Plays sounds as you type
- Gives you the option of displaying the standard keyboard layout as one of your keyboard selections

Changing Touch Settings

You can change any and all of the touch settings by following these steps:

1. In the PC Settings window, tap or click General.
2. Scroll down to display the Touch Keyboard settings.
3. Adjust the command slider of any of the settings you want to disable by dragging the slider from the right to the left.

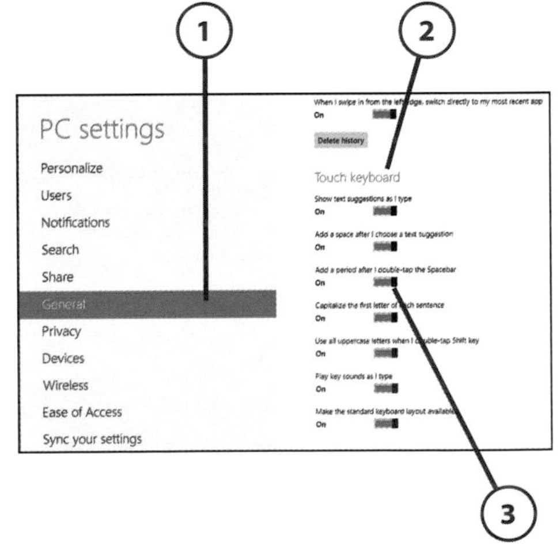

You Need the Right Touch

Of course, if you don't have a touch-capable device, you won't find these touch settings in the General tab of your version of Windows 8.

Adjusting the Mouse

Most of us don't expect too much from our mice. We want to be able to click without thinking about it. We want the right-click button to work. And when we move the mouse across the mouse pad, we want the pointer to move similarly onscreen. None of that seems too hard.

But sometimes mice are calibrated too quickly or too slow. When you double-click, the software doesn't realize what you're doing. When you move the mouse, it leaves a "trail" on the screen that is distracting and disconcerting. Luckily you can tweak the way your mouse behaves so that pointing and clicking becomes a mindless activity again.

Setting Pointer and Click Speed

You might think that having a slow mouse—where the pointer lags behind where you're pointing as you drag it across the screen—would drive you batty, but in reality, having a too-fast mouse can have the same effect. For the best possible results, you want your mouse to move like a seamless extension of our hand.

1. On the Windows 8 Start screen, type *mouse*.
2. Tap or click Settings from the Search results bar.
3. Tap or click Change Mouse Settings.

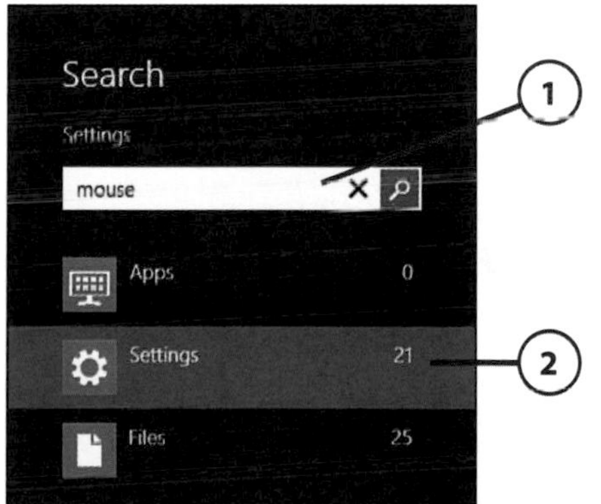

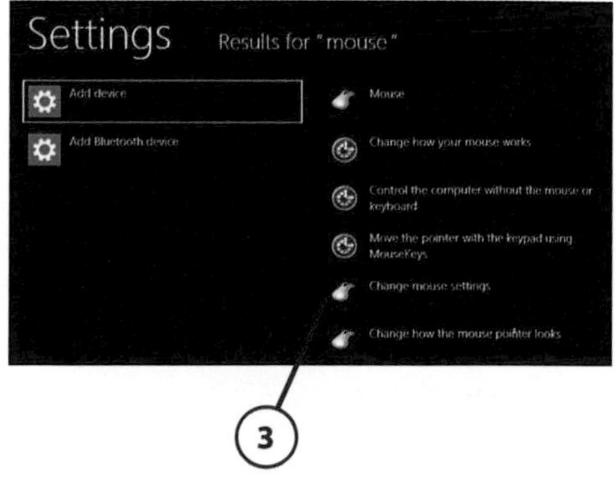

4. In the Mouse Properties dialog box, click the Pointer Options tab.
5. Adjust the slider in the Motion area to slow the movement of the pointer or increase the speed. For best results, leave the Enhance Pointer Precision check box selected.
6. If you want Windows 8 to automatically position the pointer on a default setting in a dialog box, click this check box.
7. If you like to see the "trails" of the pointer—or a series of pointers in a trail as you move the mouse—click Display Pointer Trails. You can also choose whether you want the trail to be Short or Long (or any point between the two).
8. Click Apply to save your changes.
9. Click the Buttons tab.
10. Drag the slider in the Double-Click Speed area toward Slow or Fast, depending on whether you want to increase the speed of the double-click or decrease it. If you decrease the speed, you can double-click more slowly, and Windows 8 still recognizes it as a double-click.
11. Click OK to save your settings.

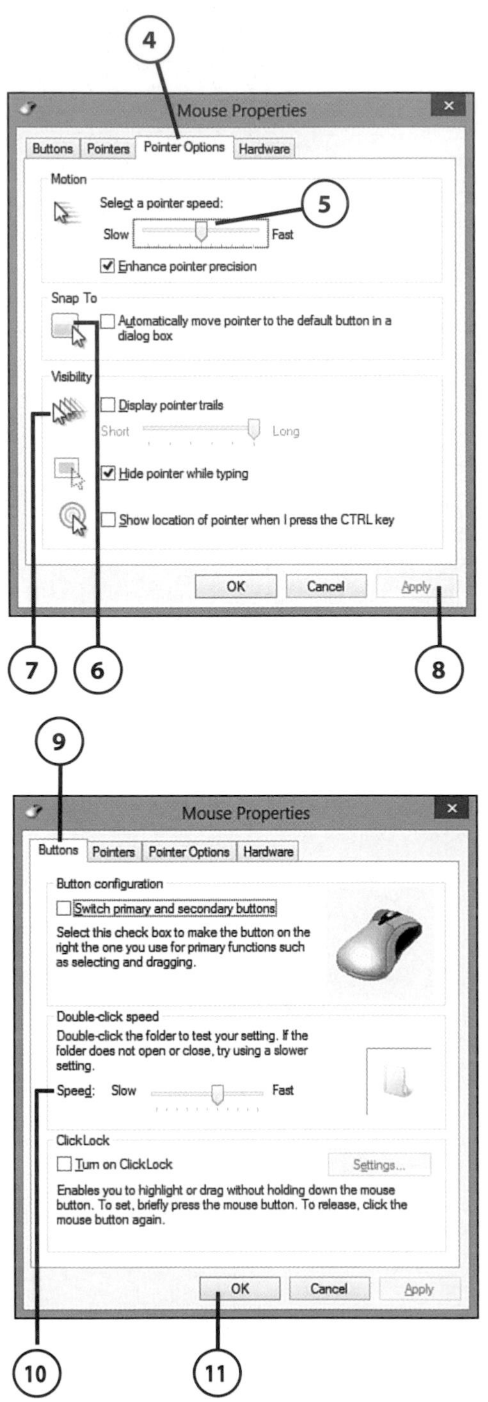

Hiding and Displaying the Pointer

By default, Windows 8 hides the mouse pointer when you are typing on the keyboard. If you don't want to suppress the display of the pointer, click to clear the Hide

Pointer While Typing check box in the Pointer Options tab of the Mouse Properties dialog box. If you opt to leave the pointer hidden while you type, you may want to click Show Location of Pointer When I Press the CTRL Key so that you can just press Ctrl to display the pointer quickly on the screen.

Changing the Way Your Mouse Buttons Work

If you're left-handed, you know how important it is to be able to change the function of the mouse buttons so that they do what you want them to do. You can change the way the mouse buttons work in Windows 8. Here's how:

1. In the Mouse Properties dialog box (see the previous section if you're not sure how to get here), click the Buttons tab.
2. Click the Switch Primary and Secondary Buttons in the Button Configuration area. The picture of the mouse on the right side of the dialog box shows the primary selection button in blue.
3. If you want to be able to highlight and drag without holding down the mouse button, click the Turn on ClickLock check box.
4. Click OK to close the Mouse Properties dialog box.

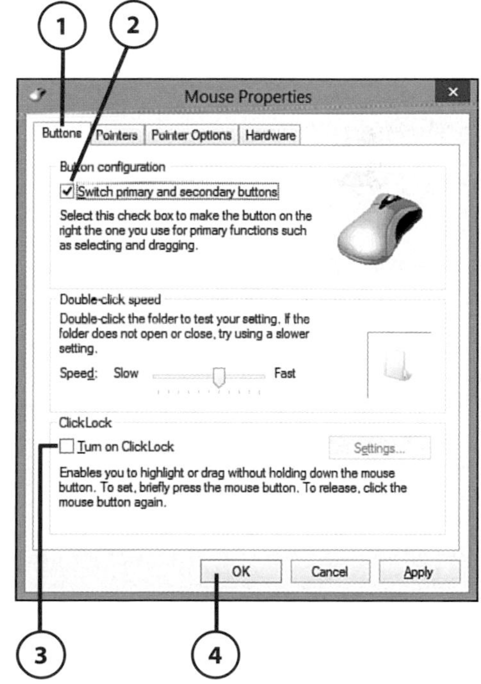

>>>Go Further

CONTROLLING THE MOUSE WHEEL

If you have a mouse that includes a mouse wheel between the mouse buttons (typically located toward the top of the mouse where you click the button), you can change the settings that control the way the wheel works in Windows 8.

On the Start screen, type *mouse wheel*, and in the Search results page, tap or click Settings. Click or tap the first item that appears, Change Mouse Wheel Settings. In the Wheel tab of the Mouse Properties dialog box, you can change the number of lines the wheel will scroll when you move it vertically, and the number of characters that will scroll when you are horizontally scrolling. Change your settings, click Apply, and then click OK to put your new settings into effect.

Turn Off Sound for Notifications

You can turn off notification sounds with just a couple of taps or clicks. Start by displaying your PC Settings (tap or click the Settings charm, and choose Change PC Settings). In the PC Settings screen, tap Notifications. Tap or click and drag the slider for Play Notification Sounds to the Off position.

Choosing Your Language

Today as our connections spread across the globe and our work moves across geographical lines, learning to work with different languages and translation tools becomes increasingly important. As a worldwide company, Microsoft has been working with language needs for a while, but they haven't been able to make the task simple for users. In Windows 8, you can use a simplified process to find and choose the language you want Windows 8 to display.

1. In the PC Settings window, tap or click General.
2. Scroll down to the Language area.
3. Tap or click the Language Preferences. The Language dialog box appears.
4. To add a new language, tap or click Add a Language at the top of the dialog box.
5. In the Add Languages dialog box, scroll down to the language you want to add.
6. Tap or click the language.
7. Tap or click Add.

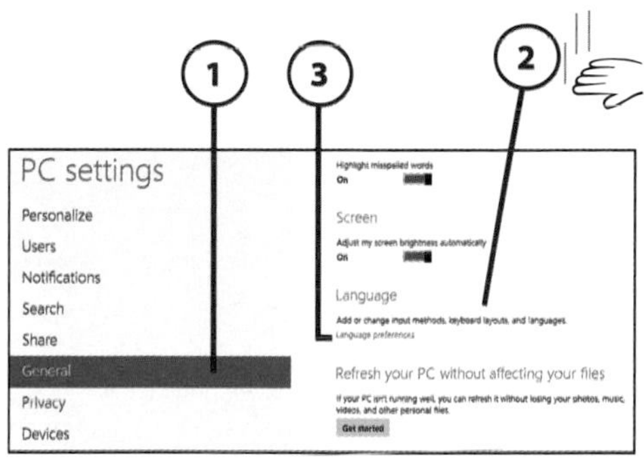

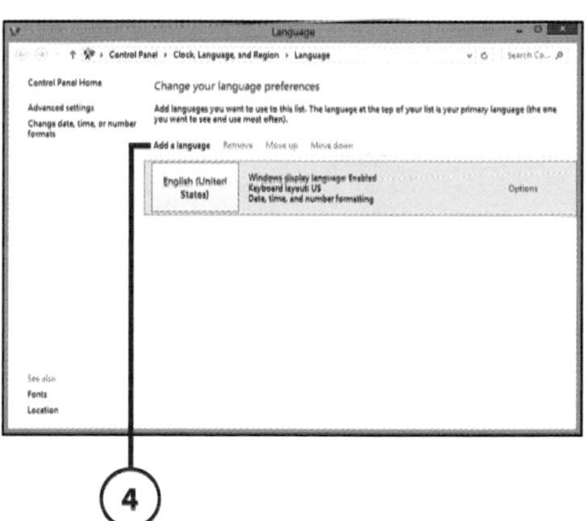

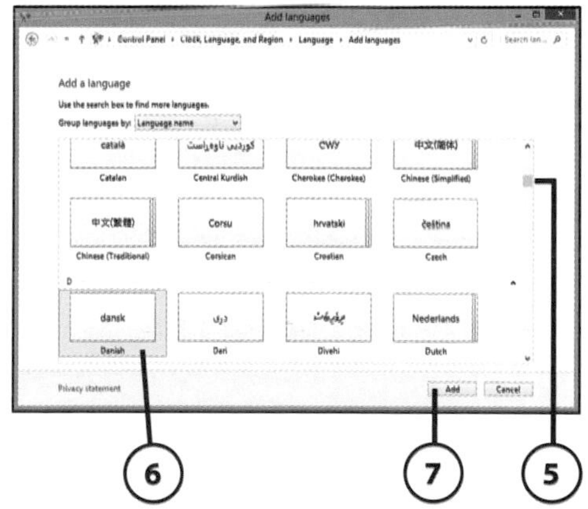

Setting Your Primary Language

By default, Windows 8 assigns the language at the top of the list in the Language dialog box as your primary language. If you want to change this, you can change the order of languages displayed by selecting the language and choosing either Move Up or Move Down in the command bar above the language list.

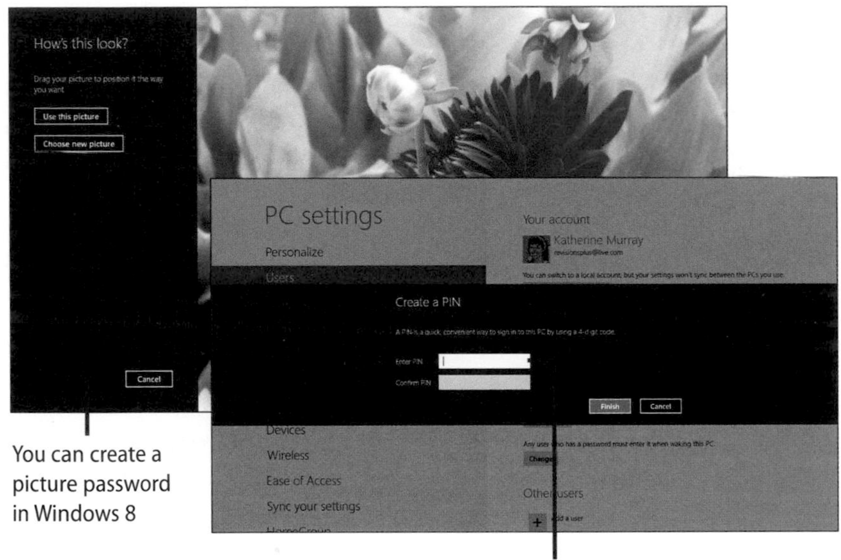

You can create a picture password in Windows 8

Create a PIN to log in quickly and easily

This chapter shows you the security features in Windows 8 by focusing on the following tasks:

- Customizing your login
- Working with the Action Center
- Using Windows Defender
- Turning on your Windows Firewall
- Working with user accounts
- Maintaining your privacy

6

Securing Your Windows 8 Computer

Today our computers seem to be attacked on many fronts. We receive phishing messages through email messages that look legitimate; we risk catching viruses when we download files; we can pick up unwanted parasites browsing the web. Thank goodness, Windows 8 is the most secure Windows operating system released to-date. Over the last few releases, Microsoft has increasingly upped the ante on security, and in Windows 7 introduced the Action Center, which notified you when anything related to security in your system needed your attention.

Windows 8 keeps the Action Center and builds on this solid foundation by adding new security measures. Now you can create a unique (and fun) picture password and customize your login PIN. If you're concerned about using your Microsoft Account (formerly called your Windows Live ID) to sign in to your computer, you can change your login to a local account, so all your files and settings are stored on your computer and not in the cloud. You can also work with Windows Defender, which is built into the operating system and not something you have to download separately.

New PCs—Security *Before* Startup

In Windows 8, PCs that are built on UEFI (Unified Extensible Firmware Interface) firmware can take advantage of enhanced security features like Secure Boot, which does a scan and ensures system elements are okay before Windows 8 even boots on your system. If you'd like to learn more about UEFI, you should check out http://www.uefi.org.

Customizing Your Login

You've already seen the Windows 8 Lock screen, which allows you to add your own picture and display the badges you care most about, so you can get the information you want before you even log in. In addition to customizing the Lock screen, you can tweak your login procedure so that Windows 8 uses the type of authentication you choose. For example, instead of a regular alphanumeric password, *you* might want to use a picture password, or create a new login PIN for your machine.

>>>Go Further

FACE RECOGNITION IN WINDOWS 8

Imagine walking into your office and sitting down in front of your computer and hearing a voice, smooth as silk: "Glad to have you back—did you have a nice lunch?"

No password required. No login. No thumbprint.

Windows 8 just recognized your face. When you get up and walk away from your computer, the PC locks everything down tight because it notices you're gone.

Think this is some far-off-in-the-distance feature? Not so! The inner workings of Windows include code that supports the recognition of "human presence," using your computer's webcam. So when you walk into the room, your Windows 8 computer (using Kinect sensors) will be able to sense your presence. Then when you sit down, the webcam can scan your face and compare the scan with the facial information stored in your user profile. If those things match, you are logged in automatically and can get right to work.

If someone else walks up, or you get up and leave your office, the computer continues reading the environment and responding accordingly. When you get up and walk away, the computer sleeps. When another user walks up, the computer scans her face and checks it against the system's user accounts—if she is recognized, she can be logged in automatically.

Yes, it's still speculation, but it's coming closer every day. In fact, a search on *face recognition in Windows 8* brings up some interesting forum posts, where users who had installed Windows 8 Consumer Preview were getting prompted to enter a "face recognition password" (which of course they didn't have).

The future isn't as far out as you thought.

Changing a Password

By default, Windows 8 asks you to log in with your Windows Live ID and password. You can, however, change your password at any time or choose different types of passwords (for example, a picture password or a PIN logon) to help with authentication.

1. On your Windows 8 Start screen, swipe or click to display the Charms bar.
2. Tap or click Settings.
3. Tap or click Change PC Settings.
4. In the PC Settings window, tap or click Users on the left side of the screen.
5. In the right side of the window, tap or click Change Your Password.

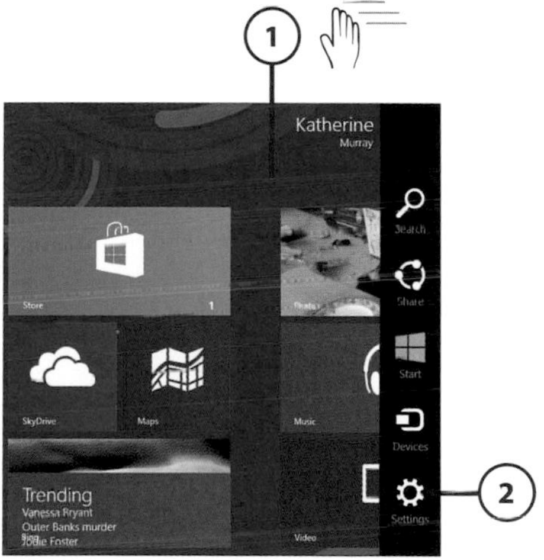

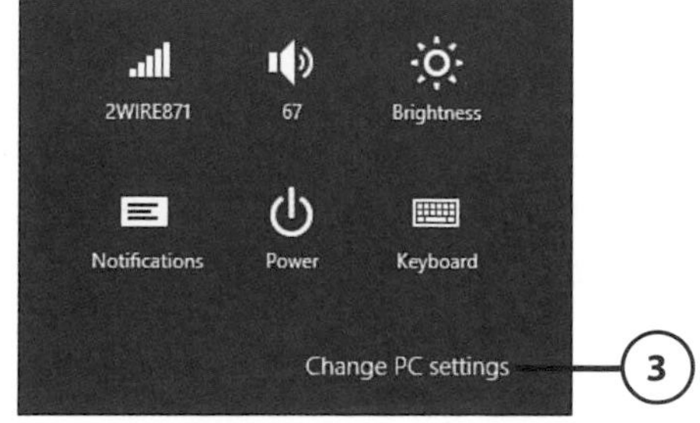

6. In the Change Your Password screen, tap or click in the Old Password box and type your old password.
7. Tap or click to move the insertion point to the New Password box and enter a new password.
8. Retype the new password in the Re-Enter Password box.
9. Tap or click Next. Windows 8 lets you know that you've successfully changed your password, and you can click Finish to return to the PC Settings window.

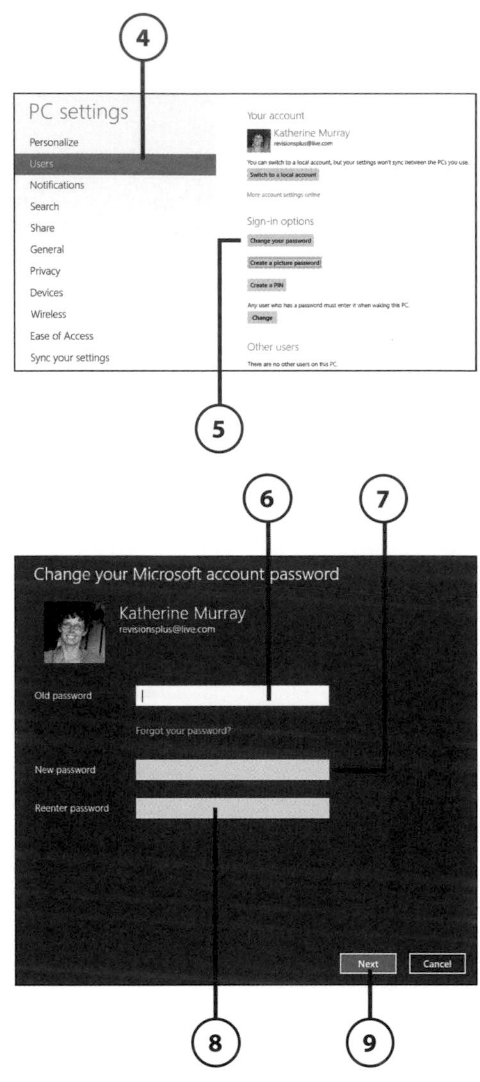

Account Trouble?

If you were using your Windows Live account as the logon for your Windows 8 computer, you may be able to get help if you have trouble accessing your account or changing your password. When you click the Can't Access Your Account? link, Windows 8 provides you with a link you can use to get account help online. Click the link to access the web help.

What Makes a Strong Password?

A strong password is at least eight characters long and doesn't include any recognizable words or number sequences. What's more, you should vary the capitalization of letters, mixing the upper- and lowercase letters. Windows 8 remembers your password as case sensitive, which means that 62GoT38 is a different password than 62gOt38.

Creating a Picture Password

In Windows 8, you can set a picture password if you want to. This type of password gives you a unique new way to set up security for your touch-based computer or monitor. You actually use one of your own pictures and a specific gesture that you trace on the picture to let Windows 8 know that it's really you logging in to your computer. For example, you might use your finger or mouse pointer to trace a shape on the photo and then draw a line to the lower-right corner. Windows 8 records this gesture and when you log in using your picture password, any gesture other than the one you recorded won't unlock your computer. Here are the steps to add your own picture password.

1. In the PC Settings window, tap or click Users.
2. Select Create a Picture Password. Windows 8 prompts you to enter your current password.
3. Type your current password.
4. Click or tap OK. The Welcome to Picture Password window appears, giving you instructions about the process of creating a picture password.
5. Tap or click Choose Picture.

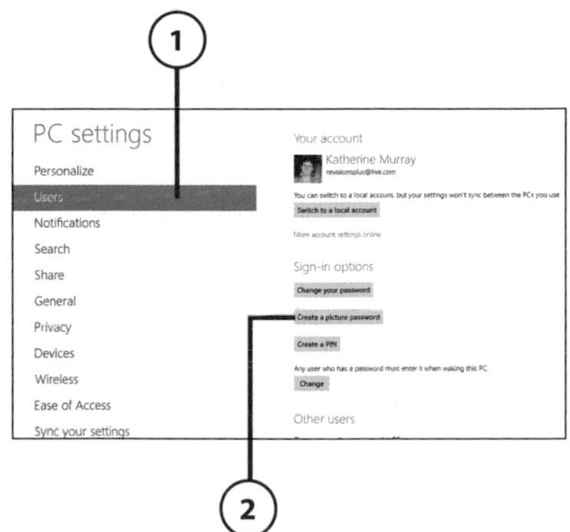

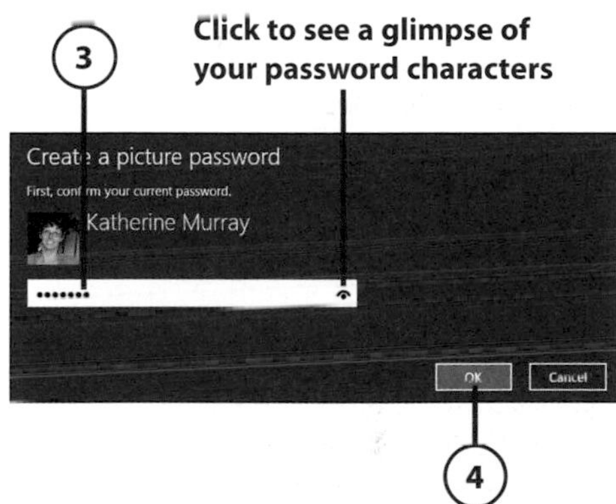

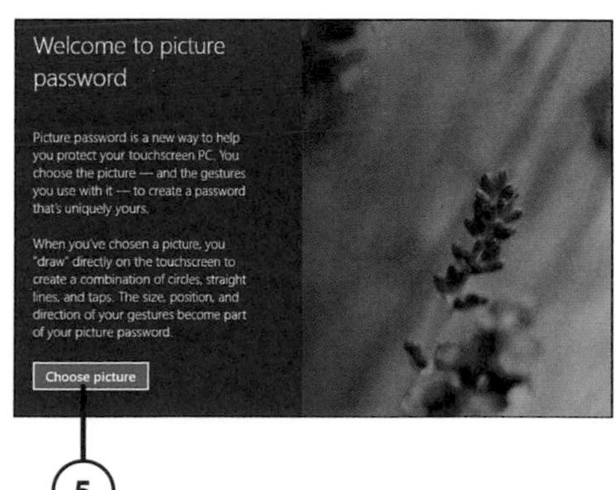

6. Tap or click the picture you want to use. A small checkmark appears in the upper-right corner of the image.
7. Click or tap Open.
8. If you want to adjust the picture, drag it to the right or left.
9. Tap or click Use This Picture.
10. If you want to choose a different image instead, tap or click Choose New Picture and repeat steps 5 through 7.
11. Using your finger or mouse, draw three gestures on the picture. For a moment after you draw on the screen, an arrow shows how Windows 8 recorded the movement. When prompted, repeat the gestures. If you don't make exactly the same gestures, Windows will prompt you to try again.

Starting Over

If you don't like the gesture you've used, you can tap or click Start Over to create new gestures.

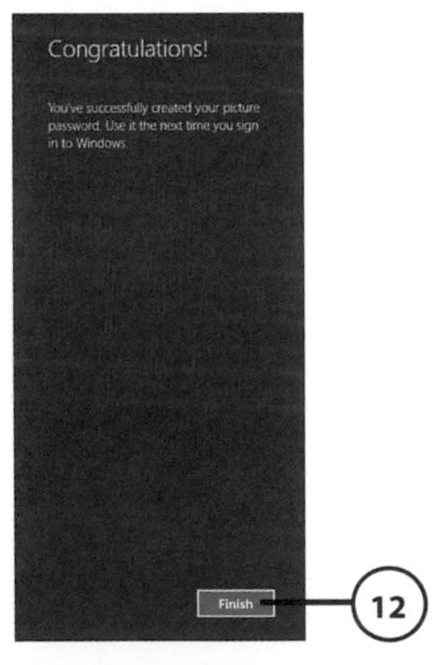

12. After you draw the gestures correctly, Windows 8 displays a Congratulations message. Tap or click Finish to save the picture password.

It's Not All Good

The Fussiness of Picture Passwords

One thing you're likely to discover very quickly: Picture passwords are very particular. Windows 8 may not record your gesture exactly as you think you entered it. If you draw an arc on the screen, Windows may close it to create a circle. Or the line you purposely skewed may show up straight. Use the Try Again option to display the gestures Windows 8 is expecting.

It can also help to use a photo that has very definite patterns or lines you can follow and remember easily. Too many curves or too much abstraction may leave you wondering about the specific gestures you need to enter.

Removing a Picture Password

As you can see, using a picture password is great if you want to ensure that you have very personalized security on your computer so that others (who might know your password) won't be able to log in as you. The downside is that the picture password is very particular and specific—so it might be hard for even you to remember!

If you want to remove your picture password, display PC Settings (by tapping or clicking Change PC Settings in the options available when you select the Settings charm) and click Users. Click or tap the Remove button that now appears to the right of the Change Picture Password button to delete the picture password you added.

Creating a PIN Logon

We're accustomed to using PINs in other areas of our lives—whether you are withdrawing money from your checking account, purchasing gas at the pump, or giving yourself a credit reward—chances are you're used to entering that short code that lets the business know you are authorized to spend the money or claim the benefit. Windows 8 now lets you create your own four-digit PIN for login, which simplifies the process and gets you to your Start screen that much faster.

Begin by displaying the PC Settings screen. Display the Charms bar and choose Settings; then tap or click Change PC Settings.

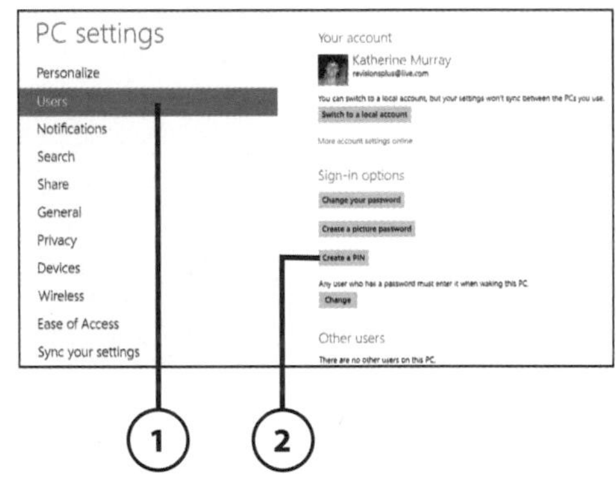

1. Tap or click Users to display your account login options.
2. Tap or click Create a PIN on the right side of the screen.
3. Windows 8 prompts you to enter your current password. Tap or click in the box and type the password.
4. Click or tap OK. The Create a PIN screen appears.

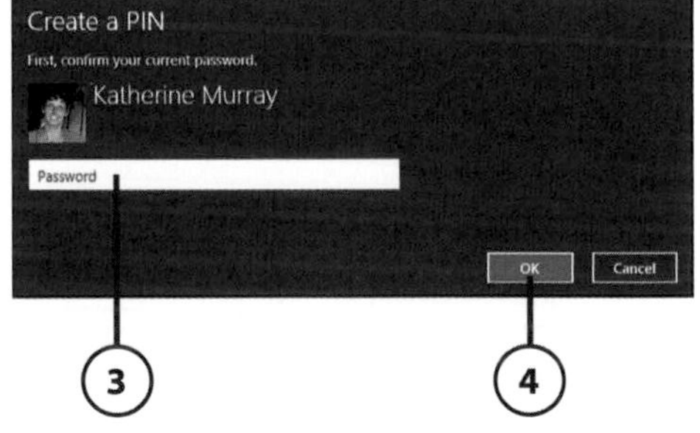

Nothing Fancy, Bub

When you create a PIN, Windows 8 insists you use only numbers. This means no alphabetic characters, punctuation symbols, or spaces.

5. Type four numbers you want to use as your PIN.

6. Tap or click in the Confirm PIN box and retype the numbers you entered.

7. Click or tap Finish. Windows 8 saves your PIN, and the next time you log on, enter the PIN instead of your password. You'll notice that Windows 8 displays the Start screen immediately, even before you press Enter!

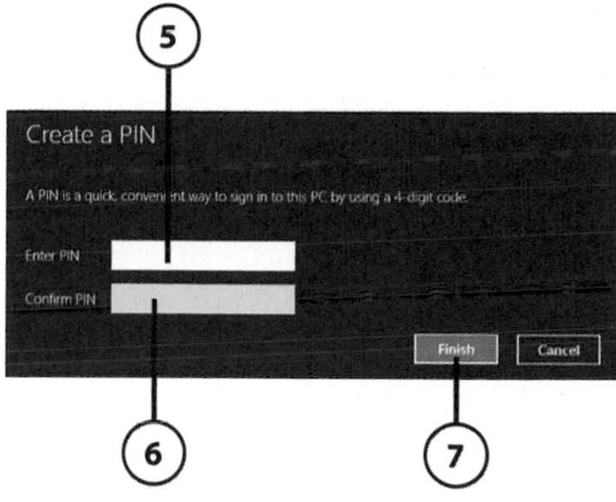

Removing a PIN

If you decide you want to remove your PIN later, you can display the User page of the PC Settings screen again, and click Remove to the right of the Change PIN button. You can, of course, also change the PIN you created by clicking Change PIN and entering and saving a new PIN.

>>>Go Further

HALT! ENTER YOUR PASSWORD!

Some people aren't crazy about the extra step of having to enter their password each time they wake Windows 8 up from a short sleep. You can actually disable this setting—if you're absolutely sure you're not putting your computer or device at risk.

Display the PC Settings screen and tap Users. Tap or click the Change button beneath Any User Who Has a Password Must Enter It When Waking This PC.

After you click or tap Change, Windows 8 applies the change automatically, but the operating system displays the following warning:

"If you change this setting, anyone can wake this PC and access the currently signed-in account without entering a password. This affects all accounts on this PC and isn't recommended if you use your PC in a public place."

So if that warning doesn't shake you up and you want to go ahead and change the setting, click or tap OK. The setting on the Users screen changes to Any User Who Has a Password Doesn't Need to Enter It When Waking This PC. (Yes, it's a bit wordy, but whatchagonnado?)

Switching to a Local Account

Windows 8 uses your Windows Live login when it creates your user account, and this can be a time-saving and efficient feature if you want to synchronize all your PC settings across your various computers—no matter how many Windows 8 PCs and devices you may have. But not everybody likes the idea that their computer is tied in an ongoing way to something so, well, Microsoft. If this bothers you, you can switch your Windows Live account to a local account, which disconnects your user account from the online synching and keeps all your settings right there on your private PC or device. When you make your account a local account, you do give up the ability to sync easily across the web, however.

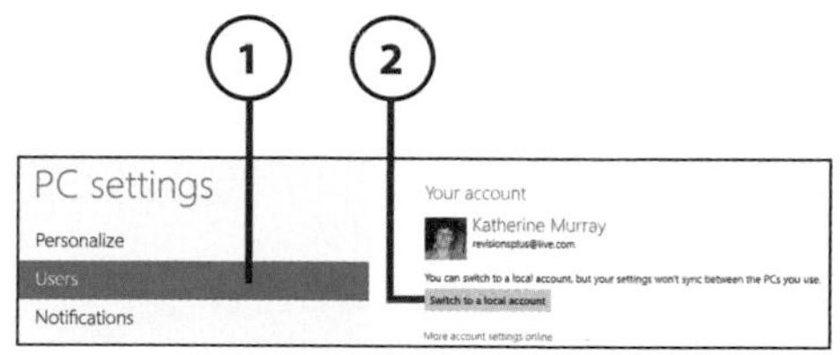

1. From the PC Settings screen, click or tap Users on the left side of the screen.
2. Tap or click Switch to a Local Account. The Change to a Local Account screen appears.
3. Windows 8 prompts you for your password. Type it in the box provided.
4. Click Next.

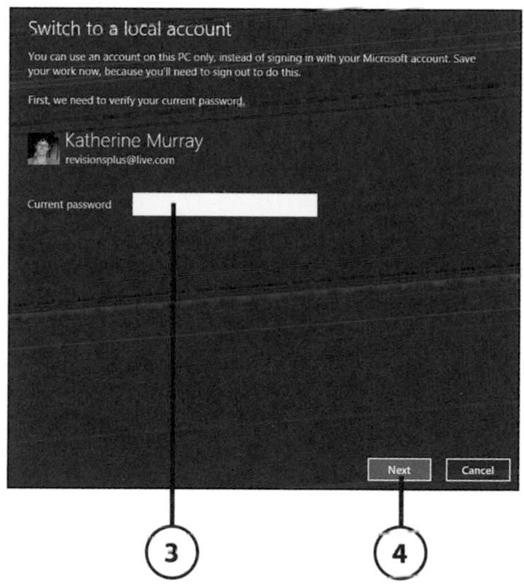

5. On the Change to a Local Account screen, enter the user name you'll use to sign in to Windows 8.
6. Type (and then retype) your password.
7. Enter a password hint to remind you of the password in case you forget it later.
8. Click Next. Windows prompts you to save any work in progress and lets you know that some apps may ask you to log in before you can view app information. Click Sign Out and Finish to complete the process.

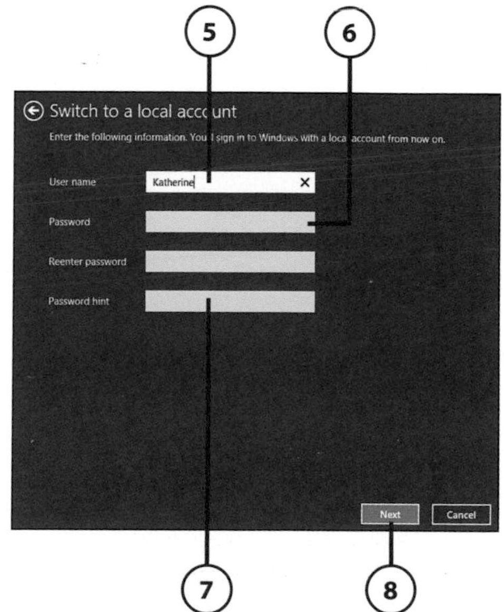

Linking Your Account Again

It may be that you find that your local account doesn't cost you anything in terms of apps that don't display properly or settings that don't synchronize. But you can switch your account back to a Microsoft account if you like, by choosing Users in the PC Settings screen and clicking or tapping Switch to a Microsoft Account. Windows 8 walks you through the process of signing back in and linking your user account settings to a Microsoft account.

It's Not All Good

What Do You Lose by Going Local?

If you want more control over the connections your computer uses, switching to a local account may be your best bet.

If you switch to a local account, you won't be able to download apps from the Windows Store, share files and photos, or sync your settings between PCs and browsers without logging in to specific apps that enable the sharing. For example, you won't be able to share photo albums through SkyDrive or get the latest app updates and notifications, unless you do it manually by logging in to your account.

Working with the Action Center

The Action Center was introduced in Windows 7 to display, in one place, the information you need about any updates your computer needs for both security and regular maintenance purposes. For example, if your antivirus program expires, the Action Center lets you know so that you can renew your subscription or find another antivirus program.

The Action Center is alive and well in Windows 8. You can use the Action Center to review the status of your system security and to set alerts so that you'll know when something important comes up. What's more, you can customize the information in the Action Center so that it displays just what you want to see when an alert is in order.

Reviewing Your System Status

You can easily see which security tools are in place on your computer, change settings, and update your software in the Action Center. You can find all the tools you need in the System and Security page of the Control Panel, but you can get to it from the Windows 8 Start screen. Here's how:

1. On the Start screen, type *action center*.
2. Tap or click Settings.
3. Tap or click Action Center.

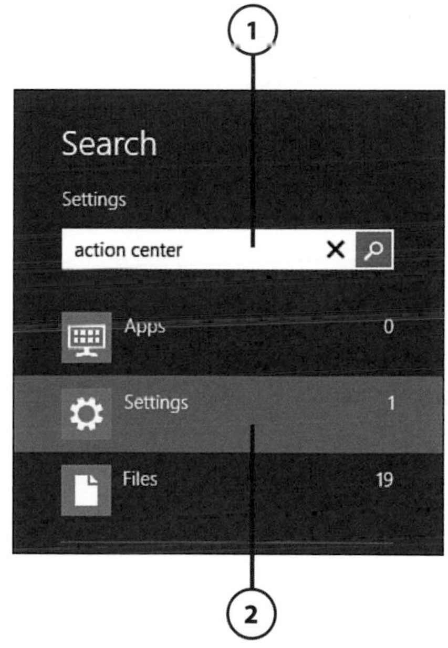

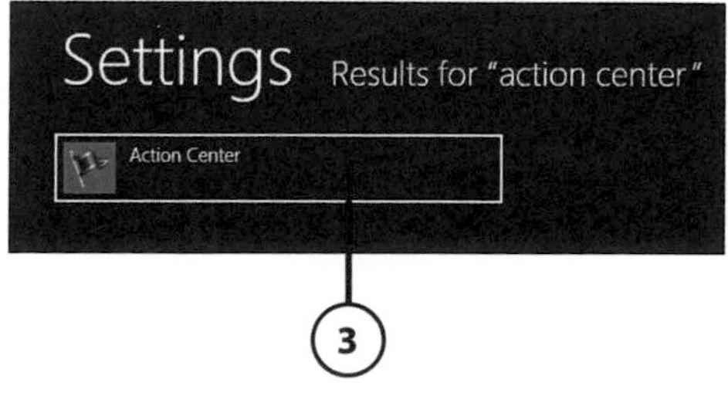

4. In the Action Center dialog box, review any messages that are displayed. The tag color to the left of the issue indicates the urgency of the issue—yellow warns you that the item should be resolved eventually; red indicates that your attention is needed immediately.
5. Click a link to get more information about the topic. The link might enable you to change settings or view more information about the displayed issue.
6. Click the button that is provided on issues you need to resolve. The name of the button and the task performed will vary depending on what Windows 8 is prompting you to do.
7. Click Ignore This Message if you want to cancel the warning message.
8. Click the down-arrow to display additional security settings and make changes as needed.

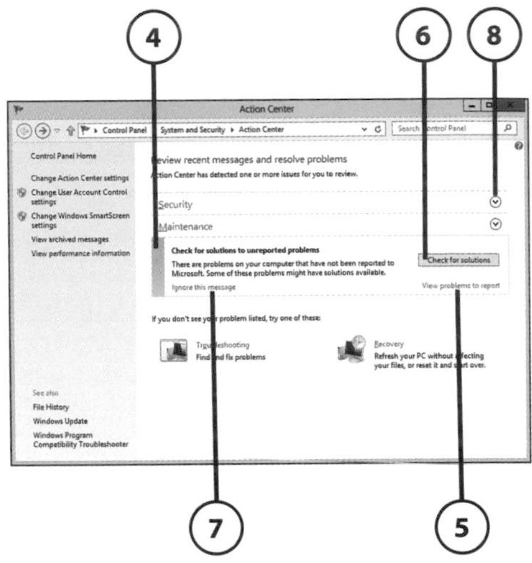

Archiving Messages

After you open and review a message displayed in the Action Center, Windows 8 archives the message and removes it from the alert list. To see old Action Center messages, click or tap View Archived Messages in the left side of the Action Center dialog box. To review an archived message, double-click (or double-tap) it. When you're finished viewing archived messages, click OK.

>>>Go Further

WHY WORRY ABOUT USER ACCOUNT CONTROL?

It's not unusual today when you're surfing the Web to encounter web sites and online programs that want to make changes to your computer. Some of these downloads are legitimate—perhaps you need the latest version of Microsoft Silverlight or Adobe Flash in order to play a movie trailer. But some programs are not so well-intentioned, and these are the ones you need User Account Control to block.

User Account Control makes it easy for you to find out when a program wants to make a change to your computer. You can set up User Account Control so you'll be notified when a program tries to change your system settings. (It's set to do this by default.) Windows 8 offers four different settings—ranging from Always Notify to Never Notify—and you can easily change the settings by clicking Change User Account Control Settings in the left panel of the Control Panel. Although User Account Control prompts can be annoying, before you disable them, remember that they're there for your protection.

Changing Action Center Alerts

Each Action Center message includes a link that gives you the next step to follow as you deal with the issue. You may choose to turn off messages about that particular issue, archive the message, or ignore the message. You can change which issues you receive alerts for so that you are notified about only the ones you want to see.

1. In the Action Center, click Change Action Center Settings.

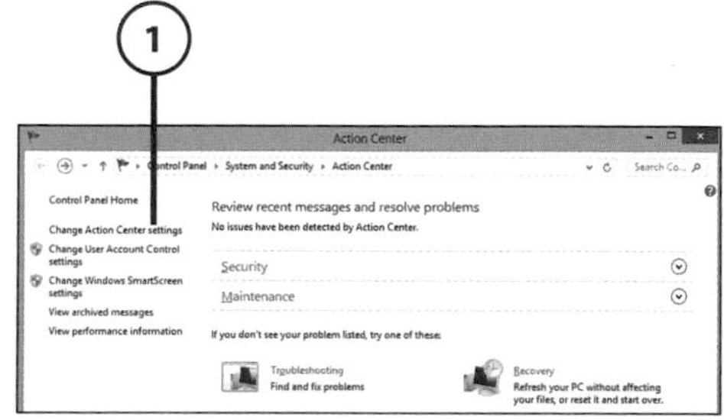

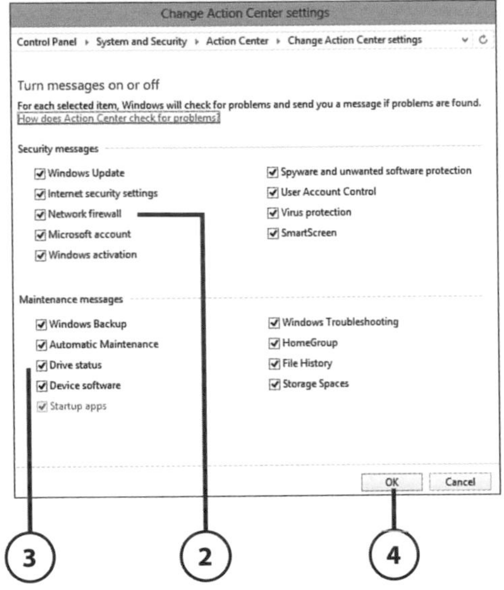

2. Click to uncheck any security item you don't want Windows 8 to check for.
3. Click to uncheck any maintenance messages you don't want Windows 8 to display.
4. Click OK.

Choice—It's Your Prerogative

Of course, you can change the items Windows 8 checks for and the messages you receive at any time. If you turn off an item and then get concerned that maybe you need it after all, simply go to the Action Center, click Change Action Center Settings again, and click to check any unmarked boxes of items you want to add. Click OK to save your settings.

Out of Sight, Out of Mind

Although being alerted for every little thing can be annoying, unless you have a specific reason for turning off an alert—for example, Windows 8 doesn't recognize the antivirus program you're using on your PC and keeps telling you there's no antivirus program installed—the best practice is to leave all the alerts turned on.

Deciding What to Do with Unrecognized Apps

Windows SmartScreen is a utility within Action Center that keeps an eye on your PC or device and alerts you before Windows 8 runs any unrecognized apps or files you've downloaded from the web. By default, Windows SmartScreen displays a warning before running an unrecognized app. You can change Windows SmartScreen settings if you want to, either to turn off the feature (not a good idea) or to require that administrator approval be given before an unrecognized app can be run.

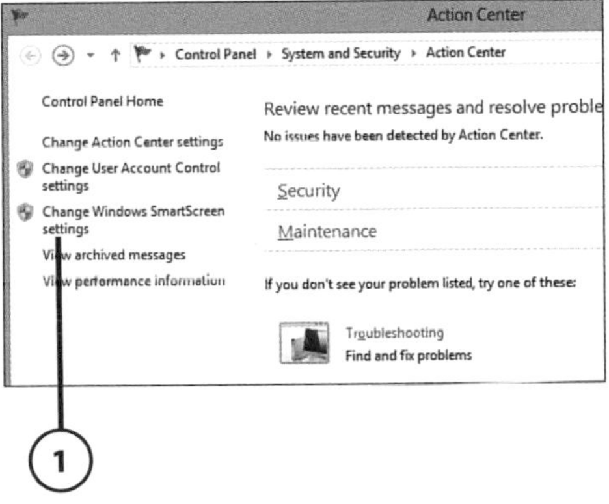

1. In the Action Center, click Change Windows SmartScreen Settings.
2. Click the new setting you want to apply.
3. Click OK.

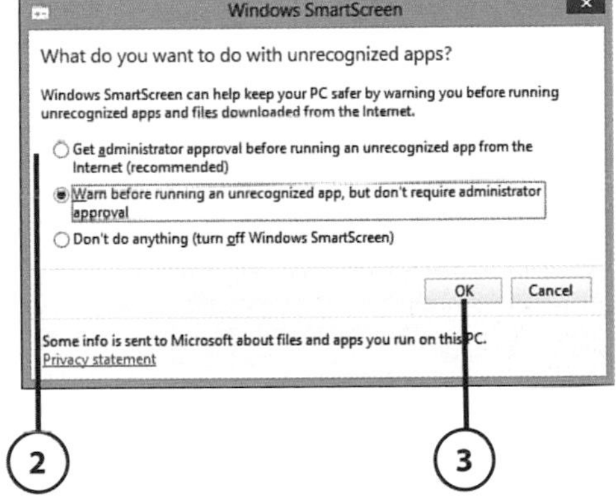

Using Windows Defender

Windows Defender is an anti-spyware utility that is already installed on your Windows 8 PC. Spyware is software that can download itself to your computer without your knowing it, and the makers of the spyware can then find out about your usage habits—or worse, get access to your important files and data. When you have Windows Defender turned on (and it should be on by default), the program runs automatically in the background as you use your computer, blocking any attempts by spyware to download files to your computer and notifying you when programs try to change your Windows settings.

You can use Windows Defender to scan your system regularly and remove any suspicious files that have been added to your computer without your knowledge.

Scanning Your PC with Windows Defender

Windows Defender is designed to scan your system every so often—at increments you choose—but you can also choose to do a scan of your PC whenever you like. You might want to do this, for example, if your system is running slowly or you are concerned about your computer's security. You can have Windows Defender scan your PC to make sure no worrisome files have snuck in under your radar.

1. On the Windows 8 Start screen, type *defender*.
2. Tap or click Apps.
3. On the Search screen, tap or click Windows Defender.

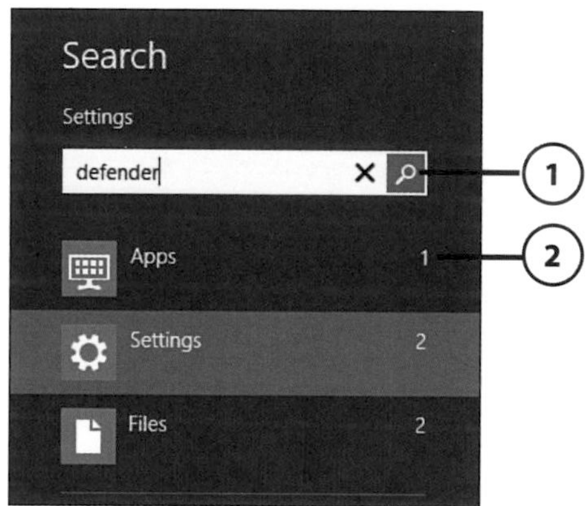

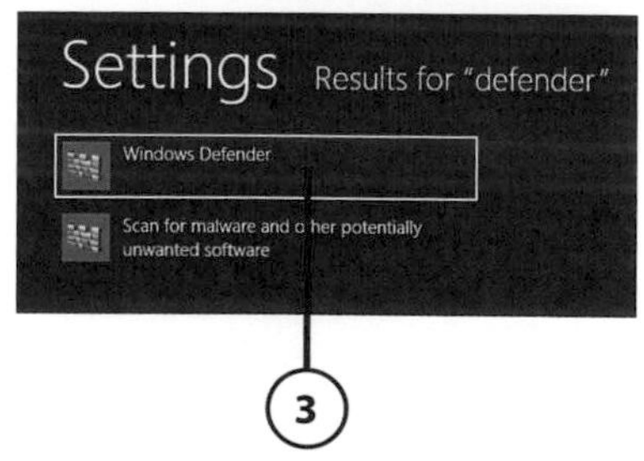

4. Choose the option you want for the type of scan you want Windows Defender to perform.
5. Tap or click the Scan Now button.

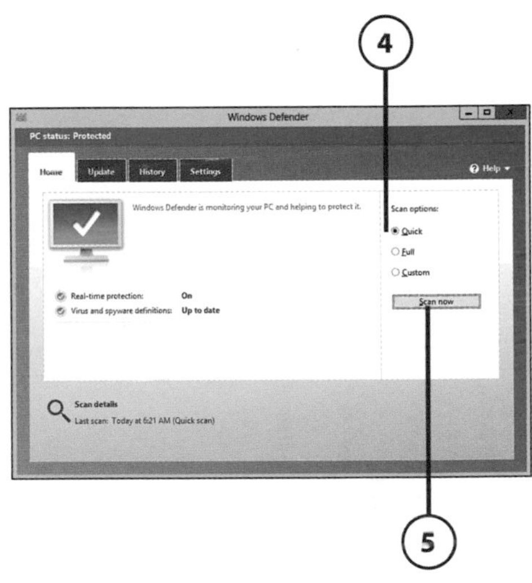

Updating Your Definitions

Windows Defender uses what's known as a definitions file to make sure it's checking for the latest viruses and spyware. Defender automatically updates the file, but you can also click or tap the Update tab in the Windows Defender dialog box and then tap or click the Update button to search for updates to the definitions file.

6. After the scan completes, click the History tab to see the scan findings.
7. You can choose the action you want to take related to found items; for example, click Remove All to delete all potentially harmful results.
8. Click the Close box to exit Defender.

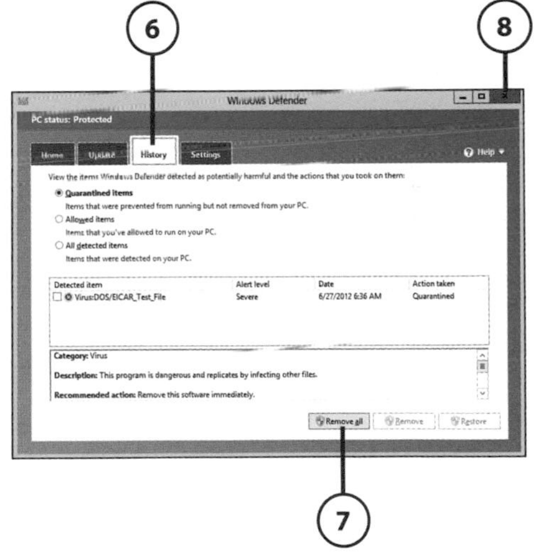

Scanning Styles in Windows Defender	
Type of Scan	**Description**
Quick Scan	Windows Defender checks all files that have been downloaded to your computer since the date of the last scan.
Full Scan	Windows Defender checks all files on all drives and folders in your computer.
Custom Scan	You can choose the drives and folders you want Windows Defender to check.

It's Not All Good

One of the challenges of working with antivirus, spyware, and malware protection programs is that they don't play nicely together. As you can imagine, they are suspicious of everyone; that's their job.

This means that if you have installed another type of antivirus or spyware program, such as Lavasoft's Ad-Aware, Windows Defender may be disabled. Or even when you download and install Microsoft Security Essentials (which includes all the basics of Windows Defender but adds a malware checker too), Windows Defender is turned off so that the other program is turned on.

If you'd rather have Windows Defender operating, you may need to uninstall the other antivirus or spyware software before you can activate Windows Defender. Yes, it's a hassle, but it's one of the prices we pay for secure systems that don't crash every few minutes.

Turning on Your Windows Firewall

A firewall checks all the information coming to your computer from the Internet or from a network you may be connected to, to see whether the sender is a trusted contact and the information can be considered safe for your computer. If any suspicious information is found, your Windows Firewall alerts you so that you can allow or block the sender based on whether or not you think it should be allowed through the firewall.

Activating the Firewall

Chances are that Windows Firewall is already turned on by default on your computer. You can, however, check the settings and turn on the utility if necessary.

1. On the Windows 8 Start screen, type *firewall*.
2. Tap or click Settings.
3. Tap or click Windows Firewall.
4. Check the Windows Firewall state to make sure your firewall is on.
5. Review the settings in the Private Networks area.
6. Click the Guest or Public Networks arrow to see settings saved for networks in public places such as coffee shops or libraries.

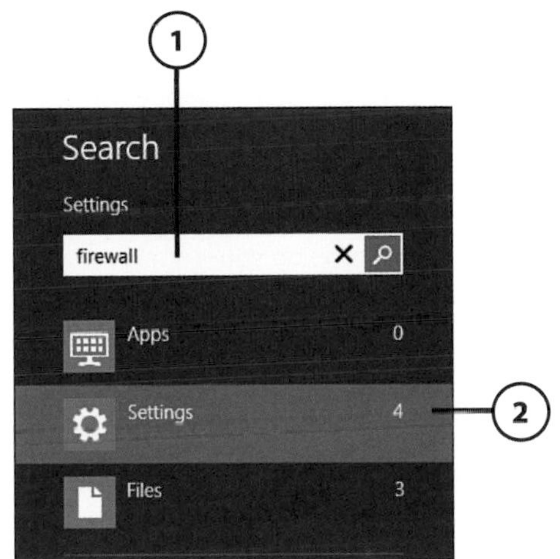

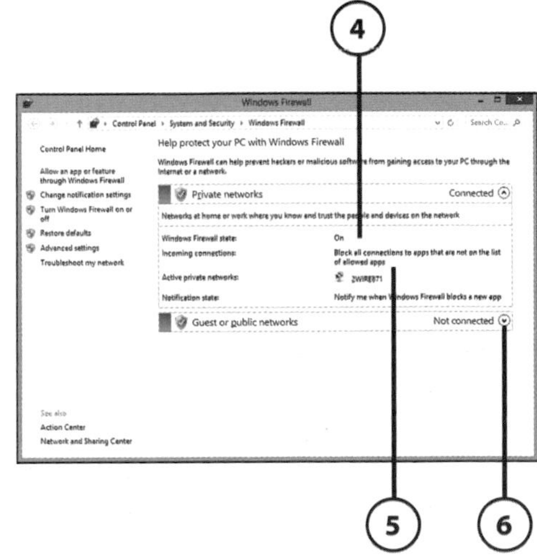

Changing Firewall Settings

When Windows Firewall is active, you are prompted each time a program tries to make changes on your computer if the sender is not on your trusted contacts list. You can change the settings for Windows Firewall so that you receive different alerts.

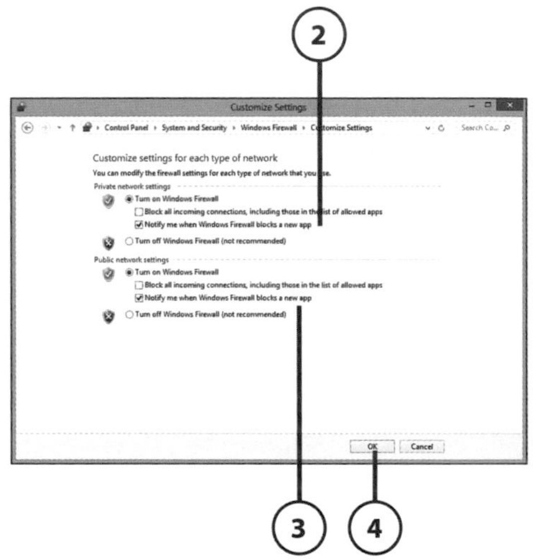

1. In the left side of the Windows Firewall dialog box, click Change Notification Settings (not pictured).
2. In the Private network area, you can choose whether you want to block incoming connections or be notified when Windows Firewall blocks an app. You can also choose to turn off Windows Firewall for your private network, but that's not recommended.
3. In the Public network settings, you can make the same choices—block everything or get notified about the programs Windows Firewall blocks—for your public network.
4. Click OK to save your changes.

Working with User Accounts

If you share your Windows 8 PC with others in your household, it's a good idea to create separate user accounts for each person who uses your computer. This helps you keep your files and programs straight, sets the permissions and color schemes you want, uses your own passwords, and limits the access others have to your personal information.

You can set user accounts with different privileges (for example, you might want to set up different accounts for your children and use parental controls to make sure they are online only during the hours it's okay with you). You can easily change and customize any user accounts you create at any time.

Add a User

Individual users can have their own user account so that specific preferences, histories, favorites, and more can be kept with that account. To add a new user, start with the PC Settings screen. Display it by choosing the Settings charm and tapping or clicking Change PC Settings.

1. Tap or click Users in the PC Settings screen.
2. In the Other Users area on the right side of the screen, tap or click the + to the left of Add a User.
3. The Add a User window appears. Enter the person's email address.
4. Click Next.

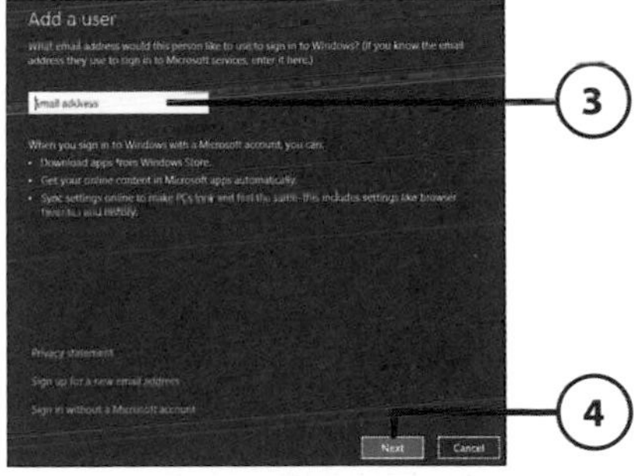

5. If the account you're creating is for a child, click the checkbox beneath the new user's profile picture placeholder to turn on Family Safety settings.
6. Click Finish. Windows 8 tells you to make sure the person knows they need to be connected to the Internet the first time they log in.

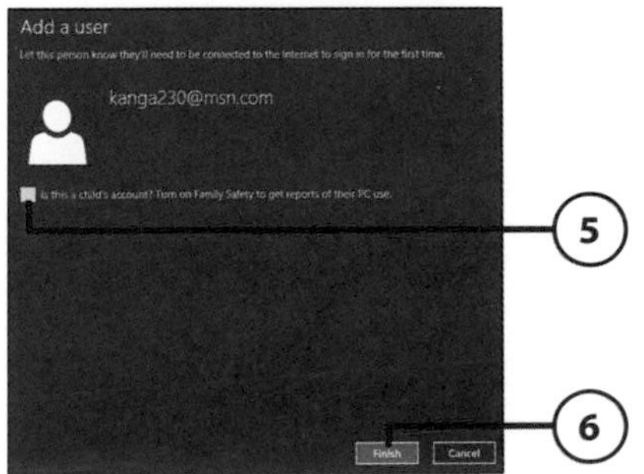

>>>Go Further

AN ACCOUNT BY ANY OTHER NAME

When you add a new user, you'll have the choice to sign the person up using his or her Microsoft Account or sign up without a Microsoft account. The difference here is that when a person signs in using a Microsoft account, all system preferences—including things like notification settings, color schemes, and more—are available on all the Windows 8 computers that person uses when they log in with their account. Using a Microsoft account also enables users to download apps from the Windows Store and save content to the cloud using SkyDrive. If the new user doesn't sign in with a Microsoft account, settings and preferences are stored only on the local machine.

Changing User Account Settings

You may want to change some of the settings for your account or the user account you've created for others. You can easily change the account name and picture, set other account controls, or even delete accounts.

1. On the Start screen, type *user account*.
2. Tap or click Settings. The Settings screen appears on the left side of the screen, showing the results of your search.
3. Tap or click User Accounts.

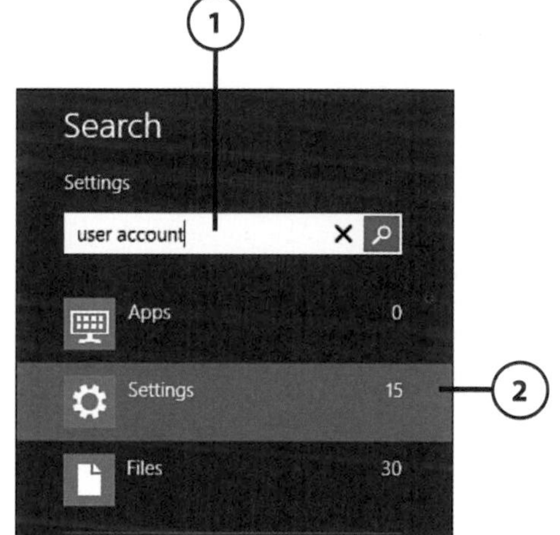

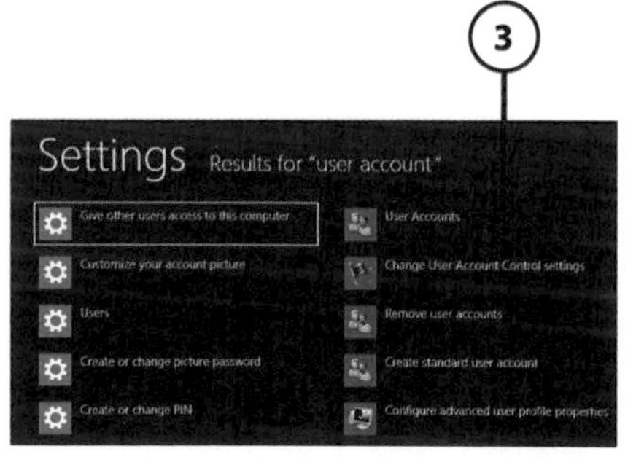

4. In the User Accounts dialog box, click or tap Change User Account Control Settings if you want to change when Windows 8 notifies you if programs are trying to make changes to your computer.
5. Tap or click Change Your Account Type if you want to change your account from Standard to Administrator or from Administrator to Standard.
6. To change the settings for another user account, click Manage Another Account.
7. In the Manage Accounts dialog box, click the user account you want to change.
8. The Change an Account dialog box appears, listing options for the ways you can modify the selected account. You can add parental controls to the user account, change the account type (from Standard to Administrator or vice versa), or delete the account.

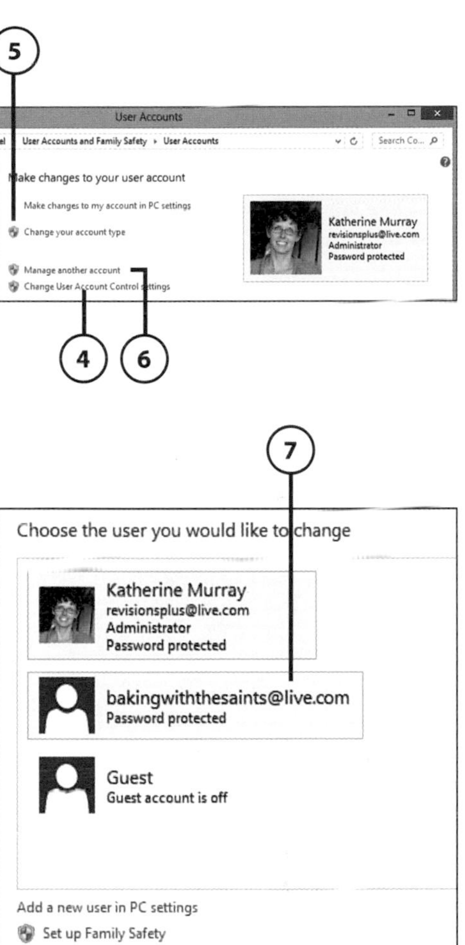

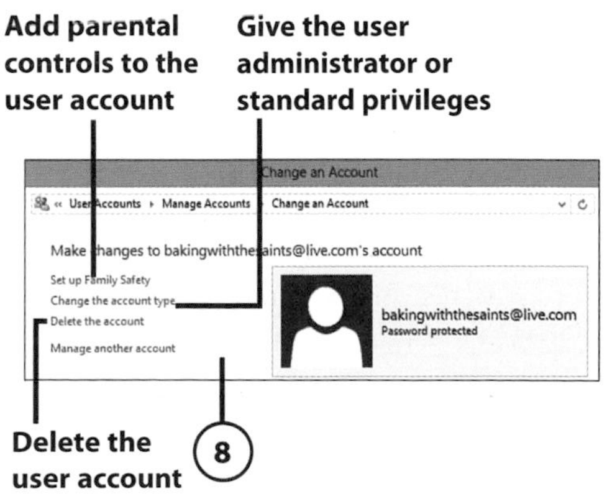

>>>Go Further

WHO'S IN CHARGE HERE?

When you change the account type of a user's account from Standard to Administrator, you are giving that user permission to change settings on the computer, to create and delete user accounts, and to have access to all files and programs. If you want to limit the permissions another user has on your computer, assign the Standard account type, which allows the user to access programs and files but limits the person's ability to make changes that could affect the computing experience of other users.

Switching Users

You can easily switch among the user accounts on your Windows 8 computer by clicking or tapping your profile in the upper-right corner of the Windows 8 Start screen. You can sign out of Windows 8, lock your computer, or change users.

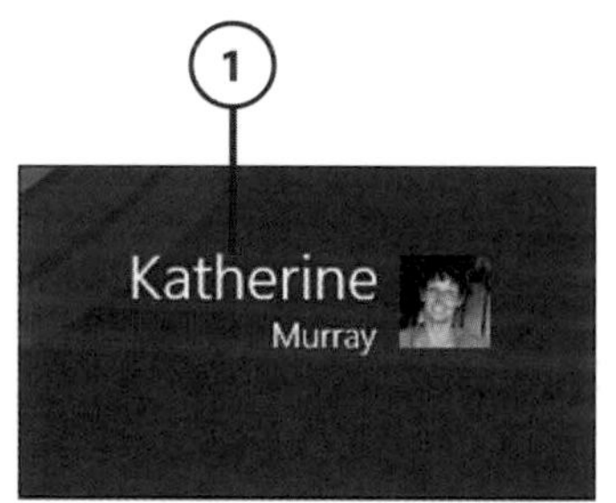

1. On the Start screen, click or tap the profile area (either your user name or picture) in the upper-right corner of the screen. A menu opens.
2. Tap or click Lock to display your Lock screen and safeguard your computer. You might choose this when leaving your computer unattended for a while.
3. Tap or click Sign Out when you want to sign out of Windows 8, perhaps so that another user can log in.

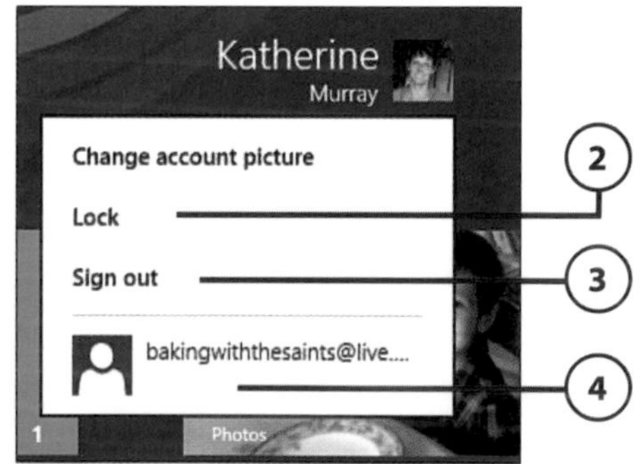

4. Tap or click another user account to display the login screen for that account. The other user can enter the account password and click Submit to log in.

On Logging Out

If you log out of Windows 8, the next time you remove the Lock screen by swiping the touch-screen or pressing any key, all user accounts on your computer appear on the next screen so that you can tap or click the one you want to use to log in. You can then enter the password that goes along with that account to display the Windows 8 desktop.

Maintaining Your Privacy

One of the hallmarks of Windows 8 is the seamless way everything seems to work together. You can easily share photos and files among apps, working with them online or off. Your apps can use your location data to set your time zone, display the weather, offer location-related search results, and much more.

On the flip side of all this sharing is an important question. How do these apps share this information and how much data do you really want to turn loose out there in cyberspace? Windows 8 lets you determine whether you want your apps to communicate with each other and share information about you—such as your location or content URLs from the apps you use—with others who are interested in gathering it.

Setting Location Privacy

To change your location privacy settings, follow these steps:

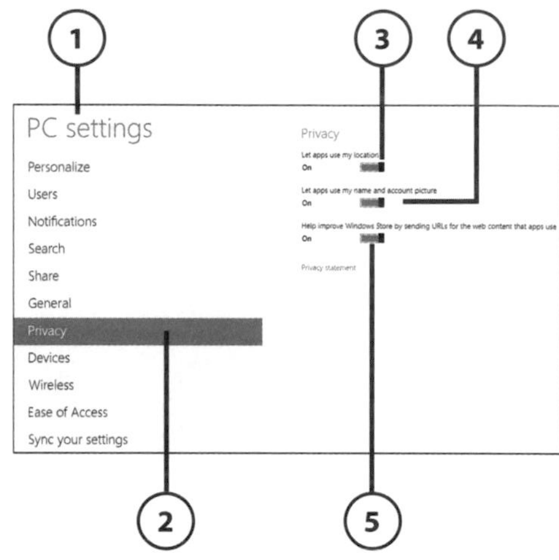

1. Display the PC Settings screen. (Tap or click the Settings charm and choose Change PC Settings.)
2. Tap or click Privacy in the list on the left side of the PC Settings window.
3. If you want to disable the location sharing that goes on among your apps, slide the top slider to the left, to the Off position.
4. To keep your name and account picture private, slide the second setting to the Off position.
5. To stop sending content URLs to the Windows Store, drag the bottom slider to the Off position.

>>>Go Further

WHAT'S IN A PRIVACY STATEMENT?

When you click the Privacy Statement link on the Privacy screen, you are taken online to the Windows page where the statement is posted. This statement explains what personal information is gathered, what your choices are about it, and how the information is used.

You can launch apps and set app options easily

Get more apps from the Windows Store

This chapter shows you how to find, launch, and work with apps in Windows 8 by showcasing these tasks:

- → Getting started with apps
- → Finding and starting apps
- → Working with apps
- → Closing apps
- → Getting new apps from the Windows Store
- → Starting and stopping a program from the desktop
- → Repairing and uninstalling programs

Exploring Windows 8 Apps

I bet I can guess the first thing you did after powering up your computer and glancing at the beautiful Windows 8 Start screen: You tapped or clicked one of the colorful tiles, just to see what it would do, right? Who can resist the app tiles on the Start screen?

Instead of a long, somewhat boring list of programs you can click or tap (like you had in the All Programs list in Windows 7), the Windows 8 Start screen displays a living panel of app choices. They're all yours for the playing. You simply need to click or tap the app you want to start, and you have plenty to choose from: Mail, Calendar, Music, Messaging, Video, Photos, People, Internet Explorer, Store, SkyDrive, Weather, Games, and more. And then of course you can download a gazillion apps you like from the Windows Store, too.

This chapter shows you all about life with apps—launching, working with, finding, downloading, and installing them. The Windows 8 experience is much different from what most people were accustomed to in Windows 7 or earlier Windows incarnations. This chapter shows you how to start programs on the Windows desktop and how to repair programs that are acting funky. For a more detailed look at the Windows desktop, check out Chapter 4, "Working with the Windows 8 Desktop."

Getting Started with Apps

Chapter 5, "Personalizing Windows 8," showed you how to change the color scheme and move app tiles around on the Start screen. Maybe you created a few app groups, too, so that you could organize your apps the way that makes the most sense to you. Windows 8 comes with a number of apps ready to use. You'll find what you need to check and send email, set appointments on your calendar, connect with others through instant messaging, catch up on the latest in your favorite social media accounts, and open Internet Explorer for some mindless browsing. These apps give you a good start on the types of tasks you'll want to accomplish in Windows 8, but this is only the beginning. You can download hundreds of apps from the Windows Store, and developers are posting new apps there all the time.

Some of the app tiles you see are *live tiles*, which continually update, showing information like the number of email messages you have to read, the current temperature in your city, the upcoming appointments on your calendar, or the headlines of your favorite news site. You learned how to change the way live tiles update—and turn off notifications entirely if you like—in Chapter 5.

What's All This "App" Business?

You may be wondering—especially if you're a bit old school—why nobody seems to be using the word "program" anymore when that's obviously what we're talking about. The word "app" (if it really can be called a word) is a shortened form of *application* or *application program*. Often in the mobile phone world, the word "app" is used to refer to a small program you can run on your phone. Following that kind of functional, easy-to-add-and-use idea, the tiles you have on your Windows 8 Start screen are referred to as apps. Instead of large, sweeping, and involved programs (like the Office suite, for example), they give you a specific set of tools to do one thing: Mail, Calendar, Photos.

Checking Out Your Apps

The easiest way to learn about the apps on your Windows 8 Start screen is to log in and swipe or scroll the screen.

1. Touch the screen and swipe to the left, or click and drag on the horizontal scroll bar to display additional apps.

2. Swipe up from the bottom of the screen or right-click along the bottom of the screen. The apps bar appears.
3. Tap or click All Apps.

4. Swipe or scroll to the left to display the full list of apps installed on your computer.

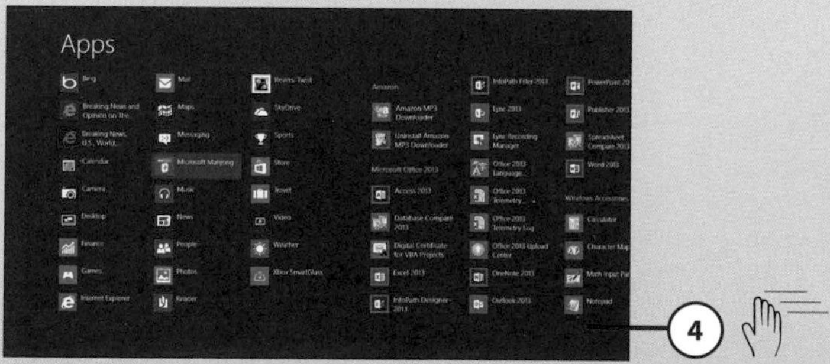

Pinning Apps to the Start Menu

As you look through all the apps on the Apps screen, you may discover a few that you'd like to add to your Start menu. You can add new apps easily—and unpin apps you no longer need—by following these steps:

1. Begin by displaying All Apps on your Windows 8 screen.
2. Swipe down on the app you want to select. Or, if you're using the mouse, right-click the app. The app options appear along the bottom of the screen.
3. Tap or click Pin to Start. The app you selected is added to the far-right end of the apps on your Start screen.

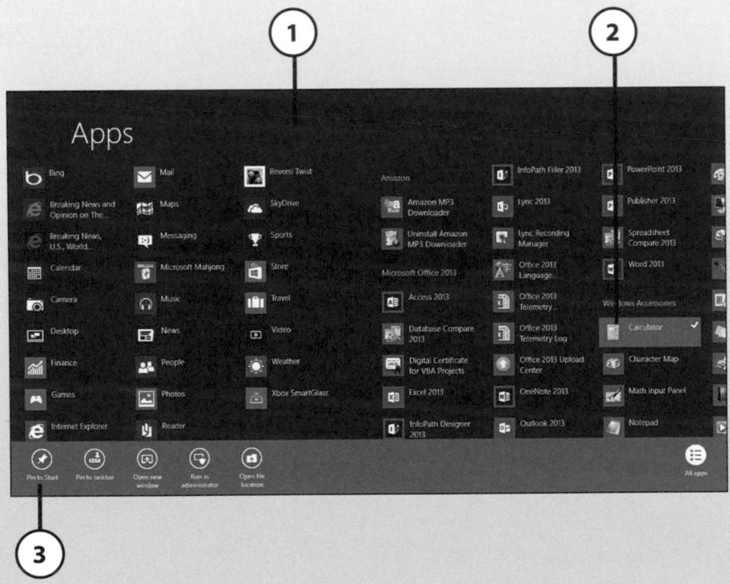

Moving Apps Around

You can easily move an app to any point on your Start screen by tapping and holding, or clicking, and dragging it to a new location. The other apps in the destination area move to make room for the new app. You can also arrange apps in groups and even name the groups so that you can easily find the apps you're looking for. For more information on moving and grouping app tiles, see Chapter 5.

>>>Go Further

PIN TO TASKBAR?

You may be wondering why, if the new Windows 8 interface is all about app tiles and easy movement, you have an option to pin the selected app to the taskbar. The taskbar is still part of your Windows desktop, which you'll display by tapping or clicking the desktop tile on your Start screen.

The taskbar on your desktop is in the same place it's always been—along the bottom of the display. The app you pin to the taskbar appears in the Quick Launch area, toward the left end of the taskbar along the bottom of the screen. To learn more about using the desktop, see Chapter 4.

Finding and Starting Apps

Windows 8 is supposed to be easy, and one of the features toward that end is instant search, available from the Start screen. When you want to find a specific item—whether that's an app, a setting, or a file—you can simply type the word or phrase you're looking for. Windows 8 is "listening" to your keystrokes behind-the-scenes and instantly displays a search results screen where you can further refine your search and launch right into the app or file you want.

Once you find the app you want, of course, starting it is as simple as tapping or clicking the appropriate tile.

Locating an App

If the app you're looking for is already on your system, Windows 8 will find it. You can simply type a few characters of the app's name and you'll be ready to go.

1. With the Start screen displayed, type the first few characters of the name of the app you're looking for. The search results screen appears immediately. If you're using a touch device, swipe in from the right to display the Charms bar and then tap in the search box. Your touch keyboard will appear, and you can type the first characters of the app's name.
2. You can choose whether the result you're looking for is an app, a setting, or a file.

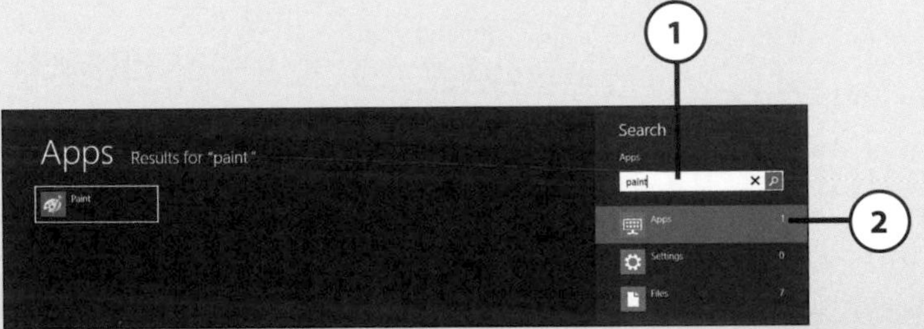

3. To search within the apps in the Apps list on the right side of the screen, tap the app you want to search.
4. Tap or click the app you want when it appears in the results list.

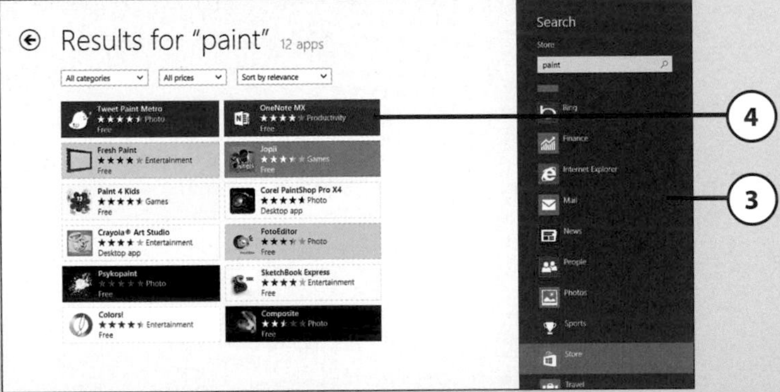

Downloading and Installing Too

You'll learn more about what to do with the apps once you've found them, if they aren't already installed on your Windows 8 computer or device, later in this chapter.

Launching an App from the Start Screen

The easiest way to start a program on your Windows 8 computer is to simply scroll to the app you want on the Start screen and tap or click the app's tile.

1. Swipe or scroll through the apps on the Windows 8 Start screen.
2. Tap or click the tile of the app you want to start.

Launching an App on the Desktop

Some apps you add to Windows 8 will launch from screen, but they will open on your desktop. This may often be the case if you're installing a legacy program—meaning a program that was available before the advent of Windows 8—and it requests permission to install a shortcut on your desktop. You can also add your favorite apps to the Windows desktop taskbar and create shortcuts for the desktop itself. (For more about making apps available on the desktop, see Chapter 4.)

1. From the Windows 8 Start screen, display your Windows desktop by scrolling to the Desktop tile and tapping or clicking it.

2. Locate the icon of the program you want to start and double-tap or double-click it. The app launches and appears on your screen.

Adding Programs at Startup

If you have certain programs you want to launch as soon as your computer starts, you can add them to your Windows Startup folder. Even though the Windows 8 Start screen is a different animal from the Windows 8 desktop, you can still add apps you use regularly to your Startup folder using File Explorer. You may need to experiment a bit to see which apps work and which don't. Dropbox, for example, loaded fine during startup, but Windows Paint (my old friend) gave me an error. To add an app to your Startup folder, use File Explorer (available on your Windows desktop) to locate the program file. Then copy and paste it in your Startup folder. The next time you log in to Windows 8 and display the desktop, your program will open automatically.

Working with Apps

One of the things I think is funny about Windows 8 is that there really aren't many *windows* around anymore. When you launch an app, it zooms to take up your full screen (even though you can tile the display to show more than one app, as you'll learn in this section).

Similarly, when you start Internet Explorer 10 from the Start screen, it now runs in what developers are calling a *modeless* window, which means you don't have any of the familiar window borders around the edge of the screen. When you launch IE10 from the Windows desktop, you get something that resembles a familiar browser window. Still, times, they are a-changing!

Switching Among Open Programs

Similar to the way you moved from one program to another in Windows 7, you can still cycle through open apps by pressing Alt+Tab in Windows 8. A small message box appears in the center of the desktop area showing you all your current open programs. Each time you press Tab while holding Alt, Windows 8 moves to the next open program available on your computer.

Exploring a Program "Window"

Depending on the type of app you open, it may appear in the Windows 8 style or in the more traditional desktop style. If the app you launch hasn't yet been designed for Windows 8, you will see a more traditional window with a title bar, scroll bars, and the like. If the app has been designed for Windows 8, the app will open in a windowless frame and fill your screen.

- **Title bar.** The title bar of the window shows you the name of the file you're working on and the name of the application program in which it was created.
- **Window controls.** In the upper-right corner of the program window, you can find three tools to change the state of the window. Minimize reduces the window to the taskbar; Restore Down reduces the window to its previous smaller size (or, if the window is already at a smaller size, it changes to Maximize, which makes the window full size); and Close, which closes the file and, if no other files are open for that program, closes the program as well.

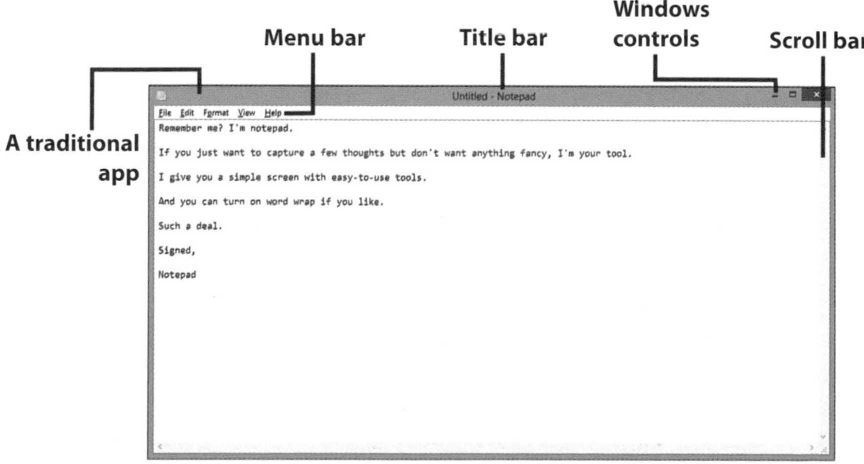

- **Ribbon or menu bar.** The Ribbon is a feature common to some legacy programs, offering the tools and options you need for working with various programs. You may instead see a menu bar listing menu names close to the top of the window. You can click a menu name to display a list of tools you can use in your program.
- **Scrollbars.** Depending on the size of your file and the type of program you are using, you may see horizontal and vertical scrollbars.
- **Work area.** The work area of the window is the place where you write documents, create worksheets, edit photos, and more. The file you open and work with appears in the work area.

Checking Out a Windows 8 App

Windows 8 apps are designed to look and act much different from a traditional app. When you tap or click a tile to launch an app that's been designed for Windows 8, the app will launch full-screen and you will navigate the program without the menu bars, Windows controls, and tools you may be accustomed to in legacy programs.

Hopefully, even though the experience is much different from traditional programs, you will find it to be intuitive and easy-to-understand. If you've been using a touch device—such as a smartphone or tablet—the gestures you use to interact with the operating system may already be second nature to you.

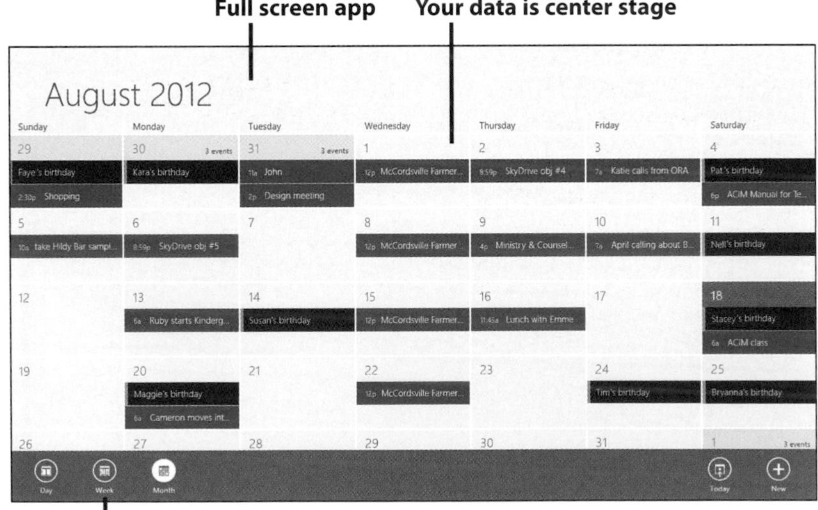

- **Full screen.** As soon as you tap an app tile to launch the program, it opens full-screen on your display.
- **Your data, center-stage.** The content of the app is really the main focus. You can tap a timeslot or appointment (in this Calendar app) to display a screen on which you can make calendar changes.
- **App options within reach.** You can easily swipe up from the bottom of the app to display the options available to you as you work with your information.

Displaying the Apps Panel

The apps panel is a new feature for navigating among apps you have open in Windows 8. Now you can "bump" your mouse against the top-left corner of the screen to display a small thumbnail of an open app. When you move the mouse downward, additional app thumbnails appear in the panel. You can then click the app you want to move to.

1. Move the mouse to the upper-left corner of the screen and "bump" the mouse against the edge. The top thumbnail appears.
2. Move the mouse downward along the left edge. Additional thumbnails appear.
3. Click the thumbnail of the app you want to display.

Moving Among Apps

The easiest way to move among different open apps is to pull them in from the left side of the screen. This kind of "app cycling" enables you to page through the different apps in order.

1. Press and drag at the left edge of the screen (either with your finger or the mouse button).
2. Drag in from the left toward the center of the screen. The next open app appears on top of the previous app.

You can continue cycling through the open apps in this way until you find the app you want.

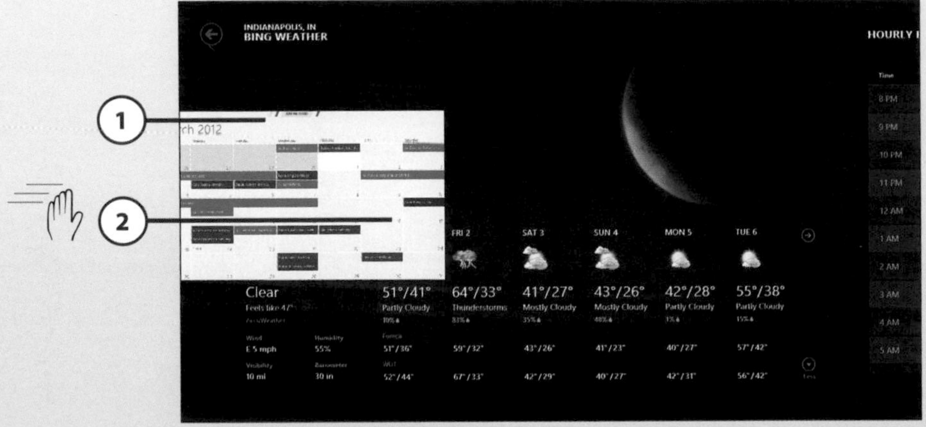

Tiling Apps

You can also tile up to two apps so that you can work with more than one on the screen at any one time. You might want to keep your Twitter app open, for example, while you're working on a report. Or perhaps you want to watch a movie while you play a game. Whatever apps you want to run in tandem, you'll tile them and place them side by side to do it. You can also still cycle through other apps, even while two are tiled. Pretty slick.

1. Open the apps you want to use.
2. To anchor an app, drag it in from the left to the right side of the screen, and flick it toward the top of your screen.

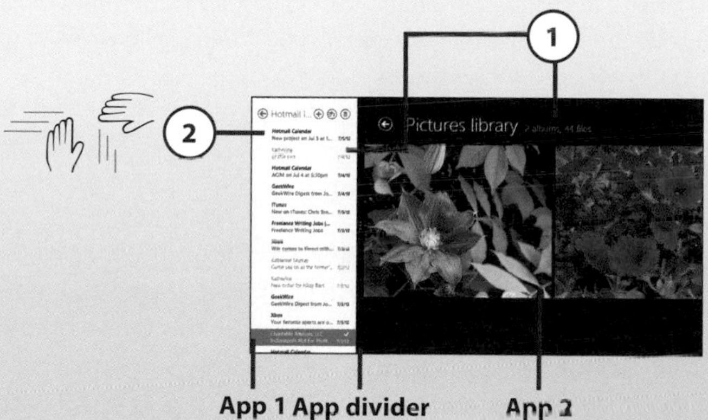

Get Me Back to Full-Screen

When you want to do away with the tiling effect, tap or click the divider and drag it to the right, off the right edge of the screen. The app that was in the left window then becomes the only app visible on your screen.

It's Not All Good

What Happened to Zune and Windows Live?

In an effort to simplify branding around a few key players—namely, Microsoft Hotmail, Microsoft SkyDrive, Windows 8, and Xbox Live for Windows—the Windows Live and Zune branding are disappearing from Windows 8 apps. Instead of seeing the name "Windows Live Calendar," you'll simply see Calendar, and so on.

The plug is being pulled on Zune, both as a brand and as a service. The actual Zune device got tossed out the window in the fall of 2011, but Windows Phone continued to update to the Zune service, and Zune software provided entertainment and media tools for subscribers. Now with Windows 8, Xbox Live for Windows is taking over the entertainment reins, with rumors that Microsoft will introduce a Spotify-like service later in 2012. That service might even be available by the time you read this.

Changing App Behavior

Windows 8 gives you the option of changing the way apps appear when you swipe in from the left edge. By default, the app you swipe in from the left will be the one you use most recently. But you can change that setting so that Windows 8 displays apps in the order you opened them. To change the default setting, display PC Settings, tap or click General, and turn off the App Switching setting named When I Swipe in from the Left Edge, Switch Directly to My Most Recent App.

Closing Apps

One of the surprising things about the earliest versions of Windows 8 was that you didn't need to close any app you had opened. Apps that aren't the current focus immediately go into suspended mode; this is one of the ways Windows 8 saves power. But not having a way to close programs just seemed odd to those of us who have been trained over the years to finish what we start, put away our toys, and exit correctly from any program we are using.

In response to the massive public confusion (okay, that may be a little bit of an exaggeration), Windows 8 developers added a close procedure to Windows 8. Now you can swipe down to put an app away, effectively removing it from memory—which, of course, it already did itself when it went into suspended mode. But now we can feel better about it.

Closing Selected Apps

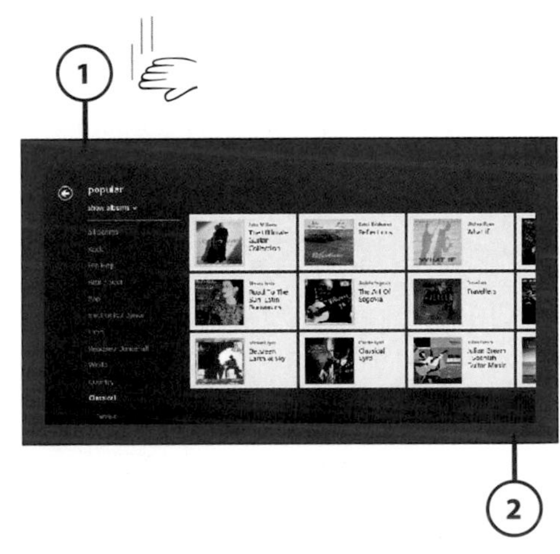

When you're ready to put away an app you've been working with, closing it is a simple matter. First, save any file you were working with and then follow these steps:

1. Touch at the top of the screen and swipe down or, if you're using a mouse, position the mouse pointer at the top of the screen, and press and hold the mouse while dragging down toward the bottom edge of the screen.
2. The app reduces to a small window, and as you swipe it downward, it disappears completely.

There you go. Closed.

Using the Task Manager

You can also close open apps by using the Task Manager. The Task Manager has been significantly revamped in Windows 8 to give you all kinds of information about how much processing power each app is using. Of course, for some of us, this type of information is overkill, so by default Windows 8 gives you the simple version of Task Manager to work with.

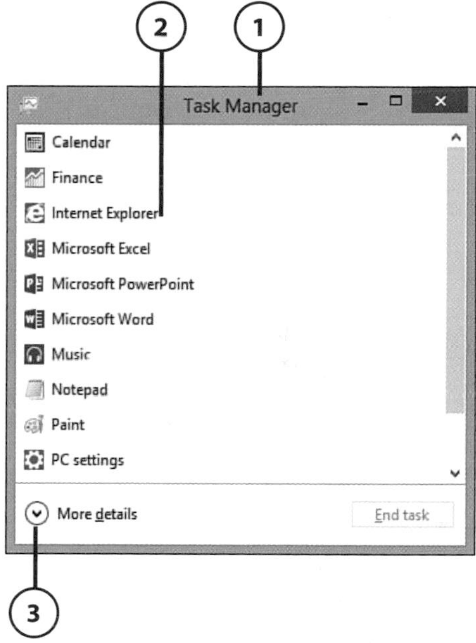

1. Press Ctrl+Alt+Delete and click Task Manager to display the Task Manager window. Or, if you're on a touch device, swipe in from the right to display the Charms bar and tap Search. Tap in the search box and your touch keyboard appears. Type *Task Manager* and the utility appears in the result list. Tap Task Manager to open it.
2. To close a specific app, tap or click the one you want to close.
3. If you want to see how much processing power each app is using, tap or click More Details.
4. Review the amount of processing power, memory, disk space, and network access each app is currently using.
5. You can also view detailed information about each app by tapping or clicking the various tabs at the top of the detailed Task Manager display.
6. To return to the simple display, tap or click Fewer Details.
7. Tap or click End Task if you want to close the selected app.

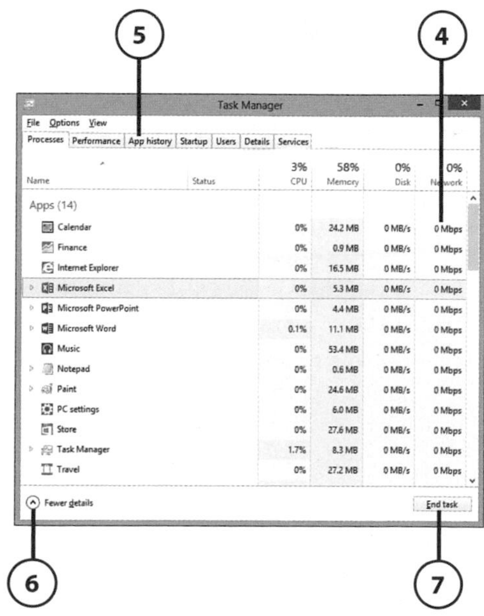

>>>Go Further

ASSESSING WHAT YOU WANT AT STARTUP

One great feature the detailed version of Task Manager offers is an evaluation of how much impact any apps you have loading automatically at startup are having on your computer's performance.

Display the Task Manager by pressing Ctrl+Alt+Delete or, on your tablet, by searching for Task Manager and tapping the utility when it appears. In the Task Manager, select More Details to see the full set of data available to you in relation to the current apps. Tap or click the Startup tab at the top of the Task Manager dialog box. In the Startup Impact column, on the far-right side of the dialog box, you see how Windows 8 rates the impact the various apps have on the startup routine. If you see an app that is rated as having a High impact, you can select it and then tap or click Disable to keep it from loading automatically. You may find that Windows 8 boots much faster after you've disabled high-impact apps.

Getting New Apps from the Windows Store

The Windows Store is a new exciting feature in Windows 8, and lots of people have been eager to get busy searching, buying, and downloading. Already the Windows Store boasts hundreds of apps in a wide range of categories. At this rate, it might rival iTunes or the Android Marketplace. It could just become your one-stop shop for all things related to Windows computers, devices, and cloud technologies.

Introducing the Windows Store

The Windows Store app tile appears in the easy-to-find location at the far-left end of your Windows 8 Start screen. The Store app tile has a live tile notification telling you the number of apps you currently have installed that now have updates available through the Windows Store.

1. Launch the Windows Store by tapping or clicking the Store app tile.
2. Scroll by swiping or using the mouse to look through apps in the following categories: Games, Social, Entertainment, Photo, Music & Video, Sports, Books & Reference, News & Weather, Health & Fitness, Food & Dining, Lifestyle, Shopping, Travel, Finance, Productivity, Tools, Security, Business, Education, and Government.
3. Tap a collection tile to see apps in a specific group of a category (for example, "Top Free" or "All Stars").
4. Tap the tile of the app you want to download.

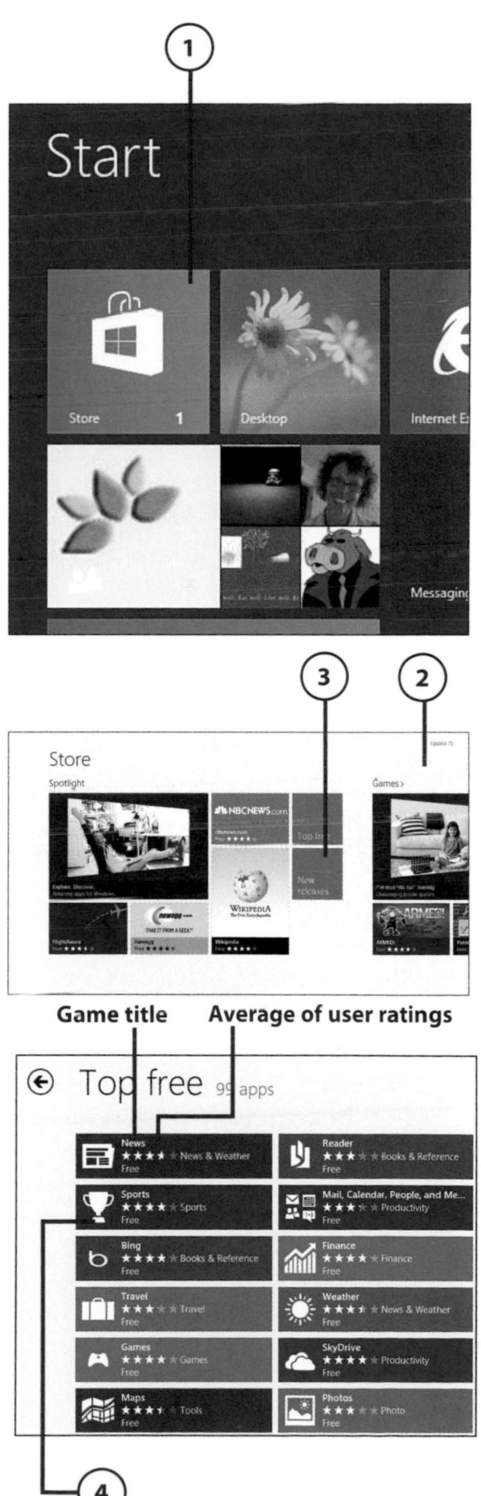

Searching for an App

You can also use the Windows 8 Search charm if you're not finding just what you were hoping for. Here are the steps:

1. Display the Windows Store.
2. Swipe in from the right to display the Windows 8 charms.
3. Tap or click Search at the top of the Charms bar.
4. Type a word or phrase that describes what you're looking for.
5. Click the Search tool. The results appear in the left side of the screen.
6. Click or tap the app you want to learn more about.

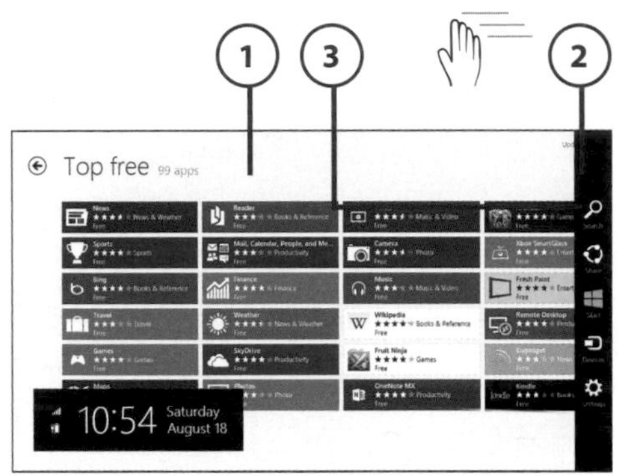

Installing an App

After you locate the app you want, you can click or tap the app tile and the app opens on the screen. You'll find out more about the app, see how users have rated it (and how many users have weighed in), and learn more about the app's specific features. The information page also shows you pictures of the app in action. If you decide this app is worth a closer look, you can install the app and the Windows Store will download and install it on your Windows 8 PC.

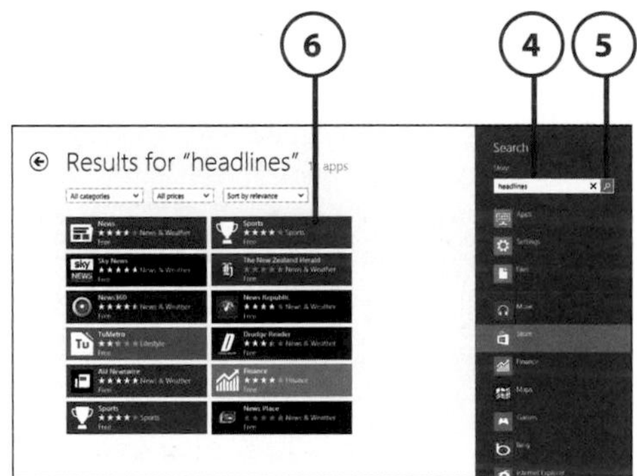

1. Scroll through the app information and determine whether you want to install the app.
2. Tap or click Install. Windows 8 displays a small "Installing" notification in the upper-right corner of your screen, and when the installation is complete, a notification lets you know.

   The new app appears on the far-right side of your Windows 8 Start screen. You can move the app to any group you like by tapping or clicking and dragging the app to that group. Then, just tap or click the app tile to launch your new app.

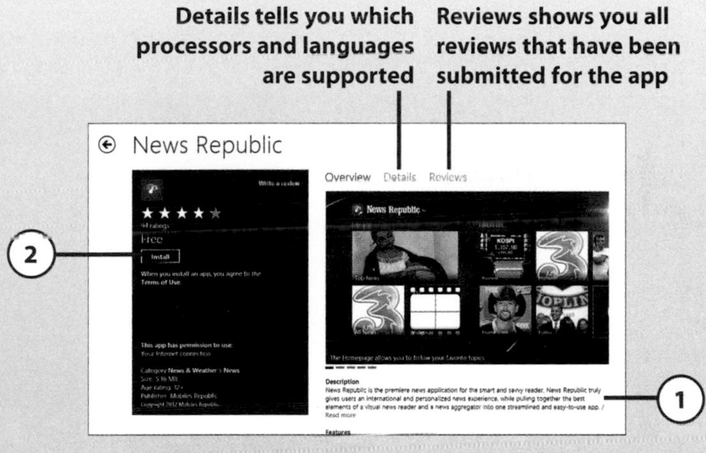
Details tells you which processors and languages are supported
Reviews shows you all reviews that have been submitted for the app
News Republic
Overview
Details
Reviews
Free
Install
2
1

Starting and Stopping a Program from the Desktop

Now that so many of your apps are available on the beautiful Windows 8 Start screen, you may be wondering what's left to work with on the Windows desktop. Actually many of the programs you run on your computer may open and work within windows on the more traditional-looking desktop. For example, when you open one of the Office 2010 apps, it launches from the Start screen, but it opens on the Windows desktop, and you have the traditional window border, complete with its tools, available for your use.

So, any computer program you used prior to Windows 8 will open and run on the Windows desktop. You can add shortcuts to the desktop if you want to launch the programs from there (you learn how to do that in Chapter 4). The easiest method may be to launch the program from the Start screen, work with it on your desktop, and close it on the desktop (or simply leave it and Windows 8 will suspend it for you).

Starting a Program from the Desktop

If you've added shortcuts to your Windows desktop or pinned an app to the taskbar so that you could launch it easily while you're working there, you have only one very simple step to take to launch the program.

1. Double-click, or double-tap, the program icon.
2. The program opens on the desktop, and you can work with it as you normally would.

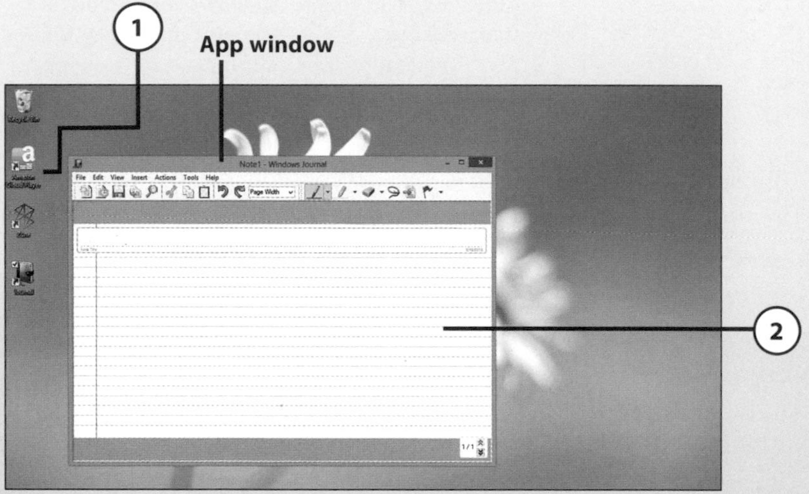

Be My BFF Program

If you want to add a favorite desktop program to the Windows 8 Start screen so that you can launch it easily from there without searching for it, try this: Right-click the program icon and tap or click Pin to Start. This adds the icon to the far-right side of the apps list on the Start screen (although you can drag the app tile anywhere you want it to appear). Now you'll be able to launch the program from the Start screen, but it will still open on the desktop.

Do More Before You Jump

As you learned in Chapter 4, jump lists give you an easy way to start a program and open a file at the same time, but you can perform other file actions as well. Right-click the file in the jump list to display a context menu that enables you to open, print, copy, or display the file properties. You can also pin the file to the list or remove it from the list altogether.

Exiting the Program

When you're ready to close the program you've been working with on the desktop, shutting it down is a simple matter. First, save any file you were working with and then follow these steps:

1. Click the File tab or, if the program is a non-Microsoft program, click the File menu. This is typically the menu farthest left on the menu bar.
2. Click Exit. Some programs may ask you to confirm that you do in fact want to close the program. If you see a prompt, click Yes to finish exiting the program.

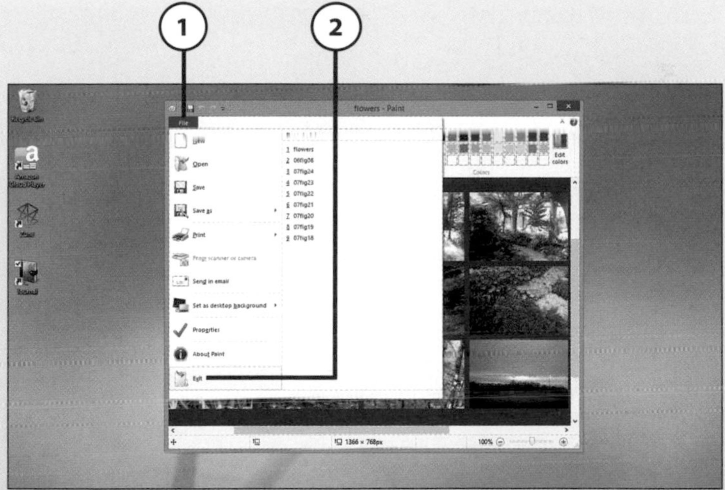

Quicker Closing

You can also exit a program by clicking the X button at the top-right corner of any open window.

Repairing and Uninstalling Programs

Windows 8 has a tool you can use—which is actually a holdover from Windows 7—that enables you to safely repair and uninstall programs. You can find what you need in the Programs category of the Control Panel.

Repairing Installations

If you have a program begins misbehaving by locking up when you open a certain template, taking forever to check for your email, or giving you errors when you try to choose a specific tool, Windows may be able to repair the installation for you. Not all programs offer Change or Repair options, but for the ones that do, you can use the tools in the Programs category of the Control Panel to correct any errors that are making your program behave inconsistently.

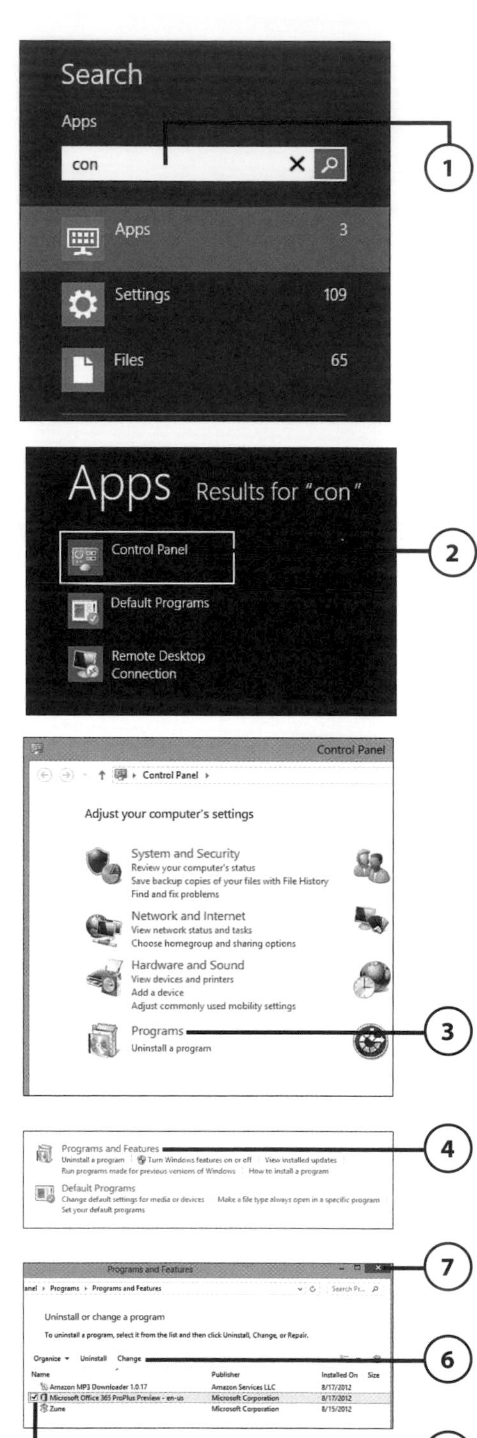

1. On the Start screen, type *con* and right away the Search tool appears and results are shown in the Apps side of the screen.
2. Tap or click Control Panel.
3. Tap or click Programs.
4. Tap or click Programs and Features.
5. In the program listing, click the name of the program you want to repair. The Repair option is available when you click Change in the toolbar.
6. Click Change. Windows launches the install utility to correct the problem. Choose the repair option you want Windows to use.
7. When the repair operation finishes, click the Close button to exit Control Panel.

>>>Go Further

AND DON'T FORGET TO REFRESH ONCE IN A WHILE

Windows 8 would suggest that you refresh your computer—using the new Refresh tool—if you begin having problems like slow processing speeds or quirky program behaviors. Refreshing your PC wipes away settings and configurations that could be causing problems, but it won't do anything to your programs or data: All is well. You can run Refresh by tapping the Settings charm, choosing Change PC Settings, and tapping or clicking General. Scroll down to the Refresh Your PC Without Affecting Your Files area and tap Get Started to begin the refresh process.

You learn more about this refreshing process in Chapter 2, "Preparing Your Windows 8 PC and Devices."

Uninstalling Programs

You can also remove programs you no longer need to free up space on your hard drive and allow room for other programs. When you know you don't need one of your programs anymore, you can uninstall it easily.

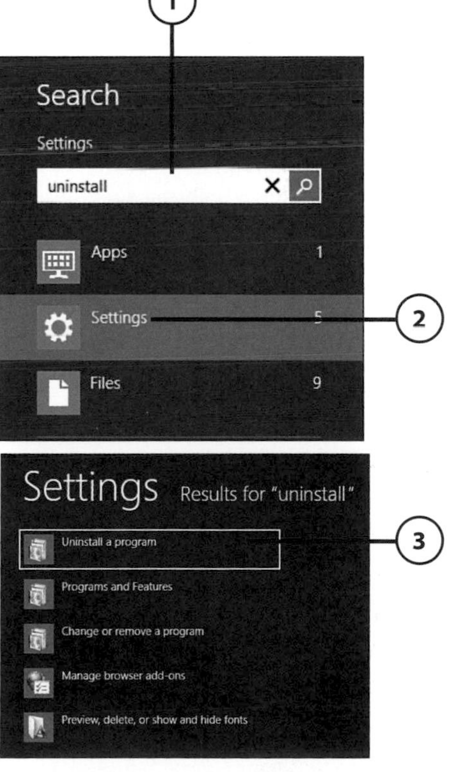

1. On the Start screen, type *uninstall*. The Search screen appears.
2. Tap Settings.
3. Tap Uninstall a Program. The Program and Features dialog box appears, listing the programs you have installed. Notice that your apps do not appear in this list. (You'll learn how to uninstall apps in the next section.)

4. Tap or click the name of the program you want to uninstall.
5. Tap or click Uninstall. Windows launches a wizard that will remove the program from your computer.

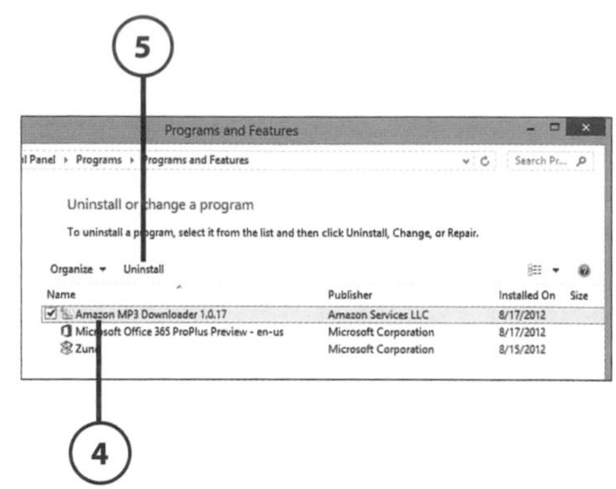

Uninstalling Apps

In Chapter 3, "Beginning with the Start Screen," you learned how to remove an app from the Windows 8 Start screen to free up room for other apps. The process for uninstalling an app you no longer want in Windows 8 is a similar process. Here's how to do it:

1. On the Start screen, choose the app you want to uninstall by swiping down on the app tile or right-clicking it.
2. The apps bar appears along the bottom of the Start screen. To uninstall the app, tap or click Uninstall.
3. Windows 8 lets you know what you're removing. Tap or click Uninstall to complete the process.

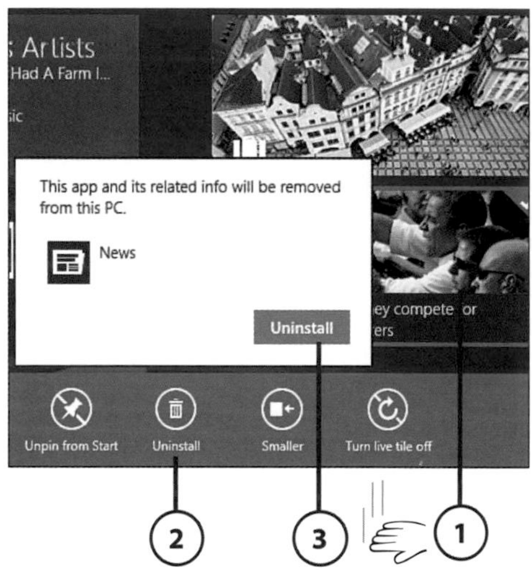

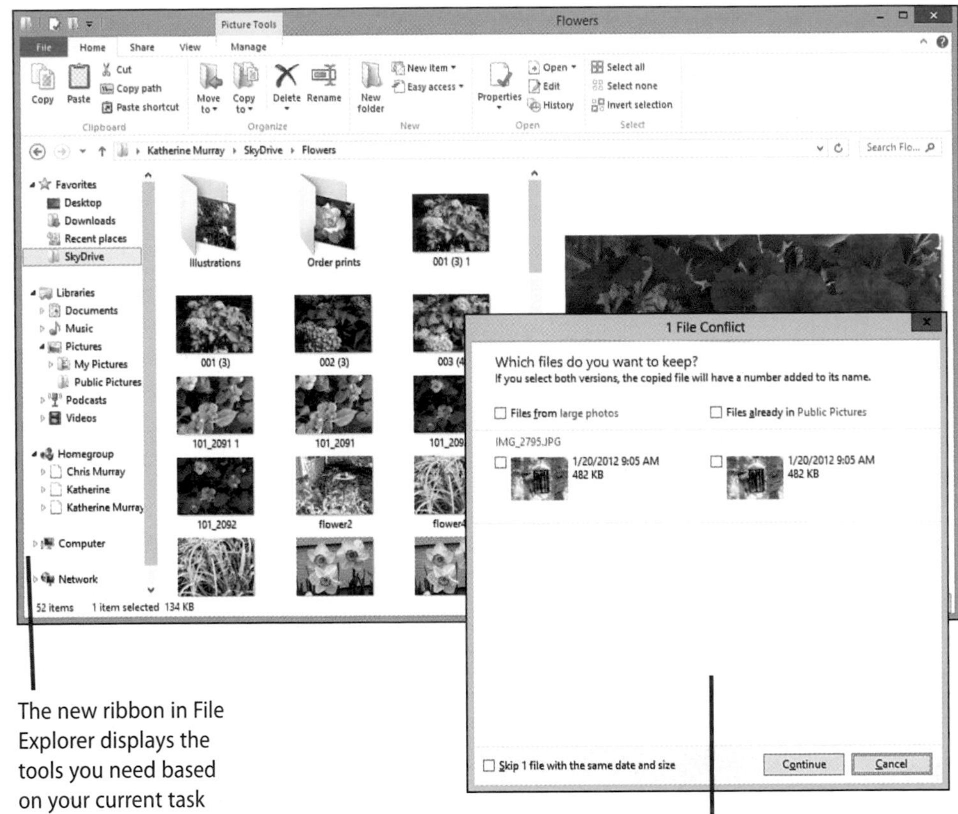

The new ribbon in File Explorer displays the tools you need based on your current task

File Explorer helps you resolve file conflicts during copy operations

This chapter shows you how to use File Explorer to work with libraries, folders, and files by exploring these tasks:

- Getting started with File Explorer
- Using the ribbon
- Working with Windows 8 libraries
- Managing your files and folders
- Copying, moving, and sharing files and folders

Managing Files with File Explorer

You'll use File Explorer to find, move, organize, and share files and folders on your computer and in the cloud. Even though you can get to File Explorer only through the Windows desktop (meaning it doesn't get its own tile on the Start screen by default), it is still an important part of Windows 8. Many of the features and much of the functionality of File Explorer is similar to what you'll find in Windows 7. You'll rely on File Explorer to help you organize, arrange, view, and work with the files and folders you create, Whenever you need to work with files—individually or as a group—you'll turn to File Explorer to select, move, copy, rename, and share files and folders. Windows 8 does bring some welcomed changes to File Explorer; now the tool has its own ribbon and includes a number of streamlined procedures.

In this chapter, you'll learn the basics of using this tool to keep your files and folders in order.

Getting Started with File Explorer

To display File Explorer, you'll need to start on your Windows 8 desktop, unless you've previously added the File Explorer tile to your Start screen (which isn't a bad idea if you use the tool a lot).

Add File Explorer to the Start Screen

Swipe up from the bottom of your touch screen or right-click toward the bottom of the screen to display the apps bar. Tap or click All Apps. Scroll to the far right end of the apps list, and swipe down on or right-click the File Explorer icon. In the apps bar, tap or click Pin to Start. Now File Explorer will appear as a tile on your Start screen and you can launch the tool without displaying your Windows 8 desktop. To find out more about how to pin an app to the Start screen, see Chapter 7, "Exploring Windows 8 Apps."

Starting File Explorer

The easiest way to launch File Explorer is to click or tap the Folder icon in the Quick Launch bar on the left side of the taskbar on the Windows 8 desktop. File Explorer opens in a window on your screen. The first time you start File Explorer, the ribbon is hidden. Display it by clicking Expand the Ribbon in the upper-right corner of File Explorer.

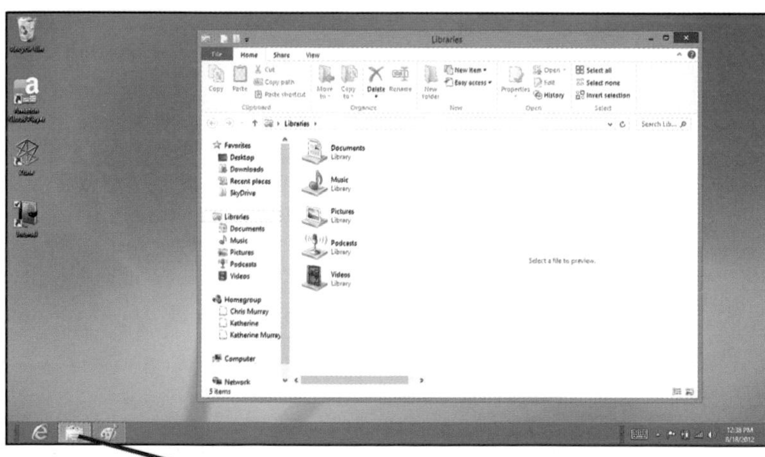

Click or tap the File Explorer icon

Exploring the Explorer Screen

Although the ribbon adds some aesthetic and functional value to File Explorer, much of what the program offers was available in Windows 7 as well. Here are the key elements on the File Explorer screen that you'll be working with:

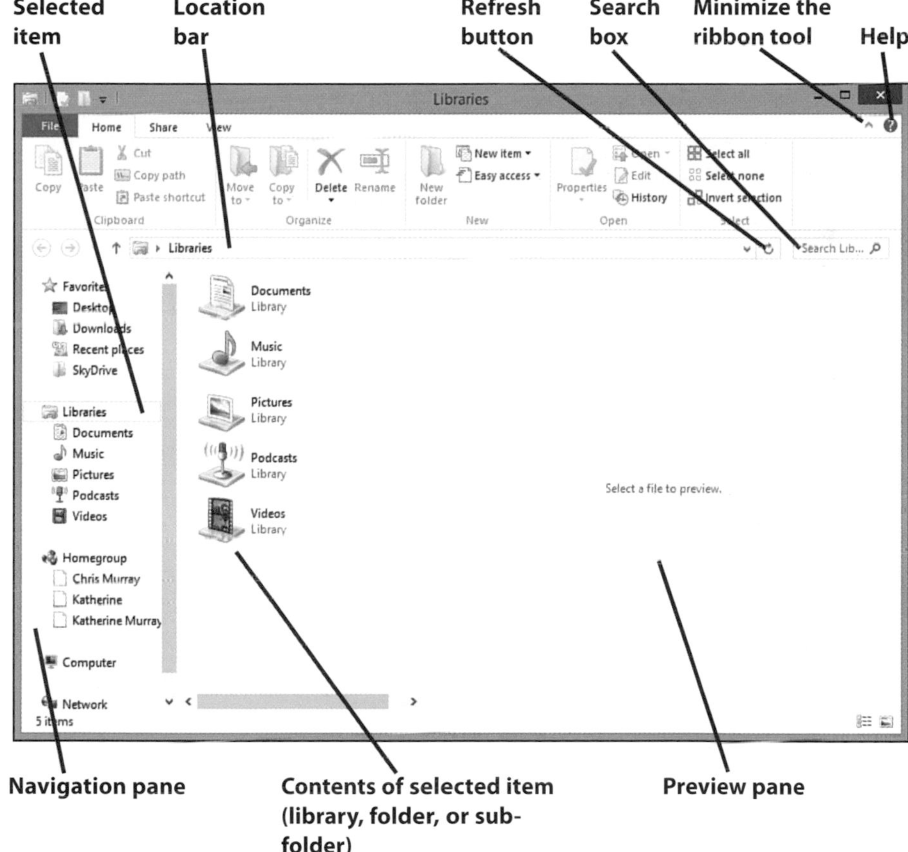

- **Location bar.** The Location bar shows the library, folder, and any sub-folders that contain the currently selected file.
- **Refresh button.** The Refresh button updates the display to show the files in the current folder.
- **Search box.** You can use the search box to find folders, files, and libraries in File Explorer.
- **Preview pane.** The Preview pane displays a preview of the contents of the file.

- **Navigation pane.** The Navigation pane displays your favorites, libraries, and folders and files on your computer.
- **Minimize the ribbon**. Use this tool to both hide and redisplay the File Explorer ribbon.
- **Get Help.** Click Get Help to display a pop-up window of help information related to the task you were performing in File Explorer.

Switching Between the Preview and Details Pane

You'll use the panel on the left side of File Explorer to get more information about a file you're working with. File Explorer includes two views—the Preview pane and the Details pane—that act as a toggle. When you click or tap the View tab and display the Preview pane, you see a preview of the contents of the file. When you tap or click Details pane, the Preview pane is replaced by a pane that shows you when the file was last modified, the size of the file, whether the file is shared, and other file details.

Navigating File Explorer

Several different tools help you find the files and folders you need in File Explorer. You use the Navigation pane, on the left side of the Explorer window, to tap or click the library, folder, or subfolder you want to view. (You can also copy and move folders by dragging them in the Navigation pane.) The Location bar, at the top of the window, makes it easy for you to enter a file location and move directly to a folder you want; or you can use the Back, Forward, or Up buttons on the left side of the Location bar to move to folders in close proximity to your current one.

1. In File Explorer, tap or click the arrow to the left of the library you want to view. Any subfolders in that library appear.
2. Select the folder with the files you want to view.
3. Tap or click the file you want. Information about the file appears in the pane on the right side of the Explorer window. The view that is displayed—the Preview pane or the Details pane—depends on which view you selected the last time you used File Explorer.

Changing the File Explorer Layout

You can hide and redisplay the different panes in File Explorer: Details pane, Preview page, and Navigation pane. Tap or click the View tab and in the Panes group on the left of the ribbon, select the pane you want to display. If you deselect both the Preview pane and the Details pane, the center pane will extend to show only the files and subfolders in the currently selected folder. You can also tap or click the Navigation pane arrow to display a menu of options for changing the way the Navigation pane displays folders and favorites. To redisplay a pane you've hidden, tap or click the pane to select the one you want to show.

Using the Ribbon

Slowly but surely, the ribbon, which made its debut in Office, is moving into everything we do. Now File Explorer has a ribbon across the top of the Explorer window, and whether you're using a mouse-based system or a touch-capable device, you'll be able to click and tap your way to easy file management. There are four basic tabs (File, Home, Share, and View) as well as contextual tabs (such as the Library, Picture, Manage, and Shortcut Tools tabs), which offer you tools and options related to the specific task you're performing or the item you've selected.

Learning the Ribbon Layout

The tabs in File Explorer group all the tools you need for working with your files and folders:

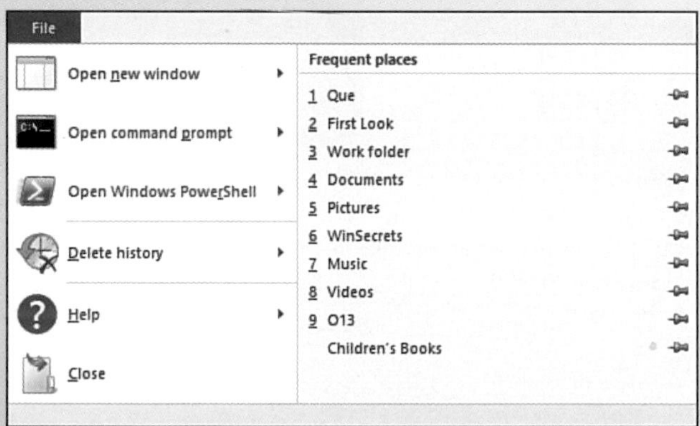

The File tab gives you access to the folders you use frequently. You can also work with the command prompt, delete the file history, display help, and close File Explorer.

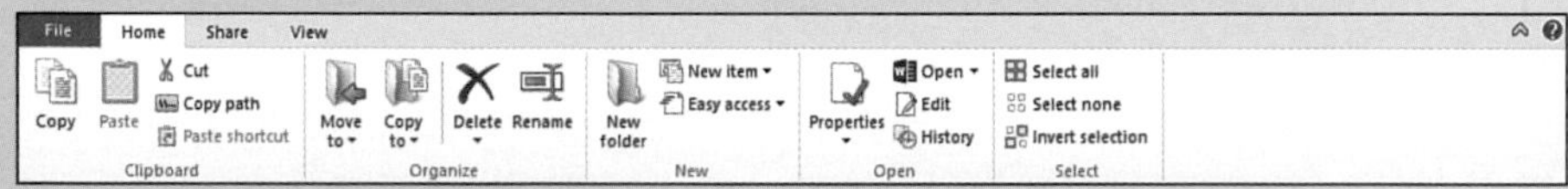

The Home tab provides common tools you'll use for copying and pasting files and paths; moving, deleting, and renaming files and folders; adding folders; opening files and folders; displaying file and folder properties; and selecting files and folders.

The Share tab contains tools for sharing the content you've selected, whether you want to email the files or folders, compress them into a ZIP file, share them with your HomeGroup, or fine-tune the security settings assigned to the file or folder.

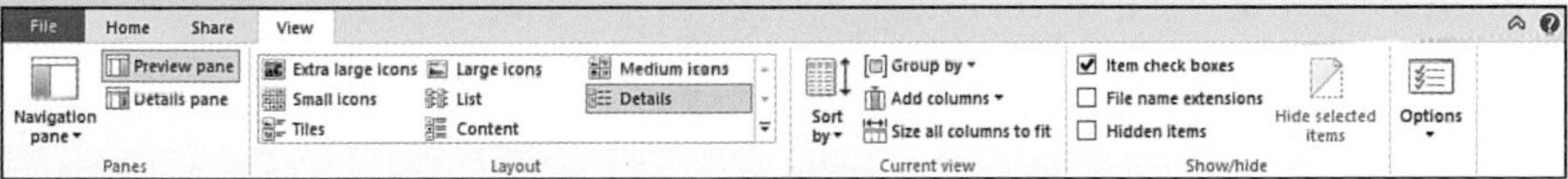

The View tab includes tools you can use to change the way the File Explorer window appears. You can use the tools in the View tab to set File Explorer up the way you want it, displaying the Navigation pane, either the Preview or Details pane, the size of the icons you want to use, and the data that will be either hidden or displayed. You can also add columns, sort files, and choose from a number of different layouts in the File Explorer screen.

Recognizing Contextual Tabs

You'll know when you're looking at a contextual tab on the File Explorer ribbon because it looks different from the regular tabs. The regular tabs are white and gray—the selected tab appears white, and the other tabs appear gray. But when you've selected a file, folder, or other object in File Explorer, a contextual tab related to the item you selected appears in a light orange shade along the top of the ribbon. When you click the contextual tab, you'll find tools that enable you to work specifically with the file or folder you've selected.

Showing and Hiding the File Explorer Ribbon

Some people aren't too crazy about the ribbon in other places. The ribbon was first introduced with Office 2007, and tweaked in Office 2010. Some users feel the ribbon takes up too much room on the screen, so Microsoft made the ribbon easy to hide, if that's your preference.

1. You can hide the ribbon by tapping the Minimize the Ribbon tool.

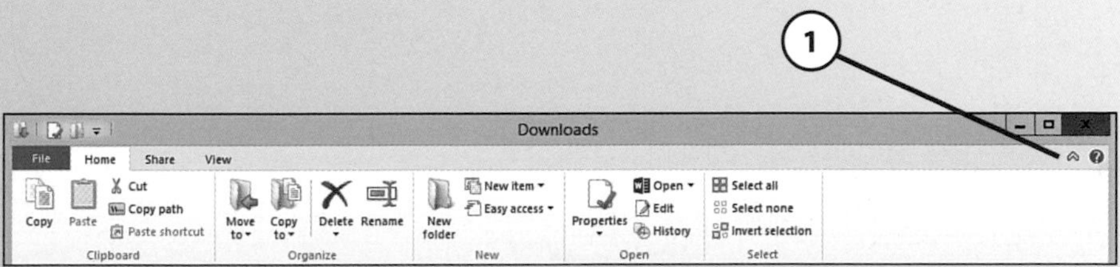

2. Display the ribbon by tapping or clicking the same tool, which is now called the Expand the Ribbon tool.

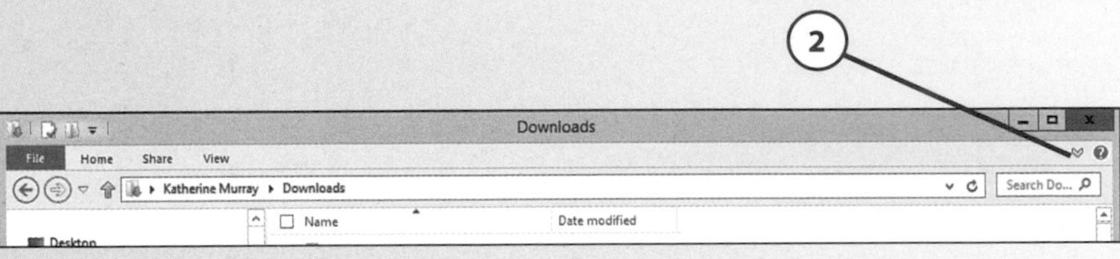

>>>Go Further

MORE TOOLS WITHIN REACH: THE QUICK ACCESS TOOLBAR

File Explorer also has a Quick Access toolbar in the upper-left corner of the Explorer window. The Quick Access toolbar gives you a small, customizable set of tools you can get to easily. It's always within easy clicking or tapping reach.

By default, the Quick Access toolbar in File Explorer shows only the Properties and New Folder tools, but you can tap or click the Customize Quick Access Toolbar arrow next to the New Folder tool to display options that enable you to add Undo, Redo, Delete, and Rename tools if you like. To add a tool, simply click or tap the one you want to add to the toolbar. To remove a tool, tap or click the arrow again and then tap or click a selected tool to remove the checkmark. The tool is removed from the toolbar.

You can also choose a different position for the Quick Access toolbar by tapping or clicking the Customize arrow and selecting Show Below the Ribbon. This moves the Quick Access toolbar so that it appears beneath the ribbon but above the Location bar. There's also a command that suppresses the display of the ribbon in the Quick Access toolbar menu; to hide the ribbon, click or tap Minimize the Ribbon.

Get the Scoop on Your Tools

File Explorer now also has new hotkey tool tips that tell you the name of the tool, give you a short description, and in some cases, displays the shortcut key for using the tool. All you need to do is hover the mouse over an item you're wondering about.

Working with Windows 8 Libraries

Along the left side of File Explorer, in the Navigation pane, you'll find a Libraries folder that includes four items by default: Documents, Music, Pictures, and Videos. Libraries in Windows 8 are different from actual folders in which specific files are stored; instead, they are indexed locations of a specific type of files which brings them all together so that you can find them easily. When you click a library to view its contents, what you're really seeing are links to the files stored in their respective folders.

You can use the libraries Windows 8 sets up for you, and you can also create your own libraries.

Clickable Locations

The various library and folder names in the Location bar are clickable, which means that you can move directly back to the library or to another folder by clicking the item you want in the Location bar. You can also click one of the arrows between the folder names to display a list of folders you can select. Simply click the one you want and move right to it. Nice.

You are likely to use some libraries more than others. All the files you create are available by default in your My Documents library, for example, so you will probably be looking for files in that folder fairly often. Your pictures may be in your My Pictures folder, and—you guessed it—your music files go in the My Music folder.

Are My Folders Repeating Themselves?

You may notice that the various Windows 8 libraries have both a "Public Pictures" and "My Pictures" folder in the Pictures library, and a "My Documents" and a "Public Documents" folder in the Documents library. In these cases, the files stored in the "My" folders are those that are for your eyes only; you haven't shared them with anyone. The items stored in the Public folder have been shared with others freely and can be accessed by other computers on your HomeGroup or users with the necessary permissions.

Adding Folders to Libraries

You can easily add folders to a library if Windows 8 seems to be overlooking a folder you want to include.

1. In File Explorer, click or tap the folder in the Navigation pane that contains the folder you want to add.
2. Right-click or tap and hold the folder in the center panel. The options list that appears shows the Include in Library option. (If you don't see this option, it means that the folder is already included in a Windows 8 library.)
3. Click or tap the Include in Library arrow.
4. Click or tap the library to which you want to add the folder. File Explorer displays a message letting you know the folder is being included in the library you selected. The new folder appears in the subfolders below the library name in the Navigation pane and will remain in that library.

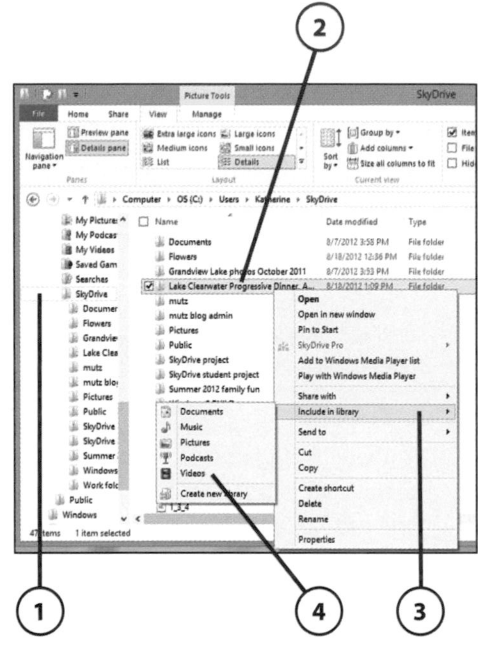

Nothing Really Moved

Even though it may look as though the folder you added to the library is now in a new location, in reality nothing moved. File Explorer maintains a link to the folder that contains the files so that you can access them easily any time you choose to work with that library.

Creating a Library

Because a library is essentially a stored, indexed search that keeps together all your favorite files of a certain type, you can create your own libraries if your interests differ from the libraries Windows 8 has already provided for you. When you are adding a folder to a library, you may decide instead to make it its own library. You could create a library that collects links to all the folders you are using for a specific project, for example.

1. In File Explorer, click the item containing the folder you want to use to create the library.
2. Click the folder.
3. Click the Include in Library arrow.
4. Click Create New Library. File Explorer automatically adds the folder you selected in the Library area of the Navigation pane, and you can click the folder name to display the contents of the folder.

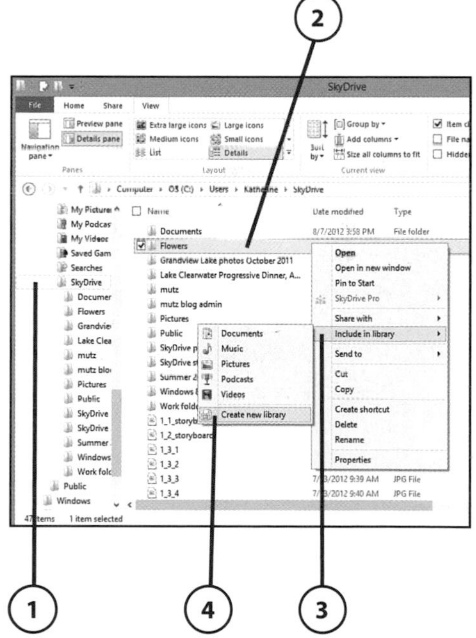

It's Not All Good

LIBRARY WRANGLING

File Explorer no doubt needs some kind of organizing mechanism to keep us from creating libraries all over the place with folders that are already in libraries. But one slightly frustrating aspect about libraries is that you can't easily create a new library from a folder that's already included in one of the default libraries. You can, however, remove the folder from the library (using the technique in the next section) and then select the folder again and create a new library.

Removing Folders from a Library

You can remove a folder from the library when you don't need it anymore. Maybe you completed the project you were working on and won't be using the same folders anymore. Here's how to remove a file from the library.

1. Click the library you want to remove in the Navigation pane. The Library Tools Manage contextual tab appears.
2. Click Manage Library in the Manage group.

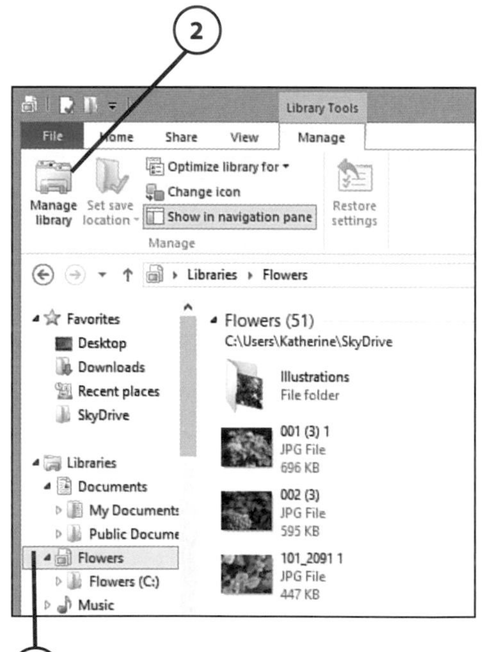

3. In the Library Locations dialog box, click or tap the folder you want to remove from the library.
4. Click or tap Remove.
5. Click OK. File Explorer removes the folder from the library for you.

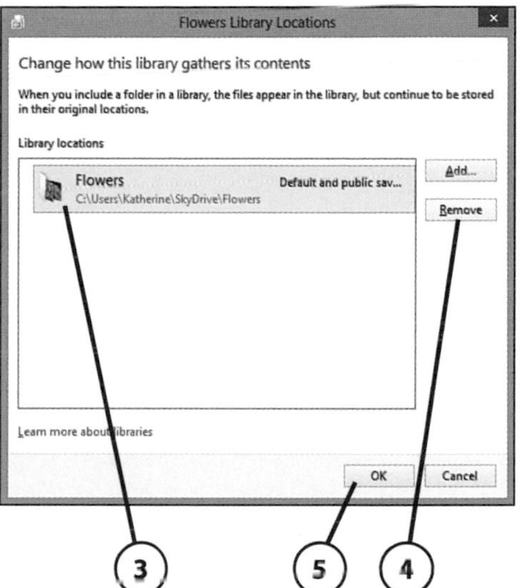

Fast Removal

You can also remove a folder quickly from a library by right-clicking the folder in the library and choosing Remove Location from Library.

Your Files Are Safe

Remember that removing a folder from a library doesn't do anything at all to the files contained in the library. Because a library is really an indexed collection of links to the various folders and files related to that topic, only the link is removed when you remove a library.

Arranging Library Display

Chances are your libraries contain lots of files, and that means you need to think about the best way to display them so that you can easily find what you need. File Explorer gives you the ability to filter your files so they are displayed in the order you prefer. You might choose to arrange the files by Author, Date Modified, Tag, Type, or Name, for example.

1. Click or tap the library folder you want to arrange in the Navigation pane.
2. Right-click, or tap, hold, and release a blank area in the center of the screen. An options list appears.
3. Click or tap the Arrange By option in the Library pane at the top of the center column.
4. Click the setting that arranges the files the way you want them to appear. Author lists the files and folders alphabetically by author; Date Modified lists files with the most recently modified files shown first; Tag arranges files alphabetically according to any tags you've assigned to the file; Type shows the files organized by file type; and Name lists the files alphabetically (from A to Z).

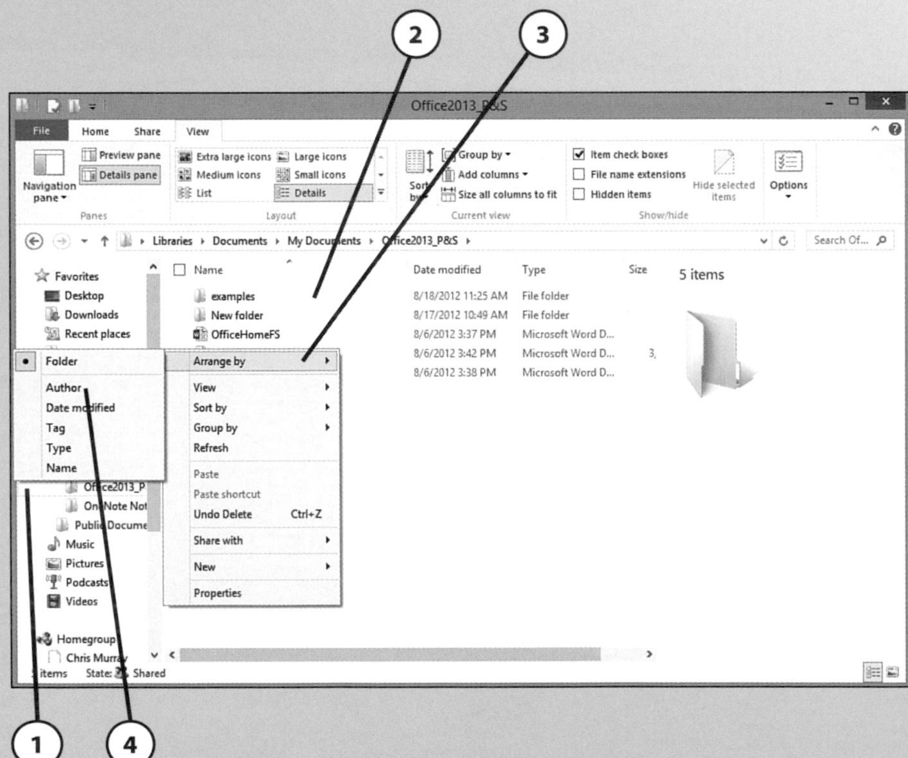

5. You can continue to fine-tune the display by clicking the column names at the top of the display list in the center column and choosing additional sort criteria.

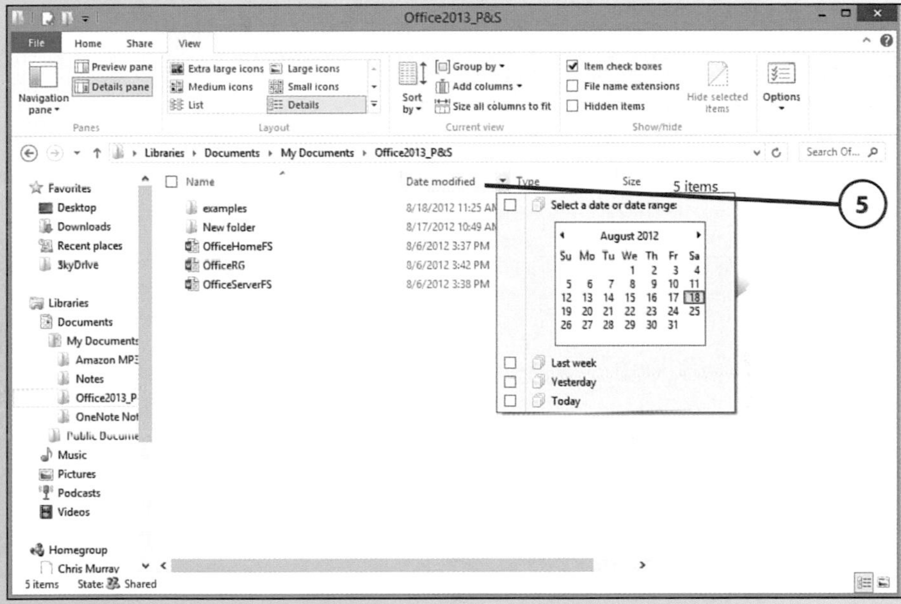

>>>Go Further

ADDING AND REMOVING COLUMNS

You can display additional details about the files you're viewing in File Explorer—and use those columns to arrange the file list—by clicking Add Columns in the Current View group of the View tab.

When you click Add Columns, you'll see a checkmark to the left of all the columns already included in the current view. For example, you might see checks in front of Date Modified, Type, Size, Tags, and Authors. Other items—such as Date Created, Folder Path, Categories, and Title— don't have checks. You can add them to your file display by clicking them. This enables you to show all files related to a particular topic, for example, or browse through files that were all created after a particular date.

You can click Choose Columns in the Add Columns list to add specific column items to your display. The long list of choices you'll see include items such as Country/region, Cell phone, Contributors, Lens Model, Status, and much more. In this way, you can customize the look and feel of your File Explorer view so that it gives you all the information you need about your files in a way that matches the way you like to work.

Managing Your Files and Folders

A lot of what you do in File Explorer involves finding, organizing, and sharing your files. You will probably work with document files, picture files, music files, video files, and more. Knowing how to locate, select, copy, move, sort, and get information about your files is an important part of staying organized and up-to-speed with all the data you're collecting. Organizing your folders so they are where you can get to them easily will help you find what you need quickly so you can get back to work (or play).

Finding Files and Folders

Finding the files and folders you're looking for in File Explorer is super simple. You can enter a word or phrase in the Search box for a simple search, or refine your search by searching for a specific date, kind of file, size, or other file properties.

1. Begin by tapping or clicking the library (for example, Documents, Music, Pictures, or Videos) or the drive where you want to search.
2. Tap or click in the search box and type a word or phrase to describe what you're searching for. The Search Tools Search contextual tab appears above the ribbon.
3. In the Location group, tap or click whether you want to search your entire computer, search the current folder, or include all subfolders in your search.

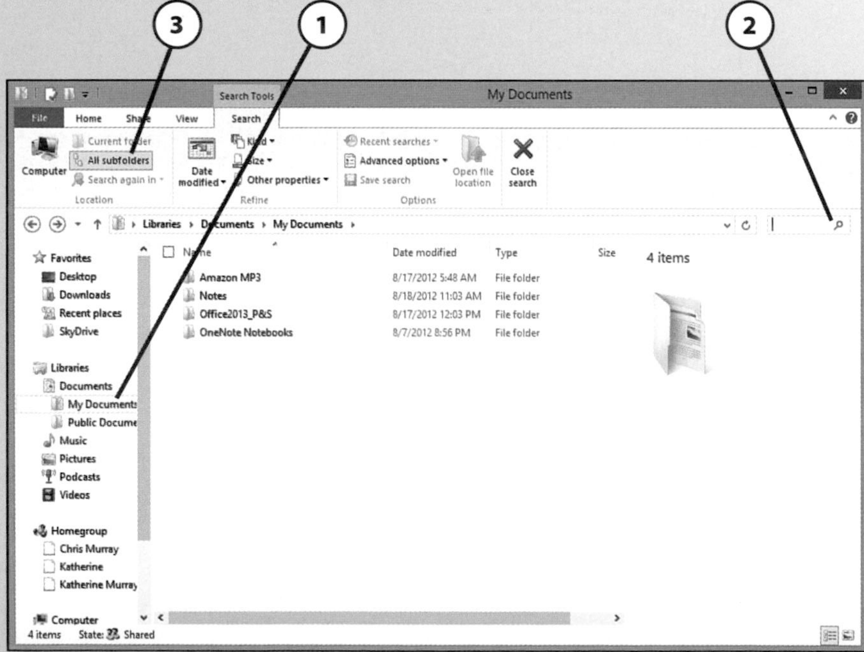

4. In the Refine group of the Search Tools Search tab, tap or click a search filter if you want to apply one: Date Modified, Kind, Size, or Other Properties.

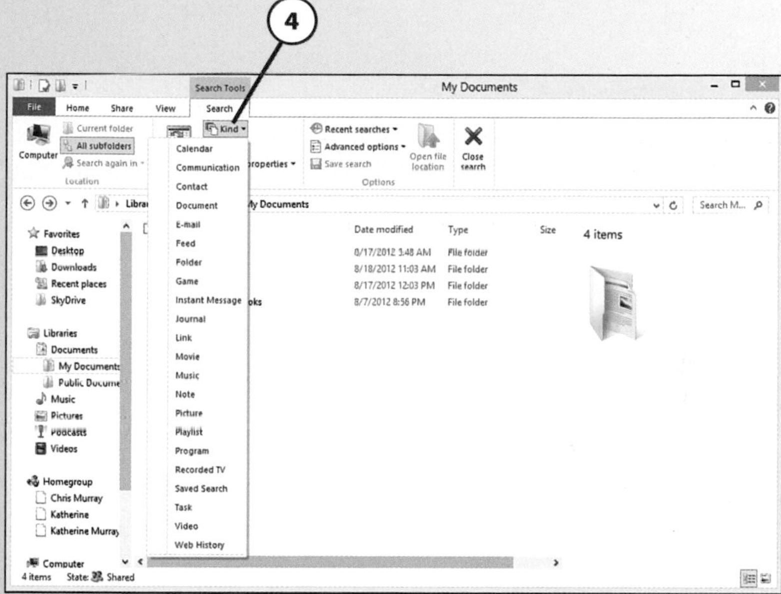

5. Tap or click the search result you want to see.
6. If you want to repeat the search in a different location, choose Search Again in the Location group and click or tap your choice.

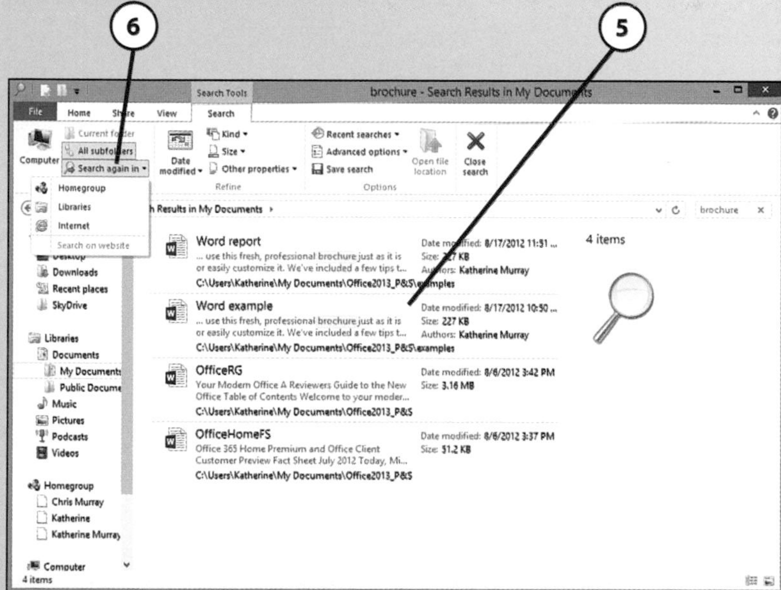

Finding Specific File Types

When you want to find files in a specific format—for example, .jpg, .wmv, .docx, or .mp3—use the Type filter in the Other Properties tool in the Refine group. When you click Type, File Explorer displays a list box of file formats you can choose to narrow your search, and you can tap or click the one that fits what you're searching for.

>>>Go Further

SAVING YOUR SEARCHES

If you find that you often perform the same searches—perhaps you search for the latest podcasts or look for the newest video clips that have been added to your computer—you can save the search so that you can use it again later.

Enter the search information as usual, and then, when the search results appear in the File Explorer window, tap or click Save Search in the Options group of the Search Tools Search tab. The Save As dialog box appears. Type a filename for the saved search and tap or click Save.

Now you can use the search at any time by tapping or clicking the saved search in the Favorites area at the top of the Navigation pane.

Selecting Files and Folders

The Home tab of File Explorer gives you the tools you need to select files and folders easily.

1. In the Navigation pane, click or tap the drive, library, or folder where you want to select files.
2. Click or tap the Home tab.
3. If you want to select all contents of the selected folder, tap or click Select All in the Select group.
4. If you want to deselect any files or folders you've previously selected, click or tap Select None.

5. If you have previously selected multiple files (by pressing Ctrl and clicking files or tapping multiple selections) and want to change the selection to all those that were previously unselected, tap or click Invert Selection.

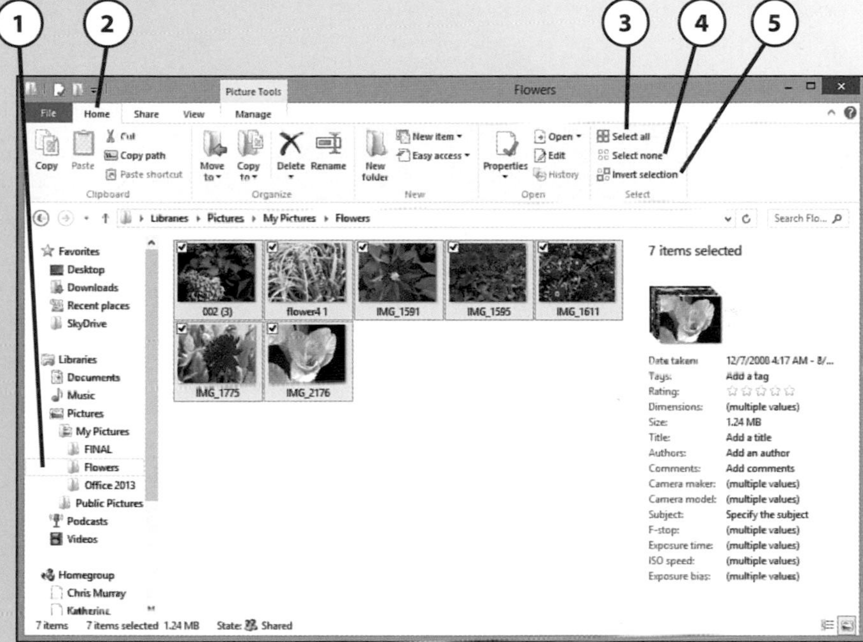

Viewing File Information

You can change the way you view the files in the folders and libraries you select by using the tools in the View tab.

The Panes group on the far-left side of the ribbon contains tools you can use to preview the selected file or display details about the file you've chosen.

1. Click or tap the library or folder containing the file you want to see.
2. Use Search if necessary to locate the file.
3. Click or tap the View tab.
4. Tap or click Preview Pane in the Panes group if you want to see a preview of the file.

5. Tap or click Details Pane if you want to see the details of the file.

What Do You Mean, *Details*?

The Details pane of File Explorer gives you information about the selected file. You can see the filename, size, and the date it was last modified. You can also see any tags that have been assigned to the file, review the authors' names, and in some cases, see any rating that has been applied to the file.

Tagging Files

And the information in the Details pane isn't just for viewing—you can also change the information and save it while you're there. By just clicking or tapping in the Tags area and typing the tags you want to add, you can categorize your files so that you can find them more easily when you search for them later.

1. Display the file you want to tag in File Explorer.
2. In the Details pane, tap or click in the Tags field. Type tags that you can use to identify or categorize the file, separating multiple tags with semicolons.
3. Click or tap Save.

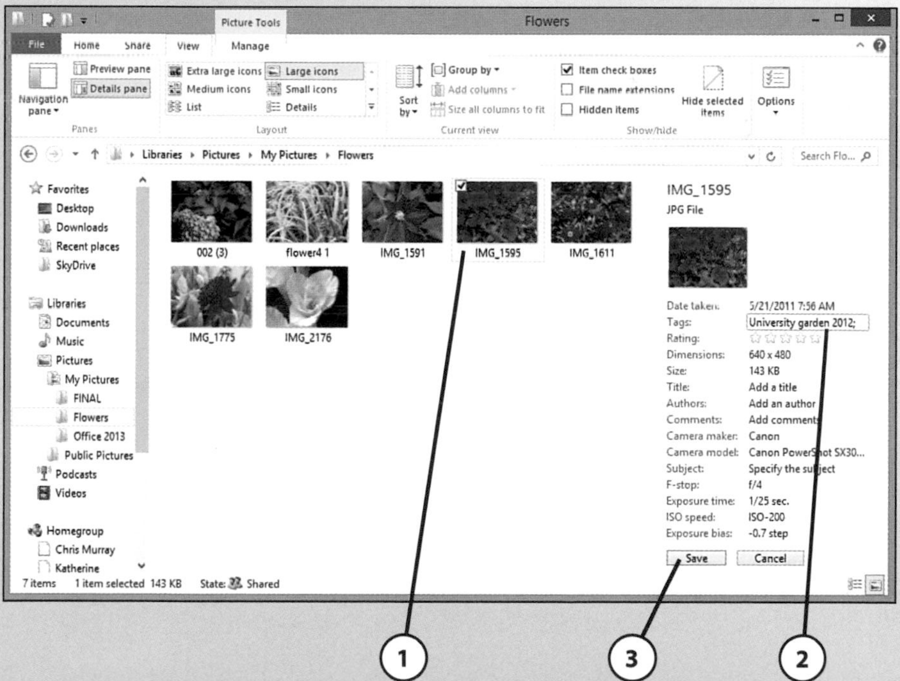

Tagging Again Later

The next time you add tags, when you tap or click in the Tag field and start typing, File Explorer displays a list box, suggesting tags that you've entered previously. Click or tap the check box of any tag you want to add, and click or tap Save to save the tags.

>>>Go Further

RATING FILES

In the Details pane of your picture files, you can also assign a rating value to your image files. Rating the files on your computer helps you prioritize the ones you love over the ones you don't. This can help you choose the right files when you're searching, for example, for the best photos you have of a particular event. If you've rated the files, you can search for the files with the highest rating, which will give you a results list that is the cream of the crop. Select the file you want to rate in File Explorer and then click or tap the number of stars (one to five) you want to assign to the image. Tap or click Save to save your rating.

Copying, Moving, and Sharing Files and Folders

One of the big stories for File Explorer involves the new Copy process, which helps you easily copy files large and small, and resolve conflicts between files that may have the same name. Now File Explorer gives you more information about the file you're copying and helps you resolve any copy conflicts by showing thumbnails of the files involved.

Keeping a Close Eye on Your Copying

When you want to copy files from one place to another in File Explorer, you can simply navigate to the folder containing the files you want, select them, and use Copy To.

1. In the Navigation pane, click or tap the folder containing the files you want to copy.
2. Select the files or folders you want to copy.
3. Click or tap the Home tab.
4. Click or tap Copy To. A list of copy destination appears
5. Click the folder where you want to paste the files. File Explorer immediately copies the selected files to the location you selected.
6. If you want to create a new folder or scroll through a list of possible folders, select the file you want to copy, click Copy To, and select Choose Location. The Copy Items dialog box appears.

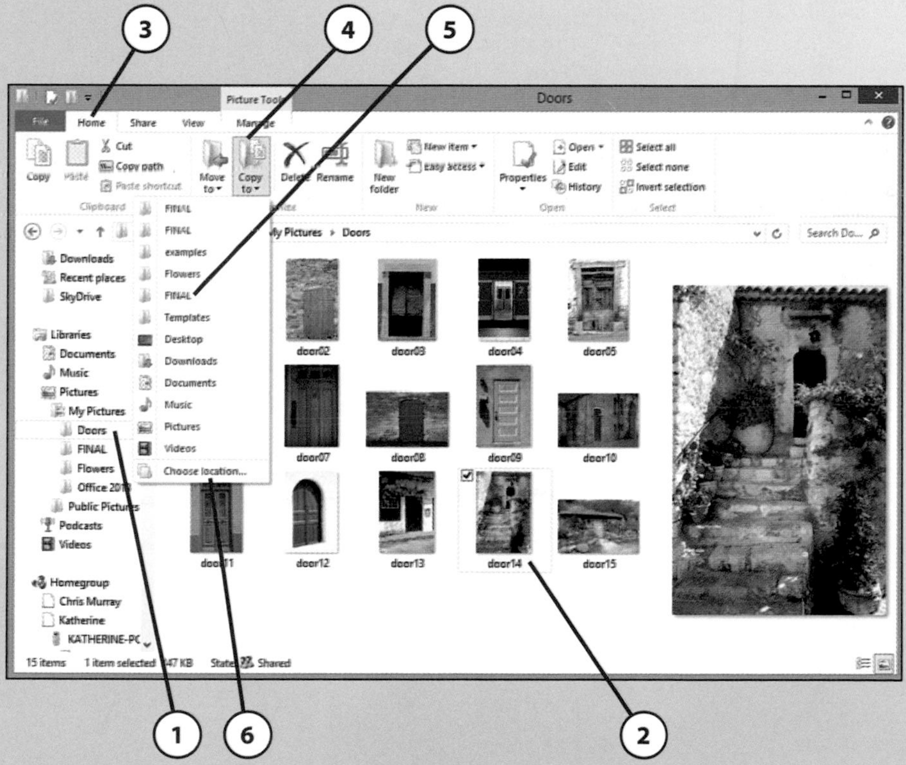

7. Click the arrow to display subfolders.
8. Click the folder where you want to copy the selected files.
9. Click Make New Folder if you want to copy the files to a new folder.
10. Click Copy to complete the operation.

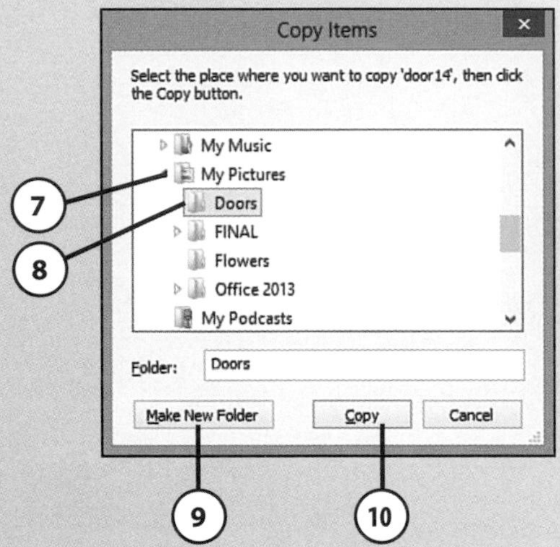

Solving Copy Conflicts

Another new change for the File Explorer copy process is the way in which the utility resolves conflicts when two files have the same name. This can happen easily when you are moving files from one computer to another—which file is the most recent one? File Explorer helps you make the call in the Replace or Skip Files dialog box.

1. Paste the files as usual in the new location. If files already exist in that folder with the same names, the Replace or Skip Files dialog box appears.
2. Click or tap Replace the File in the Destination if you want to replace the existing files with the ones you are pasting into the folder.
3. Click or tap Skip This File if you want to keep the existing file in the current folder.
4. If you want to compare the files, click or tap Compare Info for Both Files.
5. If you want to choose to keep the files in one of the folders displayed, click the checkbox to the left of your choice.
6. Compare the creation dates and times, as well as the file sizes, to determine which files you want to keep. Click or tap the checkboxes of those files.
7. Click or tap Continue. File Explorer completes the copy operation using the file you selected.

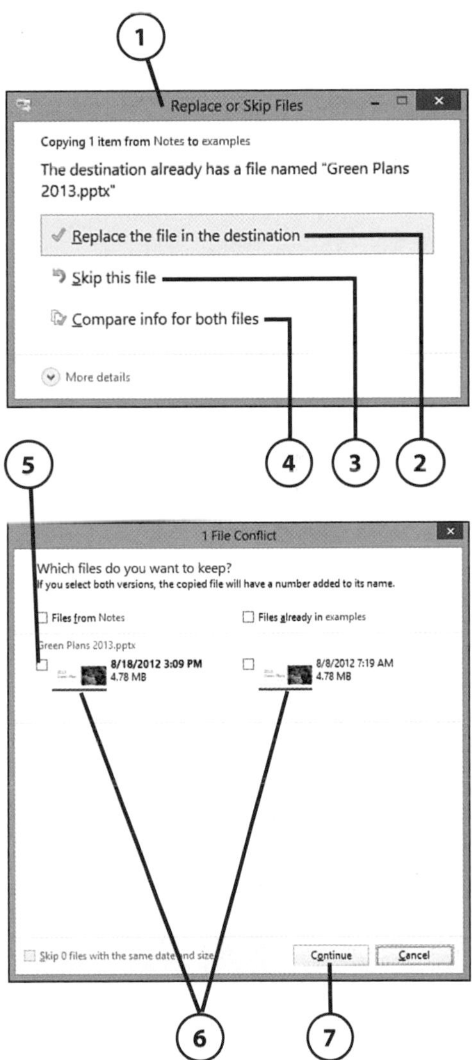

Sharing Files

When you're ready to share your files with friends, family, and coworkers, select the file or group of files you want to share and tap or click the Share tab. You'll find tools that enable you to print, email, fax, burn to disc, or share the files with others in your HomeGroup or who have accounts on your computer.

1. Select the file or files you want to share.
2. Click or tap the Share tab.
3. In the Send group, choose whether you want to Email, Zip, Burn to Disc, Print, or Fax your selection.
4. In the Share With group, choose the groups or users from the list with whom you want to share the files.
5. If you want to stop sharing selected files, click Stop Sharing.
6. Fine-tune your security settings by clicking or tapping Advanced Security and adjusting the permission levels assigned to those you're sharing the files with.

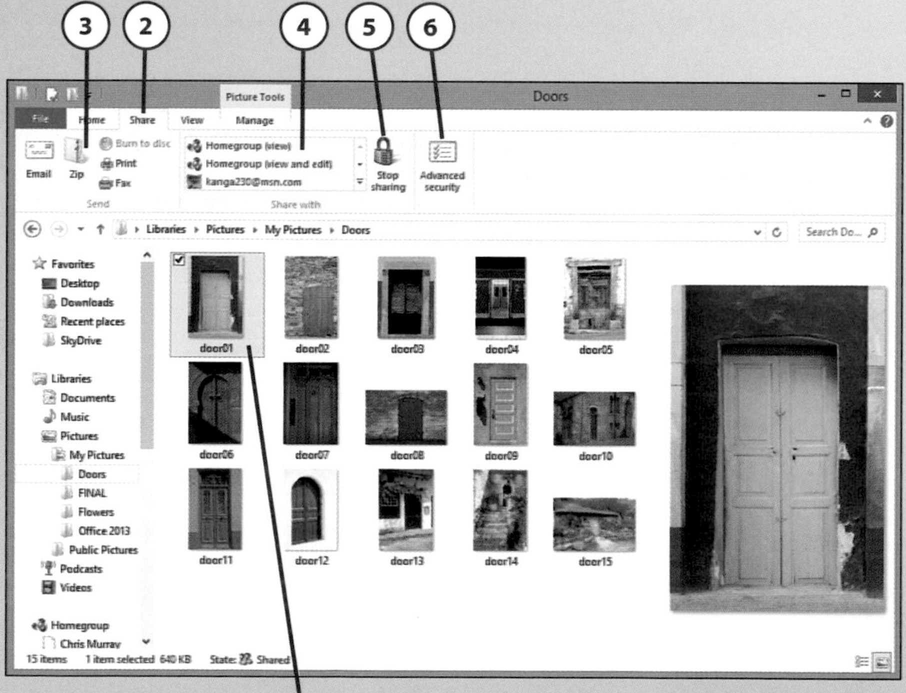

Sync Your File Explorer Settings

When you choose the Sync Your Settings tool in the PC Settings screen, you'll now be able to sync your File Explorer options and preferences along with the other Windows 8 settings that are synched from computer to computer. This feature is only available if you log in to your computer using your Microsoft Account. Find out more about syncing your settings in Chapter 6, "Securing Your Windows 8 Computer."

Moving Files: Looks Familiar

Moving files is very similar to copying files. You simply navigate to the folder containing the files you want to move, select them, and click Move To in the Organize group of the Home tab. You'll see the trusty folder list, where you can choose the destination folder where you want to move the files. Or you can click or tap Choose Location to display the Move Items dialog box, where you can choose a folder or subfolder—or add a new folder—you want to move the selected files to. Click Move to finish the job.

Copying and Moving Shortcut Keys

To use shortcut keys to copy and paste files, select the files you want to copy and press Ctrl+C. If you want to move the files instead of copying them, press Ctrl+X. Then, navigate to the folder where you want to place the copied or moved files, and press Ctrl+V.

Compressing and Extracting Your Files

Sometimes when you want to email a bunch of files, it's easier to compress them into one file you can attach to an email message instead of attaching 10 or 12 different documents. Once the recipient receives the compressed file, he or she needs to extract the contents. File Explorer includes tools to do both of those jobs: compressing and extracting files.

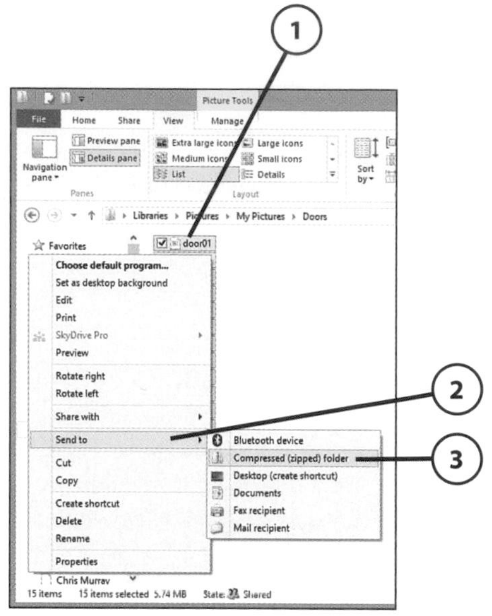

1. Select the files you want to include in the compressed file.
2. Right-click your selection and point to Send To.
3. Click Compressed (Zipped) Folder. File Explorer compresses the files and displays the zipped file with the name highlighted.
4. Type a new name for the compressed file.
5. To see and extract the contents of a compressed a file, double-click or double-tap it.
6. Click or tap Extract All. The Extract Compressed (Zipped) Folders dialog box appears.

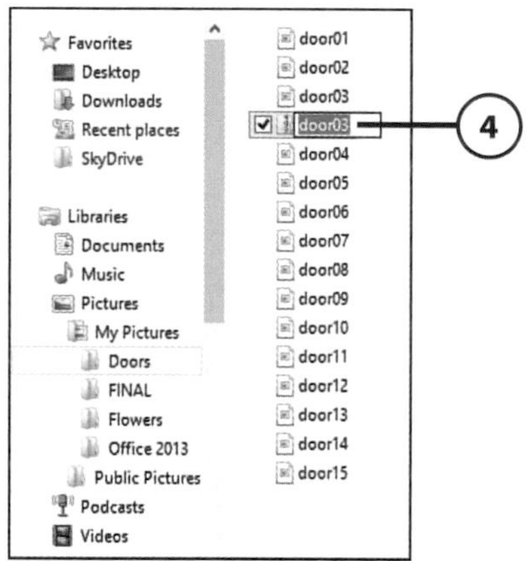

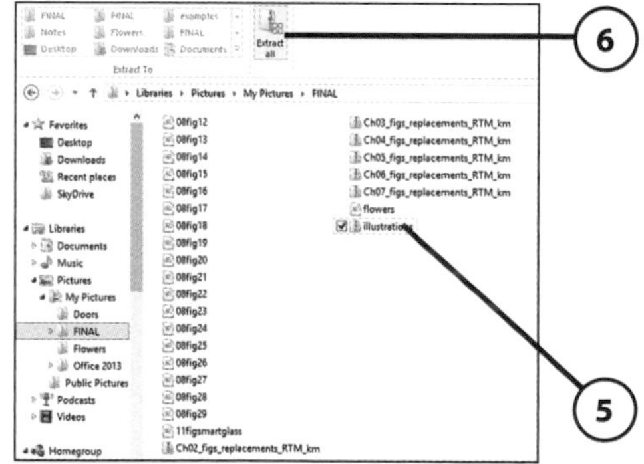

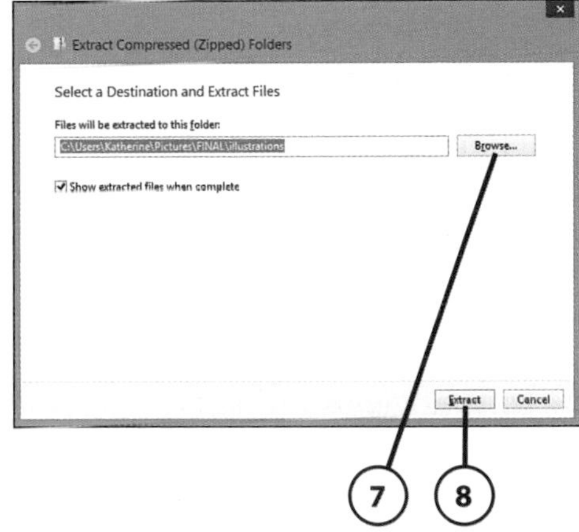

7. Click Browse if necessary to choose a folder for the extracted files. (It's okay to leave the default setting if that folder is where you want the uncompressed files to be placed.)
8. Click Extract. File Explorer extracts the files and places them in the folder you specified, ready to use.

Putting Files in Public Places

You can also place files in Public folders on your computer so that others who have the necessary permissions are able to view the files in that location. To move a file to a Public folder, simply drag and drop the file to that location.

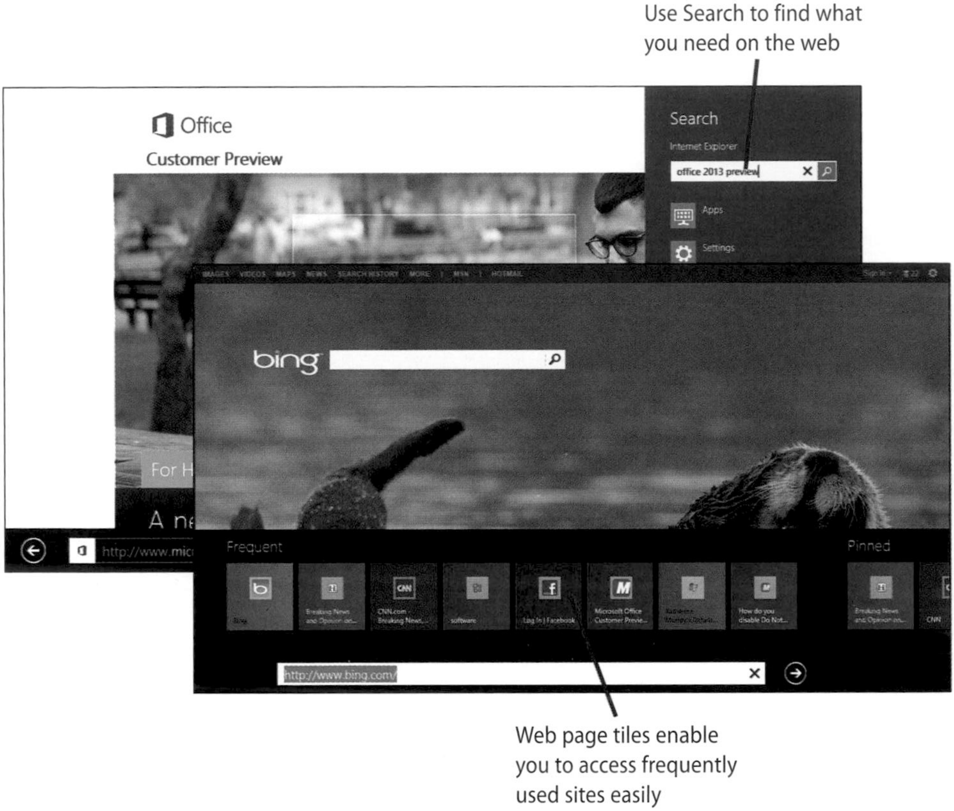
Use Search to find what you need on the web
Office
Customer Preview
Search
Internet Explorer
office 2013 preview
Apps
Settings
bing
Frequent
Pinned
http://www.bing.com/
Web page tiles enable you to access frequently used sites easily

In this chapter, you learn how to browse the web securely and find what you seek using Internet Explorer. Specifically, you learn how to use your web browser for the following tasks:

→ Introducing Internet Explorer 10

→ Browsing and searching the web—the Windows way

→ Working with tabs

→ Securing your browsing experience

Always Online with Internet Explorer 10

If you love the fast, seamless experience you get browsing the web on your phone (just don't do it while you're driving), you will love the modeless feel of Internet Explorer 10. Now in Windows 8, Internet Explorer actually has two personalities. On the one hand, IE 10 is optimized for the fast and flexible Windows 8 design, and on the other, it runs on your Windows 8 desktop, where it resembles a more traditional browsing experience, complete with a browser window and tools you'll recognize. This chapter shows you the ins and outs of these two faces of IE 10, suggesting ways you can get the most from each browsing style.

Introducing Internet Explorer 10

Like everything else in Windows 8, Internet Explorer 10 works great on touchscreens, which means you can flick and tap and pinch to your heart's content. This touch interface makes it easy for you to interact with the content you find: You can easily flick to another page, pinch to zoom in on a photo caption, and tap your way through navigation controls on the site.

The version of IE 10 you launch from your Start screen takes up your full Windows 8 screen without displaying any kind of browser window. This full-screen experience is called "modeless" browsing, because there's no bordering window with tools that enclose the browser window.

The desktop version of Internet Explorer 10 looks more like the traditional browsing experience you may be familiar with from Internet Explorer 9. You'll find the familiar browser window with tools you'll recognize as you surf the web from the desktop. Whether you choose to go "modeless" or "traditional," you'll find that IE 10 loads pages and updates faster than ever and provides the secure tools you need to have a safe browsing experience online.

>>>Go Further

ALL ABOUT PLUG-INS AND FLASH

A plug-in is a kind of utility that adds capabilities to your web browser. For example, Macromedia Flash is a plug-in that enables you to view animations in your web browser. Although plug-ins can add functionality to your browser, they also can be a security risk for your computer. For that reason, IE 10 on the Start screen is designed not to allow plug-ins of any kind, which makes for a smoother, faster, more secure browsing experience. But after some consideration, Microsoft added Adobe Flash support into the bowels of IE 10 (not as a plug-in) so you can play media objects that require Flash. This is great when you're viewing video clips from news sites or YouTube. But it's a bit ironic that Microsoft's own Silverlight is not supported by IE 10. You'll get bumped to the desktop version of the browser for that.

Starting Internet Explorer

By now you know the drill. Launch Internet Explorer 10 from your Windows 8 Start screen by tapping or clicking the Internet Explorer tile.

Tap or click to launch Internet Explorer 10 in the Windows 8 style

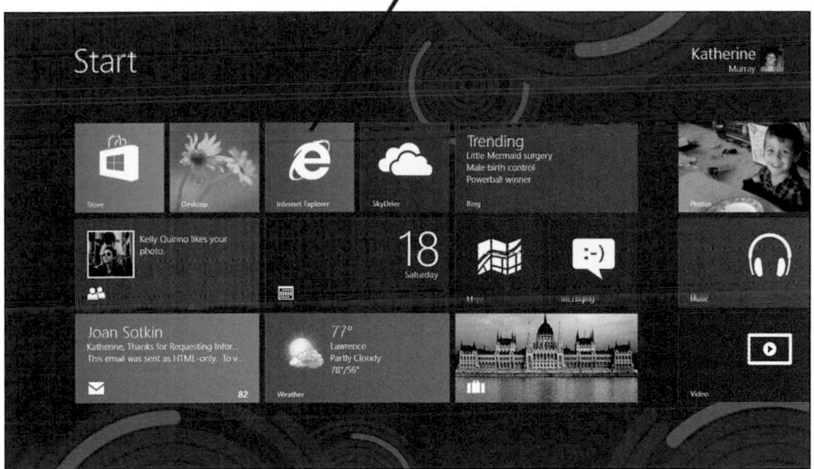

If you launch Internet Explorer 10 from your Windows 8 desktop, you'll click or tap the IE 10 logo on the left side of the taskbar.

Click or tap the IE 10 logo to launch

A Look Around the Internet Explorer Window(s)

No matter which browser you use, you'll find that each has its own unique personality with its own quirks and toolsets. It's not often, however, that you have two personalities in the same browser. Although Internet Explorer 10 is built on the same engine—meaning it processes information the same way and provides the same fast and efficient experience no matter which style you are using—it offers two very different browsing experiences.

IE 10: Modeless Style

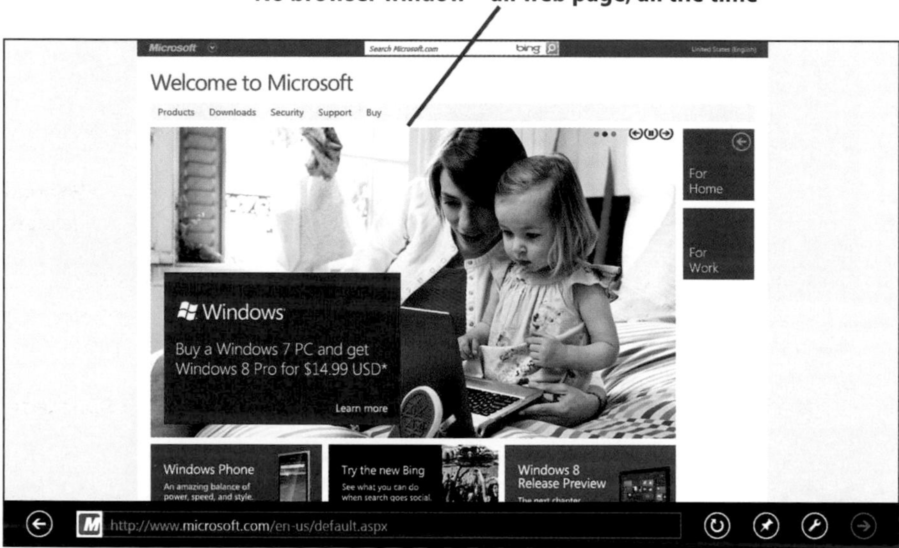

When you launch Internet Explorer 10 from the Windows 8 Start screen, the browser opens, displaying the web page without a surrounding window, making it easy for you to touch, swipe, tap, right-click, and pinch your way across the web.

To display additional pages, to see the address bar, or to work with your browser tools, you need to swipe up from the bottom of the browser window or right-click the mouse. The address bar appears at the bottom of the screen, along with navigation tiles of recently visited pages at the top of the screen.

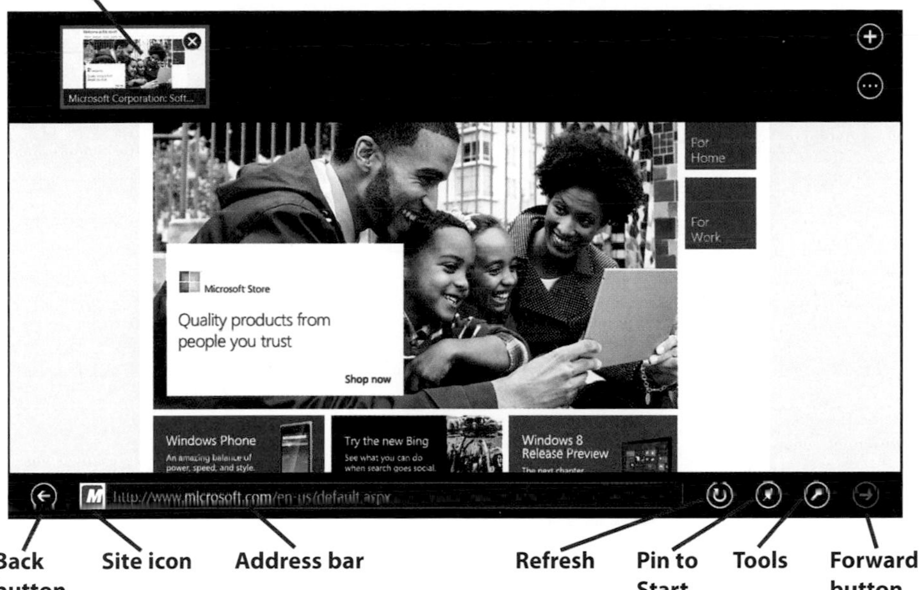

- **Navigation tiles**. These thumbnail pages show where you've visited recently. You can move to one of the displayed pages by tapping or clicking it.
- **Back button**. Click or tap Back to move to the page you viewed immediately prior to the current page.
- **Address bar**. Tap or click in the address bar and enter the address of the web page you want to view.
- **Refresh**. Update the display of the current page by tapping or clicking Refresh.
- **Pin to Start**. If you find a page you want to be able to access directly from the Windows 8 Start screen, you can tap Pin to Start. The page is added as a tile on the Start screen.
- **Tools**. You can tap or click Tools to open the page search feature so you can find content on the current page or to choose to view the page on the desktop version of IE 10.
- **Forward**. Tap or click Forward to display the next page in a series of web pages. This tool is available only if you have previously used the Back button.

Switching to the Desktop Browser

If you're viewing a web page in IE 10 and you decide you'd rather have the traditional browser window instead, you can swipe up from the bottom of the browser window, tap or click Tools and tap or click View on the desktop. The IE 10 desktop browser window opens, with the current web page displayed in the content area.

IE 10: Desktop Style

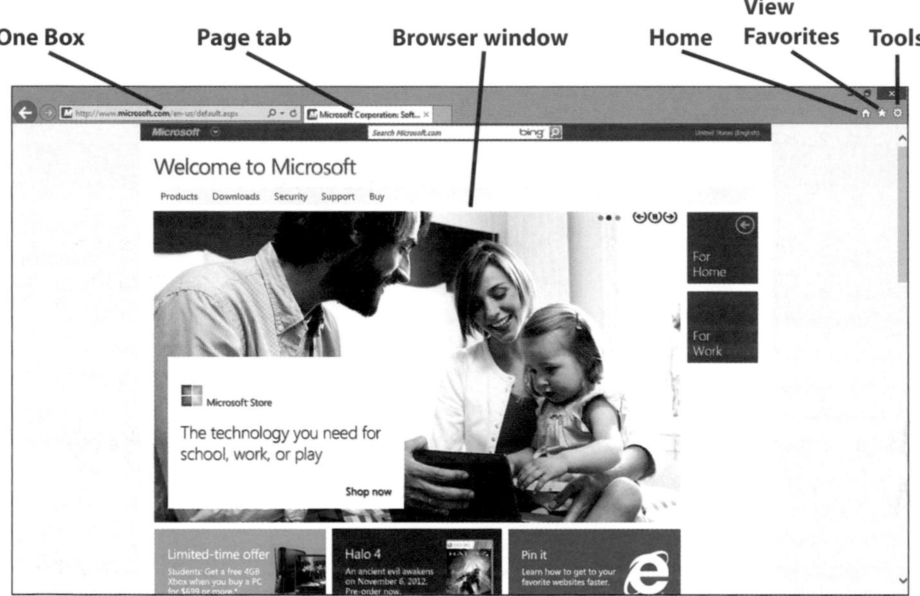

The desktop version of Internet Explorer 10, on the other hand, looks like a more traditional browser window, with the following elements that will probably look familiar:

- **One Box.** Now you can search for information or browse the web by tapping or clicking and typing in the same box. Formerly called the *address bar,* One Box enables you to surf, search, refresh the site, and display security information all in the same box.
- **Page tab.** Each web page is displayed in a separate tab, and the tabs are color-coded to help you navigate among them easily.
- **Home.** Clicking Home at any point returns you to the website you've set as your browser home page.

- **View Favorites.** Click View Favorites to access websites you've saved as your favorites or to add a new favorite to the list.
- **Tools.** Click Tools to access the various menus in Internet Explorer 10 and to print, check site security, go to your pinned sites, and set Internet options.

Making the Menus Visible

In the desktop version of IE 10, you can display traditional menus at the top of the browser window if you like. Simply tap and hold or right-click the top of the browser window; then select Menu bar. The menus appear just below One Box, where you can reach them easily.

A Peek at the Menu Bar

If your computer has a keyboard and you want the menu to appear briefly in the desktop version of IE 10 (as opposed to displaying it continually), press Alt when the menu bar is hidden. When you release the key, the menu bar appears at the top of the browser window, and after you click the option you want, the menu disappears again.

Browsing and Searching the Web—the Windows 8 Way

If you are a smartphone user, chances are that you're already browsing the web using a touch interface, so the new version of IE 10 may feel very natural to you. The version of IE 10 you launch from the Start screen enables you to tap or click your way from page to page easily. You can also swipe to advance pages, zoom in on content, and dock the display so that you can view the web alongside other open apps. Nice.

Using the Address Bar

The address bar appears when you first display a web page and reappears when you swipe up from the bottom of the IE 10 screen. To anchor the cursor in the address bar, you tap or click there. As you type in the address bar, the navigation tiles filter to show you sites from your history, favorites, and even popular URLs. With Windows 8 roaming and connected accounts, your browsing history and favorites roam with you so that you can easily access recent web pages across all of your PCs.

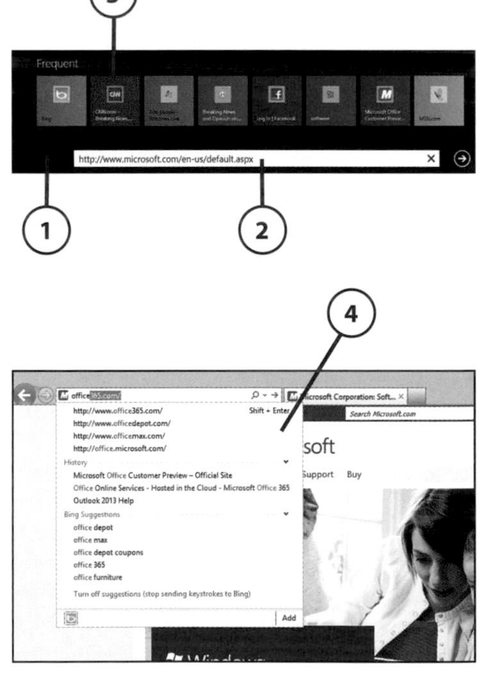

1. Click or tap in the address bar. If you're using a touch device, the touch keyboard appears so that you can type the new web address. If you're using a non-touch computer, the web address is highlighted.
2. Type the web address of the page you want to view. Internet Explorer 10 attempts to autocomplete the phrase for you, so if you want to use the site provided, tap or click the Go button. If not, just keep typing the full address.
3. You can also tap or click a tile in the Frequent area to move to the page in IE 10.
4. If you're using the desktop version, IE 10 offers suggested sites in a dropdown list when you begin to type the web address, and you can tap or click the site you want to display.

What's in a Name?

In the desktop version of IE 10, the address bar is known as One Box, where you now basically use "one box" for everything, whether you want to search, get security reports, or go directly to a web page.

>>>Go Further

KEYBOARD SHORTCUTS FOR BROWSING

If you'd rather skip the clicking and navigate through the web using your keyboard, you can use the following shortcut keys in the desktop version of IE 10:

- Press Alt+C to display your favorites, feeds, and history.
- Press Ctrl+B to organize your favorites.
- Press Ctrl+D to add another web page to your favorites.
- Press Ctrl+L to highlight the web address in One Box. (This also works in the version of IE 10 you launch from the Start screen.)
- Press Ctrl+J to display the Download Manager.

Navigating the Web

The web has been around long enough by now that you probably won't be surprised by the browser tools you'll use to navigate online. Whether you're using IE 10 from the Start screen or desktop, chances are good you already know how to move forward or backward from page to page.

Swipe across the page
bing
Popular now
Search History
Images
Videos
http://www.bing.com/
Back
Click a link
Tap a button
Forward

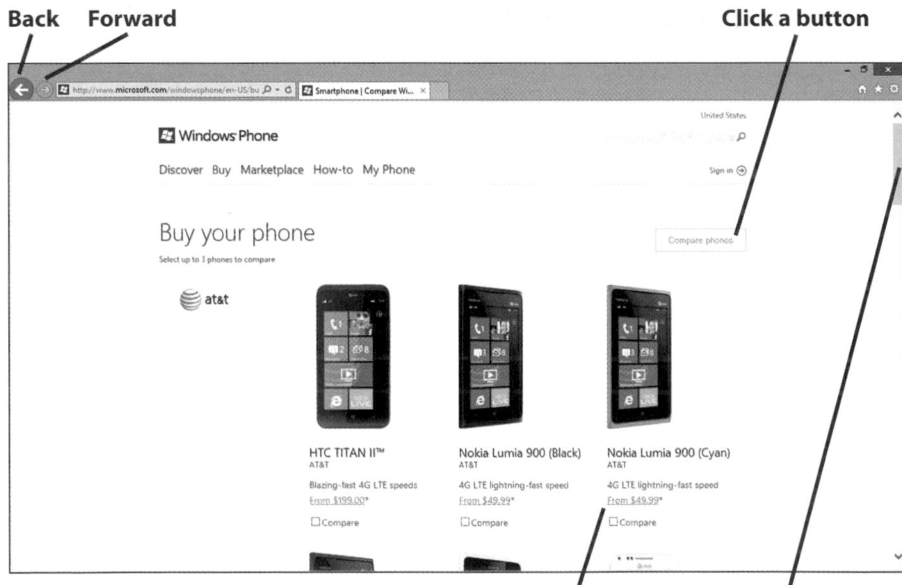

Back
Forward
Click a button
Windows Phone
Discover Buy Marketplace How-to My Phone
Buy your phone
Select up to 3 phones to compare
Compare phones
at&t
HTC TITAN II™
Nokia Lumia 900 (Black)
Nokia Lumia 900 (Cyan)
Tap a link
Scroll down the page

In both browsers, you'll use the same tools and techniques to navigate the web pages you display:

- **Back.** Tapping or clicking the Back button takes you back to the page you were previously viewing.
- **Forward.** Tapping or clicking Forward takes you to the web page you previously viewed *after* viewing the current one. This capability is helpful if you're moving back and forth between pages. If you haven't moved ahead to another page yet, this button is not available for you to click or tap.
- **Click or tap a link.** Click or tap a link on the page to move to another page or perform a web action. What that link does—for example, whether it displays a new page, opens a document, or plays a media clip—depends on what the website designer programmed the link to do.
- **Scroll or swipe down the page.** In the desktop version of IE 10, use the vertical scrollbar as you would in any other program to display content that is currently out of view along the bottom of the page. On a touch device, you can swipe up to display content that appears below the bottom margin of the window.
- **Scroll or swipe across the page.** In the desktop version of IE 10, use the horizontal scrollbar to scroll across pages that are too wide to be displayed at one time on your monitor. Using the version of IE 10 you launch from the Start screen, you can swipe to the left to show content that is out of view to the right. You can also swipe to the right or left to page through other web pages you've visited.
- **Tap or click a tool or command**. You can carry out site operations, execute commands, and access other areas of the site by tapping or clicking a button, command, or menu item.

>>>Go Further

PIN YOUR SITES WHERE YOU CAN FIND THEM LATER

If you constantly wish you had a better way to remember the sites you like to visit frequently, IE 10 has a great feature for you: pinned sites. Now you can pin a site to your Windows 8 Start menu so that you can access the site as soon as you start using Windows 8.

To pin a site to the Windows 8 Start screen, use the modeless version of IE 10 to navigate to the site you want to add, swipe up to display the address bar, and tap Pin to Start (which resembles a push pin) to the right of the address bar. IE 10 adds the site as a tile to your Windows 8 Start screen, and you'll be able to access this site directly without first opening Internet Explorer.

>>>Go Further

WHO SAYS YOU CAN'T GO BACK?

Internet Explorer 10 makes it easy to return to sites you browsed earlier—or go back to your last browsing session. If you're using the modeless version of IE 10, swipe up to display the address bar at the bottom and the navigation tiles at the top of your browser screen. Tap or click the tile you want to view.

If you're using the desktop version of IE 10, click the New Tab box to the right of the last tab open in your browsing window, and, if you want to revisit earlier sites, click Reopen Closed Tabs (on the bottom left). A list of sites you visited earlier appears. Just click the site you want to display.

If you want to return to your last browsing session, click the Reopen Last Session link, and Internet Explorer automatically opens the web page you were visiting the last time you used the browser.

Using Navigation Tiles

The modeless version of Internet Explorer 10 employs colorful tiles—similar to those you see on the Windows 8 Start screen—to help you move to your favorite and most frequently visited sites. These tiles appear when you swipe up from the bottom of the IE 10 screen or when you tap or click in the address bar.

1. Swipe up from the bottom of the screen. The address bar appears along the bottom and the open page appears as a navigation tile at the top of the display.

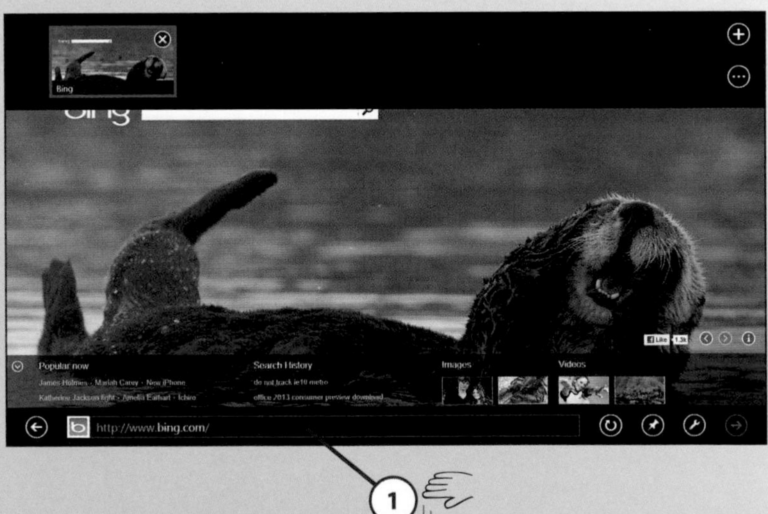

2. Tap or click in the address bar. The screen displays a list of tiles, showing your most recently visited sites. On the left, you see the 10 most frequently visited sites, and on the right, IE 10 lists any sites you've pinned to the Start screen. Note that if you tap in the address bar, the on-screen keyboard will also appear, but if you click in the address bar, only the navigation tiles will be shown.
3. Swipe to the left if necessary to display additional tiles off the right edge of the viewing area.
4. Tap or click the tile of the page you want to display, and the web page opens and fills the screen.

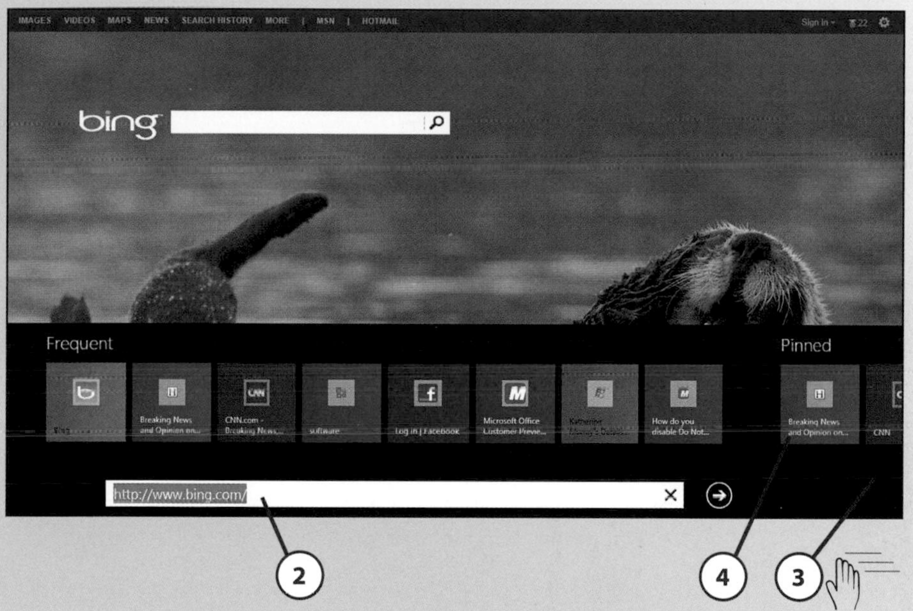

>>>Go Further

NOTIFICATIONS, SCHMOTIFICATIONS

True to the dual personality of the browsing experience in IE 10, notifications are handled in slightly different ways, depending on which version you are using. In the desktop version, messages appear in the new notification bar when you need to make a decision about a utility that is being downloaded or that is attempting to access your computer.

The most important messages you'll see will appear in gold, letting you know that the message has something to do with the safety of your computer.

The modeless version also uses the message bar approach, and the message fades away if you don't click it. If something requires more immediate attention, fly-out messages appear, similar to the update notifications you receive on the Windows 8 Start screen.

Searching for Information

If you're like many of us, you probably spend quite a bit of time with search engines. I typically start my day searching for something or other in Google or Bing. (I'm using Bing more and more lately because I love the photos they use as the search background.) With the version of IE 10 you launch from the Start screen, you can also use the Windows 8 Search charm to find what you're looking for, and the browser will automatically scour the web for you.

With the desktop version of IE 10, you can just tap or click in One Box and type what you're looking for and that functions as a search box too. Both techniques are simple and will get you to the information you're looking for.

Searching in IE 10 from the Start Screen

Searching is fast and easy in IE 10. You don't even need to open the browser if you don't want to! You could display the Search charm, type what you want to find, and tap Internet Explorer. Or, if the browser's already open, just enter the search text in the box and you're good to go.

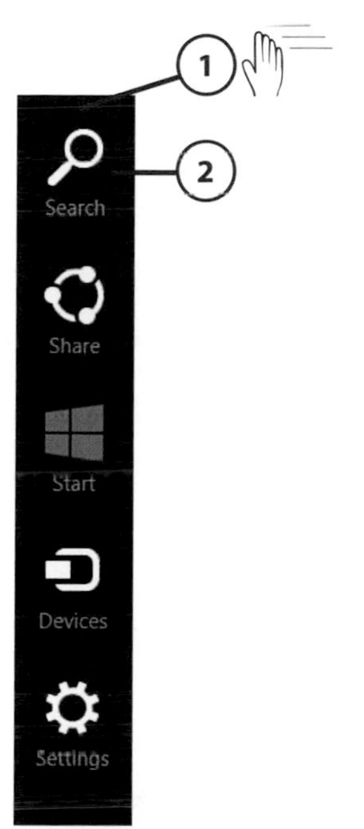

1. In IE 10, swipe in from the right to display the Charms bar.
2. Tap or click Search.
3. Tap or click in the Search box and begin to type a word or phrase that reflects what you're searching for. If you tap, Windows 8 displays the on-screen keyboard. As you type, Windows 8 displays a number of possible search phrases that include the letters you've entered.
4. To choose one of the suggested search phrases, tap or click it.
5. To search for the word or phrase you entered, tap the Search tool. The results appear in a Bing window on the left side of your screen, and you can tap or click a link that you think will have the information you seek.

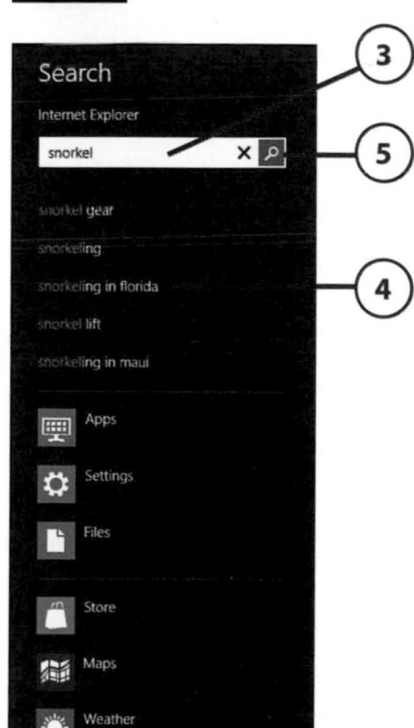

Browse, Shop, It's All the Same

One cool feature that we're sure to see more of in the Windows 8 version of IE 10 is the connection to the Windows Store. When a site you visit also has an app available that you can download to use with Windows 8, you will be able to click or tap the site icon to the left of the address bar to download the app automatically to Windows 8. Pretty slick!

Searching in IE 10 Desktop

In the desktop version of IE 10, you can click in One Box and type a word or phrase that describes what you'd like to find—for example, entering "badminton" brings suggestions like badminton rules, badminton rackets, and badminton history. Bing is the default search engine Microsoft uses to display a list of suggestions related to your search; you can click the suggestion you like to narrow your search and display a page of results with links to web pages you may want to visit.

1. Click or tap in One Box and type a word or phrase describing what you want to find.
2. Your search provider—which is Bing until you tell IE 10 otherwise—displays a list of search results, ranked from those that match your search phrase most closely to those that are not as close a match. Click or tap a link you'd like to view.

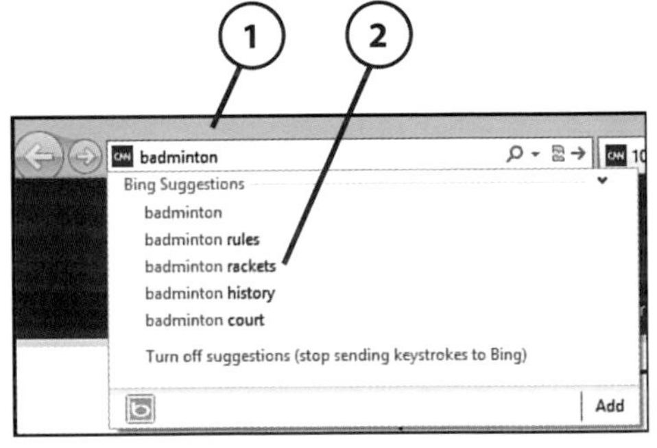

>>>Go Further

TURNING ON SUGGESTIONS

You won't see search suggestions in your IE 10 desktop browser if you haven't turned on suggestions so that Bing can do the searching for you. To turn on this feature, type the word or phrase you're looking for in the One Box at the top of the IE 10 desktop window. In the drop-down area, click or tap Turn On Suggestions (Send Keystrokes to Bing). Bing will then send the search text you entered and you'll see a list of search categories. Tap or click the one that reflects what you're looking for.

You can turn off this feature at any time by clicking or tapping Turn Off Suggestions, which appears at the bottom of the search list.

Adding Search Providers

You can add search provides to the desktop version of IE 10 so that your search goes out far and wide through your favorite search engines. After you type your search word in One Box, click or tap Add at the bottom of the results list. You are taken online to the Internet Explorer Gallery, where you can select an add-on for a search provider you'd like to include with IE 10. Note that even though the Windows 8 version of IE 10 doesn't support add-ons, the desktop version of IE 10 does.

Selecting Your Home Page

The version of IE 10 you launch from the Start screen doesn't give you an option of setting a home page. Rather, the page displayed in the browser by default is the last page you used the browser to view.

You can set a home page in IE 10 for the desktop, however. You'll find the tools you need in the Home Page area of the General tab in the Internet Options dialog box.

1. In the desktop version of IE 10, display the page you want to use as your home page.
2. Click or tap the Tools icon.
3. Select Internet Options.
4. In the Home Page area of the General tab, tap or click Use Current.
5. Select OK. Now whenever you launch IE 10, the browser opens to the web page you specified.

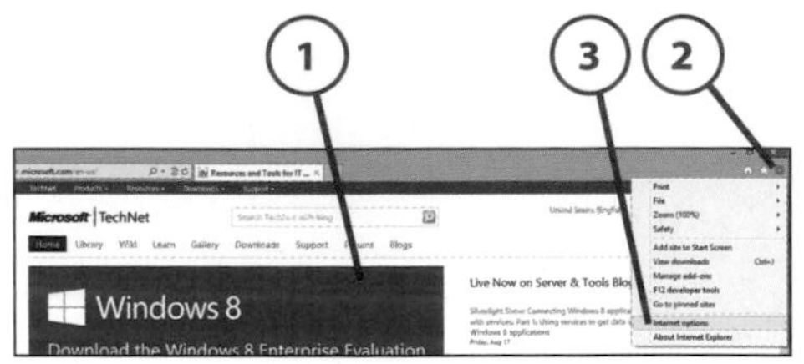

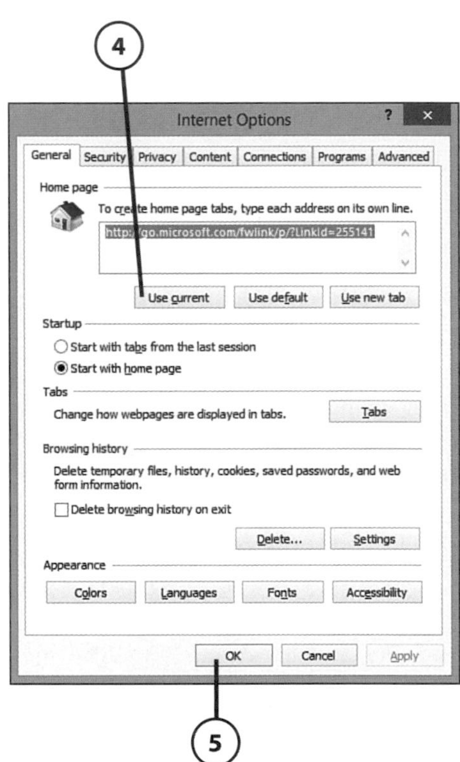

Multiple Home Pages

If you have several sites you like to check first thing in the morning, you can add them all to the Home Page area of the General tab in the Internet Options dialog box in IE 10 for the desktop. Simply put each web address on its own line and then select OK. When you launch the desktop version of IE 10 the next time, all the web pages you entered will open automatically.

Working with Tabs

Once upon a time, web browsers allowed us to have only one web page open at a time, but today we're able to have multiple pages open in different tabs in Internet Explorer. The desktop version of IE 10 shows each individual tab across the top of the browser window, but the Windows 8 version of IE 10 displays tabs as navigation tiles, which are thumbnails of the open pages, displayed at the top of your browser screen.

Using Tabs in IE 10

Tabs in the Windows 8 version of IE 10 don't look like tabs in the desktop version of IE 10. In fact, they don't look like tabs at all. When you want to display the collection of web pages you already have open, you can swipe down from the top of the screen or up from the bottom. You can also press Windows+Z or right-click the mouse to display your IE 10 tabs.

1. Swipe down from the top of the IE 10 browser window. The tab thumbnails appear.
2. To move to a specific tab, tap or click it. The page appears full-screen.
3. To close a tab you no longer want to use, tap or click the close button.
4. To add a tab, click or tap the Add Tab button.

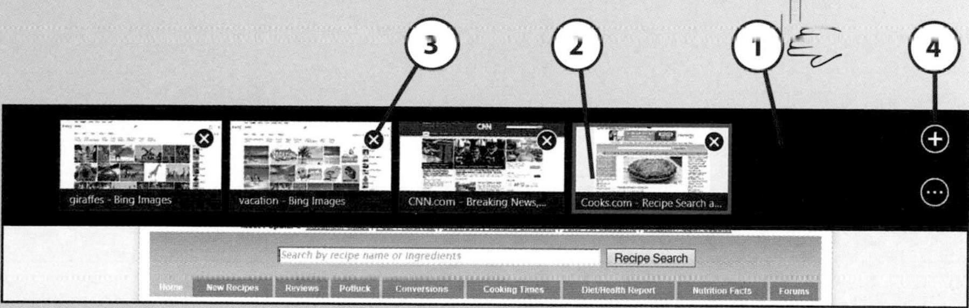

5. To close all tabs except the current one, click or tap the Tab Tools button. A small popup list appears.
6. Tap or click Close Tabs to close the extra tabs.

>>> Go Further

QUIET SURFING WITH INPRIVATE BROWSING

In some cases, you may not want to track your browsing activity for others to see. Perhaps you're shopping for a holiday gift for someone and you don't want him to inadvertently discover it. You can turn on InPrivate Browsing to tell Internet Explorer 10 to skip recording your web activity. This means that the sites you visit won't be available in your browsing history, cookies, form data, temporary Internet files, or in the usernames and passwords Internet Explorer 10 usually keeps.

You can turn on InPrivate Browsing two different ways (surprise, surprise). In the Windows 8 version of IE 10, display the tabs by swiping down from the top of the screen and tap or click the Tab Tools button; then click or tap New InPrivate Tab. If you're using the desktop version of IE 10, tap or click the Tools icon in the upper-right area of the Internet Explorer 10 window. Click or tap Safety, and then select InPrivate Browsing. Internet Explorer 10 opens a new browser session independent of the current one you have been using, and none of your browsing information is stored in the new session. When you're ready to end the InPrivate Browsing session, simply close the browser session.

Opening a New Tab in Desktop IE 10

The process of opening a tab in the desktop version of IE 10 is probably familiar. This enables you to view another web page in addition to the one—or ones—you're already viewing.

1. In the desktop version of IE 10, click or tap the New Tab button to the right of the current tab.

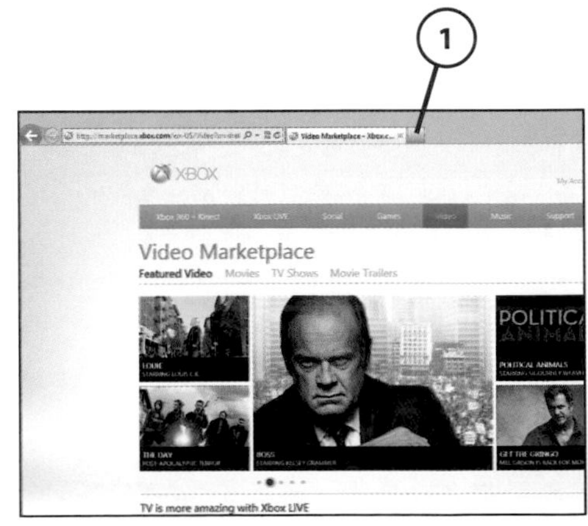

2. In the New Tab page, you can see site panels of the most recently viewed websites you've visited. You can tap or click one of the panels to go to that page.
3. You can also use the One Box to type the web address of the site you want to visit. Alternatively, you can enter a word or phrase and search for the content you want to find.

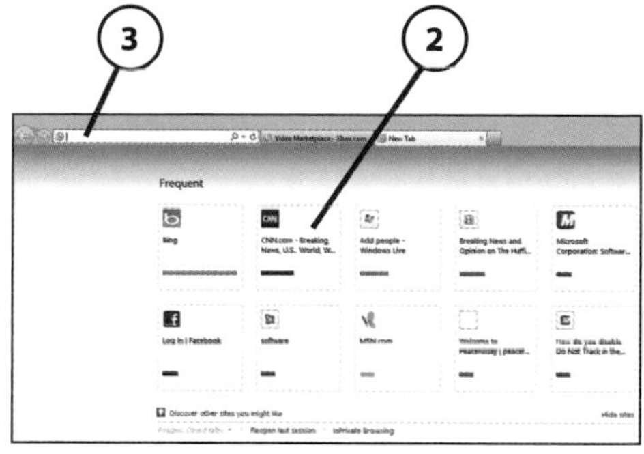

Double-Display Duty

You can view two or more pages at the same time by tapping and holding or clicking a tab and dragging it toward the center of the Internet Explorer 10 window. The page comes "undocked" from the browser window, and you can position it onscreen wherever you want it by tapping and holding or clicking, then dragging the top of the window.

Securing Your Browsing Experience

Internet Explorer 10 is touted as the most secure browser yet from Microsoft, offering all kinds of security technologies, such as SmartScreen, Application Reputation, InPrivate browsing, Tracking Protection, and hang detection and recovery. The Windows 8 version of IE 10 doesn't use add-ons, which can sometimes introduce security risks, although you are still able to use add-ons with the desktop version of IE 10.

One new security feature in IE 10 is Enhanced Protected mode, which isolates the website content that appears in each tab. Now InPrivate browsing is also segregated per tab, so your browsing is more secure and private than ever.

>>>Go Further

WHAT'S ALL THE FUSS ABOUT DO NOT TRACK?

Another security measure included with Windows 8 is the Do Not Track feature, which was initially enabled by default (but was disabled in the release version of Windows 8). Do Not Track is a setting that tells web pages you visit that you have opted not to have your browsing habits recorded. This is a good thing for consumer privacy (and the U.S. administration is pushing for this type of safeguard to enhance user safety), but online advertisers who sell ads based on traffic statistics and user browsing data are up in arms about the possibility.

To turn on the Do Not Track feature in your version of Internet Explorer 10, click or tap Tools in IE 10 desktop, choose Internet Options, and choose the Advanced tab. Scroll down to the Security area and click to add a checkmark to the Always Send Do Not Track Header checkbox. Click OK. After you make the change, you'll need to restart your computer to put the new setting into effect. But you'll have the comfort of knowing that at least your data isn't helping to sell goods to unsuspecting consumers.

Deleting Cookies

It's a good idea in the desktop version of IE 10 to regularly clean off the cookies that have accumulated on your computer, both to keep their drain on your computer's memory low and to weed out any potentially sneaky cookies that could be sending information back to the site that placed them.

1. In the desktop version of IE 10, tap or click Tools. The Tools list appears.
2. Point to Safety.
3. Select Delete Browsing History. The Delete Browsing History dialog box appears.

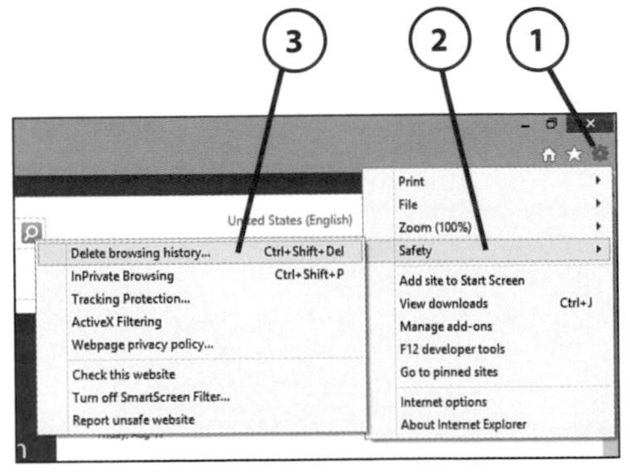

4. The first item in the dialog box, Preserve Favorites Website Data, retains information—cookies and all—related to sites that you have marked as Favorites. In most cases, you should leave this item selected.
5. Review the list of checked and unchecked items. The checked items are deleted; the unchecked items are not. Change the items as needed to suit your preference. You may, for example, want to delete all the form data you have entered in online forms; if so, check the Form Data check box.
6. Click or tap Delete to delete the cookies and other information you've selected.

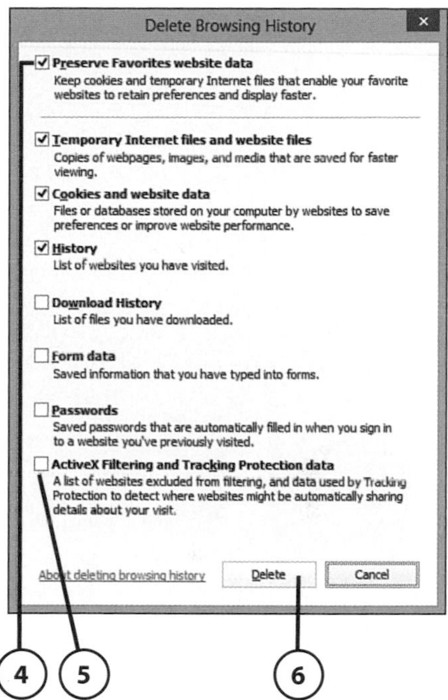

Delete Browsing History
Preserve Favorites website data
Keep cookies and temporary Internet files that enable your favorite websites to retain preferences and display faster.
Temporary Internet files and website files
Copies of webpages, images, and media that are saved for faster viewing.
Cookies and website data
Files or databases stored on your computer by websites to save preferences or improve website performance.
History
List of websites you have visited.
Download History
List of files you have downloaded.
Form data
Saved information that you have typed into forms.
Passwords
Saved passwords that are automatically filled in when you sign in to a website you've previously visited.
ActiveX Filtering and Tracking Protection data
A list of websites excluded from filtering, and data used by Tracking Protection to detect where websites might be automatically sharing details about your visit.
About deleting browsing history
Delete
Cancel
4
5
6

>>>Go Further

SO WHAT ARE COOKIES, ANYWAY?

The websites you visit want you to come back (and buy something—from them or one of their advertisers), so they want you to have a personalized experience on their site. This means they want to make visiting their site a pleasant experience for you, so they save information about your time on the site—your preferences, your username and password, if you created them—in what's known as a cookie, and the cookie is stored on your computer. Then, whenever you return to that site, your preferences are there to personalize your web experience with the items you said you like. Pretty clever, right?

But some cookies can do more than save your preferences. They may also track your web activities, and that borders on infringing upon your privacy. In Internet Explorer 10, you can control the cookies stored on your computer by deleting them, limiting them, or blocking all of them.

Gather your friends and family into one place in the People app

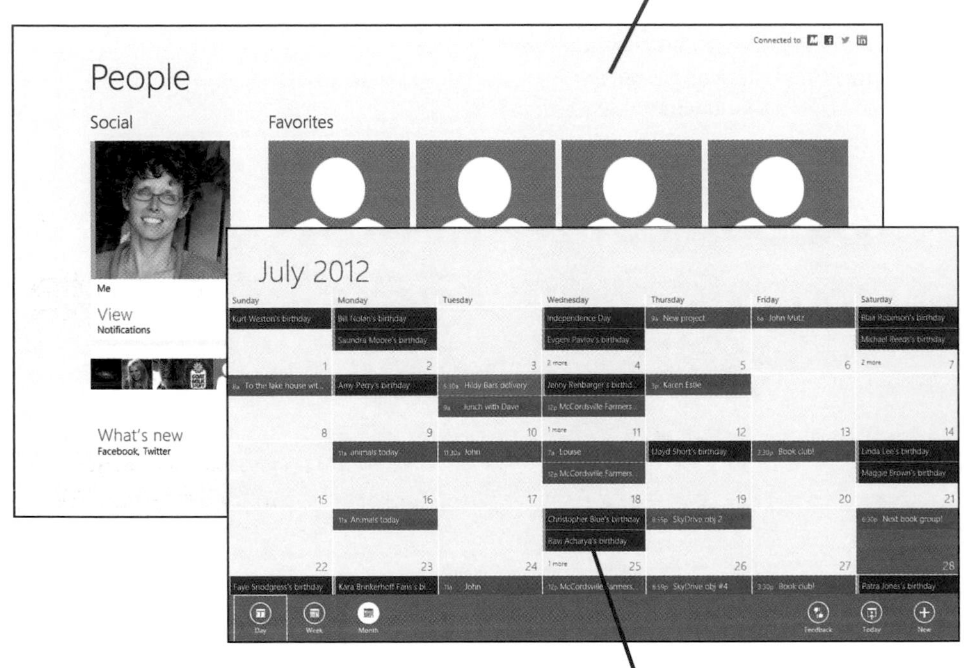

Use the Calendar app to see all your important dates at a glance

In this chapter, you learn to use the People app and the Mail, Calendar, and Messaging apps to keep your connection strong with these tasks:

- → Getting social with the People app
- → Staying in touch through email
- → Keeping your dates straight with the Calendar app
- → Messaging: When you need instant contact

Connect and Communicate with Windows 8

Once upon a time, we used our computers to accomplish functional but—well, let's face it—boring things. We wrote letters. We crunched numbers. We typed data into a form.

Ho hum.

And then social media appeared on the scene. Suddenly we are in touch with friends, family, and colleagues. We can see pictures, watch video, listen to music, and post on each other's pages. Oh, and don't forget "liking" someone's post. This has become a big part of our social culture, and Windows 8 incorporates it as the People app so that it becomes a normal part of our everyday communication.

The app you'll use for email has also been simplified and streamlined in Windows 8. The contacts you add in the People hub are available to you both as you email others and as you send instant messages to contacts using the Messaging app. This chapter spotlights ways you can stay in touch with others using the apps included in Windows 8.

Getting Social with the People App

The People app brings together all your contacts from your various social media accounts and displays them all in one lovely alphabetical list, ready for you to tap or click to contact. You can find out what's going on with a specific contact, get a news feed of status updates, and view or update your own social media information.

Getting Started with the People App

You'll find the People app toward the left of the Windows 8 Start screen. If you've moved your tiles around, as described in Chapter 3, "Beginning with the Start Screen," you may have to do a little scrolling to find your People app. Look for the app with the icon showing two people in the bottom-left corner.

1. On the Windows 8 Start screen, tap the People app.

2. Tap or click Me to display your profile information and recent updates.
3. Click or tap View Notifications to see how others have interacted with your posts and updates.

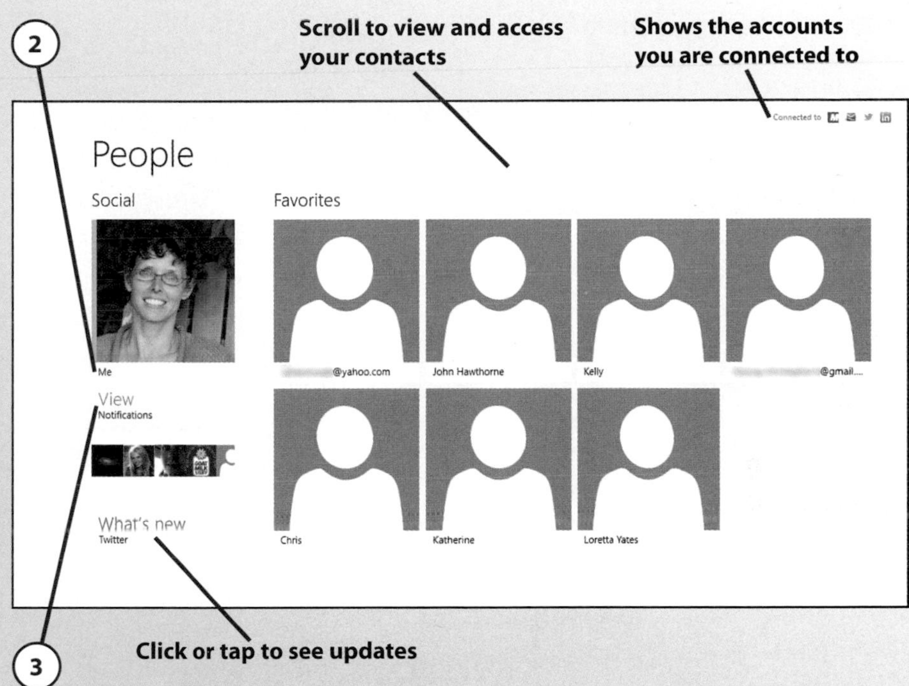

4. Swipe up from the bottom of the screen to display the apps bar.
5. Click or tap Edit. Your Microsoft Account profile opens, and you can make a variety of changes that will then be reflected in your People app.

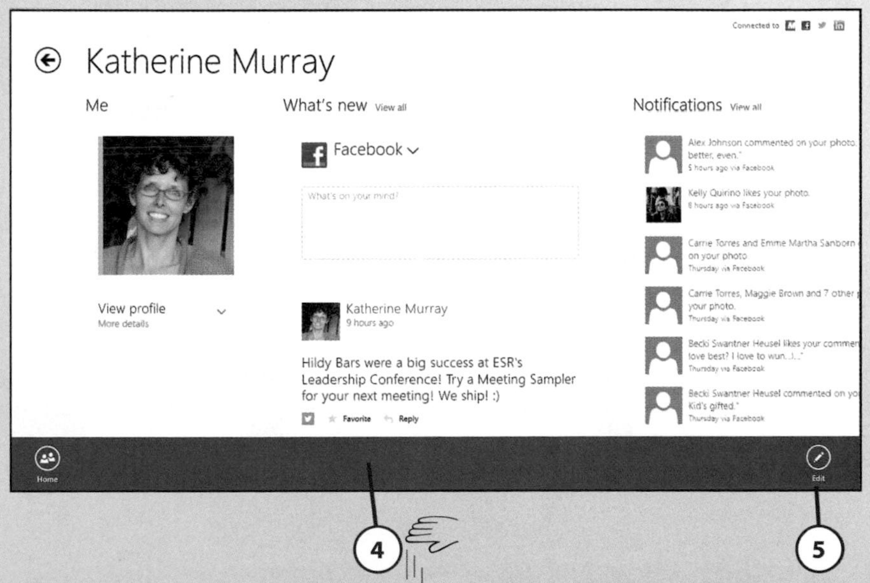

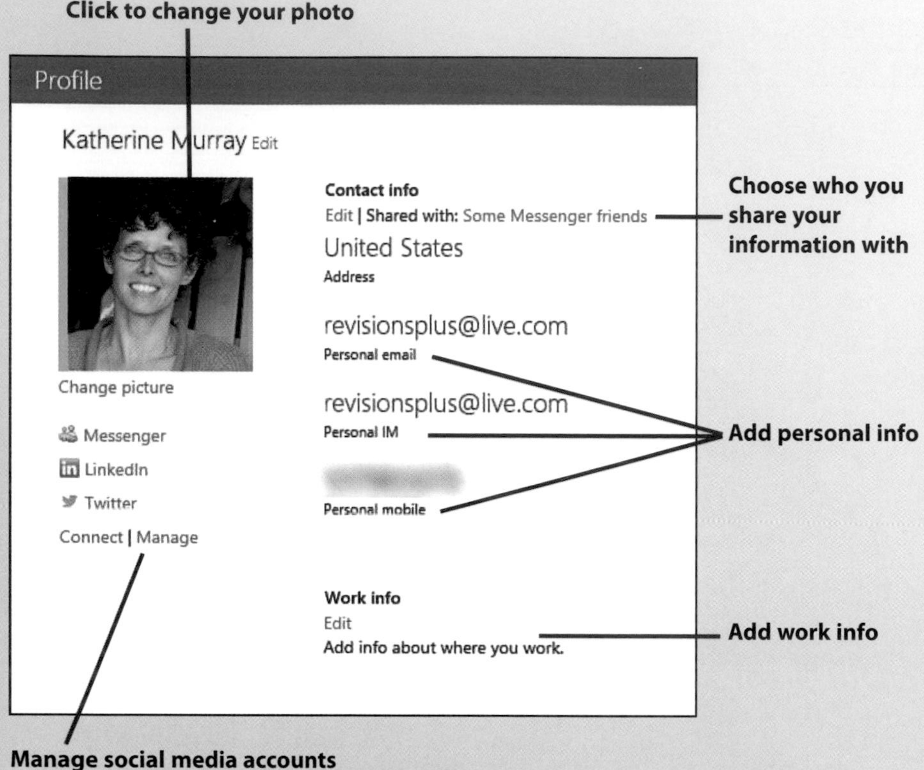

Updating Your Profile Info

What you post in your profile—and who you share it with—is your call. Your social media accounts and Windows 8 don't need access to your contact information, location, or interests in order to function properly. You can set the permissions on your profile so that it can be seen by only you, some friends, all friends, your friends and *their* friends, or everyone. To change the permissions on your profile, click the link to the right of Shared With in your profile information online.

Connecting Your Social Media Accounts

Your first step involves telling Windows 8 where to find the various social media accounts you want to include in the People app.

1. In the People app, tap or click the Connected To line in the top-right corner of the People app. The Accounts panel opens, showing your current account connections.
2. Click the Add an Account link.
3. In the Add an Account area, tap the account you'd like to connect to your People app.

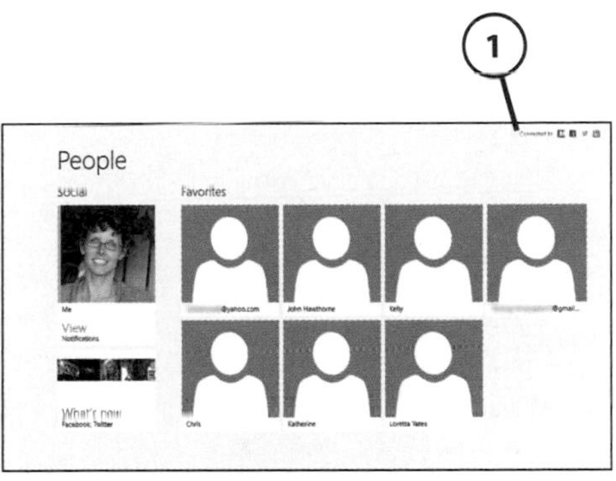

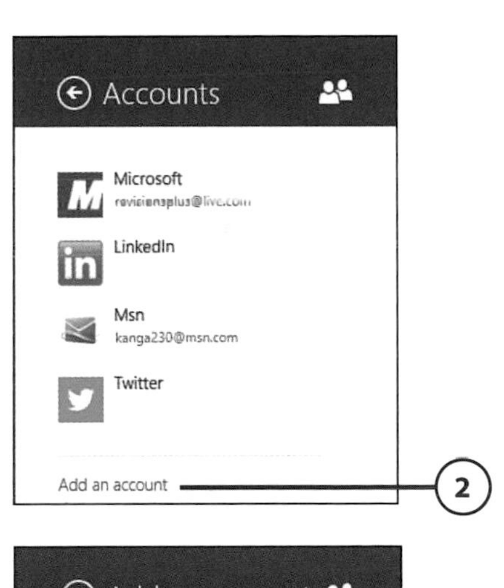

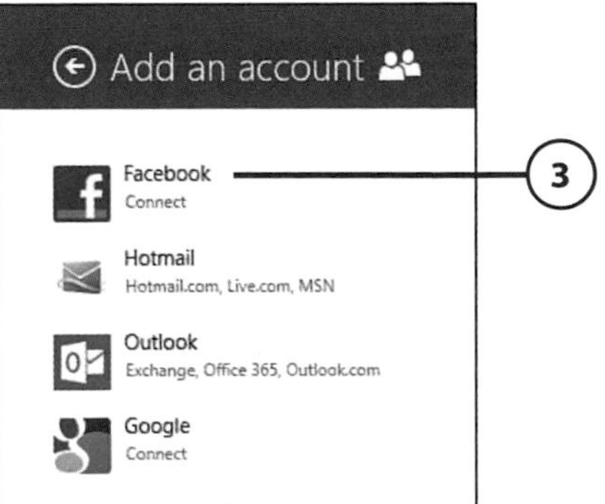

4. Click or tap Connect.
5. Enter your email address.
6. Type your password.
7. Click or tap Keep Me Logged In so that you won't need to enter login information again.
8. Tap or click Log In. Windows 8 makes the connection to your social media account.

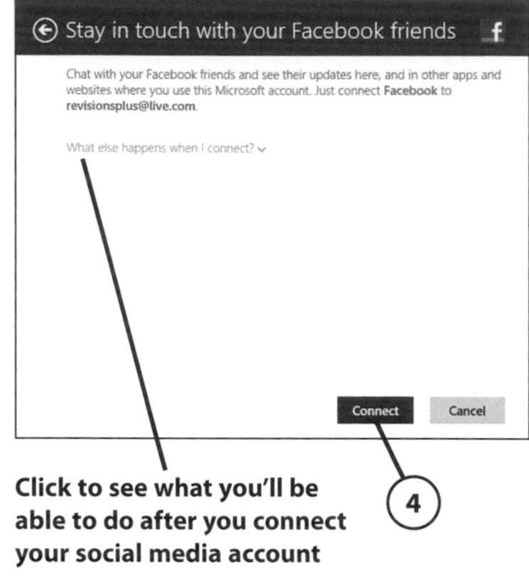

Click to see what you'll be able to do after you connect your social media account

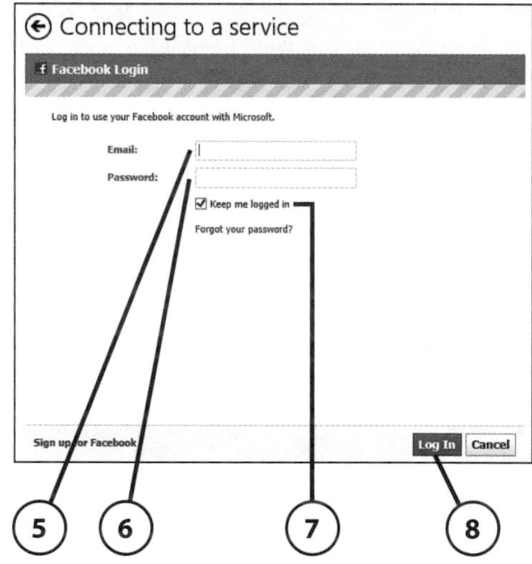

Vive la Difference

Depending on the account you choose to add to your People app, the process for connecting it to Windows 8 may be slightly different. You will be asked for your email address or login and password, and you may be asked to confirm that you're giving permission for this app to access your computer. In any case, the process is simple, and you should be up and running in just a matter of minutes.

9. Click Done to finish adding the account. You can repeat the process for as many social media accounts as you'd like to add.

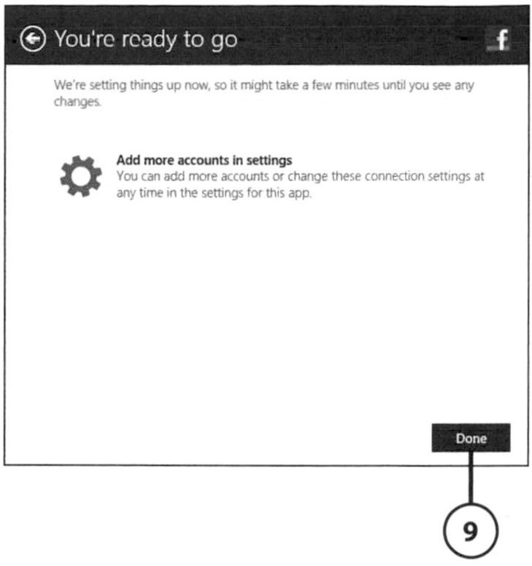

Getting a New Facebook Account

If you don't currently have a Facebook account, you can create one at this point. Click or tap the Sign Up for Facebook link at the bottom of the Connecting to a Service screen. Facebook will walk you through the process of creating a new account that you can link to your People app.

>>>Go Further

WHAT WILL I BE ABLE TO SEE?

Different social media apps allow you to do different types of things in the People app (they're all somewhat different, after all). Here's a quick list of what you'll be able to do with some of the main social media apps in Windows 8:

- When you connect Facebook, you'll be able to chat with your Facebook friends from within Windows 8, update your Facebook status, and share documents and photos with your Facebook friends. You'll also be able to view in Windows 8 the photos you upload to your Facebook account.
- When you connect Twitter, you'll be able to post new tweets, read tweets from your timeline as you would in Twitter, view the people you follow, choose to follow new people, and update your Twitter profile. You won't be able to see any direct messages you receive or view your Twitter password.
- With LinkedIn, you'll be able to update your LinkedIn status, share documents and photos, and view your LinkedIn contacts.

You can also add accounts from Hotmail, Outlook, and Google to your People app to make the most of all your online contacts and reach all your friends and family through a single, organized app.

Viewing Status Updates

The great thing about the People app is that it can give you up-to-the-minute updates on friends and family no matter which social media site they may be using. This means you can see Facebook updates, tweets, and more, all in one handy display.

1. Display the People app, and tap or click What's New. The updates are listed with the most recent updates on the left.
2. Scroll to the left to display status updates from all your connected social media accounts.
3. Click or tap an update you want to read more about.

4. Tap or click to like the post.
5. Click or tap Add a Comment to enter a comment and then press Enter.

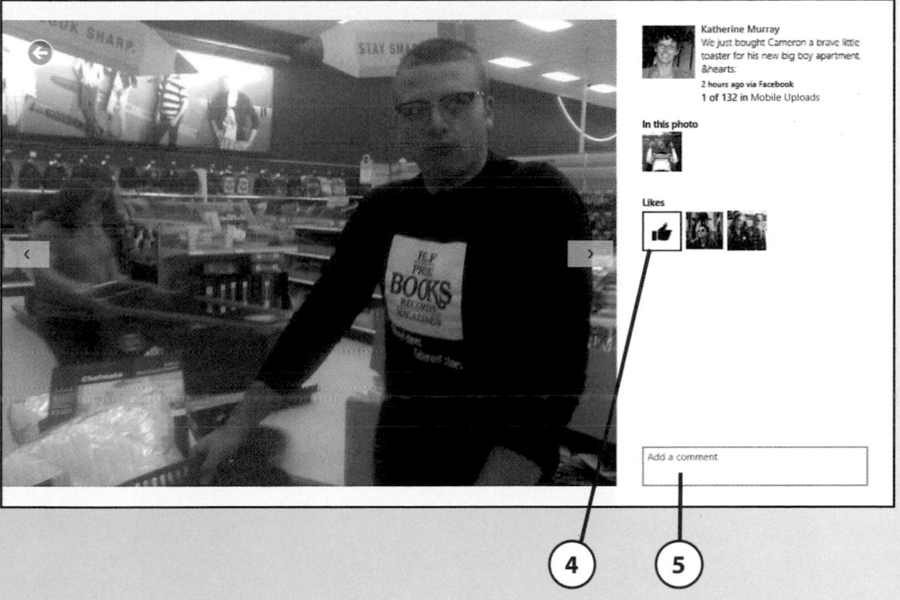

Responding to Posts, Tweets, and More

The actions that are available to you after you click or tap a social media update one of your contacts have posted will depend, of course, on the social media account they're using. If you tap an update from Facebook, you can Like or comment on the post. If you tap an update from Twitter, you can add it to your Favorites, retweet it, or respond to the tweet.

It's Not All Good

TOO MANY UPDATES!

If you find yourself drowning in status updates and you're not really seeing the ones you want to see, you can have the People app filter the updates for you. Swipe up from the bottom of the screen (or right-click along the bottom) to display the apps bar. Tap Filter on the far-right side of the bar. You can then choose the social media account you want to see, which limits the number of updates displayed in the What's New screen.

Adding a New Contact

You can easily add a new contact to the People app, which then makes that person available in your Mail app or the Messaging app.

1. Launch the People app.
2. Swipe up from the bottom or right-click near the bottom of the screen. The apps bar appears.
3. Tap or click New.

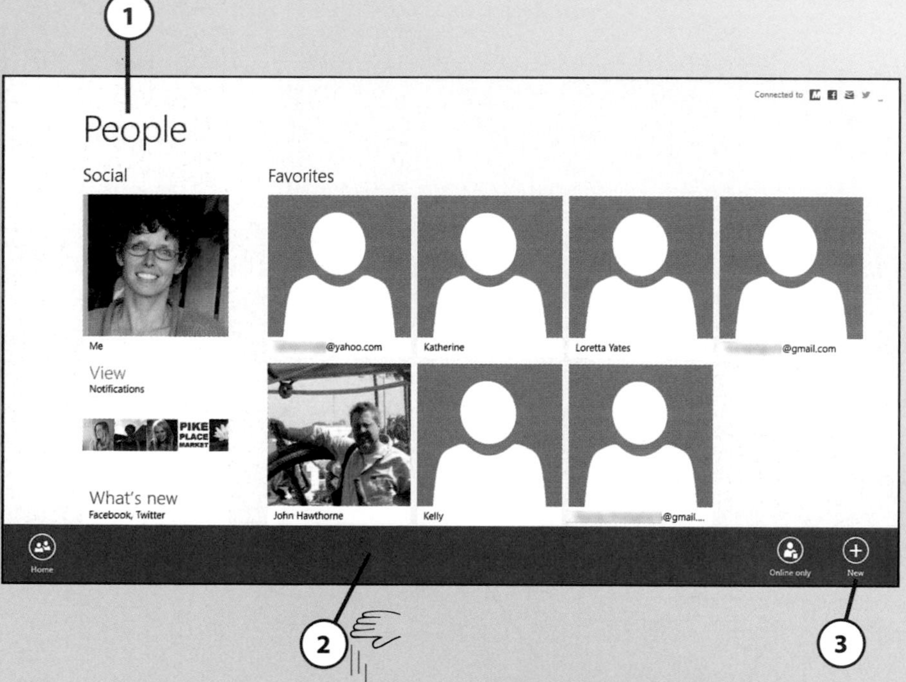

4. Choose the account for the contact by clicking or tapping the arrow and selecting your choice.
5. Enter the first name and last name of the contact.
6. If you want to add additional information—like the phonetic spelling of the first name—tap or click the Name control to see a list of fields you can add.
7. Enter the email address for the new contact.
8. Add Address information if you like.

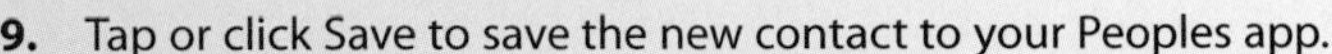

9. Tap or click Save to save the new contact to your Peoples app.

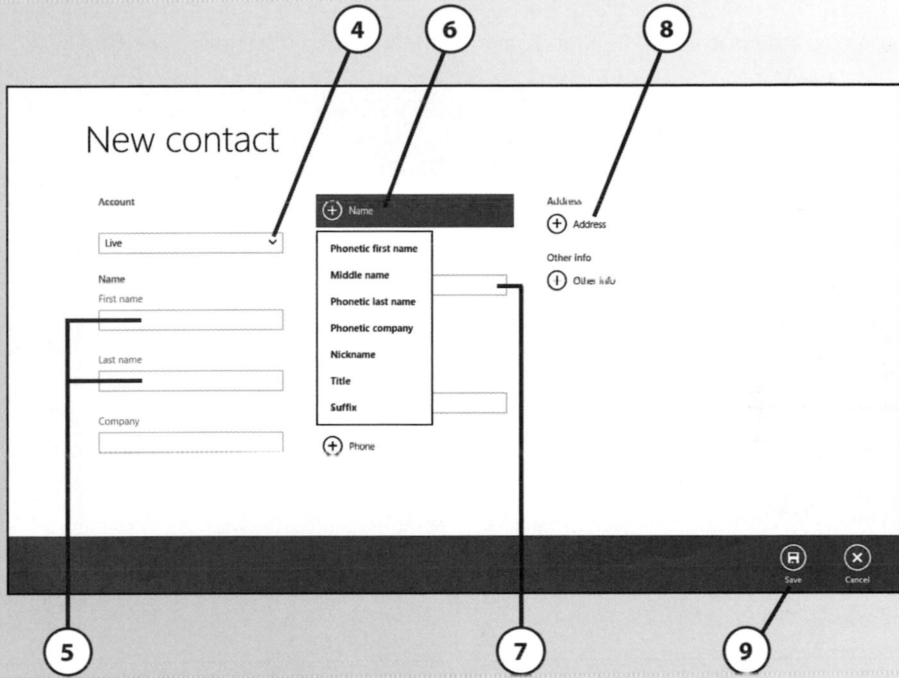

Searching for a Contact

If you're having a hard time finding someone in your contact list by scrolling through the list (that's part of the price you pay for being so popular), you can easily search for the contact in the People app.

1. Launch the People app on your Windows 8 Start screen.
2. Type the first name of the person you want to find. The Search panel appears and the letters you type are in the search box. Tap or click Search.
3. Choose the contact in the results list you were looking for.

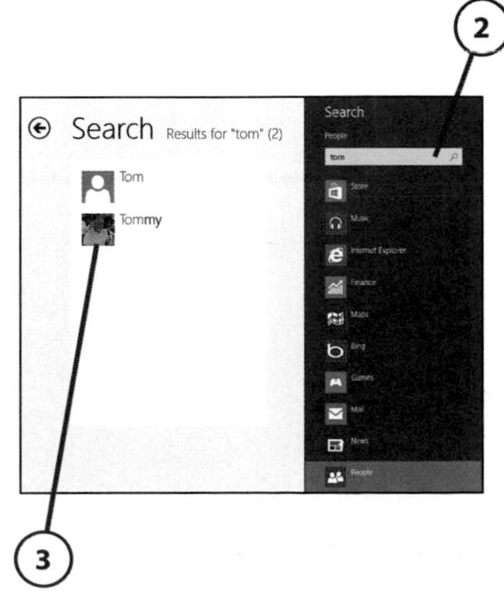

Staying in Touch Through Email

Email is now included as a part of your operating system, thanks to the Mail app in Windows 8. The Mail app is simplified and straightforward, and you can read, respond, and manage your email easily, whether you're using a touch-based system or the mouse and keyboard to get around.

Adding an Email Account

First, you need to let Windows 8 know about your email account so that you can download and respond to the messages you receive. When you first installed and launched Windows 8, Windows asked you for your Microsoft Account (formerly called your Windows Live ID), so chances are that at least that web-based email account is already activated in the Mail hub. You can add other accounts too, so that you receive the messages that really matter on your Windows 8 system, whether you're sitting in your office or out and about in the world.

1. Tap Mail in the Windows 8 Start screen to display the Mail app.
2. Swipe in from the right or move the mouse to the right side of the screen to display the Charms bar.
3. Tap or click Settings.

4. Click or tap Accounts.
5. Tap or click Add an Account.
6. Click or tap the account type you want to add.
7. Enter your email address.
8. Type your password.
9. Click Connect.

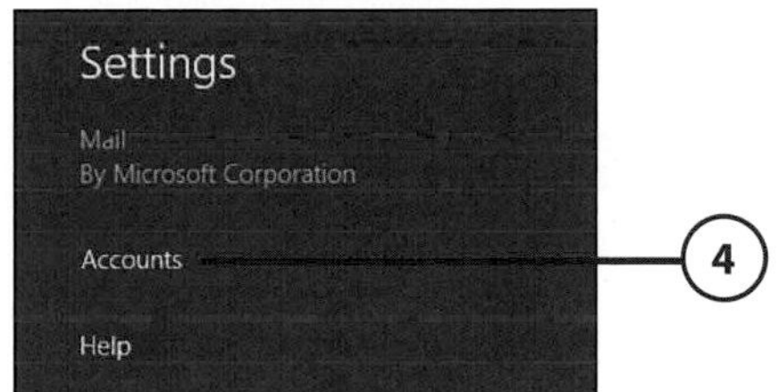

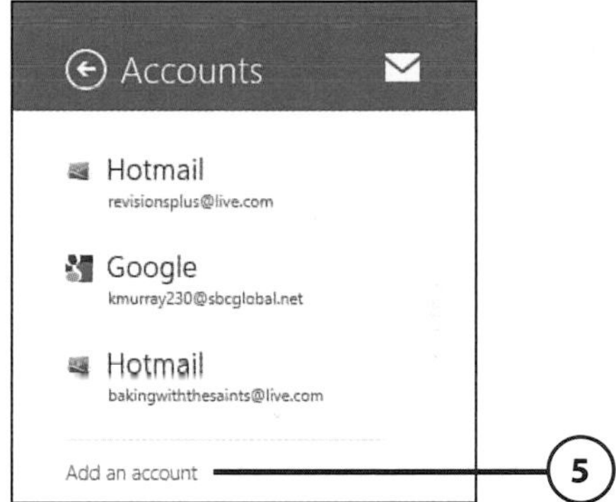

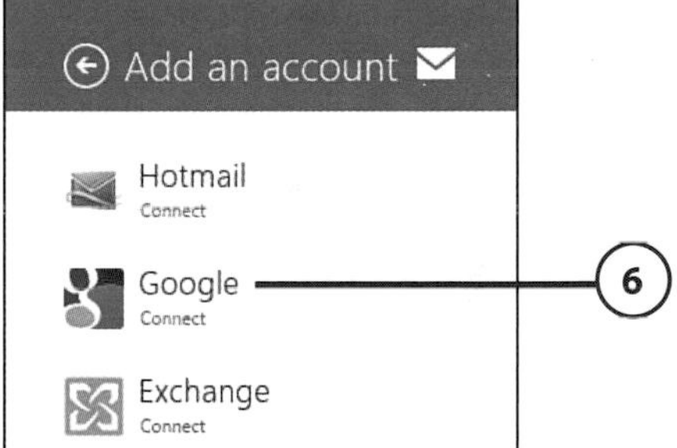

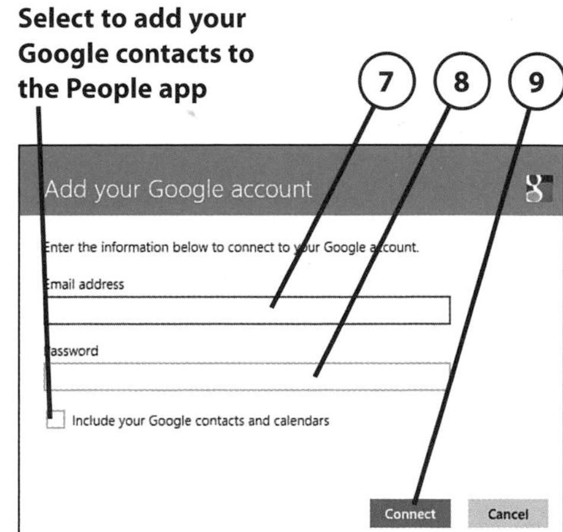

>>>Go Further

CHANGING ACCOUNT SETTINGS

You can tweak the settings of your email account to specify how often you want to check for new content, what types of information you want to download, and whether the account shows notifications on your Windows 8 desktop or Lock screen. You can also remove the account if you like.

Display the Mail app window and tap the account you want to modify in the left column of the Mail window. Swipe in or click the right side of the screen to display the Charms bar; tap Settings. Tap or click Accounts, and then tap the account you want to change. You can modify the account name, let Windows 8 know when you want to download content, and choose the items you want to sync (you can choose Sync, Contacts, or Calendar). You can change notifications by sliding the Show Notifications for This Account from Off to On.

When you want to return to the Mail app, simply click outside the settings area and it closes.

Checking Out the Mail Window

The Mail app presents a streamlined, easy-to-navigate screen that enables you to review your mail quickly, click the message you want to read through, organize your mail into folders, and respond easily to the message at hand.

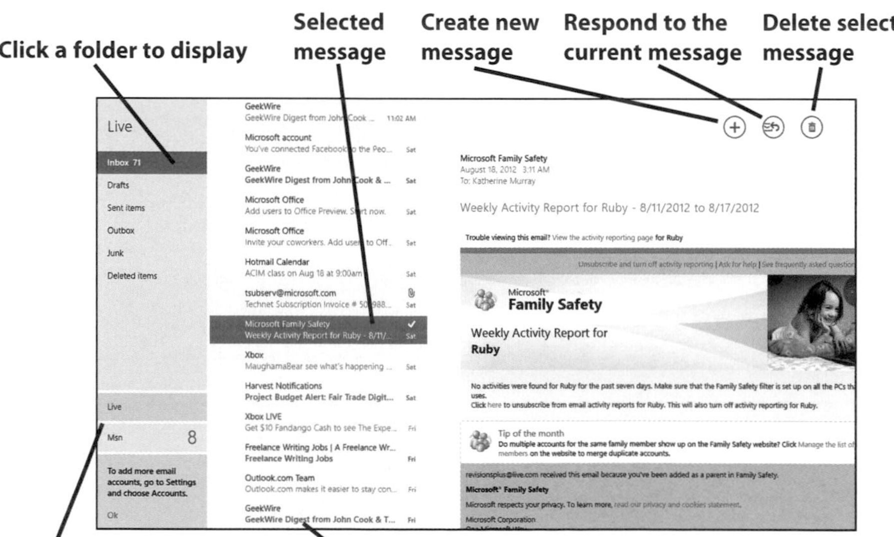

Composing an Email Message

When you're ready to create a new email message, the task is simple. Tap or click the New icon in the upper-right corner of the Mail window, and a blank message opens. You can then choose the contact you want to send the message to, add a subject line, and compose the message you want to send. You can also attach files, insert pictures, and more. Here's how:

1. In the Mail app window, tap or click New.

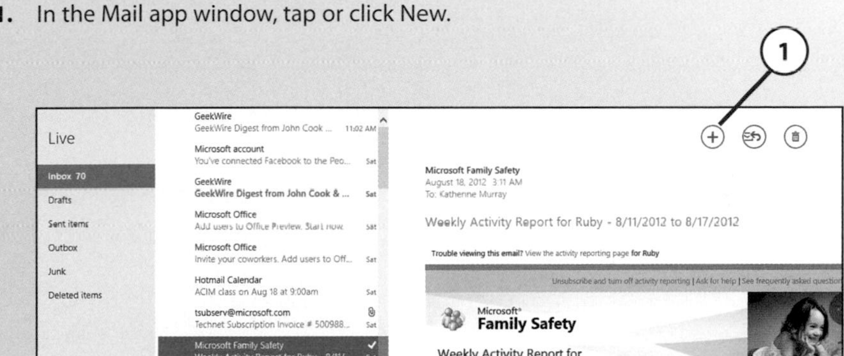

2. Click or tap in the To box and begin to type the contact's name. The names of individuals in your People app appear; you can click to select the name you want to use.
3. You can also click the + sign at the end of the box to display the People app so that you can click the contact you want and click Add to add the contact address to the To line.
4. Click in the Add a Subject line and type a message subject.
5. Click in the message area and type your message.
6. Click Show More to add a blind copy line or set the priority of the message.
7. Click Send to send the message.
8. Or, click Close to delete the message without sending it.

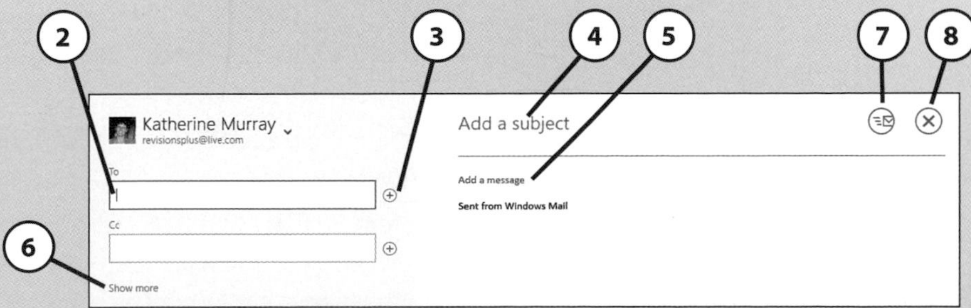

Attaching a File to a Message

If you need to send along a document, picture, or other file with the email message you're sending, you can add it as an attachment using a tool in the apps bar.

1. Create your email message as normal.
2. Swipe up from the bottom of the screen.
3. Tap or click Attachments.
4. Navigate to the folder containing the file you want to attach.
5. Select the file.
6. Click or tap Attach.
7. Click Send to send the message.

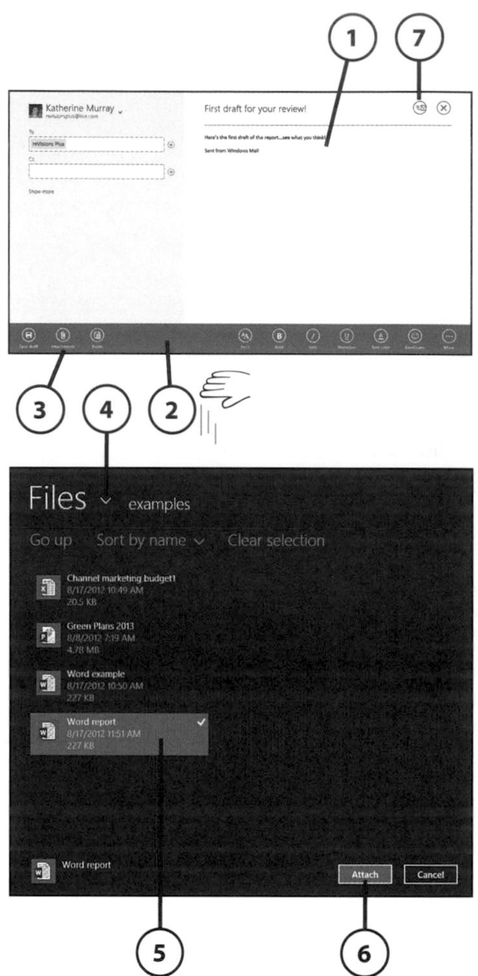

Organizing Your Email

If you're like most of us, you receive dozens—if not hundreds—of messages each day that you have to decide what to do with. Some may be junk mail; others may be notices that don't really apply to you. Others are messages you need to keep—perhaps notes about upcoming meetings, or deadlines, or fun plans. You can organize your mail by filing it away in folders you create, or you can pin a message to your task list so you'll remember to follow-up on it sooner rather than later.

1. In the Mail app, tap the message you want to move.
2. Swipe up or right-click the bottom of the screen.
3. Tap or click Move.

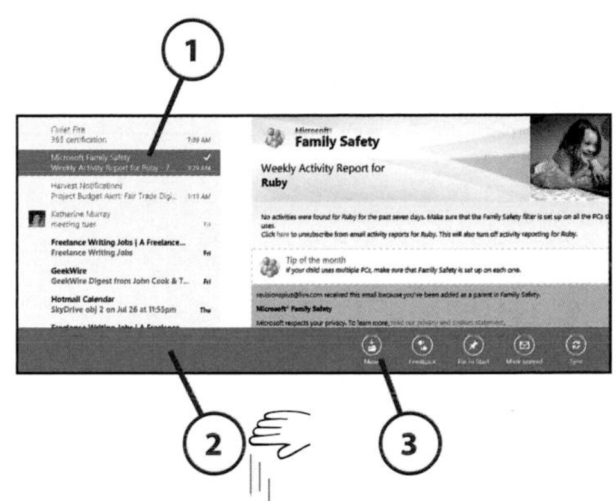

Marking Mail as Junk

It's just part of emailing today—you are going to get junk mail. To get rid of the junk mail you receive, select the message, swipe up from the bottom of the Mail window, and tap or click Move. The Inbox display changes and the folders on the left are highlighted. Tap or click Junk and the mail you selected moves to that folder.

Keeping Your Dates Straight with the Calendar App

Whether you're using your desktop PC or you're zooming around the countryside with your tablet, you need to know when your appointments are, who they're with, where you need to be, and when. The Windows 8 Calendar app can give you all that information, not only when you tap or click the app to open it on your screen, but anytime you glance at your Windows 8 computer. Because the Calendar app offers live notifications, you can have Windows 8 display your appointments on the Lock screen of your computer, so you don't even have to log in to see what's next in your day.

Checking Today's Appointments

The first place you'll see your calendar information is on the Lock screen of your computer. You'll also notice the live tile updates on the Calendar app tile on the Start screen. You can tap the Calendar app to display your calendar, which opens by default in monthly view.

1. On the Windows 8 Start screen, tap or click the Calendar app.

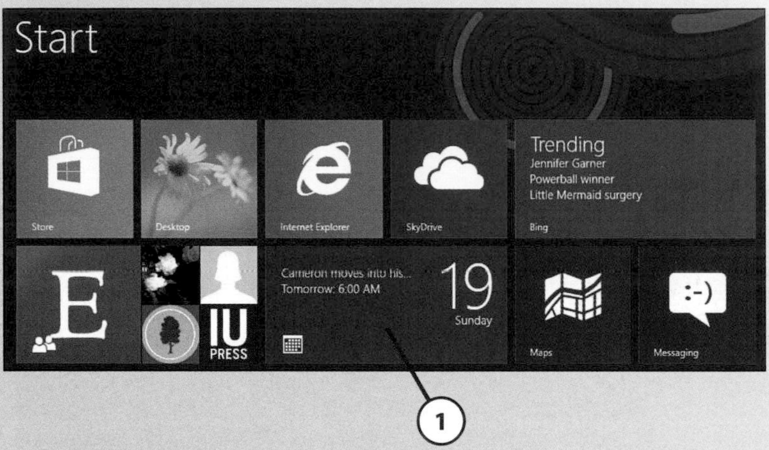

2. Swipe up from the bottom of the screen or right-click toward the bottom of the screen to display the apps bar.
3. Tap Day to switch the view to show the current day, as well as tomorrow.

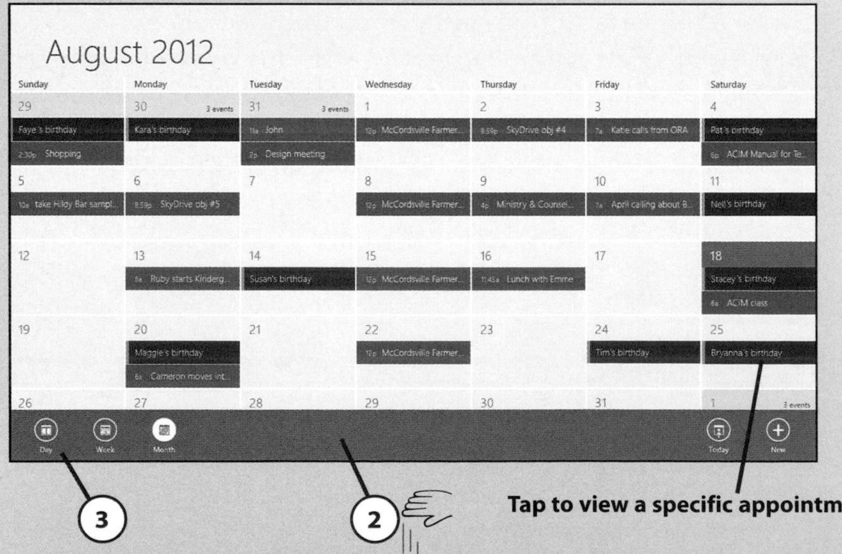

4. Scroll up to review appointments later in the day.
5. Tap to review a specific appointment.

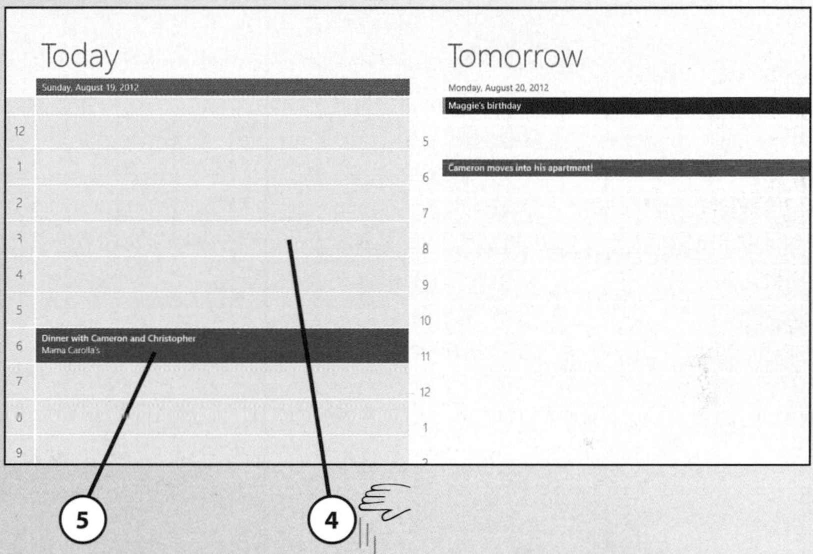

Adding a New Appointment

Creating a new appointment takes just a couple of taps or clicks and a little typing. You swipe up to display the apps bar and tap or click New, and then enter the information relevant to the appointment you're noting.

1. In the Calendar app, swipe up to display the apps bar.
2. Tap New. A blank appointment form opens so that you can enter information about the appointment.

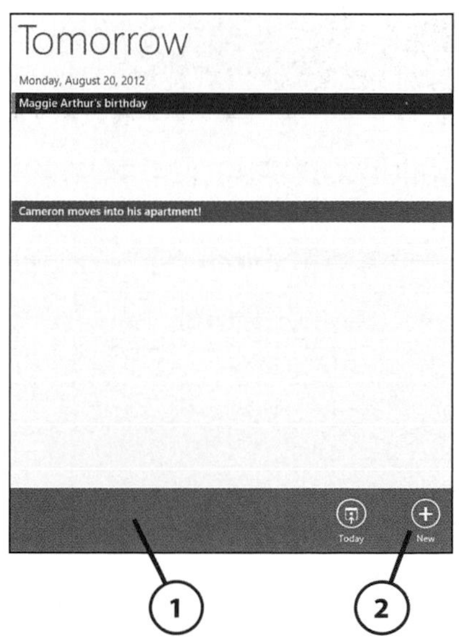

3. Type a title for the appointment.
4. Enter a message describing the appointment.
5. Choose the date for the appointment.
6. Select the start time.
7. Choose the duration of the appointment.
8. Enter the location where it will be held.
9. Choose the calendar on which you want to save the appointment.
10. Tap or click Save.

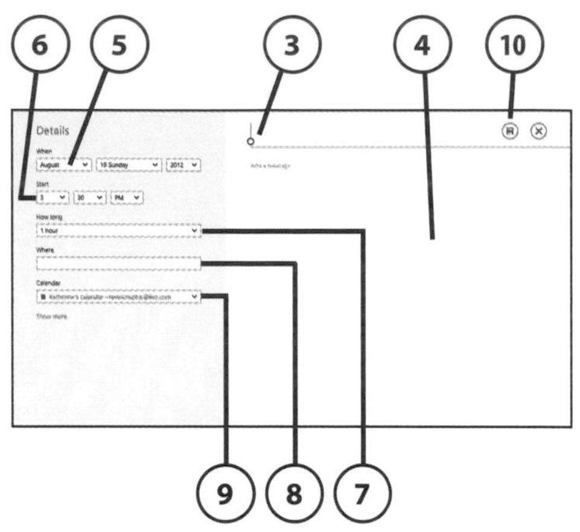

Getting Specific with It

Click or tap Show More if you want to enter additional details about your appointment. For example, you can set the appointment to recur, choose when you want to receive reminders, and invite people to the event.

Making an Appointment Private

If you want to make sure that an appointment doesn't show up on a shared or public calendar, scroll down and click the Private checkbox at the bottom of the left panel in the new appointment screen. You'll be able to see the appointment in your calendar, but others who have permission to view your calendar will not see it.

>>>Go Further

INVITING OTHERS TO YOUR SHINDIG

While you're filling in the details for your new appointment, you can invite others to participate. In the panel on the left side of the appointment window, tap or click in the Who box, and type the email addresses of the people you'd like to invite.

After you're finished filling out the appointment form, tap Send to send the invitation to everyone involved. Each person receives an invitation with Accept, Tentative, Decline, Propose New Time, and Respond at the top so that they can take immediate action in response to your invitation.

Messaging: When You Need Instant Contact

In the past, we had the means to send instant messages from Windows if we wanted to download and install Windows Live Messenger as an extra utility. But now, Messaging is built right into Windows and is present as an app on the Start screen.

A Quick Look at the Messenger Window

When you first launch Messenger, you'll see the list of conversations you've already had on the left side of your screen. The center column shows the flow of the selected conversation, and the column on the right shows your profile picture and gives your status (online or offline).

Following the Conversation

You can read through those conversations by tapping the one you want to view. If you want to continue that conversation and send another message, tap or click in the message box at the bottom of the screen.

1. In the Windows 8 Start screen, tap or click Messaging.

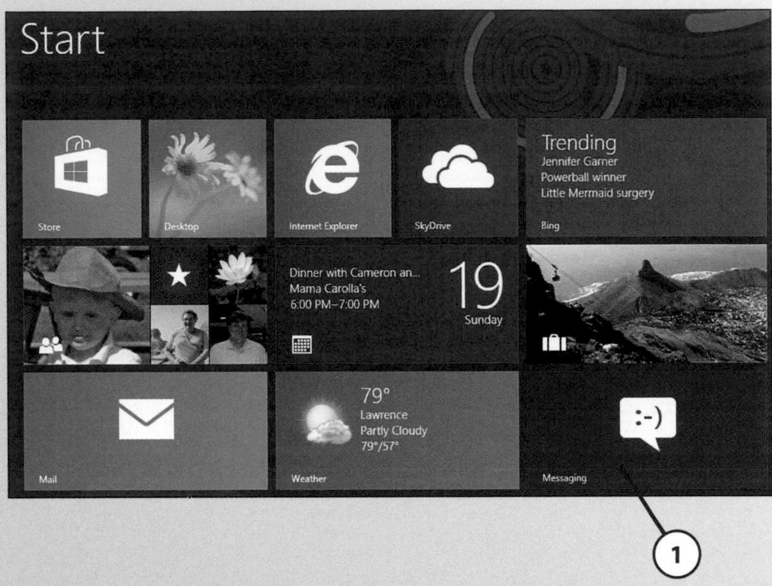

2. Tap the conversation you'd like to continue.
3. Review the message you received most recently.
4. Tap or click in the message box and type your message. You can send the message by pressing Enter.

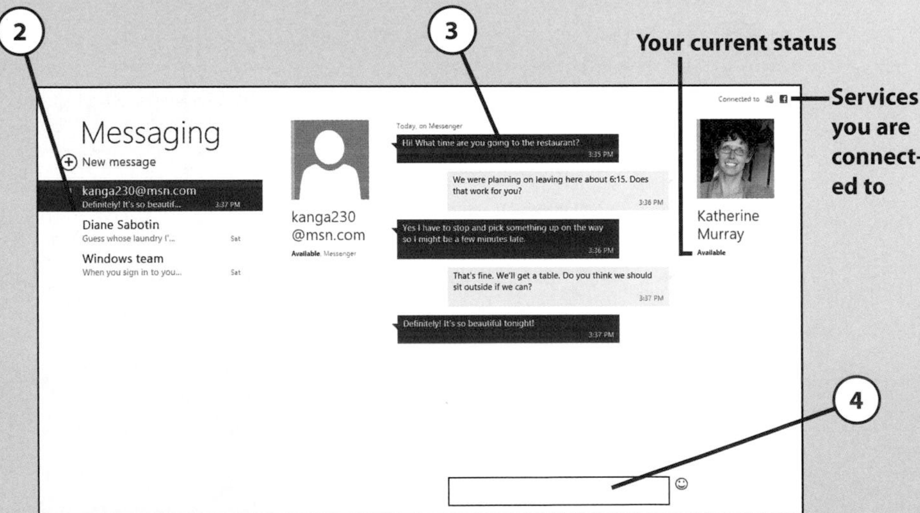

Creating a New Instant Message

When you want to send a new instant message to a friend or family member, you click or tap New Message in the upper-left corner of the Messaging window. You can then choose the person you want to send a message to from your contacts in the People app. Scroll to the person you want to select, tap their contact info, and tap or click Select. The contact is added to the list of contacts on the left.

1. In the Messaging window, tap or click New Message. The People app appears.
2. Tap or click the person you want to send an Instant message to.
3. Click or tap Choose.

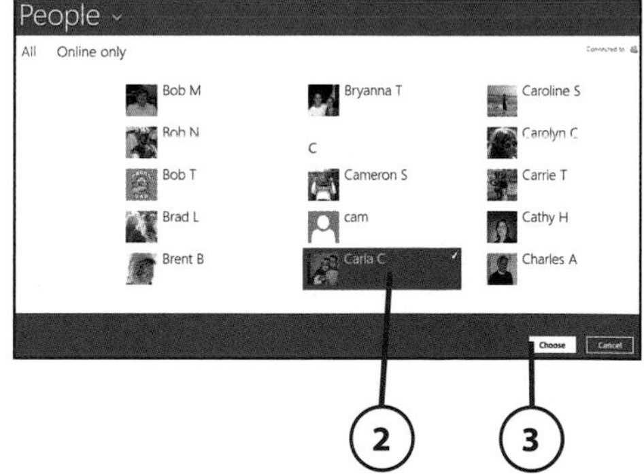

4. Enter the text you'd like to send.
5. If you want to send an emoticon, tap or click the icon to the right of the text box.
6. Tap or click the emoticon you'd like to add to your note, and press Enter to send.

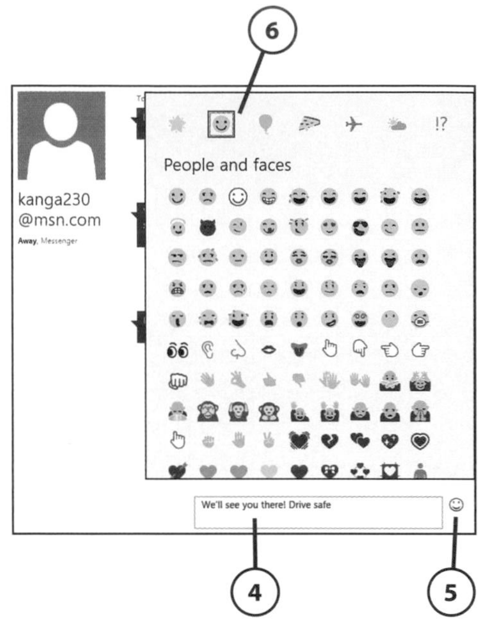

You Can Only Message with Online Friends

When you search through your contacts using the People app, you usually have a choice between viewing All contacts or viewing only those who happen to be online at that time. When you're working with the Messaging app, Online Only is selected for you, because you can't send instant messages to someone who isn't currently online.

>>>Go Further

INVITING NEW CONTACTS

You can invite new friends or family members to connect with you in the Messaging app. When you click Invite in the Messaging screen, the Add a New Friend option appears. Tap or click it and you are taken online, where you can enter the email address of the contact you want to add. Click Next to send the invitation.

You can also click the Add People to Your Contacts List if you want to connect your contacts from Facebook, LinkedIn, and Twitter.

Bring all your photos together with the Photos app

Find, preview, and buy or rent movies using the Video app

In this chapter, you learn how to set up your photos, music, video, and games in Windows 8 by learning about these tasks:

- → Let there be photos!
- → Grooving to your tunes
- → Watching and sharing video in Windows 8
- → Games in Windows 8

Get Entertained with Windows 8 Photos, Music, Movies, and Xbox

Let's forget about all the productivity features and security enhancements in Windows 8 for a moment: Windows 8 is also about media in a big way. Now in Windows 8, you can use the Photos, Music, Video, and Games apps to work in all the fun stuff—photos, games, songs, and movies—that you love to do. You can also use the Camera app to capture images, videos, or audio on your PC if you have a webcam or a camera built-in. There's a lot of happy ground to cover here, so let's get started.

Let There Be Photos!

If you're like me, you probably take photos of just about everything, now that cameras are part of our daily life (thanks to cellphone cameras). Taking photos is now a natural part of the way we communicate with friends, family, and colleagues. In addition to describing something to others—whether we do that in person, on the phone, or by email—now we can *show* them what we're talking about, using images we capture on our phones, computers, or digital cameras.

Pictures are also a big part of the way we connect in social media as we share pictures with each other, tag friends and family members in group images, and post photos in places where others can view them. Windows 8 brings together all these things we like to do with photos—capturing, gathering, organizing, and sharing them—and makes the whole process as natural as tapping or clicking a computer screen.

Adding Photo Accounts to Windows 8

When you sign in to your Windows 8 PC using your Microsoft account, your files and settings are automatically synchronized with other accounts that use that same account ID. If you've previously used your Windows Live ID to sign in to SkyDrive, for example, or you've used it to link other photo-sharing accounts like Flickr, the Windows 8 Photo app may pick up those links automatically and make your albums available right there in Windows 8. For those accounts that haven't been linked automatically, you can easily connect them to Windows 8 so that you have access to all your photos, no matter where you may have stored them.

1. On the Windows 8 Start screen, tap or click Photos. The Photos app opens, displaying a tile for your Pictures Library, along with a variety of photo-sharing accounts.

2. Tap or click the tile that says See Yours Here. This indicates that the service hasn't yet been set up to work with your Microsoft Account.
3. If you want to know how much Windows 8 will share if you connect this account, click or tap the What Else Happens When I Connect? link.
4. Click or tap Connect.
5. Tap or click in the Login box and type your user name for the account.
6. Tap or click in the Password box and add your password.
7. Click or tap Sign In.

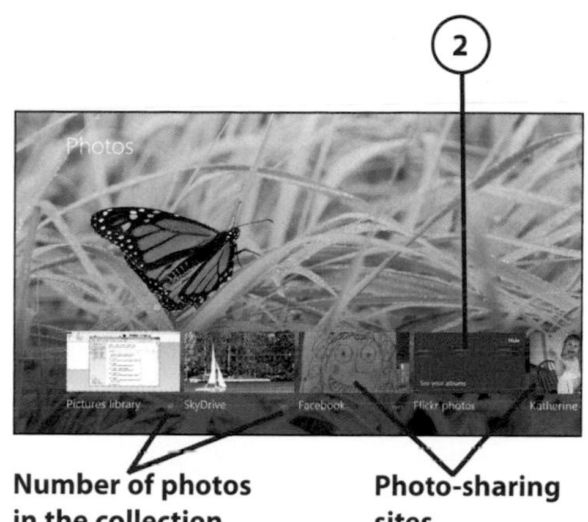

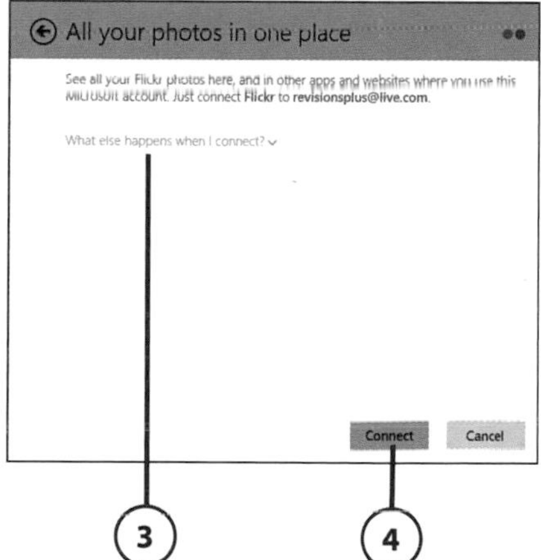

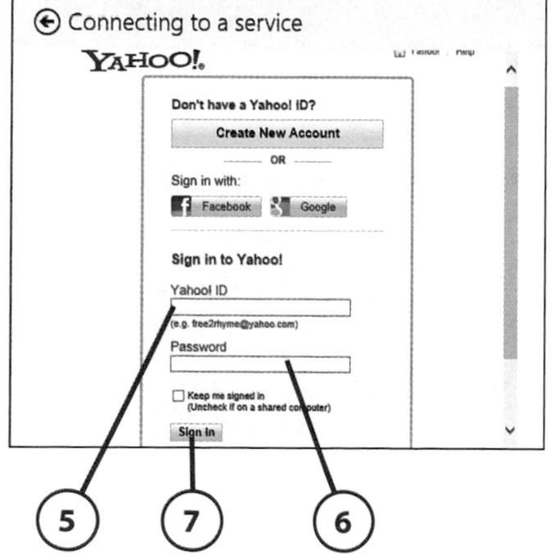

8. Read through the user agreement and click or tap OK, I'll Authorize It. When the You're Ready to Go screen appears, select Done, and your new photo account is automatically added to your Photos app.

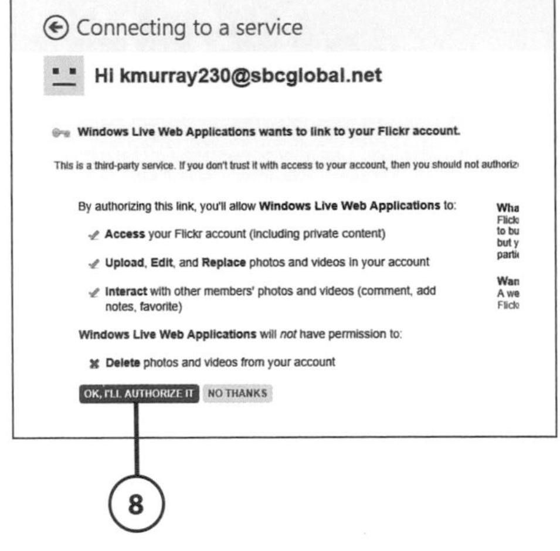

Connecting to a service
Hi kmurray230@sbcglobal.net
Windows Live Web Applications wants to link to your Flickr account.
This is a third-party service. If you don't trust it with access to your account, then you should not authoriz
By authorizing this link, you'll allow Windows Live Web Applications to:
Access your Flickr account (including private content)
Upload, Edit, and Replace photos and videos in your account
Interact with other members' photos and videos (comment, add notes, favorite)
Windows Live Web Applications will not have permission to:
Delete photos and videos from your account
OK, I'LL AUTHORIZE IT
NO THANKS
8

Download Photos from Your Phone

If you're using a Windows Phone, when you connect your phone to your Windows 8 PC, Zune launches and begins syncing your files automatically. You'll find your newly added photos in a folder added to My Pictures, named for the device.

Viewing and Selecting Your Photos

After you make your photos available in the Photos app, you can choose the albums you want to view and scroll through your photos easily. Finding photos and viewing them individually is a piece of cake too.

1. In the Photos app window, tap the collection containing the photos you want to view.

2. The albums that are part of that photo-sharing site appear in the Photos app. To see the other albums that are not displayed on the first page, swipe to the left.
3. Tap or click the album with the photos you want to view.
4. Tap or click a photo you want to view.

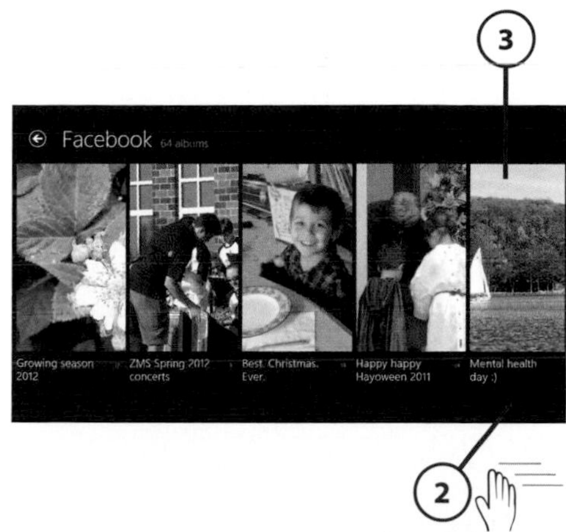

Setting Photo Options

After you select a photo in the Windows 8 Photo app, photo options become available in the apps bar that enable you to work with the photo in various ways. You can set the photo as the Photo app tile so that it appears in the tile on your Windows 8 Start screen, you can choose to use the photo as your Windows 8 Lock screen, you can view the image in its online app, you can delete the photo, you can offer feedback about the photo (thumbs up or thumbs down), or you can display the photo as part of a slideshow.

1. When a photo you like is displayed on your screen, swipe up from the bottom of the screen or right-click to display the apps bar.
2. Click or tap Set As. A list of options appears.
3. Tap or click App Tile to make this photo the image shown on the Photos app tile on the Windows 8 Start screen.
4. Tap or click Lock Screen to use this image as your Lock screen photo.
5. Tap or click App Background to display this photo as the background of the first page of the Photos app.

Fickle App Images

If you love taking photos, you may have a new photo favorite every 15 minutes. You can change the photo used for your app tile on your Windows 8 Start screen as often as you like—daily, hourly, or even more often, if you're so inclined. Just display your favorite photo in full-screen view and then swipe up from the bottom of the screen (or double-click) and tap or click Set As and choose App Tile. You can change the photo options so the images displayed on the app tile are shuffled, which will continually display new images, like an app tile slide show. With the Photos app open on the screen, swipe in from the right to display the Charms bar and tap or click Settings. Tap or click Options. Change the setting for Shuffle Photos on the App Tile from Off to On. When you return to the Start screen, the pictures on your app tile will refresh every few seconds.

Displaying a Slideshow

You can display a slideshow of all images in the current album while you're viewing your photos in the Photos app.

1. Display the album that you'd like to view in a slideshow.
2. Swipe up from the bottom or right-click to display the apps bar containing your photo options.
3. Tap or click Slide Show. The first photo in the album appears full-screen and after a few seconds, the next photo appears, and then the next. You can stop the slideshow by pressing Esc or by redisplaying the apps bar.

>>>Go Further

MANAGING YOUR SLIDESHOW IN THE PICTURE LIBRARY

You can also view and work with your photos using File Explorer, which you can access either from the Windows 8 Start screen (by clicking or tapping the File Explorer tile) or from the Windows 8 desktop (by clicking or tapping the File Explorer icon in the Quick Launch bar).

Display the folder containing the photos you want to view and select one of the photos. Click the Picture Tools Manage tab and click Slide Show in the View group. The photos begin to appear on your screen.

You can control the speed and order of the display of the photos by right-clicking the screen. A context menu appears offering you the option of choosing Shuffle or Loop for the order of the photos. You can also select Slow, Medium, or Fast for the speed of the slideshow. Click outside the context menu to hide it and continue watching the show.

Grooving to Your Tunes

In earlier versions of Windows, if you wanted to add some background music to your work—or put on some tunes for a party you were throwing—you had to go looking for Windows Media Player or Windows Media Center. Now in Windows 8, your media is front and center. You can get to your Music app right from the Windows 8 Start screen, with a simple tap or click. You can play your music in your own collection, search for the latest tunes from your favorite artists, and even purchase new music, all within the Music app.

Getting Started with the Music App

The Music app is displayed as a tile on your Windows 8 Start screen, and you launch it by tapping or clicking the app tile. Once you open the app, you'll see a screen similar to the Windows Store, where you can scroll through the various categories of tunes and purchase and download new music.

1. On the Windows 8 Start screen, tap or click the Music app tile. The Music app opens on your screen.

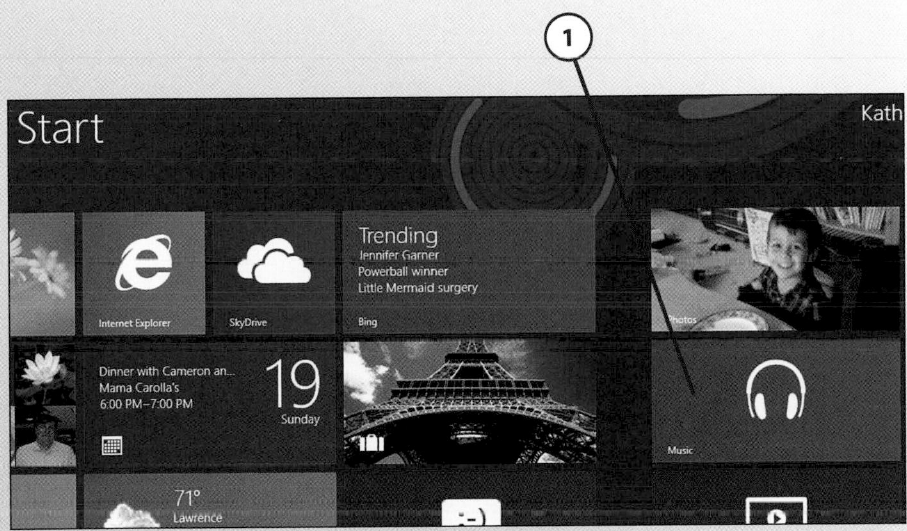

2. Scroll to the right to see all the categories in the Music app: My Music, New Releases, and Popular.

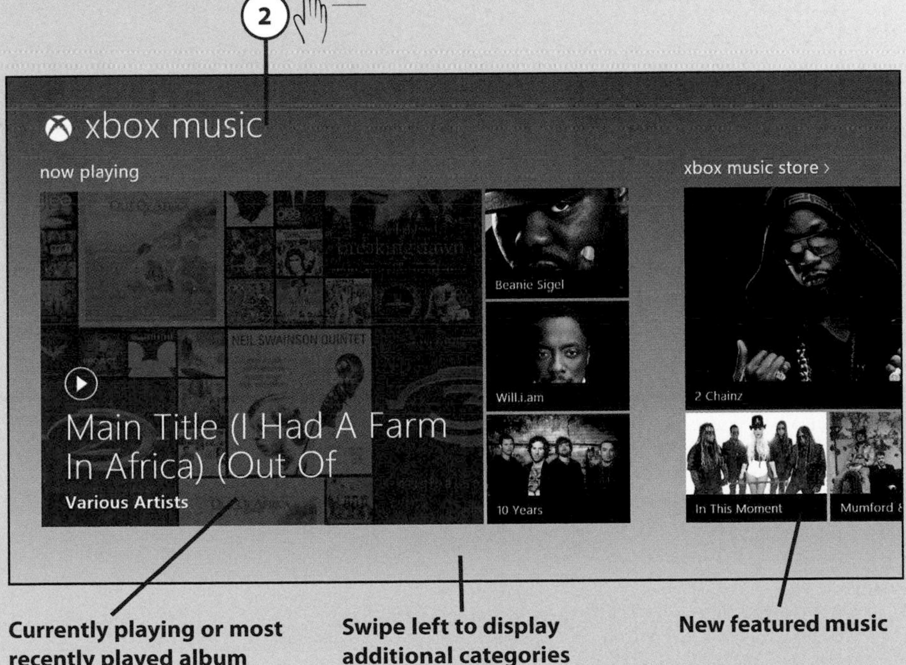

Playing Your Own Music

When you want to access the music you've already got stored on your Windows 8 PC or device, you can use the Music app to play the songs in your Music library. If your files don't appear by default in the My Music area (which means they aren't currently stored in your Music library and the Music app can't find them), you can still navigate to the tune you want to play.

1. Display the Music app and swipe to the right. Your My Music area appears.
2. Swipe up from the bottom of the screen and tap Open File.

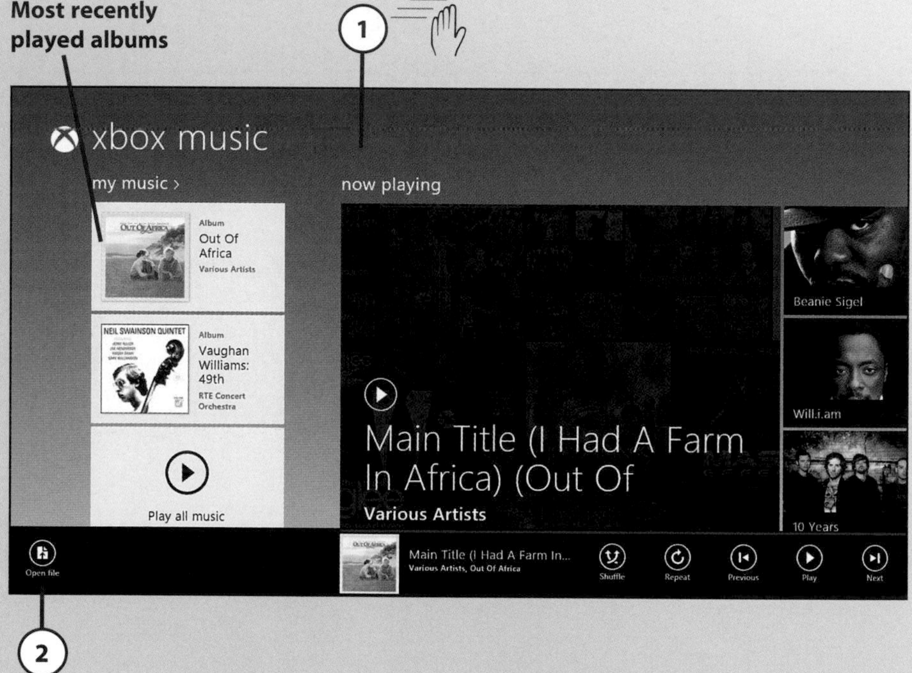

3. Click or tap the Files arrow and choose the library or Homegroup computer where the files you want are stored.
4. Tap or click the folder you need.
5. Click or tap the file.
6. Click Open. The music file begins to play.

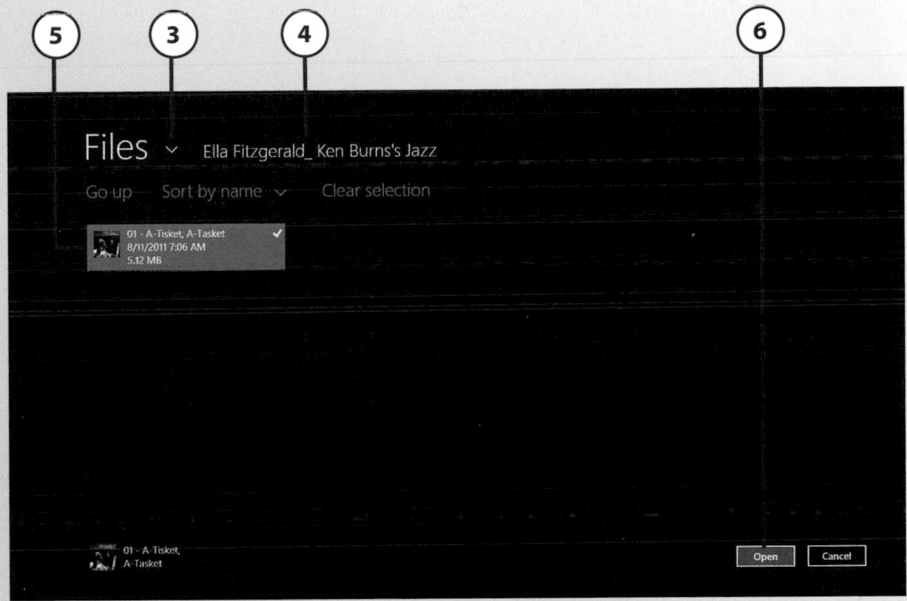

7. Control the playback by tapping or clicking pause.
8. Move ahead or back in the file by clicking the arrows.
9. Display details about the song.
10. Display your current playlist.
11. Return to the Music app while you listen to the song so you can continue browsing.

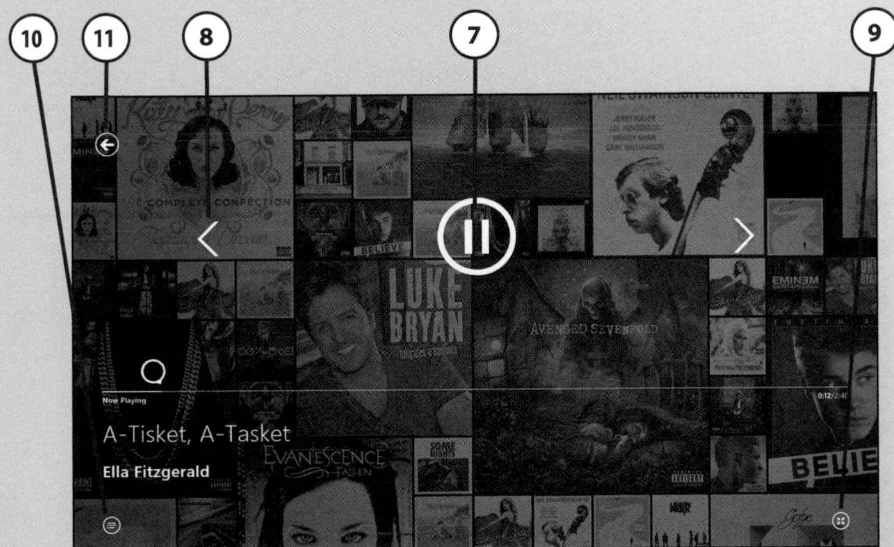

Playing Your Music

If you have music stored in your Windows 8 Music library (check this by displaying your libraries in File Explorer), the files will show up by default in the My Music area of the Music app. You can play the song you'd like to hear by tapping or clicking it. Alternatively, you can tap or click Play All Music to play the entire list of music in your Music library.

Finding Music You Like

The Music app is organized so that you can browse through songs in the genres you like most, or you can use the Search charm to locate songs by a particular artist you're partial to.

1. In the Music app window, scroll to the right and tap the Popular category. A list of categories appears along the left side of the screen.
2. Tap or click the category you want to view. Subcategories appear in the list.
3. Click or tap the subcategory that fits what you're looking for.
4. Scroll through the list to find the artist or album you'd like to hear.

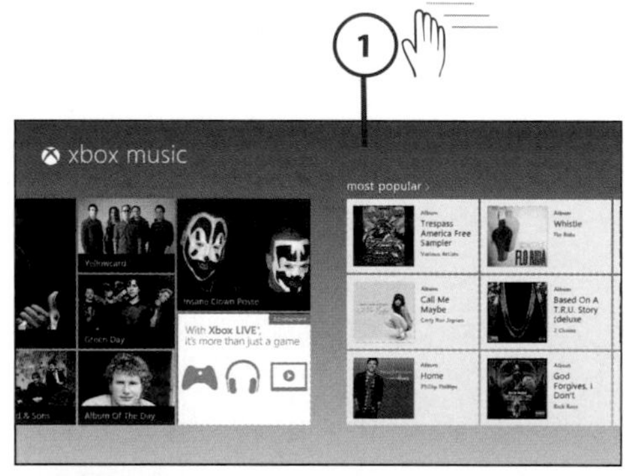

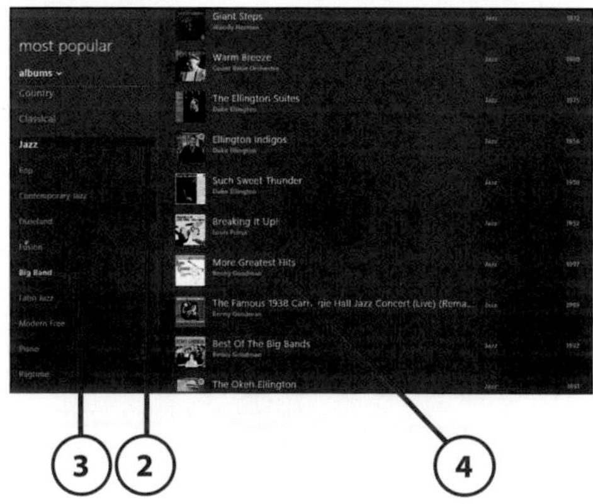

5. You can also swipe in from the right side of the screen to display the Charms bar.
6. Tap the Search charm.
7. Click or tap in the Search box and type the name of the artist you'd like to hear. A list of albums available through the Music app appears below the search box.
8. Tap the album you'd like to listen to or find out more about.

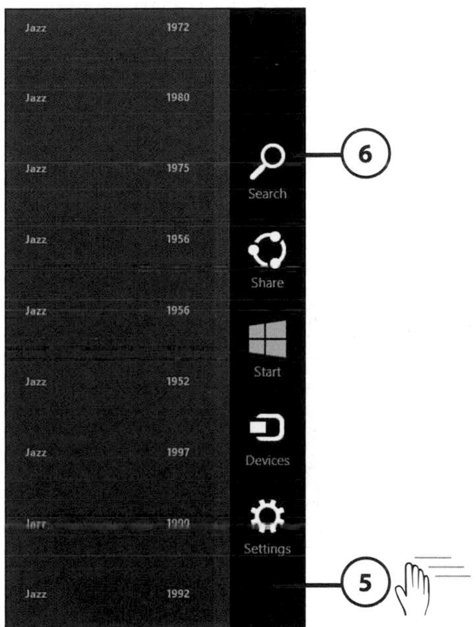

Listening to Music Previews

When you find an artist you love in the Music app, you can listen to a preview of song or an album, buy the album, or learn more about the artist. Begin by tapping the genre Popular to display the category list.

1. Tap or click the Albums arrow.
2. Tap or click Artists.

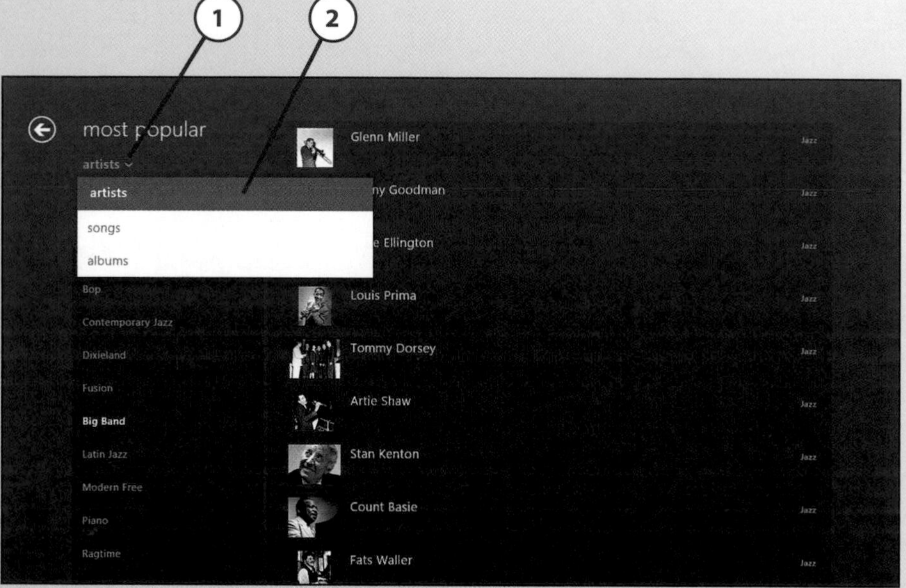

3. Tap the artist you want to listen to and the preview window opens for that artist.
4. Tap or click Preview Top Songs to listen to sound clips of the album.
5. As the songs play, sound controls as well as the name of the current song appear in the apps bar at the bottom of the screen. You can pause, listen to a different song, shuffle the song choices, or repeat a selected song.
6. Tap Explore Artist to read more about the artist and see the artist's most recent album.

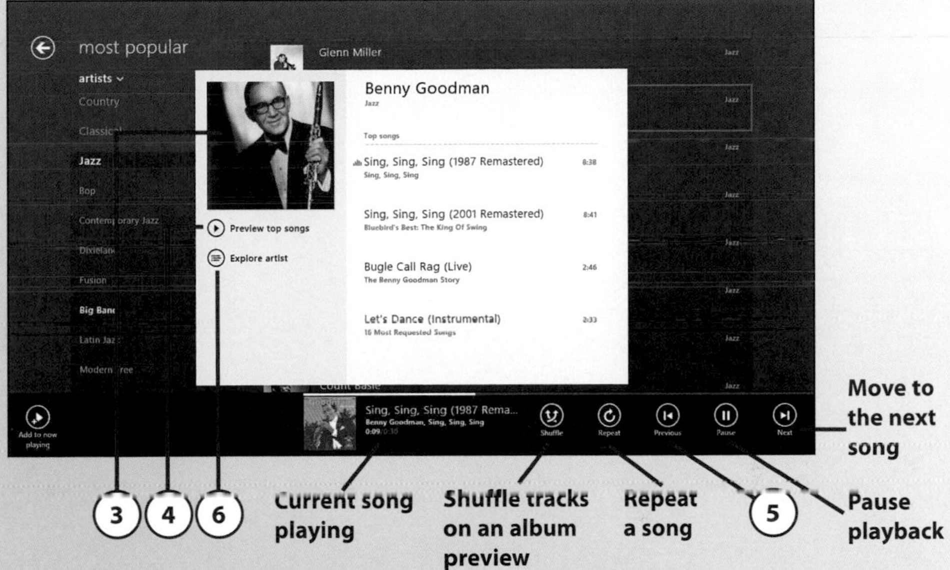

7. Tap or click the album if you'd like to preview or purchase it.
8. Click or tap the Xbox link if you want to purchase a Xbox Music Pass.
9. Click the back arrow to return to the music selections.

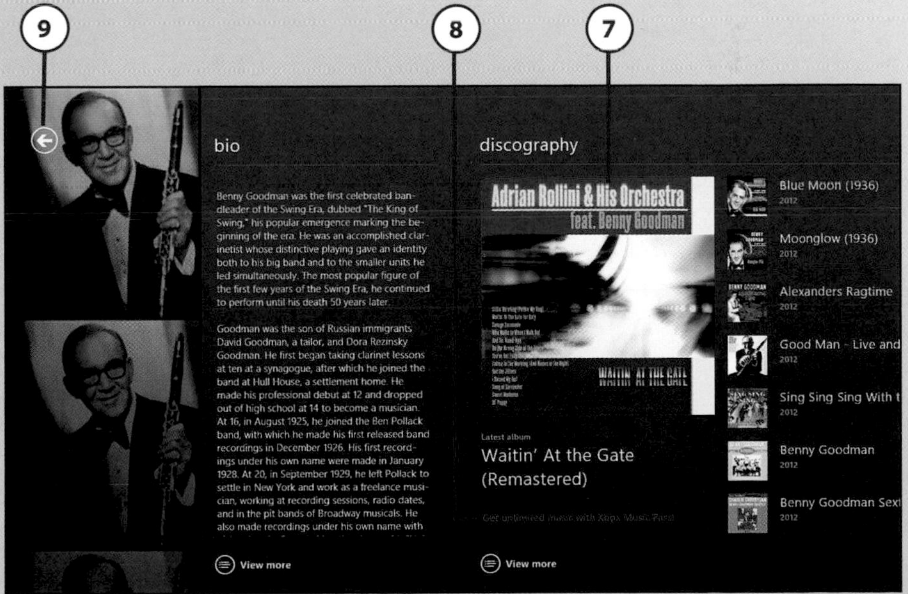

Previewing an Album

When you click or tap Preview when you're viewing an album's song list, a 30-second sample of each of the songs on the album begins to play. If you click a specific song and then click Preview, only the sample for that song will play.

Purchasing Tunes

When you find an album or a song you just have to have, purchasing it is simply a matter of using your Microsoft Points to buy it. If you don't have Microsoft Points—or you need to add more to your account—you can do that right at the point of sale.

1. When you find music you want to purchase, and tap or click Buy Album, you are taken to the Confirm Purchase screen.

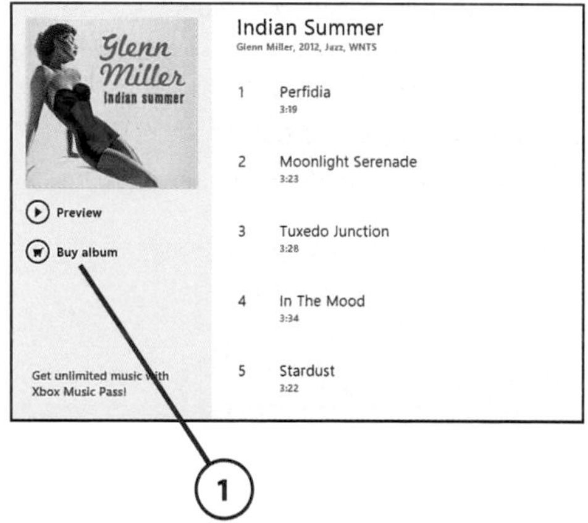

Getting Some Points

If you don't have enough Microsoft Points to purchase the album, the Music app displays the Buy Points button in place of Confirm. You will be able to purchase points and then return to this screen to buy the album with just a few simple clicks.

2. To buy the song or album, select Confirm. The Music app downloads the music to your My Music folder.
3. If you decide you'd rather not purchase the music, select Cancel to return to the previous screen.

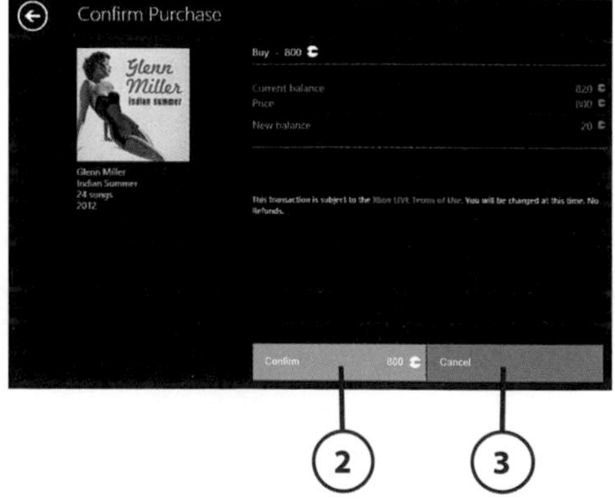

What Are Microsoft Points?

Microsoft Points are a kind of "virtual currency" that Microsoft uses for purchases of games and media. The nice thing about Microsoft Points is that they can be used no matter where in the world you are or what currency you are using. You can purchase Microsoft Points in the quantity you choose and then use them as needed for the albums, songs, videos, and games you want to buy.

Watching and Sharing Video in Windows 8

It may be tempting to watch videos and browse TV shows while you're supposed to be working on the sales presentation you need to give at next week's meeting. You'll have to disciplineyourself—to a point. The new Video app in Windows 8 is tempting, giving you access to streaming movies, television shows, and the videos you add to your own collection after purchasing them in the marketplace. You can find out more about your favorite movies and shows and even rent them online instantly and then stream them to your computer or to your Xbox.

>>>Go Further

WHERE'S MEDIA CENTER?

Microsoft removed Windows Media Center from Windows 8, much to the dismay of Media Center users who use the utility to record and view televisions shows and movies. Microsoft opted to include Windows Media Center only in Windows 8 Professional, although it is also available as a separate download, which users can purchase as an upgrade.

Windows Media Player is still a part of Windows 8, but without the ability to play DVDs. I guess we'll have to use our Xboxes to do that. Maybe that's part of the grand plan.

Exploring Video

Similar to the Photos app and the Music app, you launch the Video app by tapping or clicking the Video tile on the Windows 8 Start screen. The Video app screen resembles the configuration you saw in the Music app, with the most recent videos featured in the new releases area, the Movies Marketplace in the center, and the TV Marketplace off to the right. You can locate, preview, and buy or rent the movies and shows you want to watch.

1. Tap or click the Video app tile on the Windows 8 Start screen, and the Video app preview appears.
2. Scroll to the right to display the additional categories in latest releases, Movies Marketplace, and TV Marketplace.
3. Tap the title Movies Store if you'd like to preview movies; tap Television Store if you want to preview television shows.
4. Tap the tile of any video you'd like to know more about.

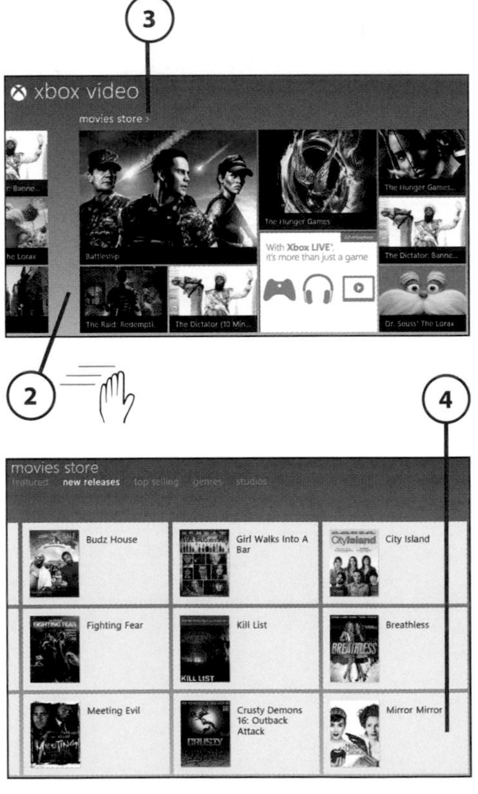

5. Tap or click to play the movie trailer.
6. Tap or click to buy or rent the video.

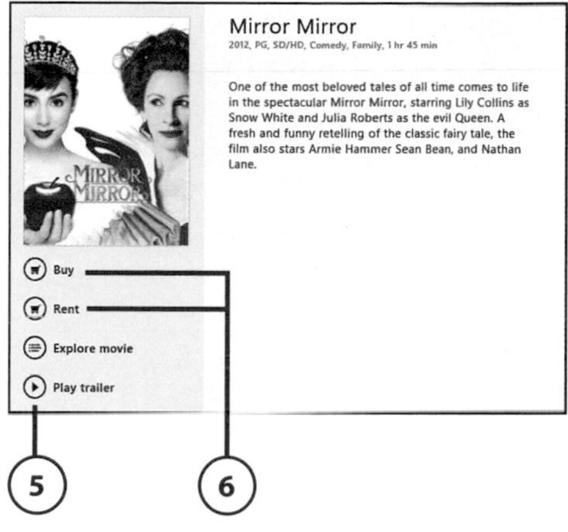

Is This an Overnight Rental?

When you rent a movie from the Movies Store, you have 14 days—or 24 hours from the time you start watching the movie—in which to view it. Since it costs $4.99 to purchase 400 Microsoft points, and current movies often cost 480 points, you may not be getting such a deal—but it is convenient to just tap a button on your Windows 8 PC and watch an Academy award-winning movie soon after it has left the theatre.

>>>Go Further

USING THE XBOX COMPANION

The Xbox Companion is available in the Windows Store. This helpful utility connects the Music and Video apps with your Xbox 360 (assuming you have one connected to your Homegroup or network). If you have an Xbox and want to connect it to the media you're using in Windows 8, you will be prompted automatically to download the Xbox Companion when you tap or click Play on Xbox. You can tap or click the Get Xbox Companion from the Store link to go directly to the Windows Store.

The Xbox Companion is a free utility; simply tap or click Install to install it on your computer. The app will appear on the far-right side of your Windows 8 Start screen.

When you tap the Xbox Companion tile, a screen appears giving you the instructions for connecting your Xbox to your Windows 8 PC. Simply log in to your account on your Xbox, and navigate to System Settings, choose Console Settings, and select Xbox Companion. Then choose Available.

Return to your Windows 8 PC and tap Connect when prompted, and your PC and your Xbox will talk to each other and synchronize your media. This makes it super simple for you to find a movie in the Movies Store, for example, and with a few easy taps, stream the movie live to your family room for everyone to enjoy.

Don't Forget Your Favorite Shows

You can use the Video app to find and stream your favorite TV episodes on your computer or your Xbox. When you tap or click TV Store, you can choose to display shows sorted into the following categories: featured, last night's shows, free TV, top selling, genres, or networks.

1. Tap or click the cover image of the series you want to view. Tap or click Explore Series to learn more about the show and choose View Seasons to display the specific episodes in the season available in the TV Store.
2. If you want to buy the whole season, tap or click Buy Season.
3. If you want to buy only a single episode, review your episode choices and tap the one you want to view.

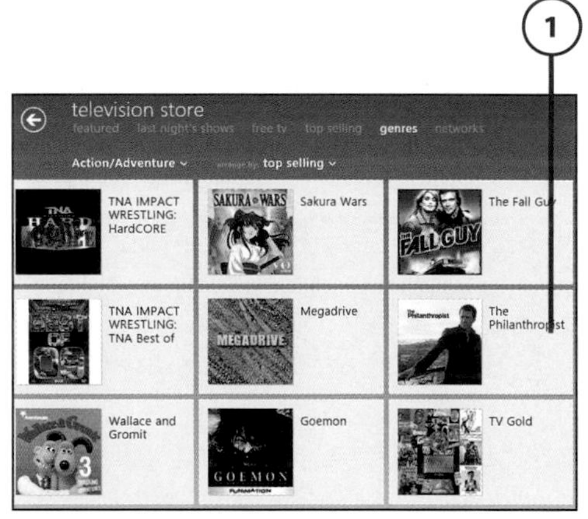

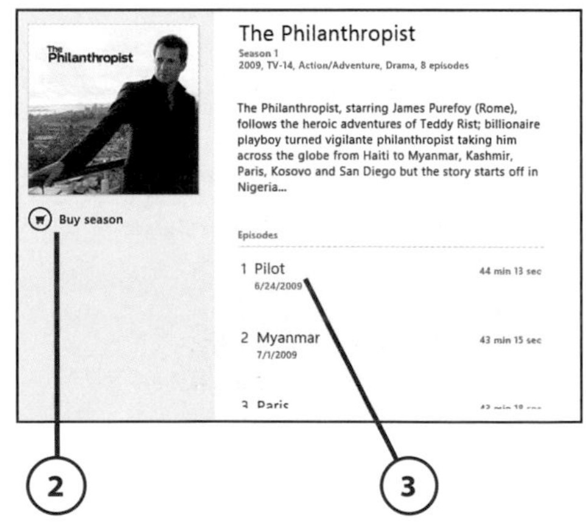

4. Tap or click Buy Episode to view the episode. The Confirm Purchase screen appears so that you can click Confirm to use your Microsoft Points to buy the show. It will then become available in your collection so that you can watch the show when you wish.

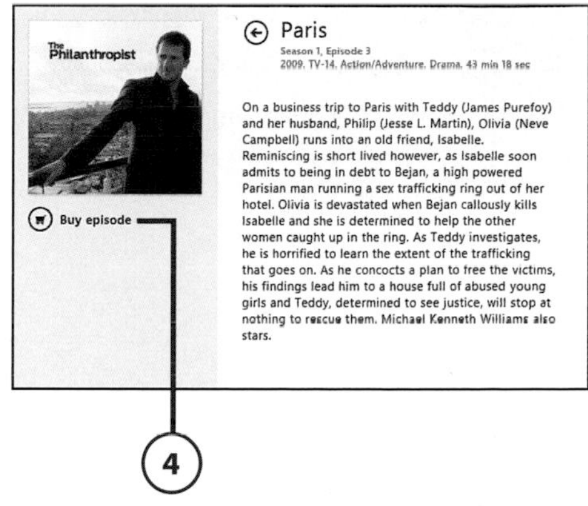

Games in Windows 8

You can use the Games app to play your favorite games, see what's hot in the world of gaming, and buy new games you'd like to try. Depending on the format of the game, you may be able to play it on your PC or the Xbox, or both. Begin by displaying the Games app by tapping the app tile on your Windows 8 Start screen.

Customizing Your Avatar

Are you as connected to your Xbox avatar as I am? It's odd how this little digital person I created and customized to suit my own online persona can make a difference when I log in to Xbox Live to play a game or two. You can personalize your avatar by choosing clothing items and features, like hairstyles, facial features, and more.

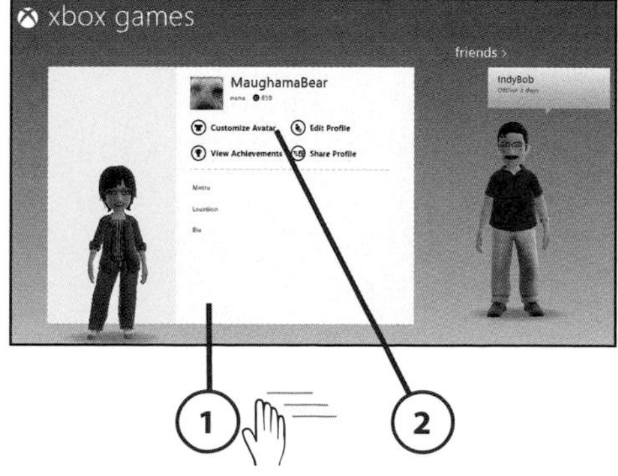

1. Scroll to the left of the Xbox Games screen to display your avatar and friends.
2. Tap or click Customize Avatar.

3. Click or tap the arrow to display a list of styles you can customize.
4. Tap or click My Features to change facial and body features of your avatar.
5. Click your choice.
6. When you're finished making changes, tap or click Save.

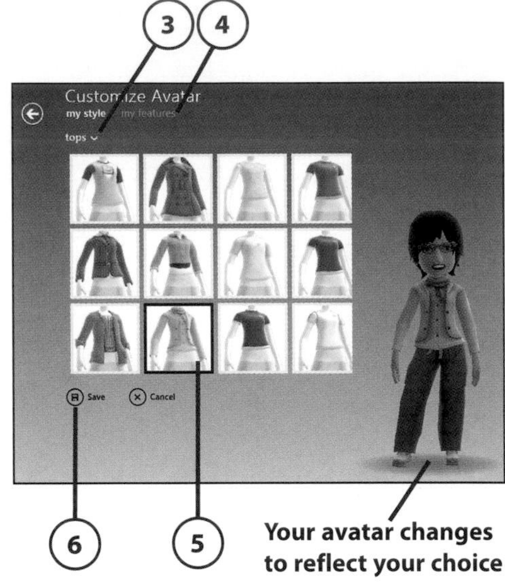

Finding and Playing Your Favorite Games

The Game Activity area of the Games app displays all the games you have purchased and played on your Xbox, Xbox Kinect, or Xbox Live accounts. You can display more information about the games or—in some cases—play the game on your PC by tapping the one you want to see.

1. Scroll to the Game Activity area of the Xbox Games screen.
2. Tap or click the tile of a game you want to play.
3. Click or tap Game Activity to see a list of recently played games and then, on that screen, tap or click the game you want to play.

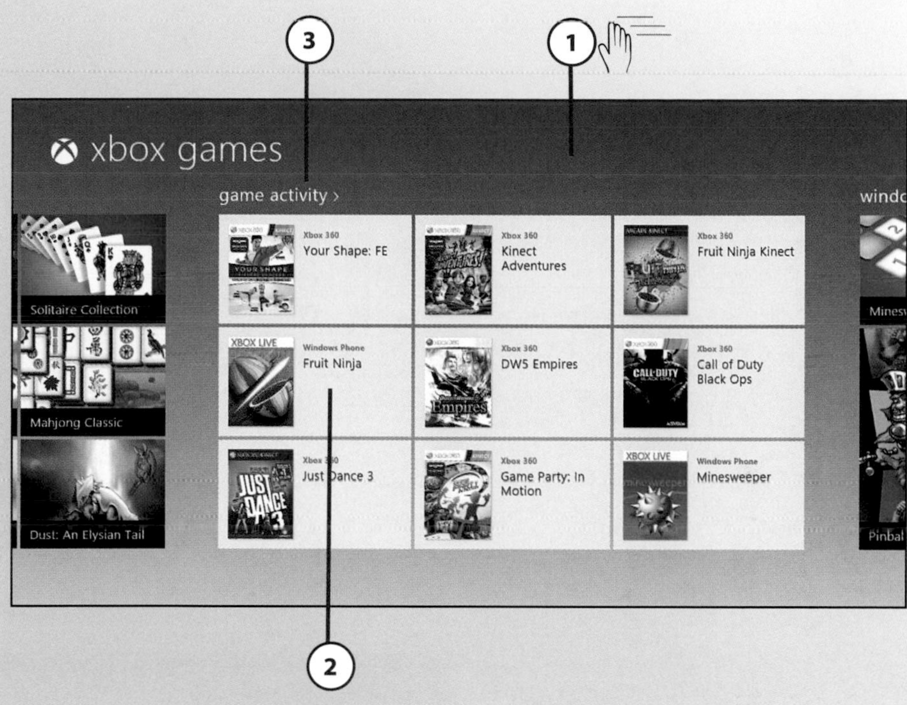

Can I Play This on My PC?

The games you can play on your computer have an Xbox Live banner at the top of the game cover. For games that can only be played on your Xbox system, you'll see either Xbox 360 Kinect or Xbox 360 at the top of the game image.

Buying or Renting a Game

You'll notice that the Xbox Live app gives you two different marketplaces. One is the Windows Games Store, and it includes only those games available with Windows 8. The other is the Xbox 360 Games Store, which gives you access to all the Xbox games available either for your PC or for your Xbox.

1. Click or tap Xbox 360 Games Store.
2. Across the top of the Games screen, you'll find a number of controls for displaying the games you're looking for. Choose from Games on Demand, Demos, Indie, or Arcade games.
3. Tap or click a game tile to display more about the game or demo.
4. Click or tap Explore Game to learn more about the game.
5. Tap or click Play on Xbox 360 to begin playing the game on your Xbox.
6. Tap or click Buy Game for Xbox 360 to purchase the game if you don't already own it.

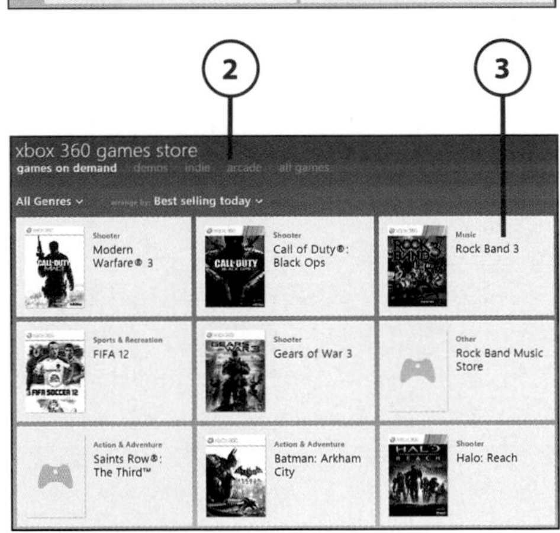

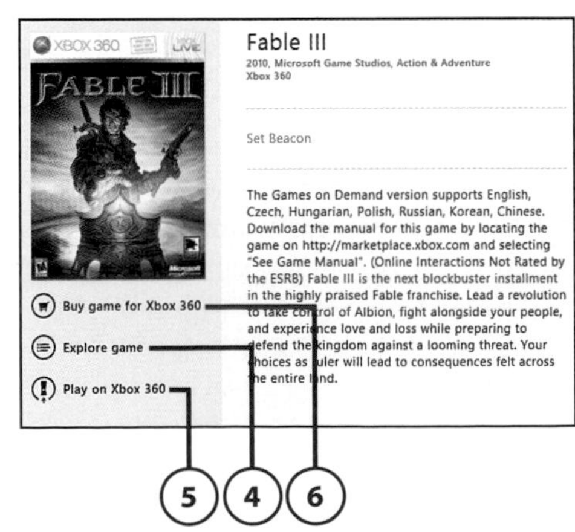

Setting Up the Companion

This is a good place to stop and make sure you've set up the Xbox Companion for your Xbox 360. If you don't have an Xbox at this point, you're limited to playing games that can be downloaded and played on your PC.

>>>Go Further

SENDING OUT A BEACON FOR YOU

You can also set a beacon to let your friends know that you're interested in playing a specific game online. Your friends and contacts in your social network and on Xbox LIVE will know that you want to play *Fable III*, for instance, and they can respond by inviting you to play a game.

To set your beacon for a specific game, display the game information and tap or click Set Beacon in the center of the game description area. A text box opens with the text "I want to play this game with friends," and you can tap or click Set to set the beacon. If you change your mind, you can click Cancel instead.

Set up sharing between your computers using a HomeGroup

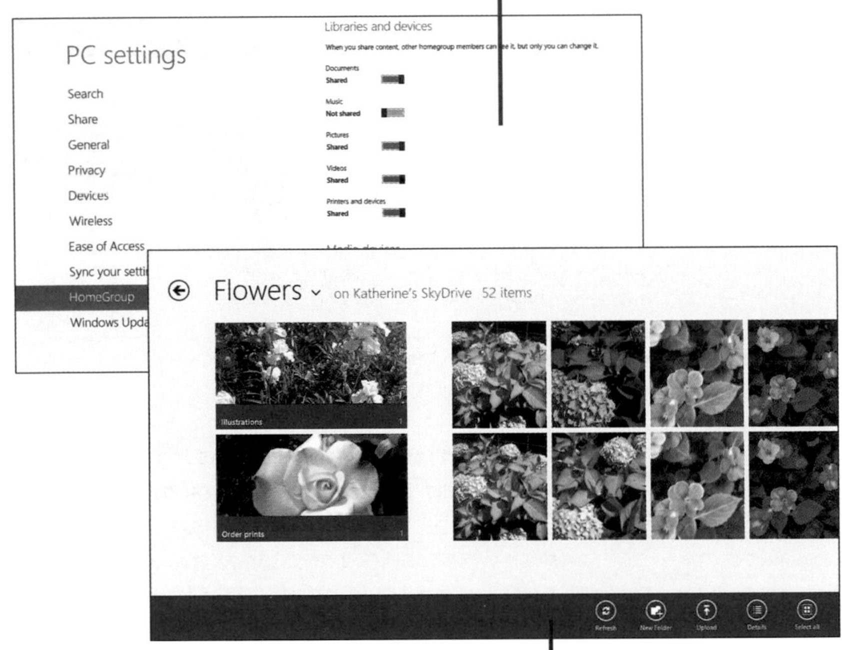

Add and access files in the cloud using SkyDrive

In this chapter, you learn to set up a network, add a HomeGroup, and save files to the cloud:

- → Setting up a home network
- → Getting started with a HomeGroup
- → Using your HomeGroup
- → Saving your files to SkyDrive

Connect with Other Computers, Devices, and the Cloud

Not too long ago, it was a real pain to set up a home network. Today it is so simple that once you get the connections established, you can access the files on a linked computer—or in the cloud—as easily as you open the folders on your own hard disk. When you are part of a HomeGroup, you can access the documents, pictures, music, and video others have shared with you. You can also choose to share your own content with others in the HomeGroup. This chapter shows you how to join a HomeGroup and set up sharing just the way you want it. You'll also find out how to save and access your files in SkyDrive.

Setting Up a Home Network

Setting up a home network enables you to easily share files, printers, and more—and connect all the computers in your house so that you can access your files from any network location. This is something you can do easily—in just a few minutes—when you have the equipment you need.

Gathering Your Equipment

To set up a wireless network, you just need a wireless router and wireless adapters for each of the computers you plan to connect to your home network. Most laptops and netbooks sold today have wireless adapters built in to their systems; you may need to purchase wireless adapters for the other PCs you want to add to your network. If your computer is in close proximity to your router, you can also connect a wired PC by cable to a port on your router, which generally supplies a faster, more reliable connection. Here's a quick introduction to the equipment you need to set up your network:

- A wireless router enables you to connect wired or wirelessly with other computers in your home. Many manufacturers offer routers designed for different needs; for example, some routers are built for the fastest access possible, whereas others are meant to support a lot of activity at once (for example, while you're browsing online and both your kids are playing online games). Although almost any router will work just fine using any modern version of Windows, if you intend to buy a new one, you should still research router types and be sure to find one that is specifically Windows 8 compatible.
- If you want or need to use a wireless connection, but your system lacks built-in wireless support, you can purchase a wireless network adapter. Many of these adapters come in the form of simple USB sticks you can plug into an open port on your PC. The adapters come with a CD that contains the software the adapter needs to be able to work. Insert the CD in your drive, and the driver should install automatically. When Windows 8 sees the new device, you should be ready to connect your home network.

And, of Course, the ISP...

In Chapter 2, "Preparing Your Windows 8 PC and Devices," you learned how to set up your Internet connection, which requires an account with an Internet service provider, so hopefully you already have this piece of the networking puzzle in place. If you haven't yet set up an account with an ISP, you need one to be able to connect to the Internet for web browsing and email.

Establishing Your Network

Begin the process by setting up your router as directed in the installation instructions that came with the router. The router may simply be plug-and-play, which means that you can connect it and Windows 8 does the rest. Depending on the router you have, you may also have a CD or DVD of software you need to run to get the necessary drivers installed for Windows 8. If so, insert the disc into your drive and follow the instructions on the screen to install the software. Once the software completes, follow these steps to get your network set up:

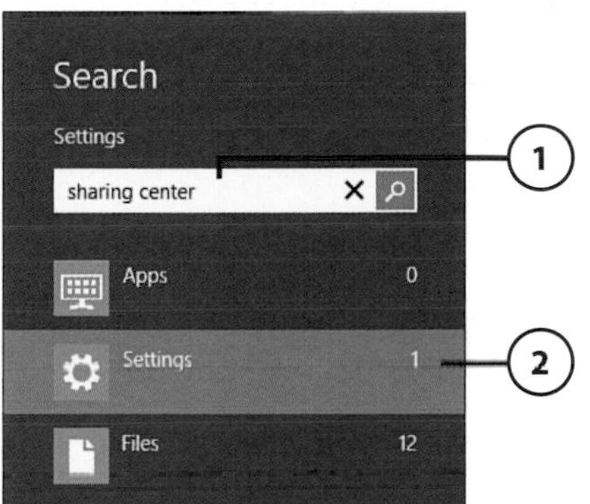

1. On the Start screen, type *sharing center*.
2. Tap or click Settings.
3. Tap or click Network and Sharing Center.
4. Tap or click Set Up a New Connection or Network.
5. Click Set Up a New Network.
6. Click Next. A wizard walks you through the rest of the process. Follow the instructions provided by the wizard, and click Finish when the process is complete.

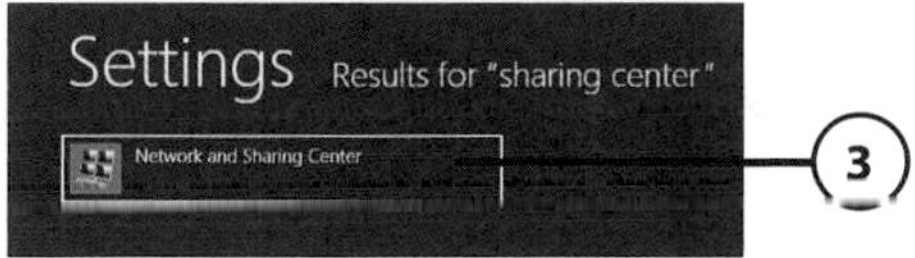

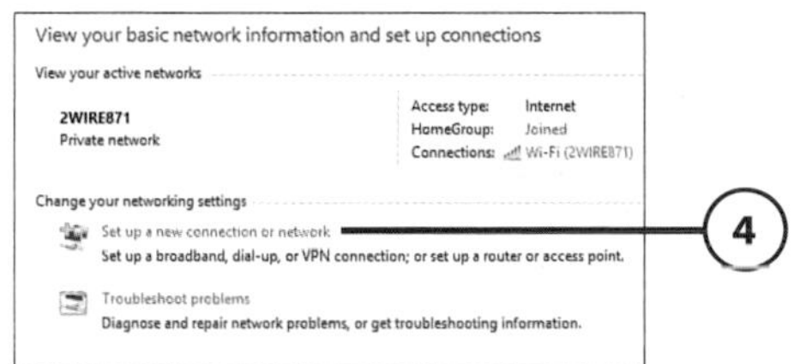

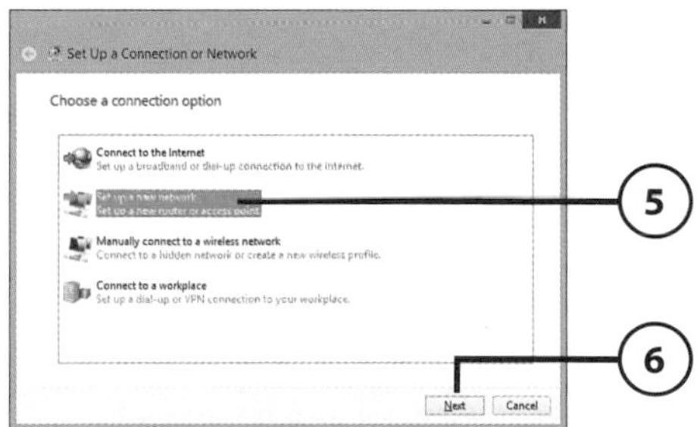

Wireless and More

Windows 8 enables you to set up other types of networks as well, including Ethernet (conventional wired), HomePNA, and Powerline networks. To find out more about setting up those additional types of networks, visit www.windows.microsoft.com and search for "network technologies."

Adding Other Computers to Your Home Network

After you add the wireless adapters to the other systems in your house and run the installation software that comes with the adapters, your Windows 8 computer should be able to recognize the wireless connection available with your wireless router. You can discover this and connect to the network by using the Settings charm.

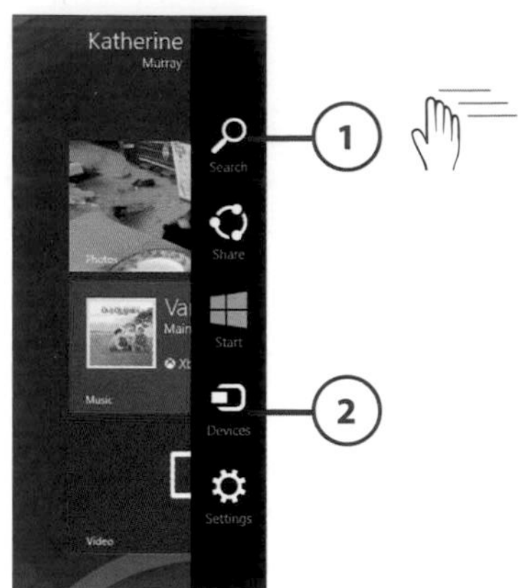

1. Swipe in from the right or point to the right edge of the screen to display the Charms bar.
2. Tap or click the Settings charm.
3. Click or tap the Network Connection icon to display the list of available connections.
4. Click or tap your network.
5. Tap or click Connect Automatically if you want Windows 8 to connect whenever your computer is in range of this connection.
6. Tap or click Connect. Windows 8 makes the connection to your network, and you will be able to access email and browse the web using Internet Explorer 10.

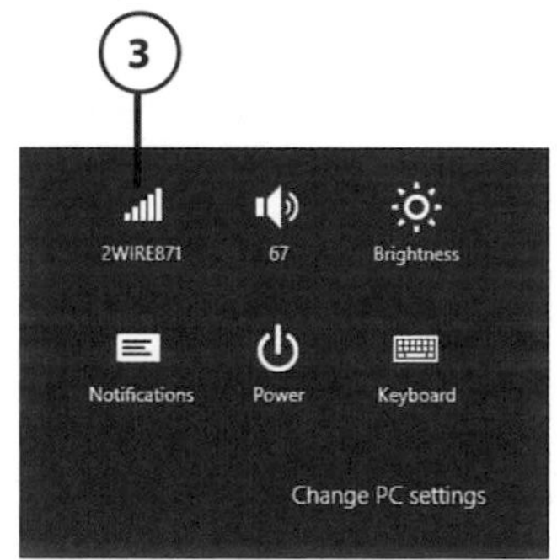

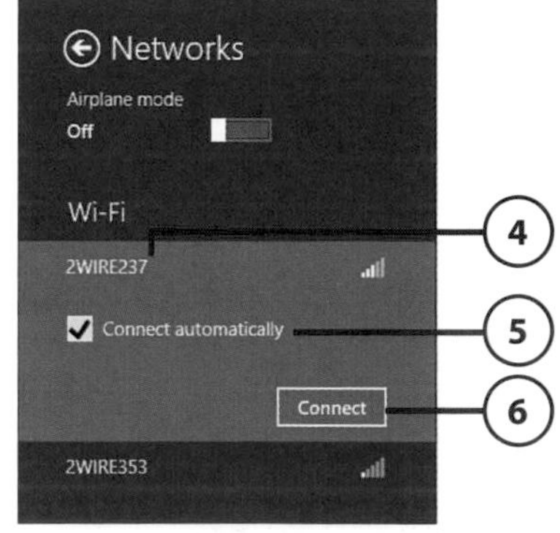

>>>Go Further

A MULTIWINDOWS NETWORK

As you learn in the next section, if all the computers on your home network use either Windows 7 or Windows 8, you can create a HomeGroup to share files, music, videos, and more. That's the easiest way to set up file and printer sharing in Windows 8.

HomeGroups aren't available, however, if you have a variety of computers running a variety of older Windows operating systems. For example, if you want to include a Windows XP computer and a Windows Vista computer in your network, you need to create a workgroup so your computers can all find and access each other on the network.

To find the workgroup name on your computers, open File Explorer and right-click Computer. Click Properties, click Change Settings to the right of Computer Name in the Computer Name, Domain, and Workgroup Settings area. In the System Properties dialog box, click the Change button to change the workgroup name. Make sure that all your computers have the same workgroup name.

Next, make sure that you have the same type of network set up in Windows XP and Windows Vista. The correct setting for your home network is Home (surprise, surprise). Adjust password protection as needed, and, when all is said and done, you should be able to see and access the other computers in the Network area of File Explorer.

Getting Started with a HomeGroup

A HomeGroup gives you a simple way to share music, media, and other libraries on your Windows 8 PC with other computers in your home. This means someone using the living room PC can watch a video clip that is on your computer in your office upstairs; your Xbox 360 can play music and slide shows from another computer; and you can share printers and other resources that you set up as part of your HomeGroup.

Setting up a HomeGroup is a simple task in Windows 8. There's a HomeGroup category in PC Settings that enables you to join a HomeGroup and adjust HomeGroup settings for the computers and devices participating. You can let Windows 8 know whether you want to share documents, music, pictures, videos, and printers and other devices on the network.

Setting Up a HomeGroup

By default, Windows 8 sets up a new HomeGroup automatically for your home network or, if you already have an existing HomeGroup on your home network (suppose, for example, that you have a Windows 7 desktop PC on which Windows 7 already created a HomeGroup), Windows 8 will ask whether you want to join the existing HomeGroup. You can then go to the other computers in your home and add them (which is covered in the next section, "Joining a HomeGroup"). To view the HomeGroup that Windows has already set up, follow these steps:

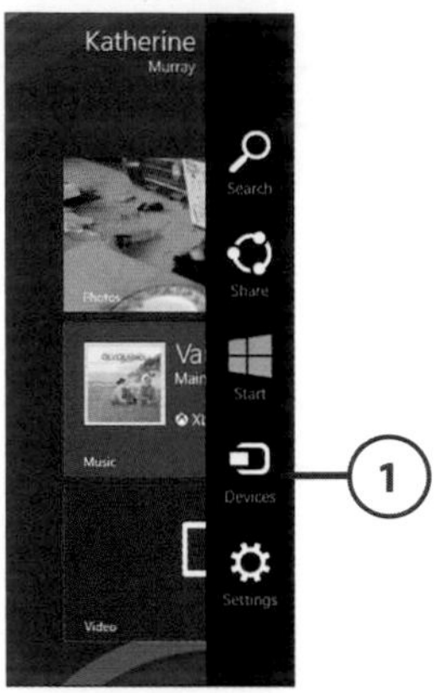

1. Display the Charms bar and tap or click Settings.
2. Tap or click Change PC Settings.
3. In PC Settings, scroll down and click or tap HomeGroup.
4. Review the settings for Libraries and Devices.
5. To turn on sharing for a particular item, drag the slider from the left to the right.
6. To turn off sharing, drag the slider from the right to the left.
7. In Media Devices, turn sharing on if you want TVs and game consoles, like the Xbox 360, to be able to access the content on your computer.

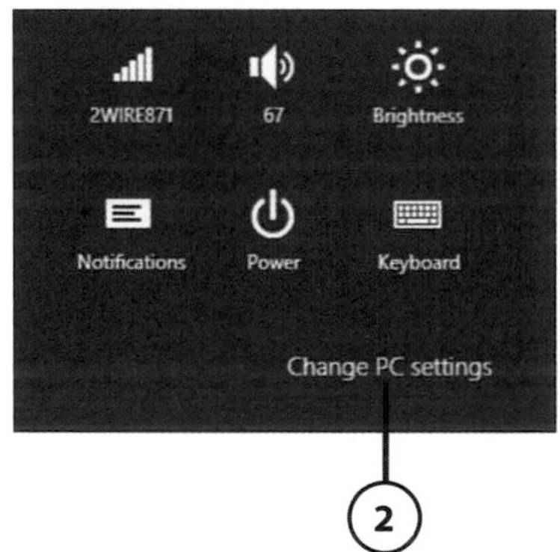

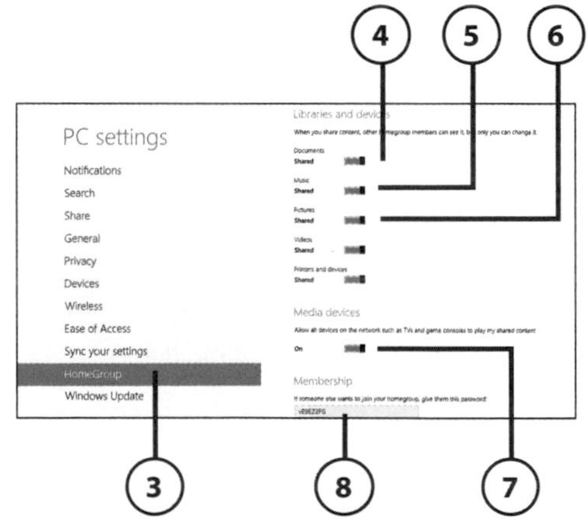

8. If you plan to set up other computers in your home so they can access this HomeGroup, write down the Membership password to enter on the other computers when prompted.

New Files in Shared Libraries

When you indicate the libraries you want to share, this means that all files—present and future—that are part of those libraries will be shared. So if you add files to the libraries later, others in your HomeGroup will also be able to access those new files.

Joining a HomeGroup

After you set up the HomeGroup that has been created on your home network, you can easily add other computers to the group. You need the password you noted in the preceding section as you set up the other computers on the HomeGroup. Use the following steps to add your other computers to your HomeGroup:

1. Display the HomeGroup page in PC Settings.
2. Click Join. Windows 8 connects you to the existing HomeGroup and displays the various shared settings in the Libraries and Devices and Media Devices area.
3. Turn on sharing of any content type you want to share with others in your HomeGroup.

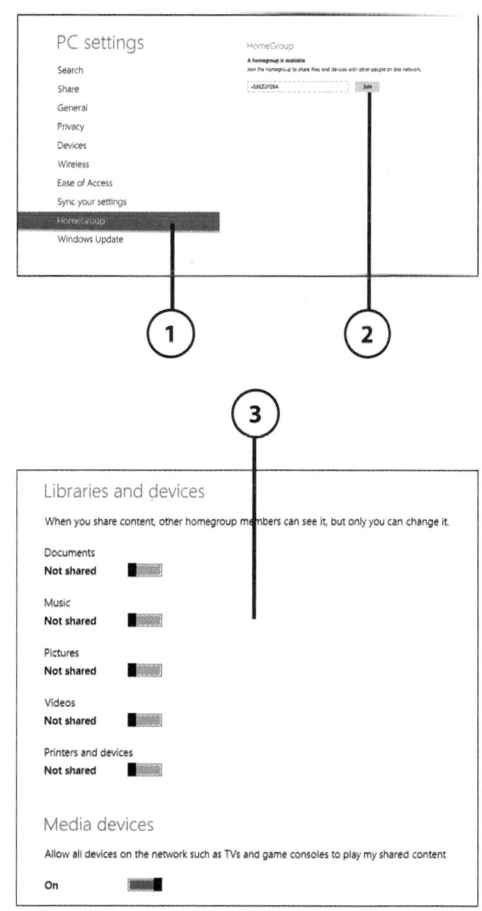

Synchronize Your Watches

Because all computers in a HomeGroup must have synchronized clocks, make sure that all your computers are set to use Internet time so you can be sure the time is accurate. You can set the time to Internet time by clicking Date and Time in the Control Panel and clicking the Internet Time tab, clicking Change Settings, and, in the Internet Time Settings dialog box, tapping or clicking the Update Now button. Finally, click or tap OK to save your changes.

Using Your HomeGroup

Each computer in your HomeGroup has its own set of shared settings. For example, you might share only Documents and Music on your computer, but someone else in your house might want to share all content types. The actual content you can access depends on what each user chooses to share when setting up or joining the workgroup, however. If one user decides not to share her music, for example, the other computers in the HomeGroup aren't able to access the music on that particular PC.

Viewing Your HomeGroup

You can easily access the various computers in your HomeGroup by using File Explorer. The HomeGroup appears in the navigation pane on the left side of the screen, just below your libraries.

1. Tap or click the Desktop tile on the Start screen.
2. Tap or click the File Explorer icon in the Quick Launch area of the Desktop taskbar. File Explorer launches.
3. Click or tap HomeGroup in the left pane. The computers in your HomeGroup appear in the Details pane.

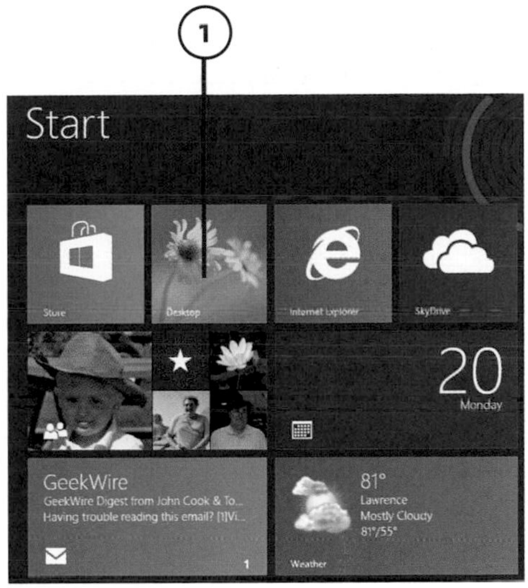

Visible HomeGroup Computers

Note that the HomeGroup computers you can see when you're viewing the HomeGroup in File Explorer do not include the one you're using. Instead, File Explorer shows you the other HomeGroup computers on your network. This enables you to view and choose files on those computers through the HomeGroup, while still accessing the files on your own computer using the traditional route—clicking your own Documents, Music, Pictures, or Videos libraries.

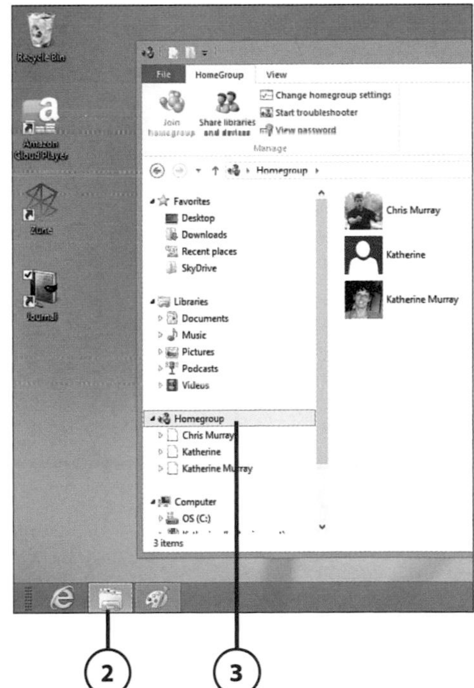

Accessing Files on Shared Computers

Once you know where to find the other computers on your HomeGroup, you can easily access the files and folders that have been shared with you. Here's how:

1. In File Explorer, click or tap HomeGroup in the left pane.
2. Click the library you want to view.

3. Click the arrow of the folder you want to display any subfolders, and tap or click the subfolder containing the file you want to see.
4. In the center column, click the file you want to view or play. Click the tool in the ribbon at the top of the File Explorer window that matches the action you'd like to take.

Changing Your Mind About Sharing

If you decide after the fact that you would rather not share some of the libraries you've shared with your HomeGroup, you can turn off sharing of those folders. On the Windows 8 Start screen, type *homegroup* and tap or click Settings. Tap or click Choose Homegroup and Sharing Options. When the HomeGroup page of the PC Settings appears, you can change the sharing settings for your Documents, Music, Pictures, and Videos folders, as well as the sharing settings for your Printers and Devices. Additionally, you can change the sharing settings for your media devices like game consoles and TVs. Close the PC Settings window after you make your changes, and Windows 8 saves them automatically.

>>>Go Further

SHARING A PRINTER ON THE HOMEGROUP

If you have a wireless printer that connects to your router, you can print from any computer in your HomeGroup. If you are using a traditional printer connected to one of the computers by a printer cable, all is not lost.

You can still log in to the computer the printer is attached to, access the document using the HomeGroup shared files, and print from the computer with printer access. Pretty slick.

Saving Your Files to SkyDrive

Now, thanks to SkyDrive, you can save and access files in the cloud as easily as you can reach files on your own computer or on other computers in your HomeGroup. If you want to save files sporadically as you work—perhaps you created a great document design you want to save somewhere safe—you can save them to your space in the cloud, where you can access them from any computer or device that has web access. The SkyDrive app on your Windows 8 Start screen gives you easy access to your SkyDrive files, and you can easily navigate to the folder you want and store additional files there as often as you'd like.

1. On the Windows 8 Start screen, tap or click the SkyDrive app tile.

2. Your SkyDrive folders appear. Scroll in from the right to display more folders.
3. Tap or click a folder to open it.

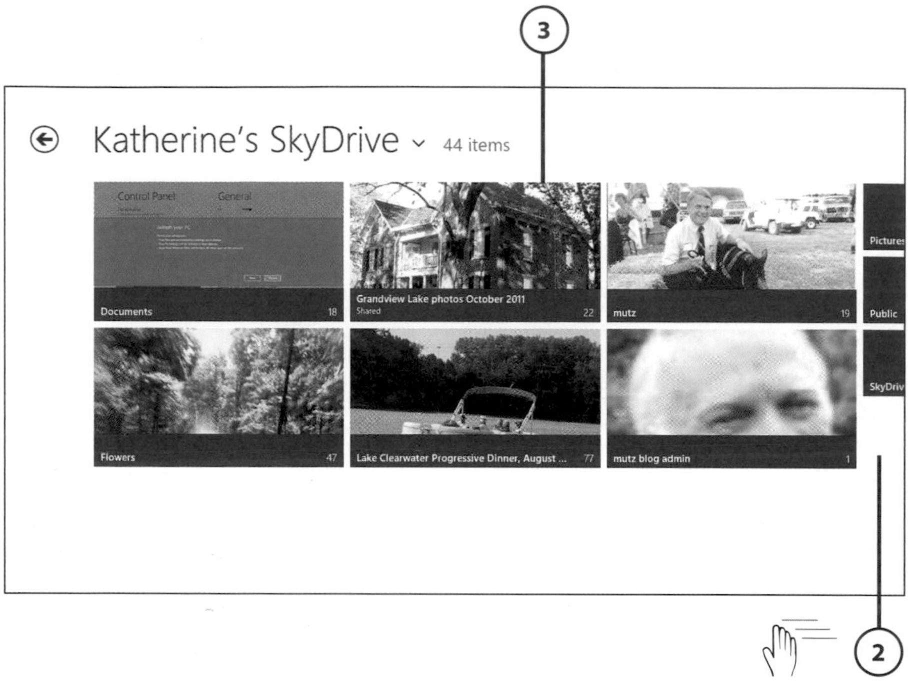

4. Swipe up from the bottom or right-click toward the bottom of the screen to display SkyDrive options.
5. Tap or click Upload.

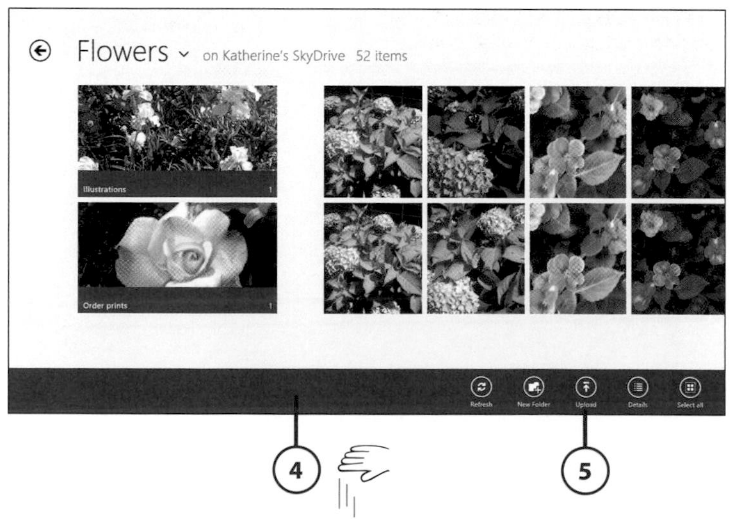

6. Click the Files arrow to display the library listing, and click the folder you want to display.
7. Swipe down or right-click individual files you want to add to SkyDrive.
8. Tap or click Add to SkyDrive. The files are uploaded to the SkyDrive folder you selected. SkyDrive gives you the status of the copy process by displaying a message in the upper-right corner of your screen.

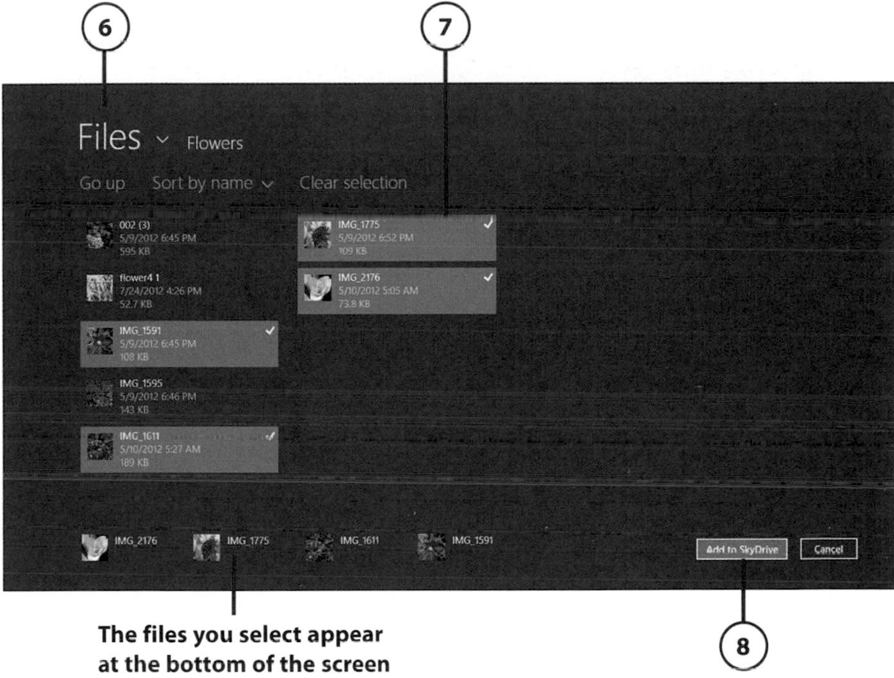

Choose how you want to install updates

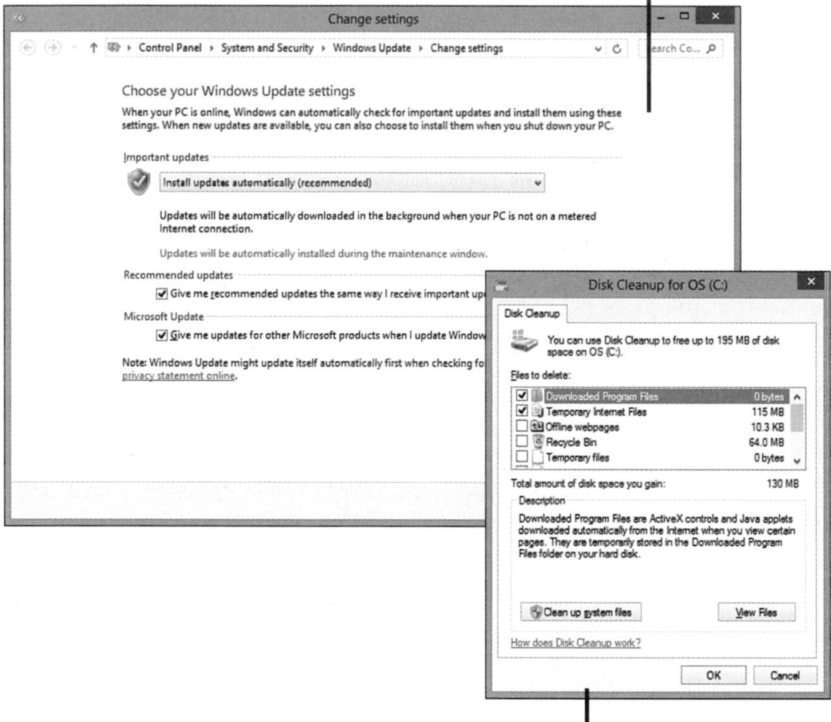

Change settings
Control Panel ▸ System and Security ▸ Windows Update ▸ Change settings
Choose your Windows Update settings
When your PC is online, Windows can automatically check for important updates and install them using these settings. When new updates are available, you can also choose to install them when you shut down your PC.
Important updates
Install updates automatically (recommended)
Updates will be automatically downloaded in the background when your PC is not on a metered Internet connection.
Updates will be automatically installed during the maintenance window.
Recommended updates
Give me recommended updates the same way I receive important up
Microsoft Update
Give me updates for other Microsoft products when I update Window
Note: Windows Update might update itself automatically first when checking fo
privacy statement online.
Disk Cleanup for OS (C:)
Disk Cleanup
You can use Disk Cleanup to free up to 195 MB of disk space on OS (C:).
Files to delete:
Downloaded Program Files 0 bytes
Temporary Internet Files 115 MB
Offline webpages 10.3 KB
Recycle Bin 64.0 MB
Temporary files 0 bytes
Total amount of disk space you gain: 130 MB
Description
Downloaded Program Files are ActiveX controls and Java applets downloaded automatically from the Internet when you view certain pages. They are temporarily stored in the Downloaded Program Files folder on your hard disk.
Clean up system files
View Files
How does Disk Cleanup work?
OK
Cancel

Remove files you no longer need

In this chapter, you learn how to care for your Windows 8 PC and solve problems when they arise by learning about these tasks:

- → Getting Windows 8 updates
- → Backing up and restoring your files
- → Using system tools
- → Being compatible with Windows 8

Windows 8 Care, Feeding, and Troubleshooting

Your Windows 8 computer—whether it's a desktop PC, a tablet, or a netbook—needs consistent care to stay healthy. In today's virus-ripe landscape, keeping your computer healthy means making sure your Windows 8 updates are current, you run anti-virus programs regularly, and your files are organized in such a way that they are making the best use of your hard disk space. This chapter introduces you to ways you can ensure that your software is up-to-date and shows you Windows 8 System Tools that will help you keep everything in order.

Getting Windows 8 Updates

One of the most important things you can do for your Windows 8 PC is make sure you're signed up to receive automatic updates. Updates can provide new security features, bug fixes, and more, so they are important for keeping your computer as up to date as possible. You can let Windows 8 know how to check for and install any available program updates, choosing, if you prefer, for the computer to do it at some point when you're not using it. When you let your computer update automatically, it downloads any new updates and installs them at the time you specified.

Turning On Automatic Updates

First you need to tell Windows 8 how you want to check for updates and install them as needed. You can have Windows 8 do it all automatically. You can also choose to have Windows 8 let you know when updates are available so that you can download and install them when you're ready.

1. On the Start screen, type *automatic*. The Search screen appears.
2. Tap or click Settings.
3. In the results area, tap or click Turn Automatic Updating On or Off.

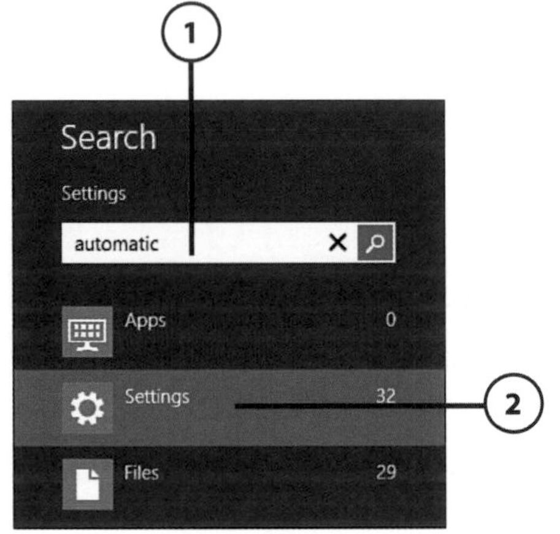

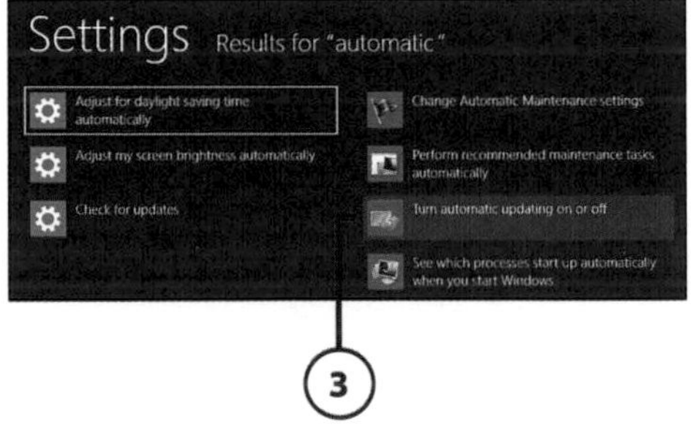

4. Tap or click the Important Updates arrow and tap or click the setting of your choice. Install Updates Automatically is selected by default; this causes Windows 8 to download and install all updates without any action from you. Your other choices are Download Updates But Let Me Choose Whether to Install Them, Check for Updates But Let Me Choose Whether to Download and Install Them, and Never Check for Updates.

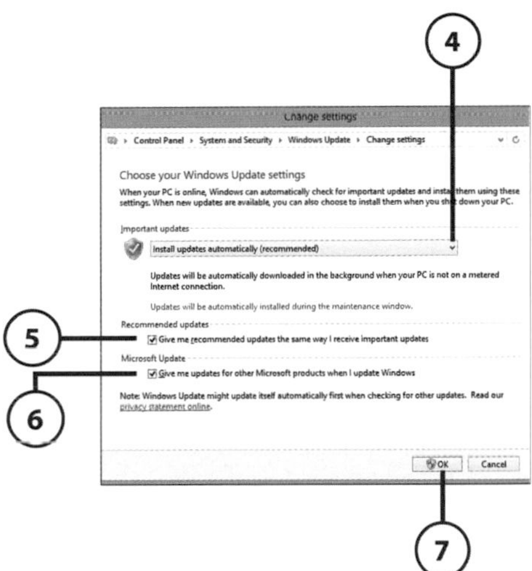

5. Click to clear the Recommended Updates check box if you want to limit the updates you receive to only those that are considered important for the functioning of the software or your PC security.

6. Click to clear the Give Me Updates for Microsoft Products check box if you don't want to receive updates for other Microsoft products and check for new software when your updates are downloaded.

7. Click OK to save your changes.

Best-Practice Updating

Microsoft recommends that you set your update schedule so that you're receiving updates at least once every week. When important updates are released, they typically arrive on the second or fourth Tuesday of the month. There are intermittent releases, however, so checking more frequently than every two weeks is a good idea.

Choosing a Time for Automatic Updates

The best tune time to schedule your program updates, of course, is the time you're not using your computer. Windows 8 enables you to choose the time you want the updates to be downloaded and installed. What's more, you can give Windows 8 permission to wake up your computer at the time you specify.

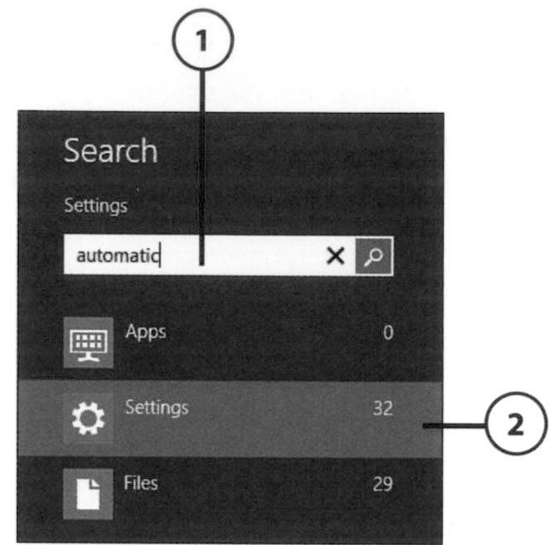

1. On the Windows 8 Start screen, type *automatic* a second time.
2. Tap or click Settings.
3. This time, tap or click Change Automatic Maintenance Settings.
4. In the Automatic Maintenance area, click the arrow to the right of Run Maintenance Tasks Daily at and click the time when you want to schedule the updates.
5. Click the Allow Scheduled Maintenance to Wake Up My Computer checkbox if you want the updates to be done whether your computer is awake or not.
6. Click OK to save your changes.

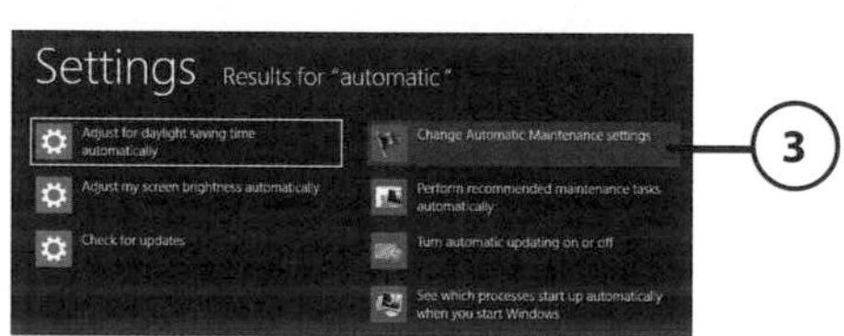

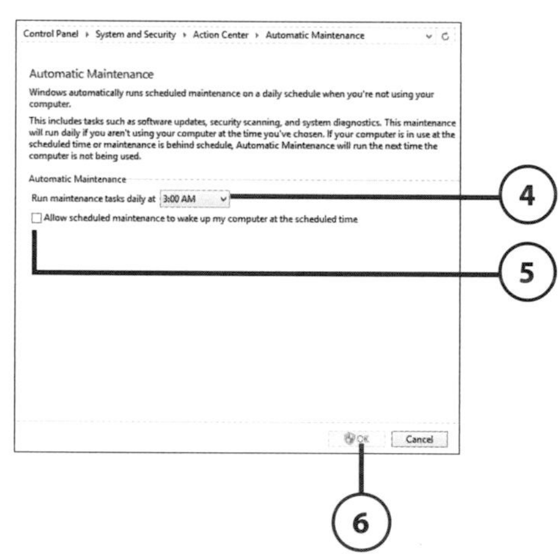

The Wake-able Computer

When you tell Windows 8 that you want it to wake up your computer to check for and install updates, be sure to leave the computer in sleep mode as opposed to turning the power off. If you turn your computer off, Windows 8 won't be able to access the computer to do the automatic updates.

Checking for Updates Manually

You can check manually for updates instead of relying solely on the automatic updating system. You might do this, for example, when you have heard that there's a new patch available for a specific feature or you have been waiting for a coming upgrade that will impact features you care about in Windows 8.

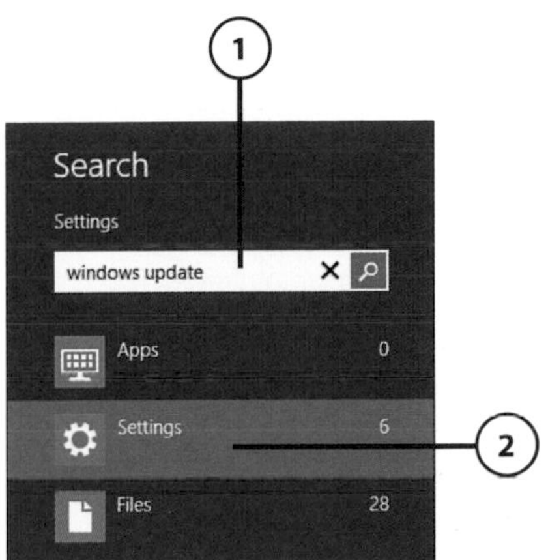

1. On the Start screen, type *windows update*.
2. Tap or click Settings.
3. Tap or click Windows Update. The PC Settings screen opens.

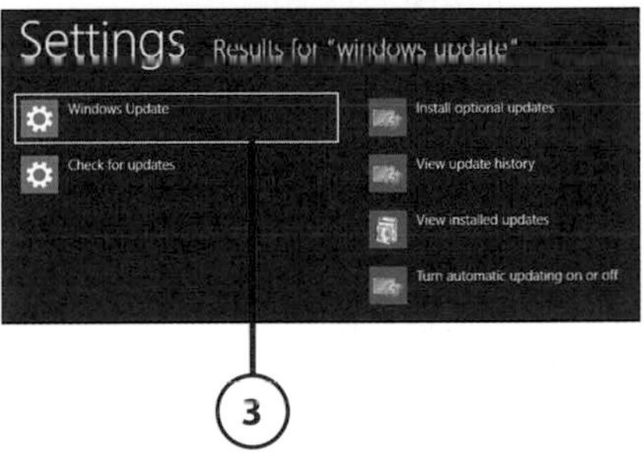

4. Tap or click Check for Updates Now. The right panel shows you the current setting of your automatic updates and lets you know the last time updates were checked. Windows 8 checks for updates and lists any found updates in the Windows Update area, where you can review and install them if you wish.

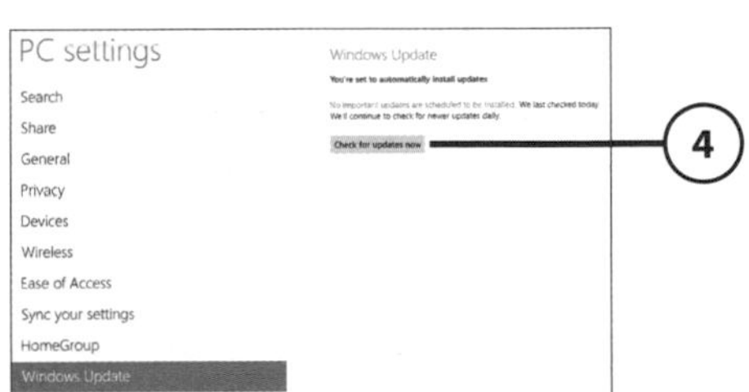

5. Even if no important updates are available, click or tap the No Important Updates Are Scheduled to Be Installed link to see additional updates you may want to install.
6. Click or tap Get More Info. The Windows Update dialog box appears.

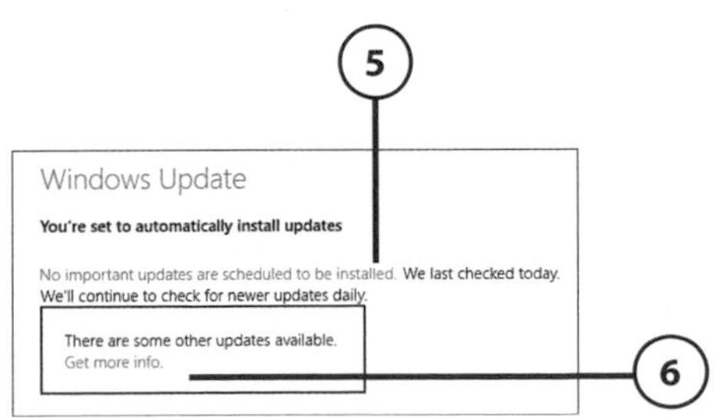

7. Click or tap the Optional Updates Are Available link.
8. Click the checkbox of any update you want to install.
9. Click Install. Depending on the update you select, you may be prompted to access license terms for the download (as is the case with Microsoft Silverlight). If you see this prompt, click or tap I Accept and click or tap Finish, and Windows 8 downloads and installs the updates without any further assistance from you.

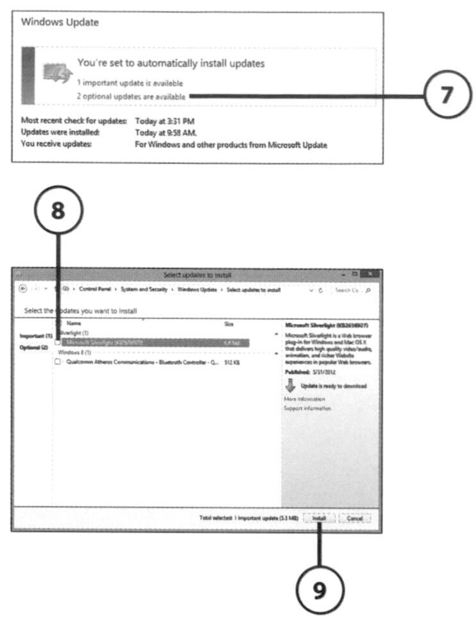

>>>Go Further

REVIEWING UPDATE HISTORY

If you're wondering what kinds of updates Windows 8 has already performed without your knowledge, you can check out the update history to see the full list. In the Windows Update window, click View Update History. A large list of updates appears, and you can get more information about individual updates that were performed by double-clicking the update name.

When you finish reviewing updates, click OK to close the Review Your Update History window.

Backing Up and Restoring Your Files

You might already be making copies of important files and tucking them away someplace safe—like copying them to an external hard disk, burning them to DVD, or saving them on a flash drive. If not, you should be. Making regular backups of your files helps you feel secure knowing that your files are protected and that you have an extra copy, just in case something happens. You can make these simple file backups yourself by using File Explorer to copy the files to the folder or device where you want to store the backup files.

Windows 8 also provides a backup utility you can use to back up everything on your hard disk. You should do this larger backup regularly—perhaps once every month or so. This ensures that your files have been saved so that if something unexpected happens to your computer—for example, you wind up with a virus that damages important files—you can restore the files from your backup and go on as usual.

Another new feature built right into Windows 8 enables you to save your files directly to the cloud, where you don't have to worry about viruses or hard disk failure. In fact, Office 2013 applications—Word, Excel, PowerPoint, OneNote, Publisher, and Access—all save your files by default to your SkyDrive account (although you can change that default so that the files are in fact saved on your computer if you choose).

Backing Up Your Files

The first step in backing up your files involves setting up the backup utility. When you do this, you tell Windows 8 where you want to save the backup files and when you want to do the backup. You can change those settings at any time, of course; but Windows 8 will take care of the backup for you automatically from here on out on the day and time you specify.

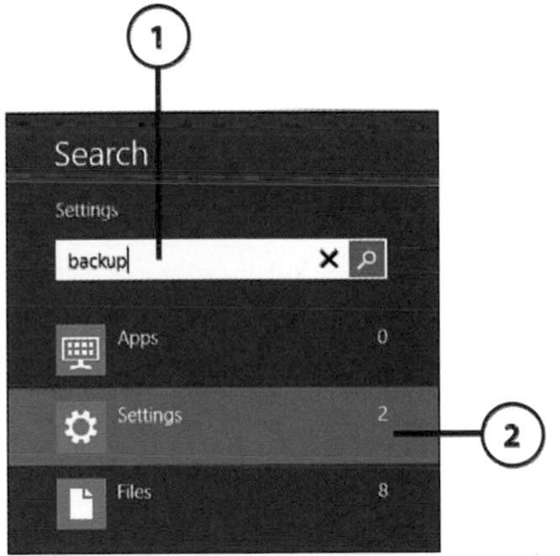

1. On the Start screen, type *backup*.
2. Click or tap Settings.
3. Tap or click Save Backup Copies of Your Files with File History. File History will want to back up your files either to an external hard drive or a network location.

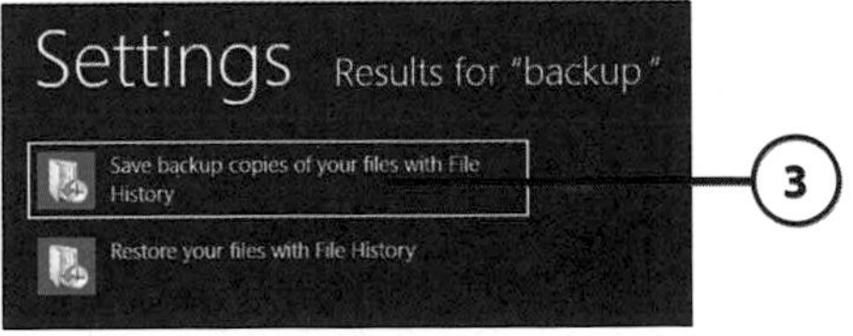

4. In the File History dialog box, the utility lists where your files will be stored. Click the destination you want to use and click Turn On.

5. If you have connected your computer to a HomeGroup, you will be prompted to choose whether you want to recommend this drive as a backup for other members of your homegroup. Windows 8 then copies the files to the destination for the first time.

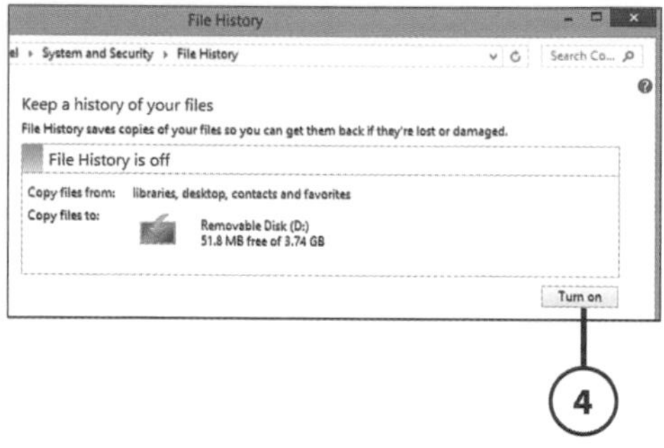

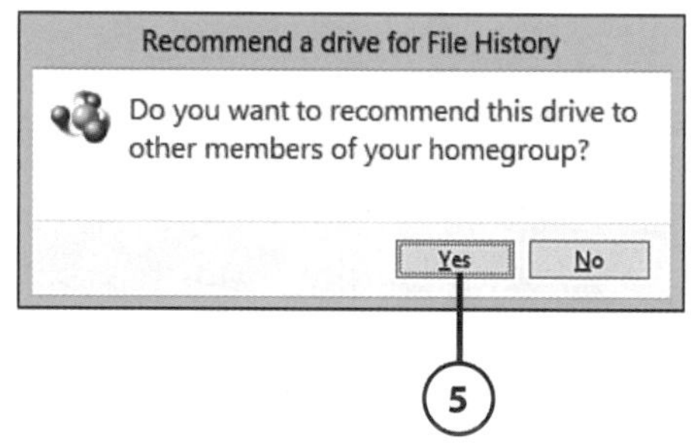

Choosing What to Back Up

You can tell Windows 8 how often you want to save files, how much space you want to devote to the backup files, and how long you want to keep file versions by clicking or tapping Advanced Settings on the left side of the File History dialog box. You can choose to save files as often as every 10 minutes or as infrequently as once a day. You can choose to allot anywhere from 2 percent to 20 percent of available disk space for your backups. And you can choose to keep files forever (which is the default) or choose from 1 month to 2 years—or until the space is needed, whichever comes first.

Restoring Files

You might not ever need the files you backed up—but it's good to have them just in case. Perhaps you accidentally deleted an important folder. Or maybe you had a computer problem and had to clean off your files, and now you're ready to put the files back. Whatever the situation, Windows 8 can easily restore your backed-up files.

1. On the Start screen, type *restore*.
2. Click or tap Settings.
3. Tap or click Restore Your Files with File History.
4. Click or tap the checkbox of the folders and libraries you want to restore.
5. Click the Restore to Original Location button.
6. If you have an existing folder with the same name as the folder you're restoring, Windows 8 will ask you whether you want to merge the folder with the existing one or skip it. Click your choice, and the files are restored.

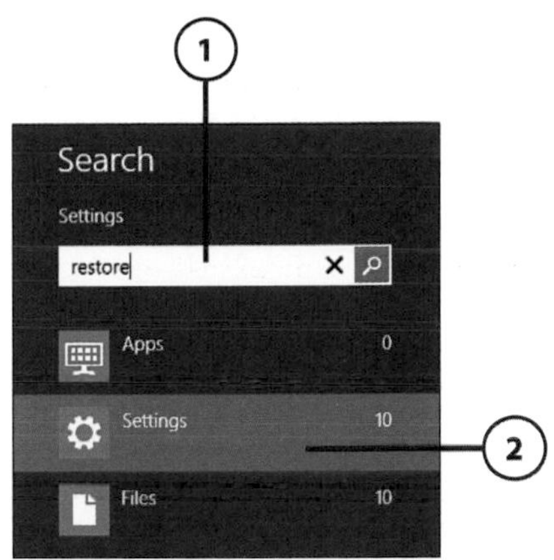

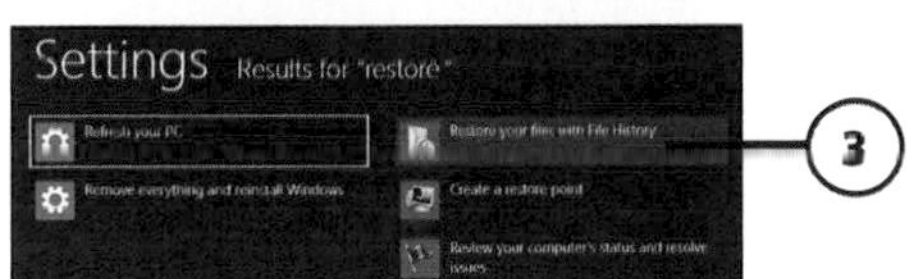

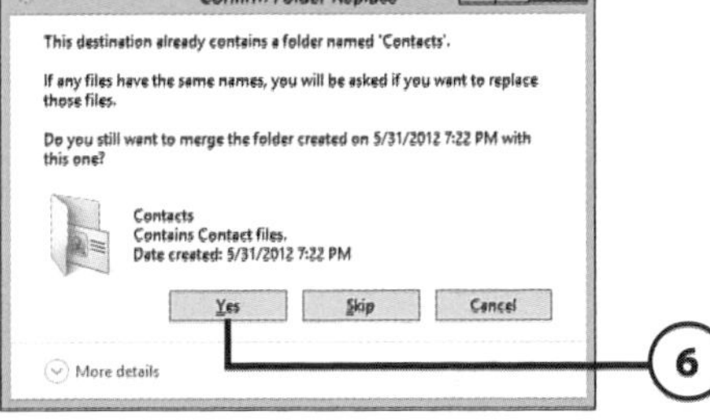

Using System Tools

Windows 8 includes two special utilities that can help you clean up your hard disk and make sure it is running as efficiently as possible: Disk Cleanup and Disk Defragmenter.

Disk Cleanup is a tool that's been around for a long time, helping computer users find and delete little bits of files that inadvertently get scattered around your hard drive. These are files like temporary Internet files, leftover files from programs you downloaded and don't need anymore, files in your Recycling Bin, and so on. When you start Disk Cleanup, the utility scans the drive you specify and then reports back, suggesting items for deletion. You can always opt out and decide not to delete the files Windows 8 suggests, but using Disk Cleanup once in a while can help you keep your computer as clean as possible.

And then there is Disk Defragmenter. As part of the normal wear and tear on a computer, file bits get scattered around the hard drive. Sure, when you look at the folders in File Explorer, everything looks nice and neat, but the way your computer is actually storing the data isn't quite that linear. Your computer knows where everything is, thanks to the way it indexes information, but over time, bits and pieces of files can be saved in various places all over the drive. And to present the file to you as a complete whole so you can work with it as usual, your computer has to do some behind-the-scenes processing. The Disk Defragmenter utility can clean up your hard drive by consolidating those bits of files and putting them back together in one place again. This can help your computer process faster and better, which is a good thing.

Let's take a closer look at each of these tools.

Cleaning Up Your Hard Disk

Disk Cleanup removes the unnecessarily files on your hard disk so that you have more room for doing things that really matter.

1. On the Start screen, type *disk cleanup*.
2. Tap or click Settings.

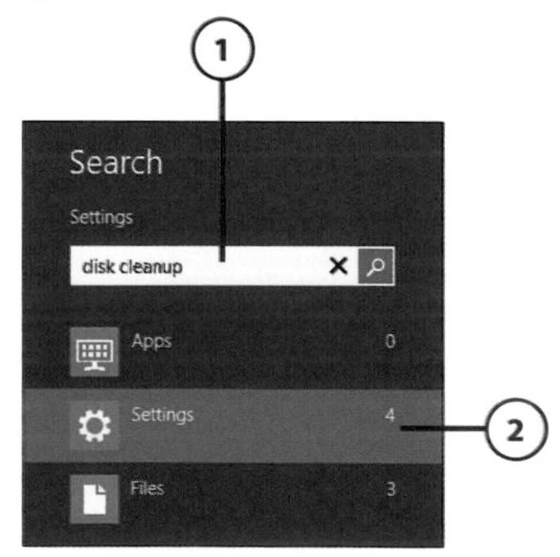

3. Click or tap Free up Disk Space by Deleting Unnecessary Files.
4. The disk checking begins as Windows 8 evaluates how much space you'll be able to free up by running Disk Cleanup. The Disk Cleanup dialog box appears, showing you which files will be deleted if you continue.
5. You can add to the files you want to delete by clicking the item's checkbox.
6. Scroll down to review the entire list of files.
7. If you want to view the files before Disk Cleanup removes them, click View Files.
8. Click OK. When Windows 8 asks you to confirm you want to delete the files, click Delete Files.

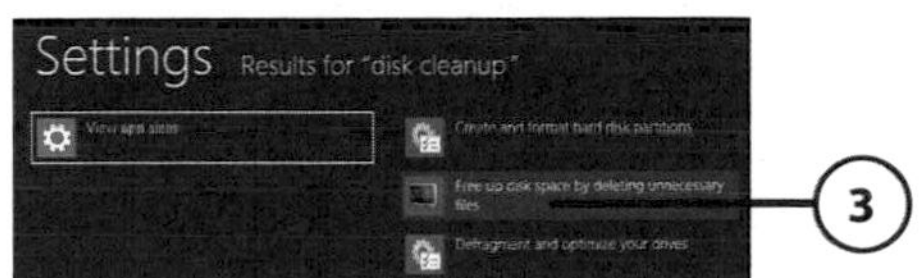

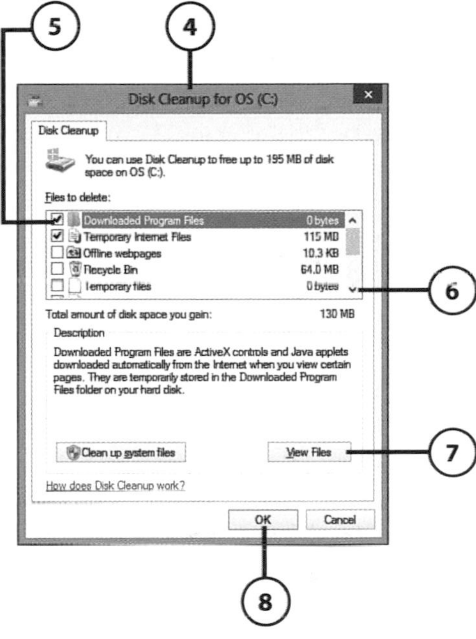

Defragmenting Your Hard Disk

Although it runs automatically by default, running the Disk Defragmenter fairly regularly—such as once every month or two—will help you ensure that you're making the most of the available storage space on your hard drive.

1. On the Windows 8 Start screen, type *defragment*.
2. Tap or click Settings.
3. Tap or click Defragment and Optimize Your Drives.
4. In the Optimize Drives dialog box, click Analyze to do a check on the selected drive to see if optimizing it will save you any space.
5. Click Optimize to defragment the selected disk.
6. After the process is finished, click Close.

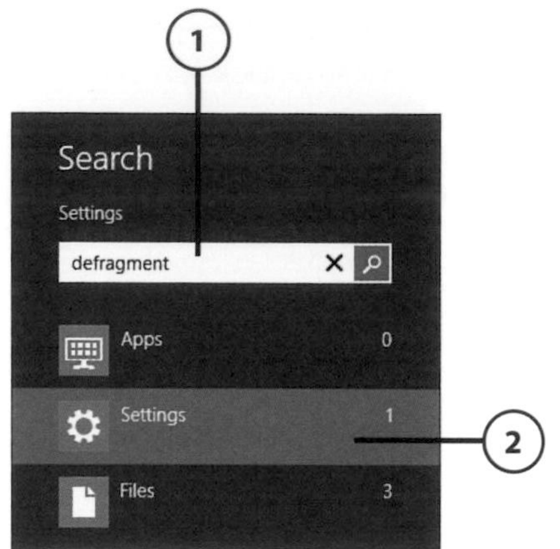

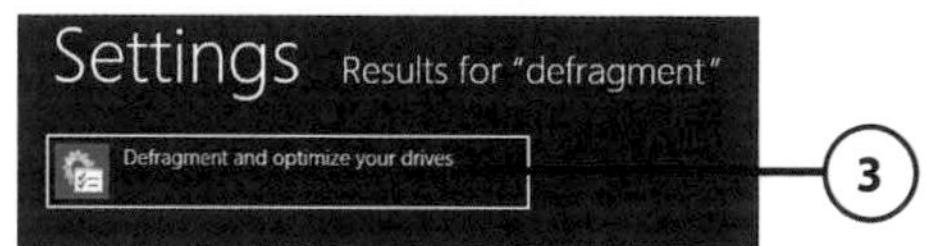

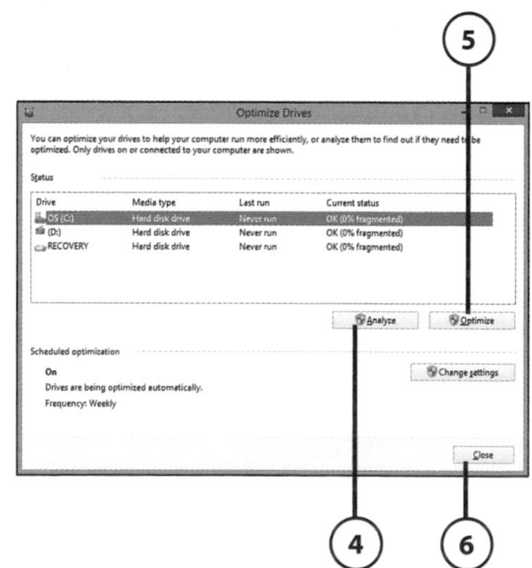

>>>Go Further

SCHEDULING REGULAR DEFRAGMENTING

You can put your PC on a steady defrag diet by having the system automatically defragment your hard drive at a specific time of the week or month. Click Change Settings in the Optimize Drives dialog box. In the Optimize Drives: Optimization Schedule dialog box, click the Run on a Schedule check box and click the Frequency you want: Daily, Weekly, or Monthly.

You can also click or tap the Choose button to select the drives you want to optimize following this schedule. Click OK to save your settings, and Disk Defragmenter will run automatically as you specified to keep your files as compact as possible.

Compatibility with Windows 8

Sure, you have a Windows 8 PC, but chances are you need to trade files and perhaps work with programs that were created long before Windows 8 came on the scene. A number of users face challenges in using software and hardware that weren't made to work with Windows 8. How can you get the programs and hardware working together to complete the tasks you need to get done? This section offers some resources that can help you resolve compatibility issues.

Using the Windows Compatibility Center

Microsoft recognizes that helping users know how to use their computers and programs together—no matter which Windows version they may be using—is an important part of supporting its product. For that reason, Microsoft has created the Windows Compatibility Center, which offers a wide range of software and hardware you can check for compatibility with Windows 8.

1. Launch IE10 and type *windows 8 compatibility center* in the address bar.
2. Click the Go button.

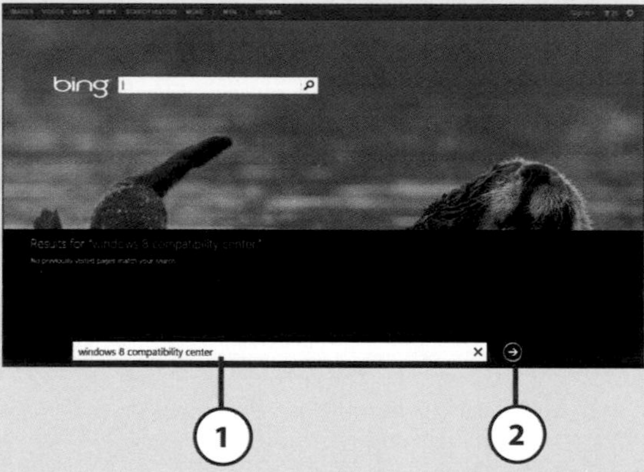

3. In the search results that appear, click the first link, Windows 8 Compatibility Center.

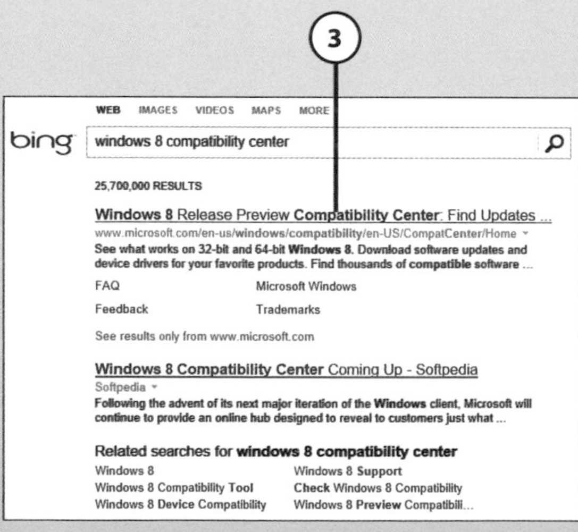

4. Type the program or hardware device you want to find on the site.
5. Click a program category to search for compatible software.
6. Scroll down to find devices that work with Windows 8.
7. Review the list of products displays to find the ones that are compatible with Windows 8. To learn more about a specific product, tap or click it, and more information about the product and its compatibility appears in the browser window.

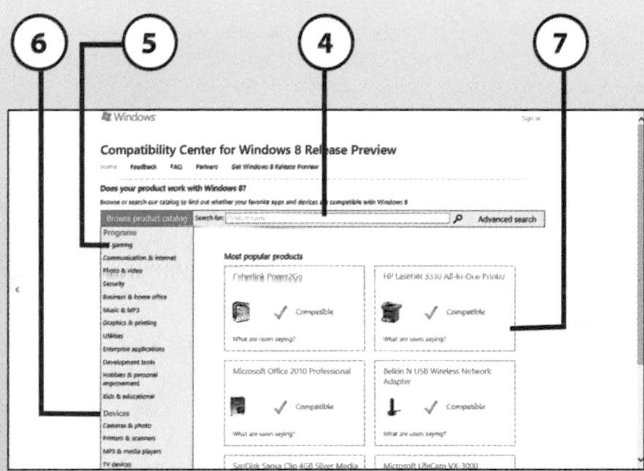

>>>Go Further

WORKING WITH WINDOWS 8 TROUBLESHOOTERS

Windows 8 includes a number of troubleshooters you can use to resolve issues you may be having with your PC or software. You can display all the different troubleshooters by typing *troubleshooter* on the Start screen and tapping Settings on the search screen. You'll see a variety of troubleshooters, ranging from tools that help you sleuth out problems with files to tools for solving memory or network problems.

If none of the troubleshooters do the trick, type *help* and tap or click the Help and Support tab to browse for the help you need or contact Windows support.

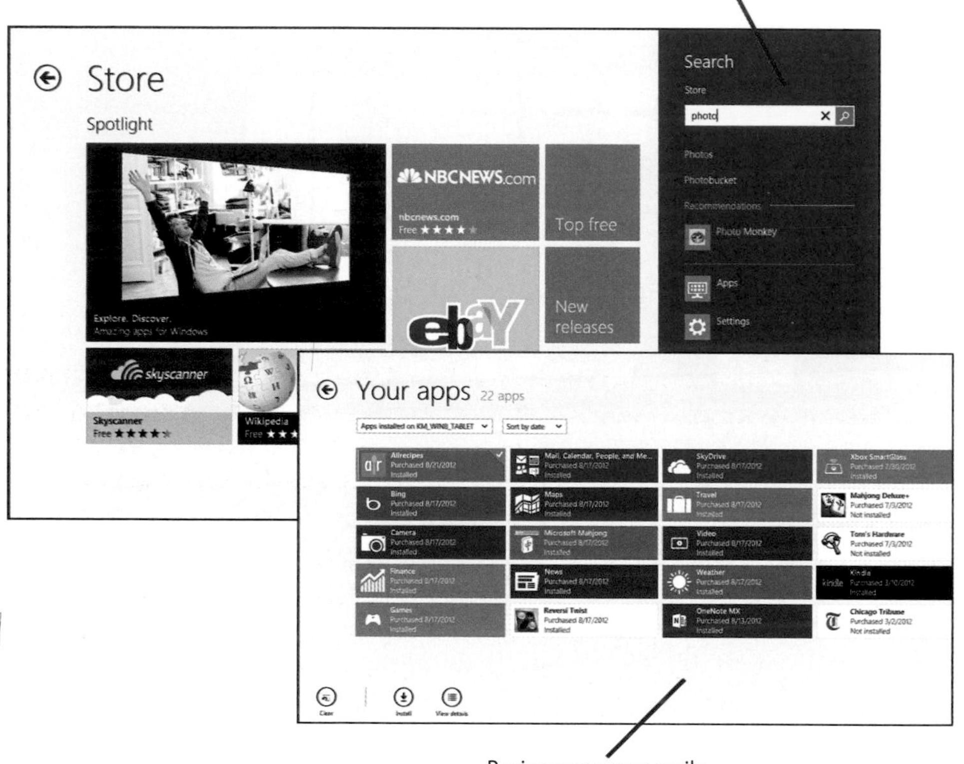
Search the Store for new favorite apps
Store
Spotlight
Search
photo
Photos
Photobucket
Recommendations
Photo Monkey
Apps
Settings
NBCNEWS.com
Top free
New releases
Explore. Discover.
Amazing apps for Windows
skyscanner
Skyscanner
Wikipedia
Your apps 22 apps
Review your apps easily and post user reviews

This appendix introduces you to Windows 8 apps and shows you around the Windows Store by exploring these topics:

- Appreciating your apps
- Checking out the Bing apps
- The Windows Store revisited
- The Windows 8 app gallery

Windows 8 App Gallery

Apps are a big story in Windows 8. They bring life from beyond your computer right to your Start screen. They offer fun, interesting information, beautiful pictures, weather forecasts, shopping, and much more, all in neat little (and sometimes updating) packages that are pleasant to see and easy to use.

And—even better—many of the apps in the Windows Store are free, too. You can browse and search for specific apps and find all sorts of information online before you download and install what you find. A growing and vibrant user community is springing up in the Windows Store as well; use the reviews others have posted to help you decide which apps you want to install and then come back and post your own reviews so that others benefit from your experience!

This appendix offers some of the common tasks you're likely to want to accomplish when you're finding, installing, and reviewing apps. You'll also learn about more than a dozen new apps in the Windows Store that were popular at the time Windows 8 launched.

Appreciating Your Apps

As you learned in Chapter 7, "Exploring Windows 8 Apps," finding, arranging, launching, and closing apps in Windows 8 is a simple task. They all work in a similar fashion—you just tap or click them to start the app—and they all display their app options when you swipe up from the bottom of your Windows 8 screen.

Although that chapter showed you how to find and work with apps, we didn't take a detailed look at all the apps you have available on your Windows 8 Start screen. (We did explore the major apps, such as Mail, People, Messaging, Music, Video, and Photos in chapters throughout this book, however.) As a quick review, here's a table of all the apps you'll find in Windows 8, along with a brief description of each one. In the section that follows, you'll learn more about the Bing apps that were covered in detail elsewhere in this book.

Introducing Your Windows 8 Apps

App Tile	App Name	Use This App To
Store	Windows Store	Browse, search, buy, and download new Windows 8 apps
	People	Keep up-to-date with friends and family on social media
Desktop	Desktop	Display your Windows 8 desktop to work with files and more
Internet Explorer	Internet Explorer	Use IE 10 to browse the web
Freelance Writing Jo... Freelance Writing Jobs Freelance Writing Jobs | A Freelance W... 2	Mail	Check your email, send new messages, and organize message you've received

App Tile	App Name	Use This App To
	Calendar	Set appointments and review your calendar for the day, week, or month
	Messaging	Trade instant messages with your online contacts
	Music	Find, preview, and purchase music or listen to your existing tunes
	Video	Search for and purchase new videos or clips on your PC or device
	Photos	Organize, view, and download photos from all your photo accounts
	News	Review today's top stories with compelling photos
	Games	Find and play your favorite Xbox LIVE games
	Weather	Check the weather in your area or in other locations you specify
	Camera	Take a snapshot or video using the webcam on your computer

App Tile	App Name	Use This App To
	Maps	Map your route to new destinations near and far
	Finance	Get the latest financial news and follow your favorite stocks
	Travel	Learn about travel destinations and read articles about favorite spots
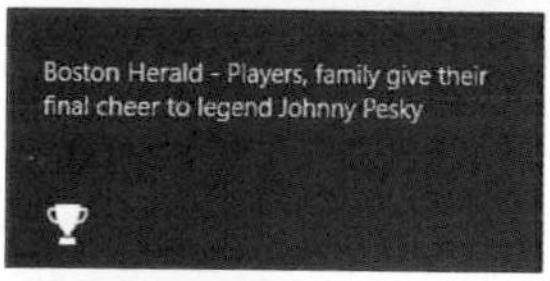	Sports	Get up-to-date sports headlines, scores, and more
	SkyDrive	Access the files stored in your own SkyDrive in the cloud

Checking Out the Bing Apps

The "Bing apps" are so called because they bring to your Windows 8 Start screen specific information related to a particular topic, using the powerful search capabilities of Bing, Microsoft's popular search engine. The Bing apps you'll find on your desktop include Finance, Weather, Maps, News, Sports, and Travel.

Bing apps are available in 12 different languages and can be used in 62 countries, which is pretty amazing given the newness of the whole app phenomenon. Bing apps of course are designed for touch interfaces but work great with a click of the mouse as well, and you can personalize and even aggregate (in some apps) the information you want to receive so you're always getting just what you want on your Start screen.

Finance App

If you're following the stock market and like to keep an eye on what's happening, you can use the Finance app to get an up-to-the-minute look at market conditions. The updating tile displays various indices, and you can easily check your favorite stocks and check all kinds of rates with a single touch or click.

The first screen you see when you launch the Finance app is the Bing Finance Today page, which offers the top financial news story as well as the current standing of the major indices. You can tap the headline to read the news story, tap the information icon to read the photo caption, or swipe to the left to display additional information, financial news, your own personal stock watchlist, and information about the big movers in the market.

Tap or click title to read article

Click or tap to read caption

Scroll to display additional financial info

Weather App

The Weather app can make you feel better about the weather forecast, whether it's going to be rainy and cold or steamy and dry today, simply because the app itself is so beautiful. The Weather app uses your location information to find the weather in your local area and displays current conditions on your updating app tile on the Start screen. When you tap or click the tile, you see a five-day forecast. You can click the arrow to display an additional five days if you like or click the arrow to display additional information like Wind, Visibility, Humidity, and Barometer, as well as forecasts from other weather services.

Swiping left displays your hour-by-hour forecast, as well as a variety of maps showing regional temperatures, Doppler radar, local precipitation, and satellite maps. Continue scrolling right, and you'll get a historical account of today's weather, including highs and lows for the month, record highs and lows in history, and the weather stats (rainfall, snow days, and rainy days) for the year so far.

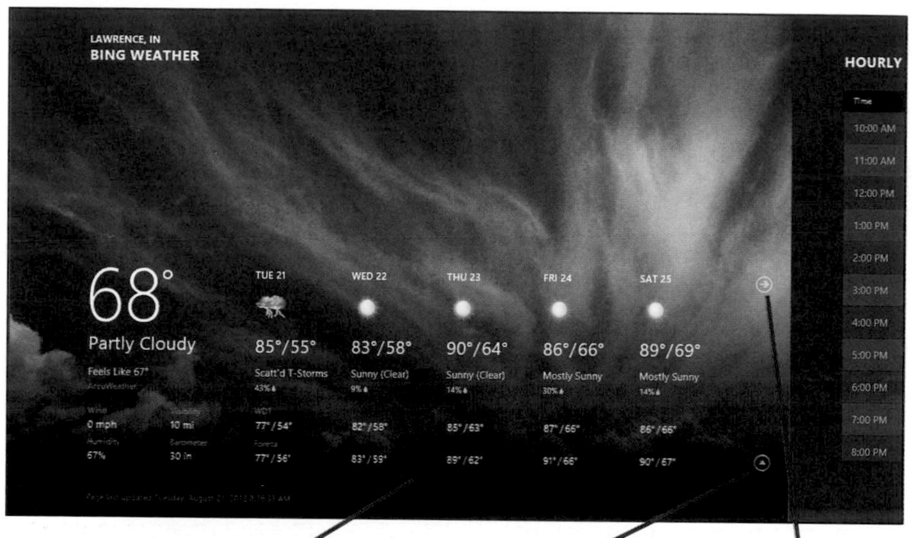

Scroll to see hour-by-hour forecasts, weather maps, and historical weather data

Show additional weather info

View five additional days

Maps App

The Maps app is a fun, functional, and fascinating app that helps you find your way to new places. You can choose from a road view or an aerial view style; you can add traffic flow; you can move quickly to your current location; and you can easily map directions from one point to another. You can zoom in and out from micro to macro with a pinch gesture or by clicking the – and + controls along the left side of the Maps window. Very slick!

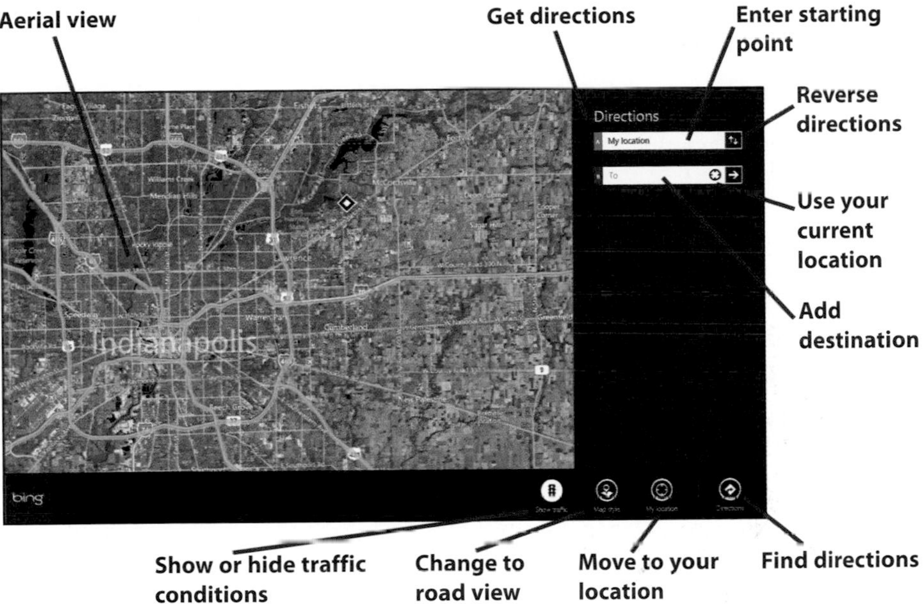

News App

The News app aggregates news stories from top news sources to give you national and world news on the topics that interest you most. You can personalize the app using the My News feature to bring you stories on your favorite subjects, such as politics, health, technology and more, or you can browse the app links to find something that catches your eye. And if you have a favorite publication, you can use the Sources feature to choose specific sources in national and world news, business, technology, entertainment, politics, sports, lifestyle, science, music, gaming, and regional news.

Once again, in the News app, you get benefit of the amazing Bing photos available through the Bing search app as well as other Bing-related apps. When you swipe up on the News app screen, instead of seeing options appear in the apps bar at the bottom of the page, you get tabs at the top, similar to what you'd see in the Windows 8 version of Internet Explorer 10.

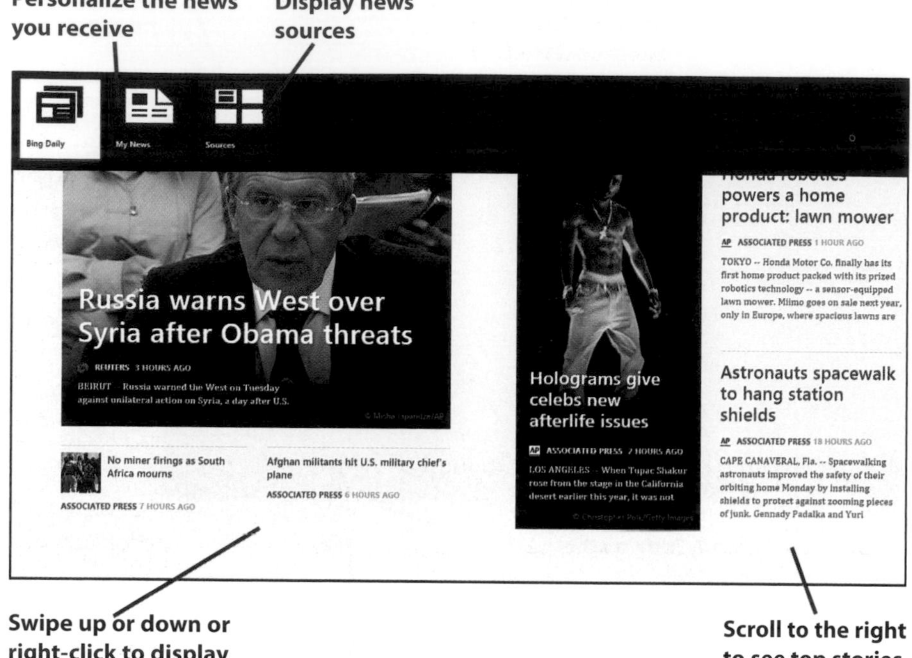
Personalize the news you receive
Display news sources
Bing Daily
My News
Sources
powers a home product: lawn mower
Russia warns West over Syria after Obama threats
Holograms give celebs new afterlife issues
Astronauts spacewalk to hang station shields
No miner firings as South Africa mourns
ASSOCIATED PRESS 7 HOURS AGO
Afghan militants hit U.S. military chief's plane
ASSOCIATED PRESS 6 HOURS AGO
Swipe up or down or right-click to display News options
Scroll to the right to see top stories

Sports App

The Bing sports app caters to sports fans of all types. When you tap or click the app tile on the Start screen, you see a compelling photo related to the major sports story of the moment. You can click or tap the title to display the full article. Scroll to the right to see additional top news stories, check schedules of your favorite teams, and browse recent magazine articles from your favorite sports sources.

You can personalize the app to track your favorite teams by swiping up or down on the screen and choosing Favorite Teams. You can also choose options related to different sporting areas or see what the best of the web has to offer in the sporting world.

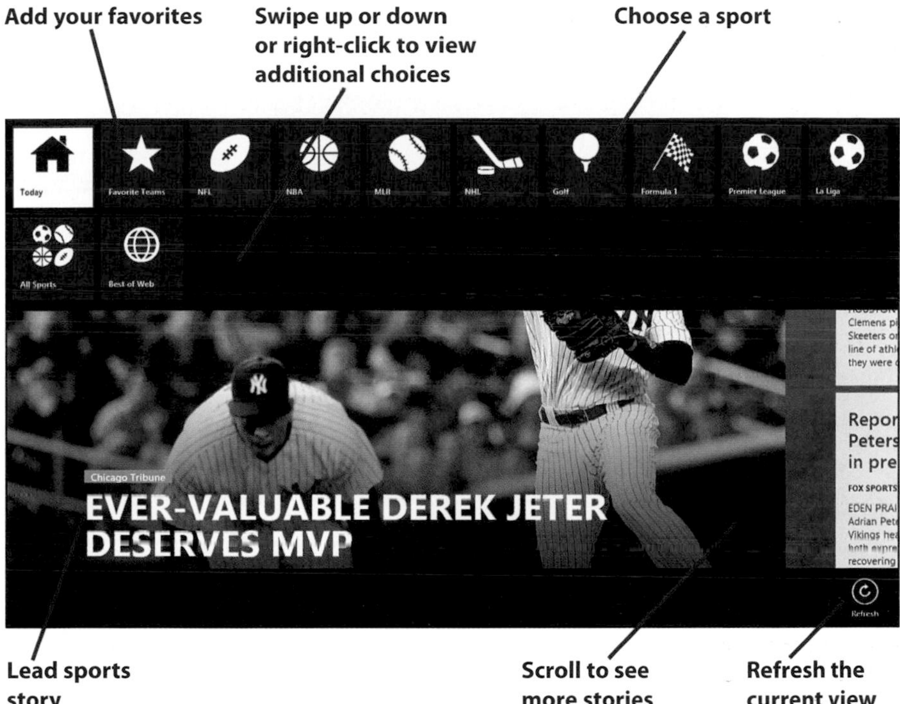

Travel App

Because of Bing's beautiful photos, the Travel app is particularly compelling, inviting you to daydream a little while you do your daily work with Windows 8. When you tap or click the Travel tile, the Bing Travel screen appears, with a lovely image to pull you in. You can tap or click on the information icon to find out more about the spot featured in the photo.

You can scroll through what the app has to offer by swiping to the left. You'll first see a grid of photos from whatever the featured destinations happen to be. Swipe up from the bottom or down from the top or right-click, and your Travel options appear at the top of the screen. You can choose to plot a destination, find a flight, look for lodging, or search online for more information and arrangements. Even though the Travel app offers a lot of inspiration, it's a practical tool too, helping you compare prices, find flights, and use filters to make your arrangements and find the features you need in your price range.

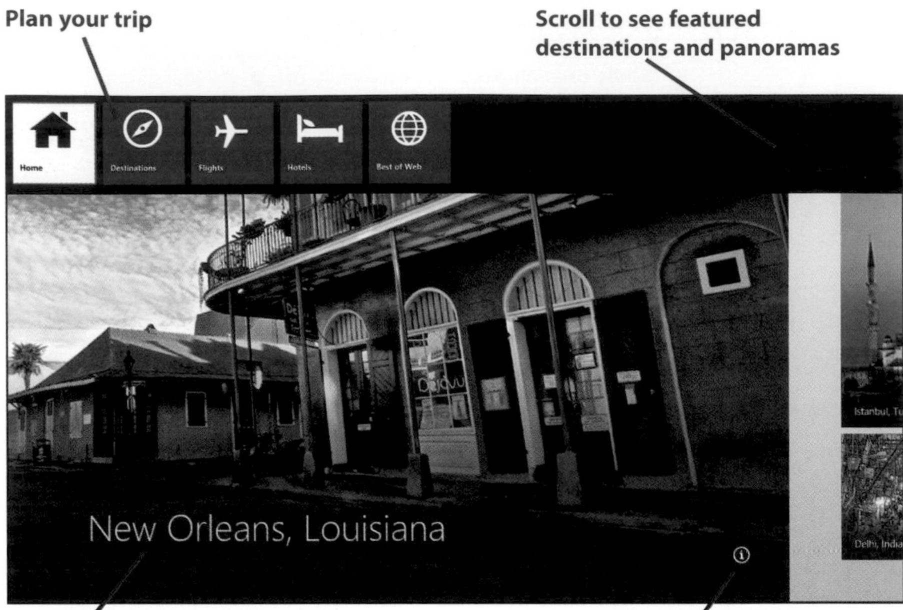

Click or tap place name to display info about the area

Tap or click to see caption and photographer credit

Continue to the right and you'll see panoramas, which are 360-degree images of a famous travel destination, like Paris, France; Barcelona, Spain; or New York, New York. To view a panorama, tap the tile you want to use and use your finger or your mouse pointer to move the image in a full circle. It really does feel like the next best thing to being there.

Scroll or swipe left or right, up or down, to get the full effect of Travel panoramas

The Windows Store Revisited

The Windows Store is something entirely new with Windows 8. You'll find all kinds of apps there, both from Microsoft and from a world-full of developers, who have been working on producing apps since Windows 8 was little more than a gleam in developers' eyes. You'll find many free apps and many apps you purchase, along with a robust user community that actively comments and recommends (or not) the apps they discover.

The Windows Store organizes the multitude of apps into the following categories:

- Spotlight
- Games
- Social
- Entertainment
- Photo
- Music & Video
- Sports
- Books & Reference
- News & Weather
- Health & Fitness
- Food & Dining
- Lifestyle
- Shopping
- Travel
- Finance
- Productivity
- Tools
- Security
- Business
- Education
- Government

Tap or click to get started with the Windows Store

Browsing Apps

If you're interested in wandering the aisles of the Windows Store or looking to discover something new, you can swipe your way through the various categories and tap or click into tiles that seem to hold promise.

1. Display the Store by tapping the Store tile on the Windows 8 Start screen.
2. Scroll to the right to browse through all the different app categories.
3. Tap or click an app category to display and browse through all apps in that category.
4. Choose Top Free to see all apps in that category that are free.
5. Click or tap New Releases to see the latest apps in that category.

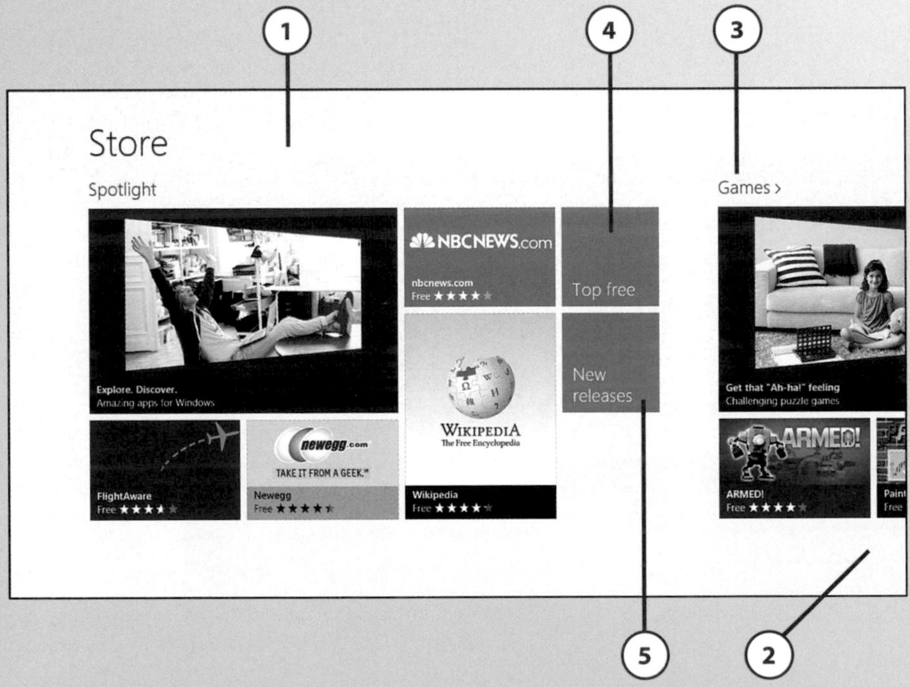

Searching for Apps

As you've seen throughout this book, searching is a simple thing in Windows 8. You'll go back to the Search charm to start the process. Then you can take your search a little farther by narrowing your search results in the Store.

1. Display the Store app and the Charms bar, and tap Search to display the Search panel.
2. Type a word or phrase representing the type of app you're looking for.
3. Tap the app Windows 8 recommends.

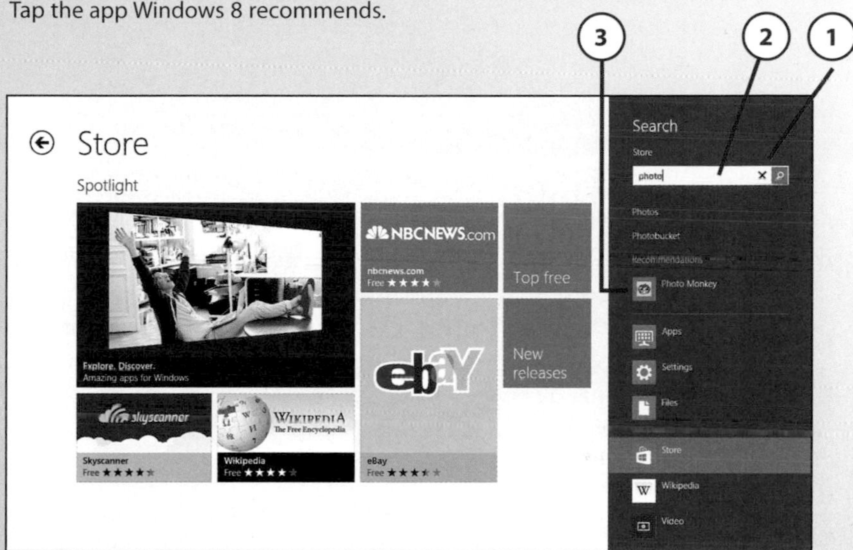

4. Alternately, tap one of the suggestions in the results list.
5. In the Store results list, further narrow the apps by choosing the price level you're searching for.
6. Sort the results by relevance to your search, by displaying the newest apps first, by the highest user ratings, by the lowest price, or by the highest price.
7. Tap or click the app you want to learn more about.

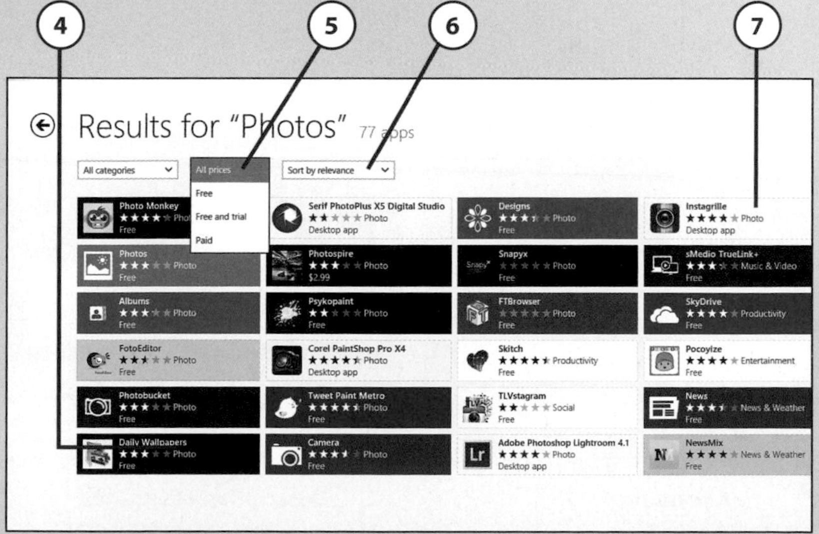

Keeping Ratings in Context

If you sort the results by the highest user ratings, be sure to check out the number of ratings that have been entered. If the app you're considering has 5 stars, that's great, but if only two people have entered ratings that isn't as big a testimony as an app that has only 4 stars but has been reviewed by 75 people.

Getting App Info

When you tap the tile of an app you're interested in, the app information is displayed full-screen so that you can find out more about the app and decide whether you'd like to download it. Each app shows you the user ratings for the app so far, displays the price (free apps say "Free"), gives you an install button, displays what permissions the app requires, and tells you the size, category, publisher, and age rating for the app.

Clicking or tapping Details gives you access to additional information about the displayed app. This might include any release notes the app publisher provides, the type of processors the app supports, and the various languages in which the app is available. Note that the information on the Details page will vary from app to app, and not all app publishers will offer similar information about every app. Begin by tapping an app you want to learn more about. The screen for that app appears.

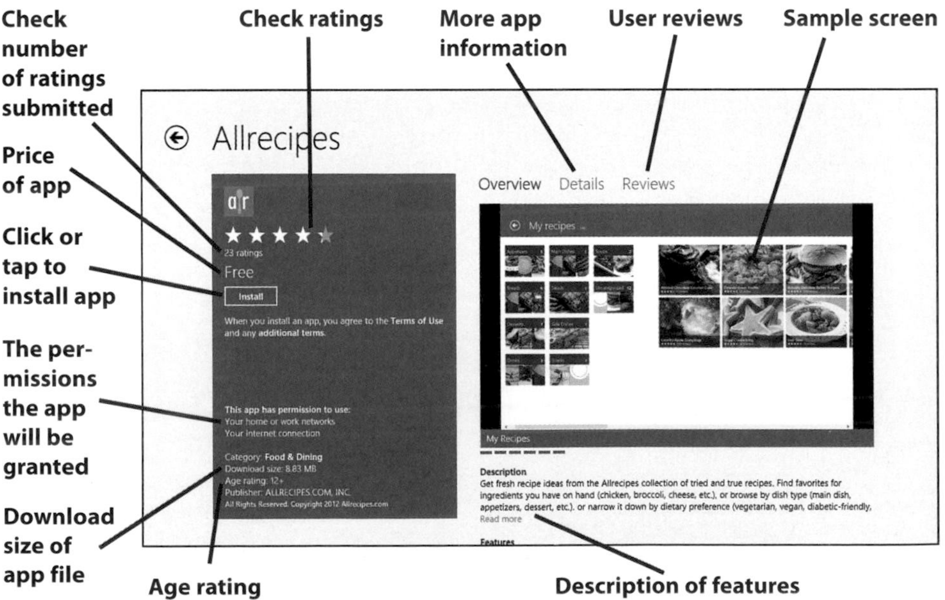

Reading App Reviews

Depending on the popularity of the app you've viewing, you might find a huge number of online reviews for the app that can help you make a choice about whether to install it on your computer. The Reviews feature is well developed, showing you at a glance how each user who posted a review rated the app, when the review was posted, and whether or not others found that particular review helpful. All this is good information to help you determine if this is the app for you.

1. Display the app you want to view.
2. Tap Reviews.
3. Check out the user ratings.
4. Read the reviews posted.
5. Indicate, if you wish, whether you found the review helpful.
6. Sort by Oldest, Highest Rated, Lowest Rated, or Most Helpful reviews.
7. Scroll down to see more reviews.

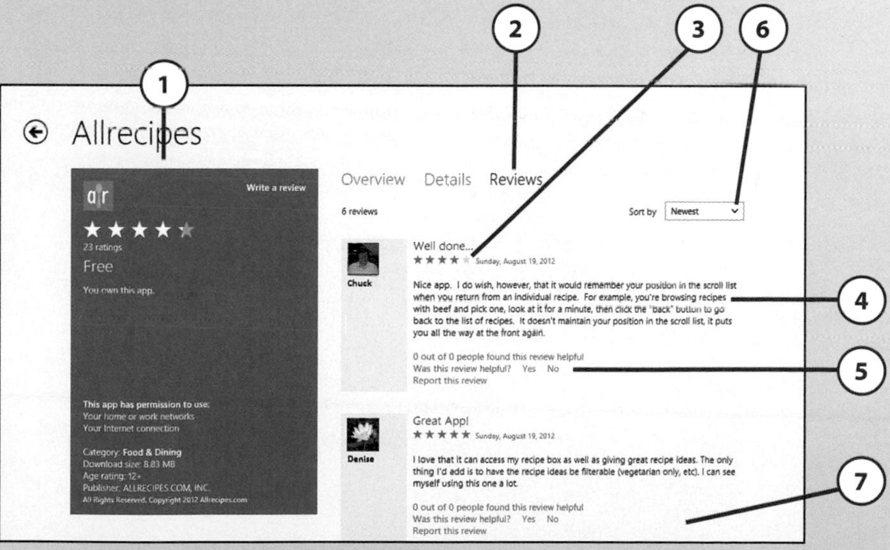

What's This Report?

The Report This Review link is for you to use if you read a review that you feel is inappropriate for the Windows Store. When you click the link, it identifies the reviewer to the folks working with the Windows Store so that they can evaluate the content and make a decision about future posts from this reviewer.

Installing Apps

When you've found an app you like and decide to install it, the how-to is simple: Tap or click Install. Windows 8 displays a small notification in the upper-right corner of your Store screen, and when the app is finished installing, you'll see a larger notification and, unless you've turned off sound notifications, hear a little chime indicating that the install is complete.

You can then press the Windows key or tap Start in the Charms bar to return to the Windows 8 Start screen and find your new app. It will appear on the far-right side of the Start screen, so swipe left, find the app tile, and tap or click it!

Windows 8 lets you know the app is installing

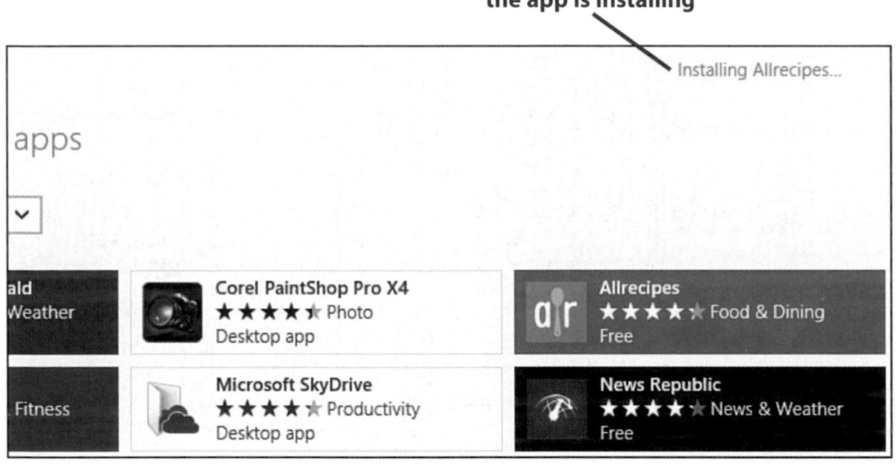

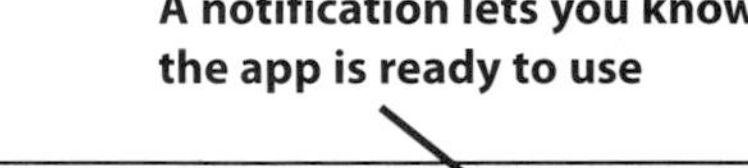

A notification lets you know the app is ready to use

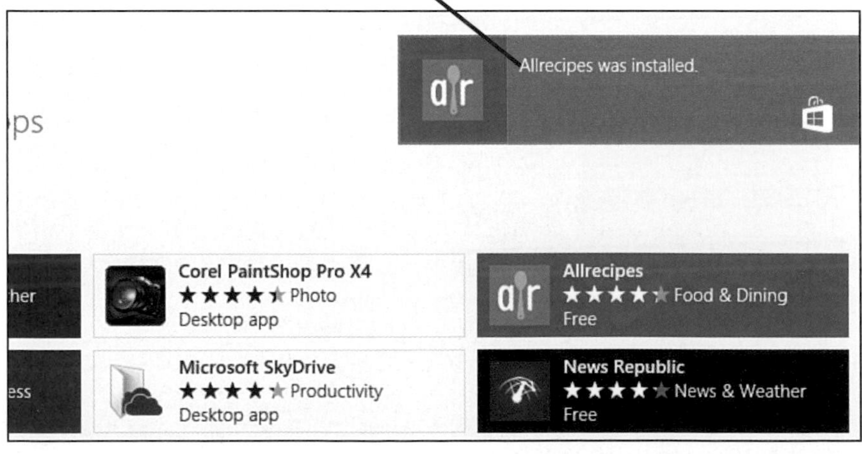

Viewing Your Apps

Apps are so easy to install that in a short period of time you may forget which ones you've installed on your computer. Luckily Windows 8 keeps track for you.

1. Display the Windows Store and swipe down from the top of the screen or right-click the mouse.
2. Tap or click Your Apps.

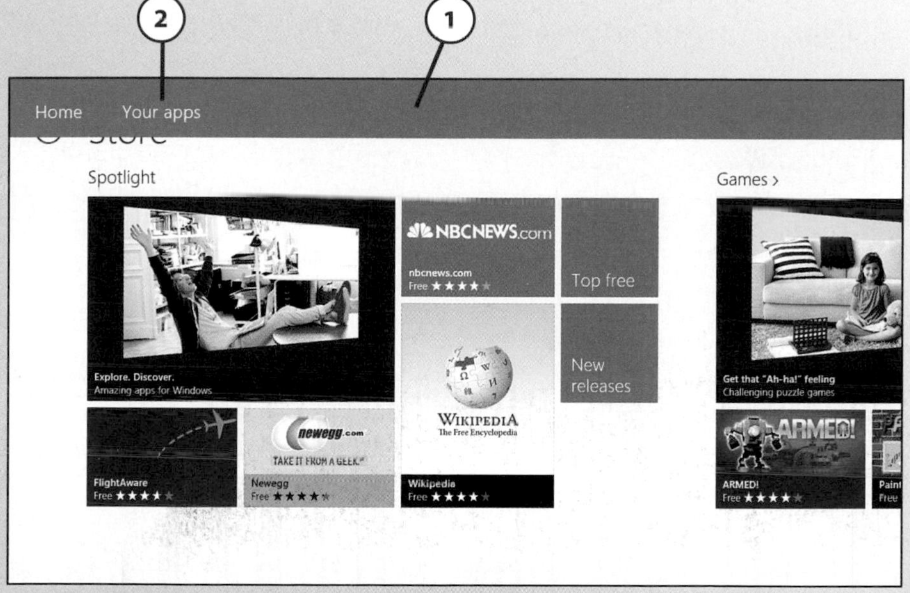

3. Click the arrow to choose which apps you want to view (apps you have downloaded but not installed or apps you've installed).
4. If you like, sort your apps by date instead of name. (By name is the default sort order.)
5. If you want to view an app in the Windows Store, tap or click View Details. (You'll use this tool when you want to add a user review, for example.)
6. If you haven't yet installed an app and want to install it now, select the app and tap or click Install.

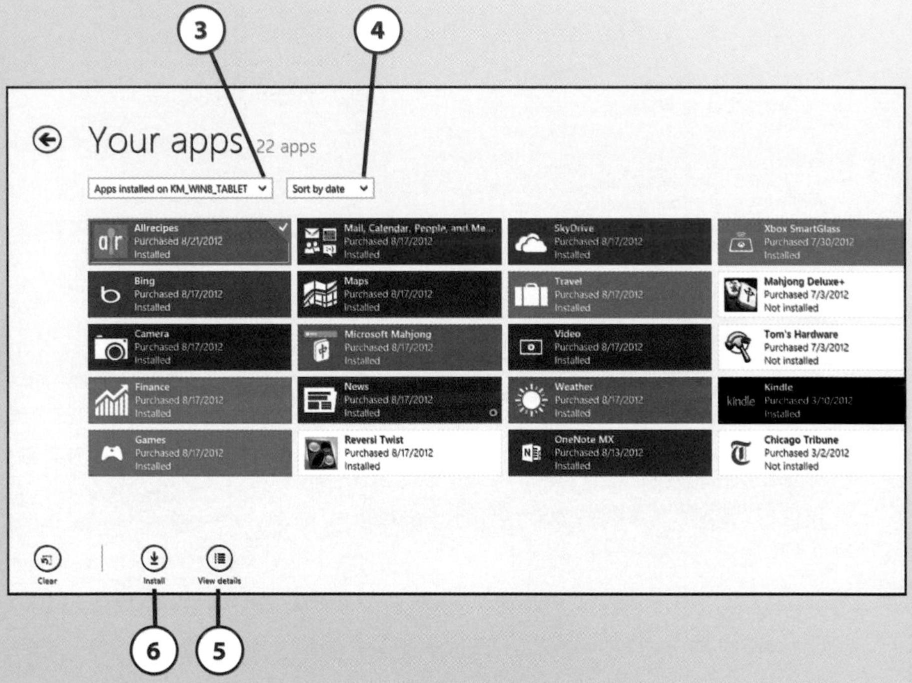

Adding Your Own Review

After you've used the app a little while, you might want to return to the Windows Store and add your own review that gives others the benefit of your experience. You'll notice, when you return to the app in the Windows Store, that there is now a Write a Review link just above and to the right of the app rating.

1. Display Your Apps as explained in the previous section and select the app you want to review.
2. Tap or click View Details.
3. Click or tap Write a Review.
4. Click the number of stars you want to assign to the app.
5. Type a title for your review.
6. Type the review you want to post. (The limit is 500 characters, so be brief.)
7. Tap or click Submit to save your review.

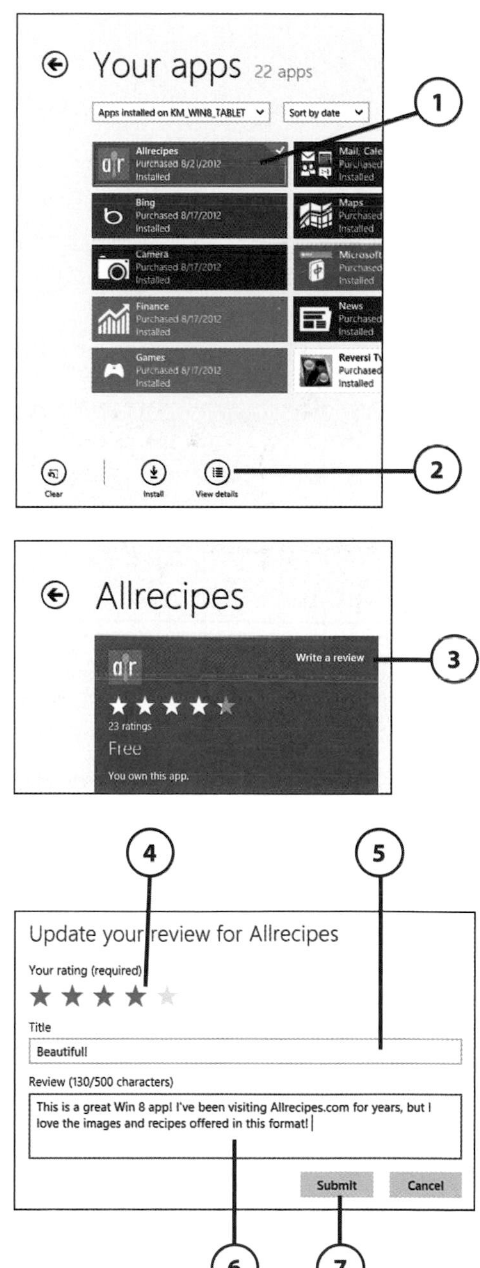

Oh, What I Meant to Say

If after you submit your review you think of something you meant to include—or something you wish you hadn't included—you can make changes by tapping or clicking Update Your Review in the app details screen. Your review will appear in the edit window and you can make any changes you'd like to make. Click or tap Submit when you're happy with the review and want to post it.

Purchasing an App

The process of locating an app is the same, whether the app is a free app or one you need to purchase. You'll see the cost of the app in the small app tile that appears as you search or browse, and when you open the app details screen for that app, the price of the app appears just below the rating stars. When you want to purchase an app, you begin the process by tapping or clicking the Buy button.

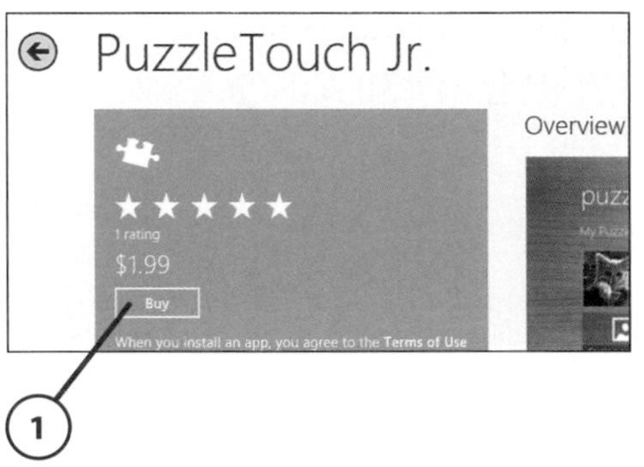

1. With the app details screen displayed in the Store window, tap or click Buy.
2. The Buy button changes to a Confirm button. To complete the sale, tap or click Confirm.

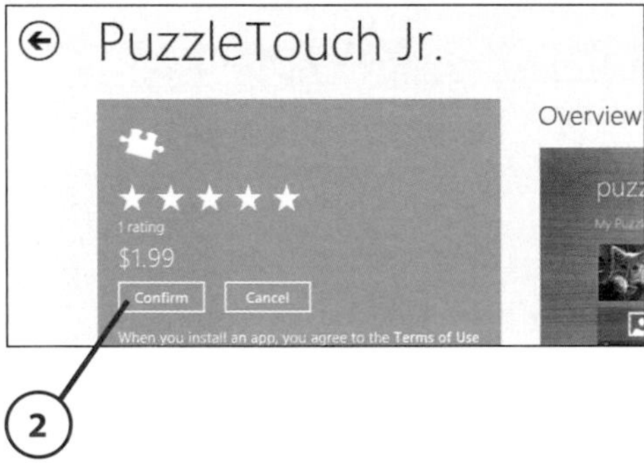

Well, Not Exactly

The Windows Store warns you that you won't be able to cancel the action once you choose Confirm, which isn't exactly accurate, because on the next screen when you are asked to enter your Microsoft account login information, you can click Cancel if you change your mind.

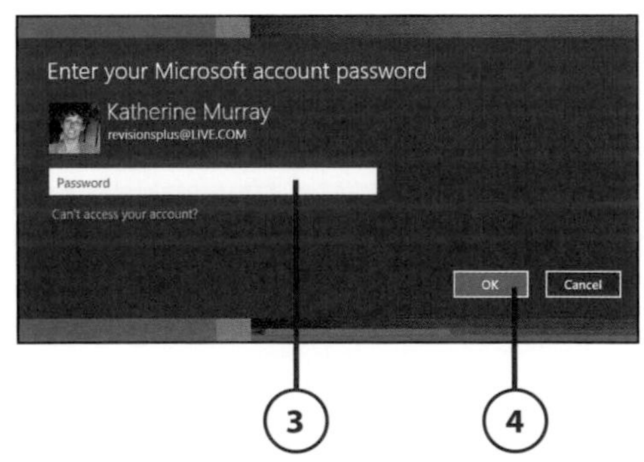

3. When prompted, type your Microsoft account password.
4. Click OK. A Payment and Billing screen appears so that you can choose the way you want to pay.

5. Choose the payment method you prefer.
6. Continue filling out the form, and at the bottom of the page, click Submit. The Windows Store then begins installing the new app you just purchased and will alert you with a notification (and a friendly chime) when it's done.

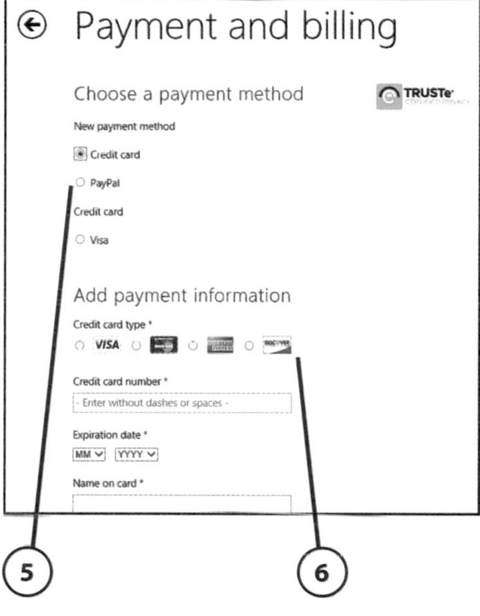

>>>Go Further

HOW DID THEY KNOW THAT?

You might find that in the Choose a Payment Method area, the Payment and Billing screen shows the last four digits of one of your credit cards and lists it as an option for you to select. When you choose that option, the rest of the form is filled in automatically with your information. Wait a minute—where did that info come from?

If you've purchased anything through Xbox or have an Xbox Live account or Zune music pass (now Xbox Music Pass), Microsoft has your credit card number on file, unless you specified otherwise. So don't panic if the info shows up. It's actually kind of nice to know you don't have to go searching for your wallet. And it also makes it w-a-a-a-a-y too easy to buy Microsoft Points when you find a game you like or a movie you want to watch in the Video app, which is probably the idea. Good one, Microsoft.

The Windows 8 App Gallery

Discovery is half the fun of shopping, don't you think? So you might find yourself lazily flicking the screen this way and that in the Windows Store, checking out new apps, reading the user reviews, and thinking about downloading free trials. We thought we'd show you a few of the apps that were new and popular when Windows 8 released. There will no doubt be more—and more, and more—as the months unfold. Some reviewers are claiming the Windows Store will give iTunes and Android a good race. We shall see.

Allrecipes

Category: Food & Dining

Cost: Free

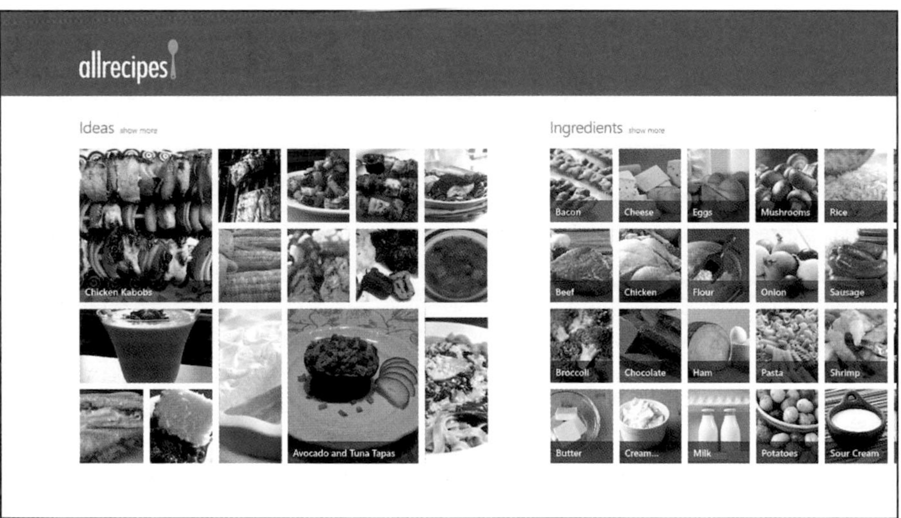

If you like to cook—or you like to eat and think, maybe, about cooking—you may love the Allrecipes app. This Windows 8 app is an offshoot of the popular website and offers fresh new recipes every day. You can search the database of more than 40,000 recipes and search by dish type or your personal preferences (vegetarian, diabetic, and so on). You can also save your favorite recipes to your own "recipe box" (this requires entering login information, which you can do without leaving Windows 8) so that you can find your favorite recipes later. (I'm going to make Praline Sweet Potatoes this Thanksgiving. Yum.)

ChaCha

Category: Tools

Cost: Free

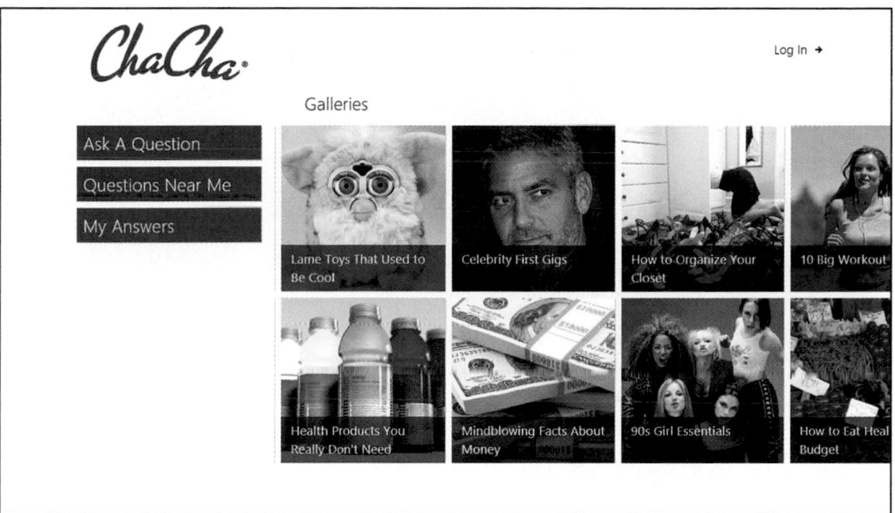

ChaCha is an unusual search app that uses real, live people to help you find the information you seek. Instead of a formal, unfriendly algorithm, a flesh-and-blood person receives your query, uses a mega-database of indexes to find just the right answer for your context, and fires it back to you with blazing speed. ChaCha is fun and free, supported by advertisers, and it's been a big hit with mobile phone users. Now ChaCha is available in the Windows Store, keeping it simple and friendly. ChaCha says you can ask any question ("Ask anything, anytime, anywhere!") and get a quick answer, which is saved to a history for you so you can always get to the information you found. ChaCha also offers an Answers Near Me feature (see next page) that enables you to find out what folks in your area are asking. When I tested out this feature I was surprised by how fascinating it is! (And by the things my neighbors are wondering about, too.)

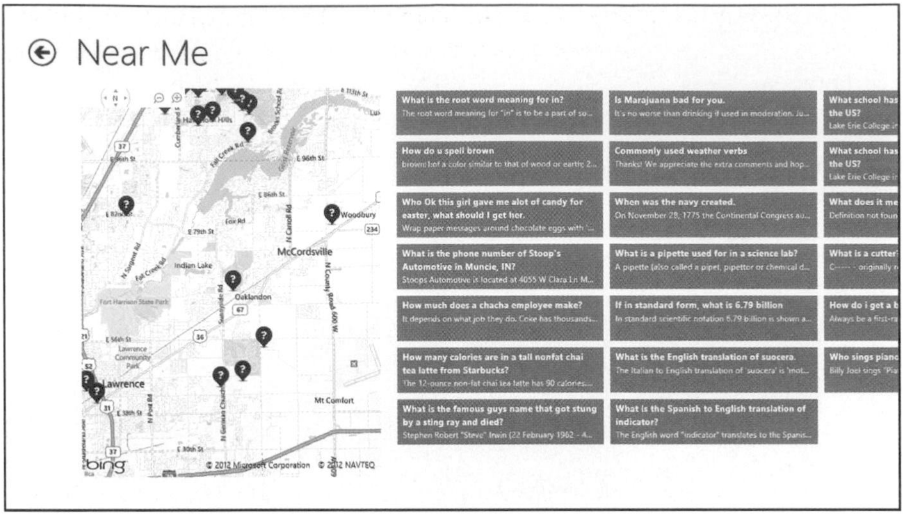

Dictionary.com

Category: Books & Reference

Cost: Free

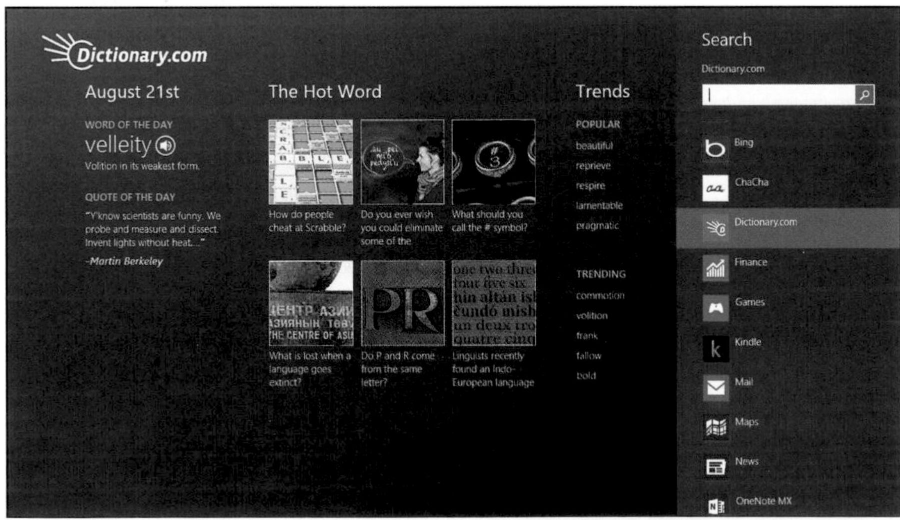

Who doesn't need a good dictionary? If you are tired of browsing the web when you need to look up a definition or check the usage of a word, why not bring the tool to you? Dictionary.com is the Windows 8 app version of the popular site, giving you tools that help you expand your vocabulary, hear how words are pronounced, find out what people are searching in your local area (this seems to be a trend), and learn other little-known facts about language and its use. When you want to search for a specific word in Dictionary.com, you use your handy-dandy Search charm to do the trick.

HowStuffWorks

Category: Entertainment

Cost: Free

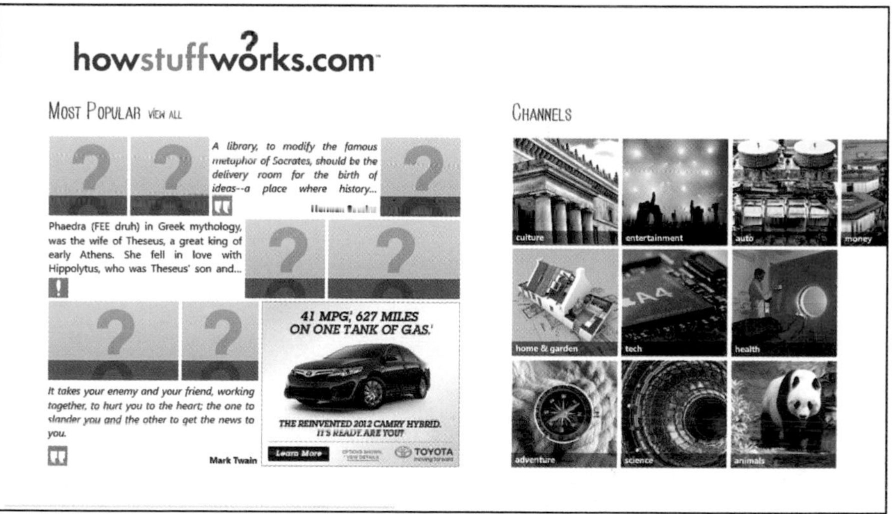

If you love to know how to do things, HowStuffWorks might be one of your favorite apps. Do-it-yourselfers and knowledge-seekers will find information organized in 10 different channels: Culture, Entertainment, Auto, Money, Home & Garden, Tech, Health, Adventure, Science, and Animals. You can also check out their "Stuff," which includes Facts & Quotes, Videos, Articles, Podcasts, Quizzes, and Countdowns, or check out one of the 15 shows you can listen to streaming through your app. You can once again use the Search charm to look for information within HowStuffWorks if there's a certain question that's keeping you up at night (or if you're just wondering).

OneNote MX Preview

Category: Productivity

Cost: Free

OneNote MX Preview is the newest version of the popular note-taking app from Microsoft. It features a sleek new design (even cooler than OneNote 2013) that includes radial menus. Radial menus are controls that are optimized for touch, so whether you are choosing fonts, colors, tools, or formats, you can spin around the dial and tap your choice. This tool is worth downloading even if all you want to do is play with the new menus. But you may just find yourself capturing notes while you're there, too.

Paint 4 Kids

Category: Games

Cost: Free

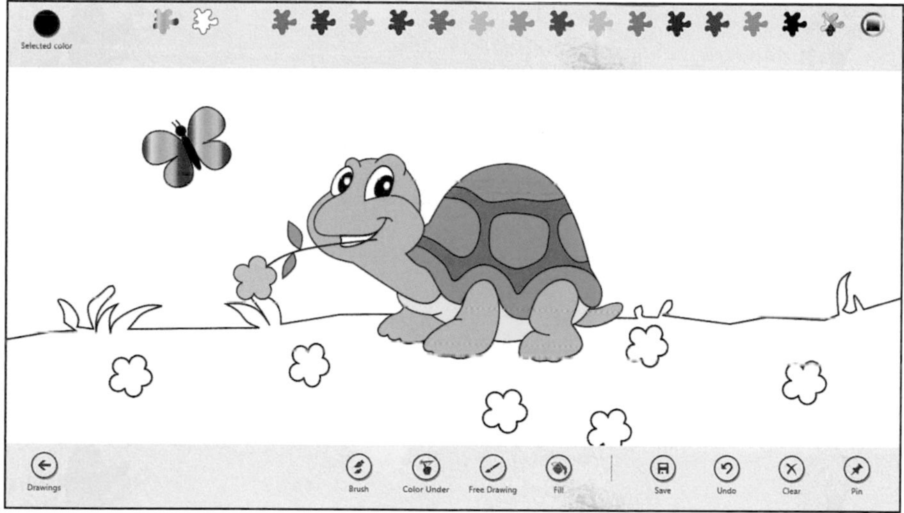

Do you still like to color? Or do you have someone in your family who does? Paint 4 Kids is a fun painting program that enables, ahem, *children* to choose paint pages from a number of categories (Pirates, Animals, Vehicles, Sea World, or Fun) or select a type of paper they'd like to use (blank, lined, or gridlined) and then paint the day away. This fun app gives users a palette with numerous colors and the ability to choose from several different tools (including a Fill tool that doesn't go out of the lines).

StumbleUpon

Category: Entertainment

Cost: Free

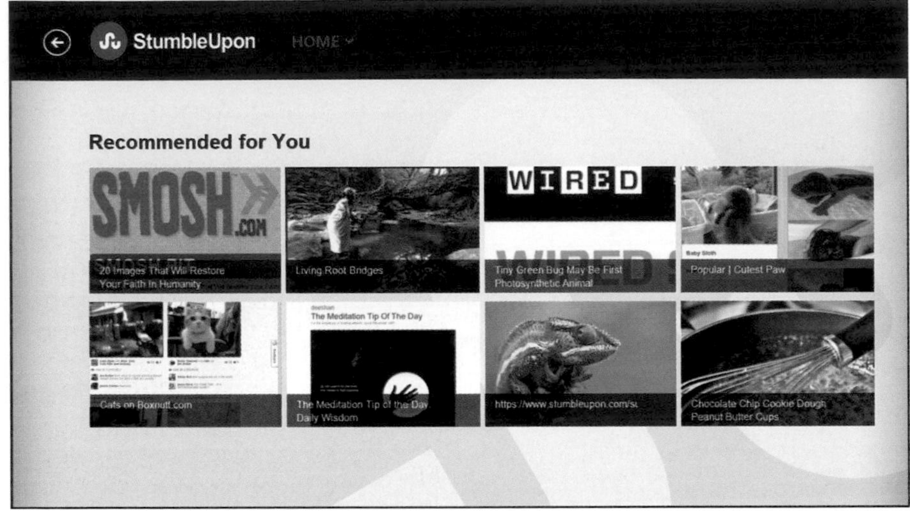

StumbleUpon is an Entertainment app that provides you with suggestions for web pages you might be interested in visiting. When you tap or click the Stumble! button, the app suggests photos, web pages, videos, and other web offerings that others who share your interests have recommended. You can begin by choosing from 500 different interests and then easily find the treasures you find. StumbleUpon does require that you join (for free) before the app can make suggestions for you. After you join, you're asked to choose at least five interests from a listing of 60 categories and click or tap Save Interests. The app then aggregates stories from all over the web that fit the interests you've selected and displays them in a beautiful (à la Windows 8) format you can tap into for more info.

Wikipedia

Category: Books & Reference

Cost: Free

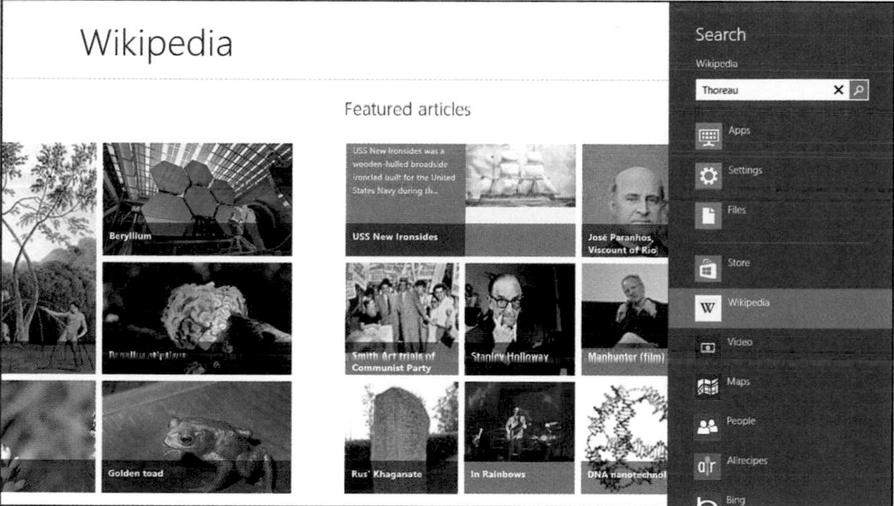

Wikipedia is another world-full of information that you may be accustomed to using online. Now you can bring it right to your Windows 8 Start screen in a free app.

The free encyclopedia boasts 20 million articles in more than 280 languages and claims to be "the most comprehensive and widely used reference work humans have ever compiled."

When you launch the Wikipedia app from your Windows 8 Start screen, you see a catalog of features, pictures, and articles, as well as the popular "On This Day" section that appears on the website home page as well. You can also review recent changes on Wikipedia or search for the content you want to find by using the Windows 8 Search charm. The clean reading layout makes it a pleasure to skim or read in-depth, no matter what topic has captured your attention.

Index

A

accessibility
  high contrast, 105
  magnifying display, 106
  Narrator, 26

accessing
  shared files/folders, 288-289
  virtual keyboard, 76

accounts
  account pictures, changing, 100-101
  email accounts, adding, 238-240
  Facebook accounts, signing up for, 233
  user accounts. *See* user accounts

Action Center
  changing Action Center alerts, 131-132
  reviewing system status, 129-130
  Windows SmartScreen, 133

activating firewall, 137

adapters, wireless network adapters, 280

Add a Device command, 37

Add a User window, 139

Add Columns command, 187

adding
  appointments, 245-246
  badges, 103
  columns to library displays, 187
  computers to home networks, 282
  contacts to People app, 236-237
  devices, 37
  email accounts, 238-240
  folders to libraries, 182
  photo accounts, 254-256
  shortcuts, 84-85
  users, 139

address bar (IE 10), 210-211

administrative tools, viewing, 63-64

administrators, 142

administrator status, checking, 52

alerts, Action Center alerts, 131-132

Allrecipes app, 330

applications. *See* apps

appointments
  adding, 245-246
  checking, 244-245

apps, 147-148. *See also* programs
  adding to taskbar, 87
  Allrecipes app, 330
  apps panel, 157
  browsing in Windows Store, 320
  Calendar app, 243, 311
    adding appointments, 245-246
    checking today's appointments, 244-245
    sending invitations, 247
  Camera app, 311

ChaCha, 331
closing, 16
from desktop, 167
selected apps, 160
with Task Manager, 161
compared to programs, 148
definition of, 148
Desktop app, 310
Dictionary.com, 332-333
Disk Cleanup, 302-303
Disk Defragmenter, 302-305
displaying, 149
docking, 15
File Explorer. *See* File Explorer
Finance app, 312-313
finding, 151-152, 164
Games app, 311
buying/renting games, 275-276
customizing avatar, 273-274
finding games, 274-275
playing games, 274-275
groups
creating, 72
naming, 73
HowStuffWorks, 333
installing, 164-165, 324
Internet Explorer. *See* Internet Explorer 10
launching, 83
at startup, 154
from desktop, 153, 165-166
from Start screen, 153
live tiles, 148
Mail app, 310
composing email, 241
email accounts, adding, 238-240
marking email as junk, 243
organizing email, 242
Maps app, 312-315
Messaging app, 311
creating instant messages, 249-250
inviting new contacts, 250
Messenger window, 247-248
moving, 150
Music app, 311
finding music, 264-265
listening to music previews, 266-267
Music app window, 260-261
playing music, 262-263
purchasing music, 268
News app, 311, 315
OneNote MX Preview, 334
Paint 4 Kids, 335
People app, 12, 310, 228-230
adding contacts, 236-237
connecting social media accounts, 231-233
profile, updating, 230
searching for contacts, 237
viewing status updates, 234-235
Photo app, 12, 311
adding photo accounts, 254-256
displaying slideshows, 259
setting photo options, 257-258
viewing and selecting photos, 256-257
pinning
to Start menu, 150
to taskbar, 151
programs versus, 60
purchasing in Windows Store, 328-329
reading app reviews in Windows Store, 323
removing from Start screen, 74
repairing, 168
reviewing in Windows Store, 327
searching, 77-78, 152, 320-321
shortcuts
adding, 84-85
deleting, 85
SkyDrive app, 312, 289-291
Sports app, 312, 316
startup impact, 162
StumbleUpon, 336
switching between, 155, 158
tiles
enabling/disabling live updates, 68
hiding notifications, 68-69
hiding personal information, 70
rearranging, 71
resizing, 67-68
tiling, 158
transferring, 50
Travel app, 312, 317-318
uninstalling, 170
unrecognized apps, 133
Video app, 311
playing movies, 270-271
renting movies, 271
watching TV shows, 272-273
viewing, 62, 322, 325-326
Weather app, 311-314
Wikipedia, 337
windows, 155-156
Windows Store, 162-163, 310, 319
browsing apps, 320
getting app info, 322
installing apps, 324
launching, 163
purchasing apps, 328-329
reading app reviews, 323
reviewing apps, 327
searching, 164
searching for apps, 320-321

updating reviews, 327
viewing apps, 325-326
apps panel, 157
archiving messages, 130
ARM, 2-3
arranging
library display, 186-187
windows, 92-93
audio
Music app
finding music, 264-265
listening to music previews, 266-267
Music app window, 260-261
playing music, 262-263
purchasing music, 268
notification sounds, turning on/off, 114
Automatic Maintenance settings, 296
automatic updates
advantages of, 293
best practices, 295
choosing time for, 296
turning on, 294-295
avatar for Games app, 273-274

B

Back button (IE 10), 213
background (desktop), choosing, 108-109
backing up files, 298-300
badges, 103
best practices for updates, 295
Bing apps, 219
Finance app, 313
Maps app, 314-315
News app, 315
Sports app, 316
Travel app, 317-318
Weather app, 313-314
boot process, Secure Boot, 118
brightness of screen, adjusting, 47
Browse for Files or Folders dialog box, 84
browser. *See* Internet Explorer 10
browsing
apps in Windows Store, 320
web. *See* Internet Explorer 10
buying
apps in Windows Store, 328-329
games, 275-276
music, 268

C

Calendar app, 243, 311
adding appointments, 245-246
checking today's appointments, 244-245
sending invitations, 247
Camera app, 311
Cascade Windows option, 92
ChaCha, 331
changing
account pictures, 100-101
Action Center alerts, 131-132
contrast, 105
email account settings, 240
File Explorer layout, 177
firewall settings, 138
Lock screen pictures, 98-100
passwords, 119-120
power options, 48-49
Start screen color, 104
text size, 30
time, 106-107
user account settings, 140-141
Charms bar, 12, 60, 64-66
Check for Updates Now command, 297
checking
administrator status, 52
appointments, 244-245
compatibility, 306
device status, 37
for updates, 297-298
choosing
automatic update schedule, 296
desktop background, 108-109
desktop themes, 109
language, 114-115
passwords, 120
power management plan, 46-47
transfer methods, 53
cleaning up hard disk, 302-303
click speed, setting, 111-112
Close button (windows), 89
closing apps, 16
from desktop, 167
selected apps, 160
with Task Manager, 161
cloud, saving files to, 289-291
color of Start screen, changing, 104
columns, adding to libraries, 187
compatibility, Windows Compatibility Center, 306
composing email, 241
compressing files, 200-201
computers, adding to home networks, 282
connecting
devices, 38-39
social media accounts, 231-233

to wireless networks, 43-45

contacts
adding to People app, 236-237
inviting, 250
searching for, 237

context for charms, 66

contrast, adjusting, 105

cookies, 224-225

copy conflicts, resolving, 196

copying files, 194-196

Copy Items dialog box, 195

Copy To command, 195

Create New Library command, 183

Create Shortcut dialog box, 84

customizing Windows 8. *See* personalizing Windows 8

Custom Scan (Windows Defender), 136

D

Daylight Savings Time, adjusting time for, 107

definitions file (Windows Defender), updating, 135

defragmenting hard disk, 304-305

Delete Browsing History command, 224

Delete Browsing History dialog box, 224-225

deleting
cookies, 224-225
shortcuts, 85

desktop, 11, 81, 310
closing apps from, 167
displaying, 82
launching apps from, 153, 165-166
personalizing, 107-109
background, 108-109
themes, 109
searching from, 77
Start screen. *See* Start screen
taskbar
adding apps to, 87
jump lists, 88-89

desktop style (IE 10)
home page, setting, 219-220
notifications, 216
overview, 208-209
tabs, 222-223
web searches, 218-219

Details pane (File Explorer), 176, 193

devices
adding, 37
checking device status, 37
connecting, 38-39
removing, 40
troubleshooting, 40-42
viewing installed devices, 36-37

Devices charm, 65

Dictionary.com, 332-333

disabling
live tile updates, 68
passwords, 126

Disk Cleanup, 302-303

Disk Defragmenter, 302-305

displaying. *See* viewing

docking apps, 15

Do Not Track feature (IE 10), 224

downloading
photos from phone, 256
Windows 8, 7

downloads, troubleshooting, 39

E

Ease of Access screen
contrast settings, 105
screen magnification setting, 106

editing app reviews, 327

email
composing, 241
email accounts, adding, 238-240
Mail window, 240
marking as junk, 243
organizing, 242

enabling live tile updates, 68

End Task command, 161

Enhanced Protected mode (IE 10), 223

Ethernet, 281

exiting. *See* closing apps

expanding ribbon, 90, 180

Expand the Ribbon command (File Explorer), 90, 180

Express Setup, 10

Extract All command, 200

extracting files, 200-201

F

Facebook
connecting with, 231-233
signing up for, 233

File Explorer, 173
adding to Start screen, 174
changing layout of, 177
Details pane, 176, 193
displaying, 174
files
compressing, 200-201
copying, 194-196
extracting, 200-201
finding, 188-190
moving, 199

rating, 194
selecting, 190-191
sharing, 198
solving copy conflicts, 196-197
tagging, 193-194
viewing file information, 191-193
folders
adding to libraries, 182
finding, 188-190
removing from libraries, 184-185
selecting, 190-191
Get Help command, 176
hotkey tool tips, 180
launching, 86, 174
libraries, 181
adding folders to, 182
arranging library display, 186-187
creating, 183
removing folders from, 184-185
Location bar, 175
navigating, 176-177
Navigation pane, 176
Preview pane, 175-176
Quick Access toolbar, 180
Refresh button, 175
ribbon
layout, 178-179
showing/hiding, 179-180
searches, saving, 190
syncing settings, 199

File History dialog box, 300

files
backing up, 298-300
compressing, 200-201
copying, 194-196
definitions files (Windows Defender), updating, 135
extracting, 200-201
finding with File Explorer, 188-190
moving, 199
rating, 194
restoring, 301
saving to SkyDrive, 289-291
searching, 76
selecting, 190-191
sharing, 198, 288-289
solving copy conflicts, 196-197
tagging, 193-194
transferring, 49-53
apps, 50
Windows Easy Transfer, 50-53
viewing file information, 191-193

File tab (File Explorer), 178

Finance app, 312-313

finding
apps, 151-152, 164, 320-321
contacts, 237
files, 188-190
folders, 188-190
games, 274-275
music, 264-265

firewalls, 136-138
activating, 137
changing firewall settings, 138

Flash, 204

folders
adding to libraries, 182
finding, 188-190
"My" folders, 181
Public folders, 201
removing from libraries, 184-185
selecting, 190-191
shared folders, accessing, 288-289

Forward button (IE 10), 213

Full Scan (Windows Defender), 136

G

games, 4
finding, 274-275
playing, 274-275
purchasing, 275-276
renting, 275-276

Games app, 311

gestures
pinch zoom, 16-17
single tap, 13
swipe left, 14
swipe right, 14-15
swiping up and down, 15-16
tap and hold, 14

Get Help command (File Explorer), 176

Get Online Help option, 31

groups
app groups
creating, 72
naming, 73
HomeGroups. *See* HomeGroups

H

hard disk
cleaning up, 302-303
defragmenting, 304-305

help
Microsoft Windows 8 website, 32
online help, 31-32, 43
printing help information, 31
Windows Community forums, 32
Windows Help and Support, 29-30

Help button, 90

Help Experience Improvement Program option, 31

Hide Ribbon tool, 90

hiding
File Explorer ribbon, 179-180
live tile notifications, 68-69

personal information on tiles, 70
pointer, 112-113
ribbon, 90

High Contrast slider, 105

HomeGroups, 283
file/folder sharing, 288-289
joining, 285
printer sharing, 289
setting up, 284
sharing settings, 288
viewing, 286-287

home networks, 279
adding computers to, 282
HomeGroups, 283
file/folder sharing, 288-289
joining, 285
printer sharing, 289
setting up, 284
sharing settings, 288
viewing, 286-287
Internet time, setting computers to, 286-287
network technologies, 281
required equipment, 280
setting up, 281
workgroups, creating, 283

HomePNA, 281

Home tab (File Explorer), 178

HowStuffWorks, 333

I

images. *See* pictures

Include in Library command, 182

InPrivate Browsing, 222

installed devices, viewing, 36-37

installing
apps, 164-165, 324
Windows 8, 7

instant messaging
creating instant messages, 249-250
inviting new contacts, 250
Messenger window, 247-248

Internet Explorer 10, 12, 203-204, 310
address bar, 210-211
desktop style
home page, setting, 219-220
notifications, 216
overview, 208-209
tabs, 222-223
web searches, 218-219
Flash, 204
InPrivate Browsing, 222
keyboard shortcuts, 211
launching, 205
navigation tiles, 214-215
navigation tools, 211-214
notifications, 216
pinned sites, 213
plug-ins, 204
searching web, 216
in IE 10 desktop, 218-219
in IE 10 from the Start screen, 217
search suggestions, 219
security, 223
cookies, 224-225
Do Not Track feature, 224
Enhanced Protected mode, 223
InPrivate Browsing, 222
tabs, 222-223

Internet Service Providers (ISPs), 280

Internet time, setting computers to, 286-287

Internet Time Settings dialog box, 286

invitations, sending, 247

inviting new contacts, 250

ISPs (Internet Service Providers), 280

J-K

joining HomeGroups, 285

jump lists, 88-89

junk, marking email as, 243

keyboards
physical keyboard, 22-23
touch keyboard, 24-26
virtual keyboard, accessing, 76

keyboard shortcuts, 23, 211

L

language, choosing, 114-115

Language dialog box, 115

launching
apps, 83
from desktop, 153, 165-166
from Start screen, 153
at startup, 154
File Explorer, 86, 174
Internet Explorer, 205
starting up computer, 10
Windows 8, 10
Windows Store, 163

left swipes, 14

libraries, 181
adding folders to, 182
arranging library display, 186-187
creating, 183
removing folders from, 184-185

Library Locations dialog box, 185

LinkedIn, connecting with, 231-233

listening to music previews, 266-267

lists, jump lists, 88-89

live tiles, 148

live updates of tiles
enabling/disabling, 68
hiding notifications, 68-69
local account, switching to, 126-128
locating. *See* finding
Location bar (File Explorer), 175
location privacy, setting, 143-144
Lock screen
personalizing, 97-102
pictures, changing, 98-100
unlocking, 15-16
login security
changing passwords, 119-120
creating picture passwords, 121-122
creating PIN logons, 124-125
face recognition, 118-119
removing picture passwords, 123
removing PINs, 125
switching to local account, 126-128

M

magnifying display, 106
Mail app, 310
composing email, 241
email accounts, adding, 238-240
Mail window, 240
marking email as junk, 243
organizing email, 242
Make Everything on Your Screen Bigger setting, 106
Manage Accounts dialog box, 141
Maps app, 312-315
marking email as junk, 243
Maximize button (windows), 89
Media Center, 269
messages. *See* email; instant messaging
Messaging app, 311
creating instant messages, 249-250
inviting new contacts, 250
Messenger window, 247-248
Microsoft Points, 269
Microsoft Surface, 5, 17
Microsoft Windows 8 website, 32
Minimize button (windows), 89
Minimize the Ribbon command (File Explorer), 176, 179
minimizing ribbon, 179
modeless windows, 154
mouse
navigating with, 18-21
personalizing, 111-114
mouse buttons, 113
mouse wheel, 114
pointer and click speed, 111-112
Mouse Properties dialog box, 112-114
mouse wheel, controlling, 114
movies
playing, 270-271
renting, 271
Movies Store, 271
moving
apps, 150
files, 199
windows, 91
Music app, 311
finding music, 264-265
listening to music previews, 266-267
Music app window, 260-261
playing music, 262-263
purchasing music, 268
"My" folders, 181

N

naming app groups, 73
Narrator, 26
navigating
File Explorer, 176-177
with mouse, 18-21
with physical keyboard, 22-23
with touch keyboard, 24-26
Navigation pane (File Explorer), 176
navigation tiles (IE 10), 214-215
navigation tools (IE 10), 211-214
networks
home networks, 279
adding computers to, 282
HomeGroups, 283-286, 286-289
Internet time, setting computers to, 286-287
network technologies, 281
required equipment, 280
setting up, 281
workgroups, creating, 283
network connections, repairing, 45
wireless networks
connecting to, 43-45
wireless network adapters, 280
News app, 311, 315

notifications
- Internet Explorer 10, 216
- live update notifications, hiding, 68-69
- notification sounds, turning on/off, 114

O

One Box, 211

OneNote MX Preview, 334

online help, 31-32, 43

opening. *See* launching

Optimize Drives dialog box, 304-305

organizing email, 242

P

Paint 4 Kids, 335

passwords
- changing, 119-120
- choosing, 120
- disabling, 126
- picture passwords
  - *creating, 121-122*
  - *removing, 123*

pausing live tile notifications, 68-69

People app, 12, 310
- adding contacts, 236-237
- connecting social media accounts, 231-233
- overview, 228-230
- profile, updating, 230
- searching for contacts, 237
- viewing status updates, 234-235

personal information on tiles, hiding, 70

personalizing Windows 8
- badges, 103
- contrast, 105
- desktop, 107-109
  - *background, 108-109*
  - *themes, 109*
- Games avatar, 273-274
- language, 114-115
- Lock screen, 97-102
- magnification, 106
- mouse, 111-114
  - *mouse buttons, 113*
  - *mouse wheel, 114*
  - *pointer and click speed, 111-112*
- Start screen color, 104
- time settings, 106-107
- touch, 110

Pg Dn key, 23

Pg Up key, 23

phone, downloading photos from, 256

Photo app, 12, 311. *See also* pictures
- adding photo accounts, 254-256
- displaying slideshows, 259
- setting photo options, 257-258
- viewing and selecting photos, 256-257

Photos app

picture passwords
- creating, 121-122
- removing, 123

pictures
- account pictures, changing, 100-101
- desktop background pictures, choosing, 108-109
- downloading from phone, 256
- Lock screen pictures, changing, 98-100
- photo accounts, adding, 254-256
- picture passwords
  - *creating, 121-122*
  - *removing, 123*
- retaking, 102
- selecting, 256-257
- setting photo options, 257-258
- storing, 102
- viewing, 256-257

pinch zoom gesture, 16-17

PIN logons
- creating, 124-125
- removing PINs, 125

pinning
- apps
  - *to Start menu, 150*
  - *to taskbar, 151*
- websites to Start menu, 213

PINs, removing, 125

Pin This Program to Taskbar option, 87

Pin to Start command, 150, 213

playing
- games, 274-275
- movies, 270-271
- music, 262-264
- TV shows, 272-273

plug-ins, 204

pointer
- hiding/displaying, 112-113
- pointer speed, setting, 111-112

Power button, 10

Powerline networks, 281

power management, 46-49
- changing power options, 48-49
- choosing power management plan, 46-47

Power Options dialog box, 47

power user commands, 22

previewing music, 266-267

Preview pane (File Explorer), 175-176

primary language, setting, 115

printers, sharing on HomeGroups, 289

printing help information, 31

privacy, 143-144
Privacy Statement, 144
private appointments, creating, 246
profiles (People app), updating, 230
Program and Features dialog box, 169
programs. *See also* apps
- compared to apps, 60, 148
- uninstalling, 169-170

Public folders, 201
purchasing
- apps in Windows Store, 328-329
- games, 275-276
- music, 260

putting Windows 8 to sleep, 27

Q-R

Quick Access Toolbar, 89, 180
Quick Scan (Windows Defender), 136

rating files, 194
reading app reviews, 323
rearranging apps, 71
Refresh button (File Explorer), 175
refreshing PC, 54-55, 169
Refresh tool, 169
Refresh Your PC option, 54-55
reinstalling Windows 8, 55-56
removing
- apps from Start screen, 74
- columns from library displays, 187
- devices, 40
- folders from libraries, 184-185
- picture passwords, 123
- PINs, 125

renting
- games, 275-276
- movies, 271

Reopen Closed Tabs command (IE 10), 214
Reopen Last Session link (IE 10), 214
repairing
- apps, 168
- network connections, 45

Repair option, 168
Replace or Skip Files dialog box, 197
Reset Your PC and Start Over option, 55-56
resizing
- thumbs keyboard, 26
- tiles, 67-68
- windows, 91, 94

Restart command, 28
restarting computer, 28
Restore Your Files with File History command, 301
restoring
- default power management settings, 47
- files, 301

retaking pictures, 102
returning to Start screen, 83
reviewing
- apps, 327
- system status, 129-130
- update history, 298

ribbon, 156
- hiding/expanding, 90
- tabs, 90

ribbon (File Explorer)
- layout, 178-179
- showing/hiding, 179-180

right swipes, 14-15
routers, wireless routers, 280

S

Save Backup Copies of Your Files with File History command, 299
saving
- File Explorer searches, 190
- files to SkyDrive, 289-291

scanning with Windows Defender, 134-136
scheduling
- automatic updates, 296
- disk defragmenting, 305

screen brightness, adjusting, 47
scrollbars, 156
scrolling in Internet Explorer 10, 213
Search box (File Explorer), 175
Search charm, 65
searching
- apps, 152, 77-78
- from desktop, 77
- for files, 76
- for contacts, 237
- in File Explorer, 190
- for settings, 76
- in Start screen, 75-78
- web, 216
  - *in IE 10 desktop, 218-219*
  - *in IE 10 from the Start screen, 217*
  - *search suggestions, 219*
- Windows Store, 164, 320-321

search providers, adding to Internet Explorer 10, 219
Secure Boot, 118
security, 117
- Action Center
  - *changing Action Center alerts, 131-132*
  - *reviewing system status, 129-130*

Windows SmartScreen, 133
Internet Explorer 10
cookies, 224-225
Do Not Track feature, 224
Enhanced Protected mode, 223
InPrivate Browsing, 222
logins
changing passwords, 119-120
creating picture passwords, 121-122
creating PIN logons, 124-125
face recognition, 118-119
removing picture passwords, 123
removing PINs, 125
switching to local account, 126-128
privacy, 143-144
Secure Boot, 118
User Account Control, 131
user accounts
adding users, 139
changing account settings, 140-141
switching users, 142-143
Windows Defender, 134-136
Windows Firewall, 136-138
activating firewall, 137
changing firewall settings, 138

selecting
files, 190-191
folders, 190-191
photos, 256-257

semantic zoom gesture, 16-17

sending
instant messages, 249-250
invitations, 247

settings. *See* personalizing Windows 8

Settings charm, 65-66

setting up
HomeGroups, 284
home networks, 281

Set Up a New Network wizard, 281

Share charm, 65

Share tab (File Explorer), 179

sharing
files/folders, 198, 288-289
printers, 289
sharing settings (HomeGroups), 288

shortcuts
adding, 84-85
deleting, 85
keyboard shortcuts, 23
copy and paste, 199
moving files, 199
mouse shortcuts, 21

Show Windows Side By Side option, 93

Show Windows Stacked option, 93

Shut down command, 28

shutting down Windows 8, 28

signing up for Facebook, 233

single tap, 13

SkyDrive, 289-291, 312

Sleep mode, 27

slideshows, displaying, 259

social media
Facebook, signing up for, 233
People app
adding contacts, 236-237
connecting social media accounts, 231-233
overview, 228-230
profile, updating, 230
searching for contacts, 237
viewing status updates, 234-235
social media accounts, connecting, 231-233

sound
Music app
finding music, 264-265
listening to music previews, 266-267
Music app window, 260-261
playing music, 262-263
purchasing music, 268
notification sounds, turning on/off, 114

Sports app, 312, 316

Standard account type, 142

standard keyboard, displaying, 25-26

Start charm, 65

starting. *See* launching

Start menu, 21
pinning apps to, 150
pinning websites to, 213

Start screen, 10-12, 59-61
adding File Explorer to, 174
administrative tools, viewing, 63-64
apps
creating groups, 72
launching, 153
naming groups, 73
rearranging, 71
removing, 74
viewing all, 62
Charms bar, 64-66
color, changing, 104
moving between desktop and Start screen, 82-83
returning to, 83
searching, 75-78
tiles
enabling/disabling live updates, 68
hiding notifications, 68-69

hiding personal information, 70
resizing, 67-68

startup, launching apps at, 154

status
administrator status, checking, 52
device status, checking, 37
status updates, viewing, 234-235
system status, reviewing, 129-130

storing pictures, 102

StumbleUpon, 336

suggestions (search), 219

swipe left gesture, 14

swipe right gesture, 14-15

swiping up and down, 15-16

switching
between apps, 155, 158
between windows, 92
to local account, 126-128
users, 142-143

Switch to a Microsoft Account option, 128

syncing File Explorer settings, 199

system status, reviewing, 129-130

system tools
Disk Cleanup, 302-303
Disk Defragmenter, 302, 304-305

T

Tab key, 23

tablets, Microsoft Surface, 5, 17

tabs (IE 10), 222-223

tagging files, 193-194

tap and hold, 14

tapping
single tap, 13
tap and hold, 14

taskbar
adding apps to, 87
jump lists, 88
pinning apps to, 151

Task Manager
closing apps with, 161
viewing startup impact of apps, 162

text size, changing, 30

themes, 109

thumbs keyboard, resizing, 26

tiles
app groups
creating, 72
naming, 73
enabling/disabling live updates, 68
notifications, hiding, 68-69
personal information, hiding, 70
rearranging, 71
resizing, 67-68

tiling apps, 158

time
automatic update times, choosing, 296
changing, 106-107
Internet time, setting computers to, 286-287

title bars, 89, 155

touch
explained, 13
hardware not optimized for Windows 8 touch, 4-5
personalizing, 110
pinch zoom, 16-17
single tap, 13
swipe left, 14
swipe right, 14-15
swiping up and down, 15-16
tap and hold, 14

touch keyboard, 24-26

touchscreens, 4-5

transferring files, 49-53
apps, 50
Windows Easy Transfer, 50-53

Travel app, 312, 317-318

Troubleshoot Computer Problems dialog box, 41

troubleshooting
copy conflicts, 196
devices, 40-42
downloads, 39
network connections, 45
Windows 8 troubleshooters, 307

turning on/off
automatic updates, 294-295
notification sounds, 114
search suggestions, 219

TV shows, playing, 272-273

Twitter, connecting with, 231-233

U

UEFI (Unified Extensible Firmware Interface), 118

Unified Extensible Firmware Interface (UEFI), 118

Uninstall a Program command, 169

uninstalling
apps, 170
programs, 169-170

unlocking Lock screen, 15-16

Unpin This Program from Taskbar option, 87

unrecognized apps, 133

up and down swipes, 15-16

updates
advantages of, 293
automatic updates
choosing time for, 296
turning on, 294-295

best practices, 295
checking for manually, 297-298
reviewing update history, 298

updating
app reviews in Windows Store, 327
definitions file (Windows Defender), 135
People app profile, 230

User Account Control, 131

user accounts
adding users, 139
changing account settings, 140-141
switching back to Microsoft account, 128
switching users, 142-143

User Accounts dialog box, 141

users
adding, 139
switching, 142-143

utilities
Disk Cleanup, 302-303
Disk Defragmenter, 302, 304-305

V

versions of Windows 8, 2-3

Video app, 311
playing movies, 270-271
renting movies, 271
watching TV shows, 272-273

viewing
administrative tools, 63-64
app info in Windows Store, 322
apps, 62, 149, 325-326
desktop, 82
File Explorer, 174
File Explorer ribbon, 179-180
file information, 191-193
HomeGroups, 286-287
installed devices, 36-37
photos, 256-257
pointer, 112-113
ribbon, 90
slideshows, 259
standard keyboard, 25-26
status updates, 234-235

View tab (File Explorer), 179

virtual keyboard, accessing, 76

W

waking up computer, 28

Weather app, 311, 313-314

web browser. *See* Internet Explorer 10

web browsing. *See* Internet Explorer 10

web searches, 216
in IE 10 desktop, 218-219
in IE 10 from the Start screen, 217
search suggestions, 219

websites, pinning to Start menu, 213

Welcome to Picture Password window, 121-122

Wikipedia, 337

windows
app windows, 155-156
arranging, 92-93
components, 89-90
modeless windows, 154
moving, 91
resizing, 91, 94
switching between, 92

Windows 8 Pro, 2

Windows Community, 32, 43

Windows Compatibility Center, 306

Windows Defender, 134-136

Windows Easy Transfer, 50-53

Windows Firewall, 136-138
activating firewall, 137
changing firewall settings, 138

Windows Help and Support, 29-30

Windows key, 23

Windows Live, 159

Windows Media Center, 269

Windows Network Diagnostics, 45

Windows RT, 2

Windows SmartScreen, 133

Windows Store, 12, 162-163, 310, 319
browsing apps, 320
getting app info, 322
installing apps, 164-165, 324
launching, 163
purchasing apps, 328-329
reading app reviews, 323
reviewing apps, 327
searching, 164, 320-321
updating reviews, 327
viewing apps, 325-326

Windows Update dialog box, 297-298

wireless networks
connecting to, 43-45
wireless network adapters, 280

wireless routers, 280

wizards, Set Up a New Network, 281

workgroups, creating, 283

X-Y-Z

Xbox Companion, 271

Xbox, using with Games app
buying/renting games, 275-276
customizing avatar, 273-274
finding games, 274-275
playing games, 274-275

Zune, 159

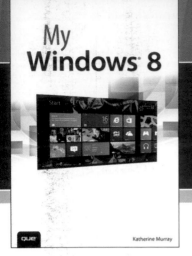